A Decent Home

Planning, Building, and Preserving Affordable Housing

Alan Mallach, FAICP

American Planning Association
Planners Press

Making Great Communities Happen

Chicago | Washington, D.C.

Copyright 2009 by the American Planning Association
122 S. Michigan Ave., Suite 1600, Chicago, IL 60603
1776 Massachusetts Ave., NW, Suite 400, Washington, D.C. 20036

ISBN (paperback): 978-1-932364-58-3
ISBN (hardbound): 978-1-932364-59-0

Library of Congress Catalog Number: 2008941235

Printed in the United States of America

All rights reserved

Contents

Acknowledgments vii

Preface ix

Chapter 1. The Case for Affordable Housing 1
    The Need for Decent Housing 2
    Affordable Housing Needs and the Private Market 10
    Is Affordable Housing a Housing Problem or an Income Problem? 17
    Conclusion 25

Chapter 2. Affordable Housing in the United States: A Short History 29
    Beginnings 29
    The Rise and Fall of Public Housing 33
    Federal Funding, Private Ownership 37
    The Age of Devolution 44
    Affordable Housing Policy Today 47

Chapter 3. Designing Affordable Housing 53
    Why Design Matters 53
    Housing for Whom? 57
    Housing That Works for People 60
    Cars, People, and Open Space 65
    Safe Spaces 69
    Designing Housing That Fits In 72

Chapter 4. Finding Sites and Gaining Approval for Affordable Housing 79
    Criteria for Selecting Sites 79
    Good Sites Are Hard to Find 85
    Getting Projects Approved 89

Chapter 5. Making the Numbers Work: Financing Affordable Housing 101
   Defining Affordability 102
   Filling the Gap 106
   Capital Grants and Tax Credit Equity 112
   Putting the Pieces Together: Subsidy Layering and the Development Pro Forma 123

Chapter 6. Developing Affordable Housing, Step-by-Step 133
   Thinking the Project Through 135
   Forming the Development Team—Finding a Site 137
   The Predevelopment Process 140
   Construction, Marketing, and Rent-up 146

Chapter 7. Concentration and Opportunity: Undoing the Exclusion of Affordable Housing 157
   The Practice of Suburban Exclusion 158
   Challenging Exclusion in the Courts 162
   State Planning Laws and Affordable Housing Mandates 165
   Conclusion 174

Chapter 8. Affordable Housing, Community Development Corporations, and Neighborhood Revitalization 177
   Affordable Housing and Poverty Concentration 179
   The Role of Community Development Corporations 186
   Toward Communities of Choice 191
   Balancing Affordable Housing and Neighborhood Revitalization 195

Chapter 9. The Risks and Rewards of Affordable Home Ownership 207
   Home Ownership—The American Dream 207
   The Costs and Benefits of Home Ownership 212
   Public and Nonprofit Strategies to Foster Lower Income Home Ownership 217
   Low-income Home Ownership and the Subprime Meltdown 228

Chapter 10. Preserving Affordable Housing 239
   Preservation: A Critical Issue 239
   The Problem of Expiring Use Restrictions 242
   Preserving Affordable Home Ownership 246
   Preserving Affordability in the Private Market 254

Chapter 11. Homelessness and Affordable Housing   263
   Who Are the Homeless?   264
   Why Are So Many People Homeless?   267
   Changing Approaches to Housing the Homeless   272
   Affordable Housing and Housing First   279

Chapter 12. Inclusionary Housing: Using the Market to Create Affordable Housing   285
   What Is Inclusionary Housing?   286
   The Legal Status of Inclusionary Housing   292
   Economics of Inclusionary Housing   295
   Making Inclusionary Housing Work   300

Chapter 13. Policies, Politics, and the Future of Affordable Housing in the United States   311
   Drivers of Housing Policy Change   312
   Shaping Future Affordable Housing Policy   319

Appendix: Resources for Further Information   347

Index   365

Acknowledgments

It is hard to know where to begin in acknowledging the many people from whom I have learned about affordable housing in the course of a career that began in the fall of 1967, with my first job in housing at the newly established New Jersey Housing Finance Agency. It has been my privilege as well as my pleasure to have worked with an extraordinary number of creative and dedicated individuals over the past 40 years. While this book reflects their knowledge and insights as much as my own experience, I do not think I would ever have reached this point without the contributions of three people in particular: Ralph Brown, who first introduced me to the endlessly fascinating nuts and bolts of affordable housing; George Sternlieb, whose questioning mind and intellectual seriousness challenged me to think critically about these issues; and Paul Davidoff, who inspired a generation of planners and housing advocates. By enlisting me in his struggle against exclusionary zoning, he helped me understand how affordable housing is also a social justice issue.

Over the years, I have gained my knowledge and understanding of housing issues from an eclectic band of scholars, practitioners, and activists, a body that includes Peter Abeles, Kenneth Anderson, Joy Aruguete, Alison Badgett, Michael Barber, Richard Bellman, Eric Belsky, Carl Bisgaier, Karen Black, Mary Brooks, Paul Brophy, Nick Brunick, Lance Jay Brown, Peter Buchsbaum, Jim Capraro, Joan Carty, Budd Chavooshian, Rick Cohen, Sean Closkey, John Davis, Frank Ford, George Galster, William Gilchrist, Janet Hanson, Chester Hartman, Alan Goodheart, Liz and Marty Johnson, Peter Kasabach, David Kinsey, Susan Lenz, Carla Lerman, David Lewis, Kermit Lind, Dede Myers, Patrick Morrisy, Harriet Newburger, Oscar Newman, Ray Ocasio, Peter O'Connor, Connie Pascale, John Payne, Kent Pipes, Alex Polikoff, George Raymond, Ruth Price, John Prior, Michael Pyatok, Kerry Quaglia, Peter Reinhart, Eugene Schneider, David Schwartz, Harold Simon, Alexander von Hoffman, Colin Ward, Sidney Willis, and Ken Zimmerman. To the many others whom I should have included and have regrettably omitted, I apologize.

I am particularly grateful to Diane Sterner, my friend and collaborator on numerous housing policy papers and advocacy efforts, and to Nico Calavita, my friend and inclusionary housing maven. I would also like belatedly to acknowledge my debt to two good friends and fellow affordable housing colleagues who died far too young—Ken Russo and Fred Travisano—and to my father, Aubrey Mallach, who spent the first years of his career as a "houser" in New York City in the 1930s, and who left me a precious legacy in the lifelong pride he took in having helped frame a new housing policy for the United States during those years. Finally, my deepest gratitude as ever goes to Robin, whose support, encouragement, and companionship sustained me in this project, as they have in so many other efforts over the years, and to whom this book is dedicated.

Preface

The most casual look at housing conditions in the United States reveals a seeming paradox. While the majority of Americans are well housed, with many owning large, well-equipped homes that are the envy of millions throughout the world, a large, less affluent minority continues to be poorly housed, living in overcrowded or substandard conditions or burdened by housing costs well beyond what they can afford without hardship. This minority, which may include a quarter to a third of the nation's population, includes not only the poor, but school teachers, nurse's aides, Wal-Mart checkout clerks, the elderly on fixed incomes, single parents with small children, and individuals with disabilities.

Few people would disagree that every household should have a home where they can live in decent conditions without being forced to spend so much of their income for shelter that their ability to provide for the other necessities of life is impaired; in other words, that they should have affordable housing. Most people would also agree that if the market is unable to provide housing that less affluent households can afford, it is a reasonable use of public or philanthropic funds to make up the difference between what it costs to provide decent housing and what less affluent households can afford to pay.

Yet as soon as the subject of affordable housing arises, it becomes a matter of confusion, misunderstanding, and controversy. Even the term itself is considered suspect by many; indeed, one recent affordable housing publication stated that "[developers] seldom use the word 'affordable.' Not only does it scare off the neighbors, it creates a self-esteem issue for residents and a public relations issue for developers."[1] Frustrated housing advocates have suggested coming up with a new name, with some suggesting "workforce housing," others "attainable housing," and one, tongue somewhat in cheek, proposing "normal people's housing."

By whatever name, people have many different reactions to affordable housing. Some suburbanites associate affordable housing with real or imaginary social pathologies, or simply with the declining cities that they left behind for greener pastures. For others, the term conjures up images of stark, oppressive public housing projects, of which St. Louis's Pruitt-Igoe public housing project, long since demolished, is still seen as a malign model. With little concrete information available, affordable housing can easily become a blank slate, a virtual reality onto which individuals can project not only their aspirations, but their fears and ambivalence.

Part of this may be the result of American society and settlement patterns, which, as the United States became an increasingly suburban nation after World War II, have tended to divide the nation sharply both by race and by economic status. It also reflects the fact that, unlike most affluent postindustrial nations, the United States lacks a generally accepted body of affordable housing policies and principles that might provide for common ground across different regions, states, and cities. Finally, it comes from the reality that affordable housing itself is not a single, easily defined object; it is more like a kaleidoscope, taking different forms depending on where it is being built, who is building it, and whom it is designed to serve.

The confusion, misinformation, and stereotypes associated with affordable housing impose a huge burden on those who deal with affordable housing issues. These individuals include professionals in related fields, such as city planners reviewing development applications, architects designing affordable housing projects, or attorneys representing developers, citizens, or local government bodies. They may be lay people who find themselves acting on development applications as members of planning or zoning commissions, public officials and citizens wanting better to understand how affordable housing proposals will affect their neighborhood, counselors or social workers helping people find affordable housing, or individuals seeking to make a contribution to their communities by volunteering to become board members of a nonprofit housing development corporation or a local Habitat chapter. All of these people have, at best, sporadic access to solid, objective information to help them in their work.

The problem is not that nothing has been written about affordable housing. On the contrary, so many books have been written that bookshelves groan under their weight. The content of these books, however, suggest the nature of the problem. They are specialized works, designed to be useful to a more or less specialized audience looking for more or less specialized information, whether it is on the architecture, the legal issues, or the management of affordable housing. What is missing on this list is a book that offers professionals and educated lay persons alike a comprehensive picture of what affordable housing is, how it works, and how it is planned and developed, to provide them with the information and insight to make thoughtful, responsible decisions.

This book is designed to fill that gap. It is intended to provide the reader with a solid understanding of affordable housing in the United States in the early years of the 21st century—not only as a collection of buildings, but also in terms of its social, economic, and political dimensions and the most important issues and controversies surrounding it. The book is designed so that those interested in the subject can read it through from beginning to end for information and, I hope, with pleasure; at the same time, it is also designed so that a reader may go directly to a particular chapter in order to learn more about a pressing issue or question. A municipal attorney may want to read about how the town might go about adopting an inclusionary zoning ordinance; a local planner, faced with an inquiry from a developer of affordable housing, may want to read the chapters on siting and design in order to frame a presentation to the town's planning commission; and a social service provider may want to better understand the relationship between homelessness in her community and the availability of affordable housing.

The book is organized into four sections, each of which addresses a different dimension of this complex and multifaceted subject. The first section (Chapters 1 and 2) provides a background to the subject, in the form of a short history of affordable housing in the United States and a discussion of why, for all our nation's economic might and the enviable conditions under which most Americans live, affordable housing has been and continues to be needed.

The second section (Chapters 3 through 6) focuses directly on the process by which affordable housing is developed. Its four chapters begin with the design of affordable housing, and continue with site selection and the local approval process. Another chapter looks at the complicated mix of grants and loans that go into the financing of affordable housing, including a detailed discussion of financing under the Low Income Housing Tax Credit, the principal vehicle by which most affordable housing is developed in the United States today. The final chapter in this section walks the reader through a step-by-step description of the development process—from the framing of the initial idea to its successful conclusion—of a hypothetical but representative project developed by a nonprofit housing organization.

The third section (Chapters 7 through 12) moves from the development process to look at the major issues and controversies surrounding affordable housing. It begins with the exclusionary practices that have kept affordable housing out of large areas of the United States, then moves on to discuss the efforts that have been made to foster greater social and economic integration, particularly in the suburbs of major metropolitan areas. Further chapters discuss the role of affordable housing and community development corporations in neighborhood revitalization, and the risks and rewards of affordable home ownership, including a discussion of how the rise and fall of subprime lending and the foreclosure crisis may affect the future.

This section continues with chapters on the preservation of affordable housing, the role of affordable housing in addressing the problems of homelessness, and the use of inclusionary housing, an increasingly important strategy that uses the market as a vehicle for increasing affordable housing supply. Each chapter discusses the policy questions associated with the issue as well as practical considerations that will be useful to individuals grappling with preserving an affordable housing development, ending homelessness in their communities, or considering enactment of an inclusionary zoning ordinance.

Finally, the book's closing section (Chapter 13) takes a look forward at the larger policy issues affecting affordable housing in the United States today, and the trends, including demographic, geographic, and environmental changes, that are likely to affect affordable housing policies in the future. This section explores the politics of affordable housing, reviewing the affordable housing policy issues that are likely to be of concern to the professionals and citizens reading this book, and finally, using a somewhat cloudy crystal ball, takes a speculative look at possible future directions for affordable housing in the coming years.

In writing about a subject as complex and fraught with controversy as affordable housing, it is difficult, but critically important, to maintain a balance between fact, analysis, and opinion. Any book on the subject that avoided opinion and interpretation would quickly become nothing more than a tedious recitation of statistics, or an equally tedious precis of government documents and regulations; conversely, a book that offered no more than opinions would be little more than a polemic, shedding heat rather than light on the subject. I have tried to avoid both extremes and to be as clear as possible about what is fact, what is analysis, and what is opinion, stating whether it is mine, based on years of experience as public official, developer, advocate, and scholar, or someone else's. I do not expect every reader to agree with every position expressed here, and indeed, would be disappointed if that were the case. However, I hope that every reader will recognize that the ideas, opinions, and positions are the product of experience and careful thought, worthy of consideration, if not deference.

I am a planner by trade, and I share the planner's conviction that well-reasoned strategies are generally preferable to ad hoc improvisation, and that actions are usually more effective and constructive when animated by solid, reliable information and a thorough understanding of the issues. I hope that readers will find that this book will not only help provide them with that understanding and information, but that it will also help them act more effectively and responsibly in addressing the issues they confront as professionals and citizens.

NOTE

1. Corcoran, Suzanne. 2005. "The Developer's Perspective," in *Affordable Housing: Designing an American Asset*. Washington, D.C.: Urban Land Institute.

CHAPTER

1

The Case for Affordable Housing

Millions of households in the United States live in substandard or overcrowded housing conditions, or face excessive economic burdens in their effort to find decent housing that meets their needs. Understanding how to meet these needs and why creating affordable housing to address these needs is so important, however, takes more than simply recognizing that these needs exist. It demands an understanding of what the needs are, why they have come into being, and why they have not and will not be fully met by the private market, either by older housing filtering down to low-income families, or through regulatory reforms that will in some fashion lower the cost of housing to the point where all Americans will be able to afford a sound, livable home or apartment. While the private market plays an important role in affordable housing, that role is limited by economic forces that are inherent in the market itself, as well as by other powerful political, cultural, and social factors.

The purpose of this chapter is to put these issues in perspective, beginning with a look at the different elements that make up the need for affordable housing in the United States today. The balance of the chapter explores the extent to which those needs can be met through the private market, examining whether the need for affordable housing is a housing or an income problem and whether it is desirable to build new affordable housing or better to meet housing needs by increasing people's income and their ability to afford housing on the private market through housing vouchers or other means of stimulating demand.

THE NEED FOR DECENT HOUSING

When Franklin Delano Roosevelt said in his second inaugural address that he saw "one-third of the nation ill-housed," he was talking about the physical condition of their housing, about the millions of families living in homes without indoor plumbing, electricity, or the many things that 21st century Americans largely take for granted. Roosevelt's assessment was still valid in 1950, when more than one out of every three tenants, and nearly a quarter of all home owners, lived in a home that was dilapidated or lacked a private toilet or hot running water. Much has changed since then. By 2000, the number of occupied homes without complete plumbing and bathroom facilities had dropped to less than one percent of the nation's housing stock. Just the same, severe housing problems are still very much part of American society in the beginning of the 21st century.

Substandard housing

Although nearly all housing today contains basic plumbing and heating, substandard conditions are still widespread, as anyone who spends time in America's inner cities or distressed rural areas can testify. Although the Census stopped measuring housing conditions in 1960,[1] the American Housing Survey[2] found in 2005 that six percent of the housing units in the United States had moderate or severe physical deficiencies, and nearly 13 percent of all low-income families lived in physically deficient housing. Seven percent of all rental units had open cracks or holes in walls, floors, or ceilings, while eight percent of renters had seen mice or rats in their unit during the preceding three months. The AHS also reported that one out of six homes or apartments, and one out of four rental units, had an external building deficiency, such as a sagging roof, cracking or crumbling foundation, or missing bricks or outside siding.

Six percent may be a small share of the total, but it amounts to more than six million homes and apartments. Despite code enforcement efforts and other steps taken by local government, this number seems to resist further improvement and has remained virtually unchanged for the past decade. These properties, of course, run the gamut of conditions. Some may need to be demolished or extensively rebuilt, while others could be

Few cities offer as dramatic a juxtaposition between wealth and poverty as Houston, Texas, where dilapidated shacks huddle in the shadow of downtown towers. This scene dates to the 1980s.

rendered sound by only modest improvements, or in some cases simply by more conscientious maintenance and upkeep.

Despite the persistence of deficient units, most lower income households live in homes or apartments that meet the basic requirements that American society has defined as being minimally acceptable: four solid walls and a roof that protect its residents from the elements; no hazards such as lead paint or asbestos; electricity for lighting and appliances; plumbing, including a flush toilet, a bath or shower, and hot and cold running water; a complete kitchen, including a sink, stove, and refrigerator; and adequate heat in cold weather.

Lower income households suffer far more from problems associated with housing cost and housing occupancy—cost burden and overcrowding—than from deficiencies in their physical accommodations. In contrast to physical conditions, these problems have not diminished over time. The number of families suffering from cost burden has increased steadily since 1950, while overcrowding, after declining between 1950 and 1980, has been rising steadily at least through 2000 (Figure 1-1).[3]

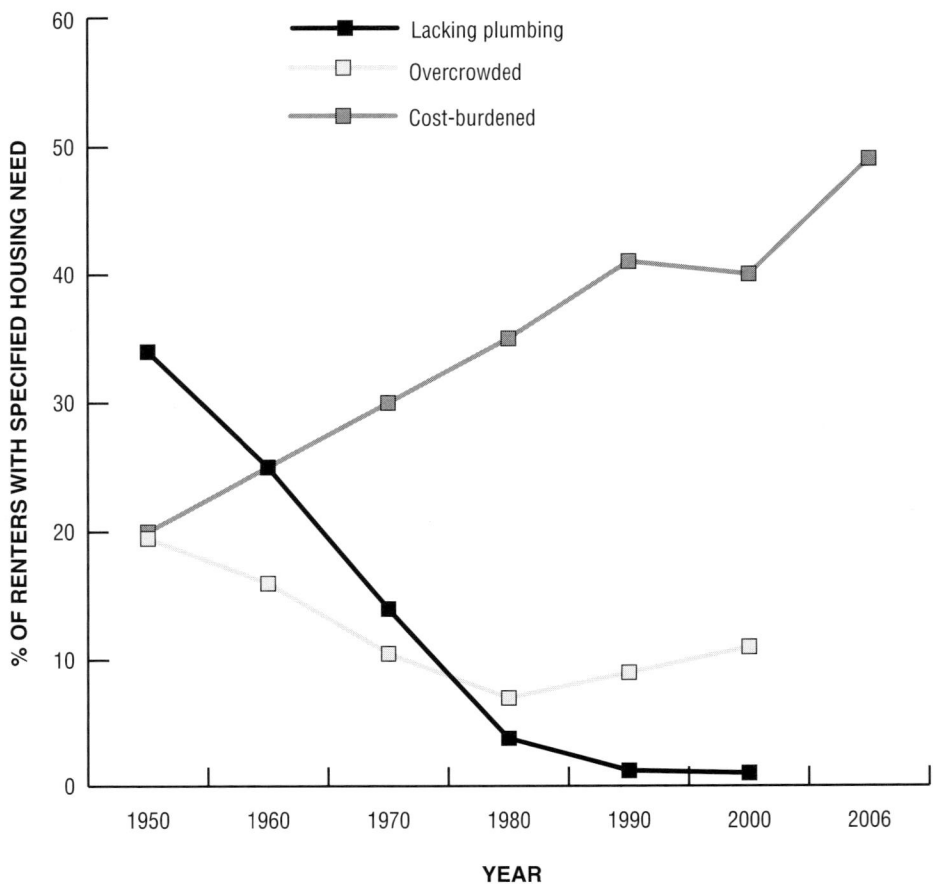

Figure 1-1 Trends in Rental Housing Needs, 1950–2006

Cost burden

The housing problem that affects the largest number of Americans today is *cost burden*. Cost burden arises when families must spend so much for housing that their ability to pay for the other necessities of life is compromised. While the weight of the burden varies widely from household to household, depending on their income and the size of their nonhousing expenses such as health care, commuting, and child rearing, the federal government and other public agencies have adopted the standard that a household spending more than 30 percent of its gross income for shelter is cost-burdened, and one spending more than 50 percent is *severely* cost-burdened.[4] For a low-income family earning $20,000 to $30,000 per year, it is easy enough to see that the amount left after taxes and annual housing costs that may be $8,000 to $10,000 will be difficult to stretch to cover the cost of putting food on the table, getting to and from work, and raising children.

Before going further, it is important to define what is meant by *low income*. Given the huge disparity in economic conditions and living costs from one part of the nation to another, government agencies dealing with housing, rather than setting a single national figure, have defined low- and moderate-income in relative terms, as a percentage of the median income in each region.[5] This book will use the federal terminology and refer to those households earning less than 50 percent of the median income for the area in which they live, adjusted for household size, as *very low-income* households, and those earning between 50 percent and 80 percent of that median as *low-income* households.[6] The sum of very low- and low-income households (all those earning 80 percent of median income or less) are referred to as *lower income* households. Lower income households make up roughly 40 percent of the nation's population.

Area median incomes, which are calculated annually by the U.S. Department of Housing and Urban Development for all metropolitan areas or rural counties in the United States, vary widely from one part of the country to another. They can be as high as $111,600 (Stamford, Connecticut) or as low as $32,100 (Yazoo County, Mississippi) for a four-person family. As a result of these regional variations, a family of four earning $55,000 in Stamford would be defined as a very low-income family, but would be considered quite well-off in Yazoo County, where a family would only be defined as very low-income if their annual income was $16,050 or less.

Cost burden disproportionately affects low-income households. Nearly two-thirds of all low-income households in the United States suffer from cost burden (Table 1-1). Renters are much more likely to be cost-burdened than are owners. In 2004, 48 percent of all renters were cost-burdened, compared to 32 percent of home owners with mortgages, and only 14 percent of home owners without mortgages. During the past decade, however, the number of home owners with cost burdens has been rising much faster than the number of cost-burdened renters, as a result of the dramatic increase in house prices in much of the nation and the growth in subprime mortgages.

In 2000, more than three-quarters of all cost-burdened households were lower income households, or nearly 22 million households. Of these, half, or 11 million, were severely burdened, spending more than

TABLE 1-1 COST BURDEN FOR LOW- AND MODERATE-INCOME HOUSEHOLDS IN 2000

INCOME RANGE	NUMBER OF HOUSEHOLDS		PERCENTAGE OF HOUSEHOLDS	
	Cost-burdened	Severely cost-burdened	Cost-burdened	Severely cost-burdened
Very low income	15,700,000	9,600,000	64.2%	39.2%
Low income	6,100,000	1,400,000	33.3	7.7
All lower income	21,800,000	11,000,000	51.0	25.8

Source: 2000 Census

TABLE 1-2 CHANGE IN PERCENTAGE OF HOUSEHOLDS THAT ARE COST-BURDENED BY INCOME RANGE, 2000–2005

INCOME RANGE	HOME OWNERS		RENTERS	
	2000	2005	2000	2005
$0–19,999	60%	68%	81%	87%
$20,000–34,999	37%	44%	38%	58%
$35,000–49,999	25%	34%	11%	25%
$50,000–74,999	14%	23%	5%	11%

Source: 2000 data from 2000 Census; 2005 data from 2005 American Community Survey

50 percent of their income on housing costs. A recent study found that "working families facing a severe housing cost burden are more likely than other working families to endure material hardships." The study found that 38 percent of those families experienced food insecurity—a euphemism for hunger—while 37 percent had a family member who lacked health insurance.[7] Their situation is very different from that of affluent families, who may spend more than is necessary in order to buy a larger or higher quality home or live in a particularly desirable community. While a wealthy household might spend 30 percent of its income for housing and still have more than enough left over to live comfortably, that option is not available for struggling, hard-pressed working families.

Although cost burdens have been rising steadily since 1950, they took a sharp upward turn between 2000 and 2005, both for renters and—even more so—for home owners, as house prices skyrocketed to unprecedented levels. The number of renters spending 30 percent or more of their income for rent went from just over 13 million to nearly 17 million in only five years, an increase of 3.6 million or 29 percent. During the same period, however, the number of cost-burdened home owners went from 12 to 21 million, an increase of over 75 percent. Since most very low-income families were already cost-burdened in 2000, the change most dramatically affected low- and moderate-income families, as shown in Table 1-2. Many low-income families, already cost-burdened, saw their burden become even greater.[8]

The increase in renter cost burden since 1950 comes partly from rent increases over that period, but even more from the growing income gap between renters and owners. In 1950, when there were nearly as many renter households in the United States as home owners, there was little difference in their incomes. The median renter earned 83 percent of the income of the median home owner. Millions of households that could afford to buy a home, including many minority and nontraditional households, were barred from home ownership by the real estate and mortgage practices of the time. As home ownership has come to be all but universally seen as a desirable goal for American households, and has become increasingly accessible through changes in mortgage products and underwriting practices, the economic gap between owners and renters has grown steadily wider. By 2005, the median income of renters had dropped to only 48 percent of that of home owners.

Between 1950 and 2005, the median monthly gross rent in the United States increased from $43 to $694, slightly more than doubling when adjusted for inflation.[9] Although this seems like a lot, it only represents an average increase of 1.5 percent per year in constant dollars. During the same period, however, renters' median incomes rose from $2,799 to $24,482, an exiguous increase of only 12 percent in constant dollars over 55 years, while the median income of home owners more than doubled. While wealthy renters may cluster in Manhattan and a few other highly desirable urban settings, renters today in the United States are disproportionately lower income households.

Overcrowding

The third category of housing need is overcrowding, which takes place where limited financial resources or inadequate housing supply force families to rent or buy housing that is too small to accommodate them adequately, or where families and individuals double up in the same house or apartment, often as a way to avoid homelessness. The federal government currently defines overcrowding as more than one person per room, and severe overcrowding as more than 1.5 persons per room. Rooms include bedrooms, the living room, and the kitchen or dining room if they are separate from the other rooms in the house or apartment, but not bathrooms, alcoves, and foyers. As a result, a family of five persons living in a typical two-bedroom apartment, which contains four rooms, is considered overcrowded, while a family of seven in the same apartment would be considered severely overcrowded.

While few people would argue with the principle that crowding too many people into a house or apartment is undesirable, defining what number is too many has changed considerably over time, even more than the changes in the standard of cost burden or housing condition. How overcrowding is defined reflects not only a society's housing conditions, but how it defines what living arrangements are acceptable; as one legal scholar has written, "Lacking a scientific basis in safety, occupancy limits instead reflect profound social and cultural biases about how a family 'should' live."[10]

A hundred years ago, in an age of large families, a unit was generally considered overcrowded only if two or more separate families were doubling up. If a family had the entire house or apartment to themselves, they were by definition not overcrowded, whatever the size of the family or the apartment. By 1940, the federal government had adopted a standard of more than two persons per room, which it reduced to 1.5 persons per room in 1950, and one person per room in 1960, where it has remained since then.[11] Other standards, such as the number of people per bedroom or per square foot of floor space, are often used for code enforcement purposes.

Overcrowding in the United States declined steadily between 1950 and 1980. In 1950, nearly 20 percent of all renters lived in overcrowded conditions, a figure that dropped to seven percent by 1980. At that point, the trend reversed course, with the percentage of renters in overcrowded conditions rising to 11 percent in 2000. As shown in Table 1-3, more than six million American households live in overcrowded conditions, nearly half in severe overcrowding. Although renters make up less than one-third of American households, they make up nearly two-thirds of overcrowded households.

Overcrowding is unevenly distributed around the United States. It is at its most pronounced in California, where nearly one out of every four

TABLE 1-3 OVERCROWDING BY TENURE

CATEGORY	OWNERS	RENTERS
1.01 to 1.50 per room	1,328,503	1,856,265
1.51 or more per room	815,232	2,057,890
Number overcrowded	2,143,735	3,914,255
Percentage overcrowded	3% of all owners	11% of all renters

Source: 2000 Census

renters lived in overcrowded conditions in 2000; in fact, 30 percent of all of the overcrowded renter households in the nation lived in California. By contrast, only one out of every 26 Iowa renters and only one out of 41 Vermont renters lived in overcrowded conditions.

Overcrowding is closely associated with high housing costs, which compel many lower income families to live in smaller units out of economic necessity, or in many cases to double up with two or more separate families sharing a single dwelling unit. Indeed, some overcrowding represents a sort of "hidden homelessness," in that many of the families who live doubled or tripled up with friends or relatives might otherwise be homeless. As early as 1986, the New York Housing Authority estimated that nearly one out of every four of their apartments contained a second family doubling up with the legal tenant.[12]

Overcrowding is also closely related to immigration. High immigration locales have much higher levels of overcrowding than communities with little immigration. In California, 43 percent of all Latino households and 51 percent of Latino renters lived in overcrowded conditions, compared to only four percent of non-Latino White families. Latino families, and to a lesser extent those of Asian origin, tend to have much higher levels of overcrowding than either non-Latino White or Black families. While much of this can be attributed to lower incomes and larger family sizes, there is also evidence that, with overcrowding perceived differently in different cultures, a higher level of household density is more acceptable among Latino families than among non-Latino families—White or African American—in the United States.[13]

Finally, not all housing needs have to do with the condition of a tenant's housing unit or the rent she must pay. Disproportionate numbers of lower income households are geographically segregated and concentrated in high-poverty areas, which, although most often urban, are also found in rural areas, particularly in the South. Although the housing units many such households occupy may meet minimum standards of living space, condition, and even affordability, the areas in which they live are often isolated, with limited access to jobs and shopping, poor public services, and poor schools. Areas of concentrated poverty not only lack opportunity, but are subject to a wide range of ills, including high crime rates, abandoned buildings, and environmental contamination. This issue represents a fundamental challenge to American social and housing policy, which must be addressed by entire regions, not just by the cities where poverty is most heavily concentrated.

AFFORDABLE HOUSING NEEDS AND THE PRIVATE MARKET

With millions of Americans still living in overcrowded or substandard housing, and 38 million households suffering from housing cost burdens, it is clear that the need for affordable housing is a problem of enough magnitude that it must be acknowledged and addressed by a society that takes pride in its ability to provide its citizens with a decent standard of living. To recognize something as a problem, however, is very different from recognizing why it has come into being and what should be done about it. In housing, as in any other area involving complex social and economic policy issues, answers to these questions are often both elusive and a source of contention.

Some people question the need for governmental or voluntary participation at all in meeting the nation's housing needs. With a robust, vibrant housing industry that has demonstrated its ability to provide decent, even luxurious, housing for the majority of the American people and make healthy profits doing so, this argument goes, the market should be able to provide—either through new construction or by older housing "filtering down"—affordable housing for all who need it.[14]

This argument hinges on a three-part chain of reasoning. First, that excessive regulation of housing construction has both driven up costs and reduced the ability of the home building industry to meet these needs; second, that if unreasonable regulations were removed, the industry would produce housing in far greater numbers and at far lower costs, thus housing the majority of those currently in need; and third, to the extent that even the most inexpensive newly constructed housing is beyond the reach of the very poor, their needs will be met by the resulting filtering down of older units at lower cost.

Each link in the chain contains a partial truth. The cumulative effect of regulations, including building codes, zoning ordinances, and environmental regulations, does affect the cost of housing and reduce the number of new homes built. If more new units were constructed, the price of older units—at least in some areas—*might* drop. To the extent that changes can reasonably be made that will permit the private market to meet *more* of the housing needs of lower income households, housing advocates should push for those changes. In the final analysis, however, the evidence does not support the argument that the private sector will ever realistically be able to meet all of the nation's affordable housing needs.

Regulation and the cost of new housing

Regulations affect housing in two fundamental respects: by adding cost or by limiting production. Modern building codes, by requiring more expensive materials or more complex construction techniques, increase the cost of building new homes. Zoning regulations, by restricting the number of units that can be built on a piece of property, both limit housing production and add costs by imposing standards for minimum house sizes, minimum front yard setbacks, and similar features. Environmental regulations such as wetlands restrictions further constrain supply by reducing the amount of land available for development, as do public open space acquisition and farmland preservation programs. The upshot is fewer and more expensive units. In New Jersey, where the regulation of housing is probably as strict as anywhere in the United States, housing production has dropped off dramatically—despite powerful market demand—since the 1950s and 1960s, while the average new house price in the first quarter of 2006 was nearly $500,000.[15]

Even if deregulation could theoretically transform the cost and volume of housing production in states like New Jersey and California, a proposition that has never been clearly established, the likelihood of the drastic deregulation that might be needed to achieve that end is so remote as to be little more than a fantasy. Regulations exist not out of perverse desires, but because they serve some widely valued purpose. Building codes exist because they reflect widely held norms of what constitute reasonable housing standards, either in terms of specific health and safety considerations or a less explicit but equally powerful social consensus of which features are needed for a decent living environment. Environmental regulations and open space preservation programs exist either because there are sound science-based reasons for preserving wetlands or barring construction in floodplains, or because the public strongly values and is willing to pay for preserving green space and the natural environment.

This is not to suggest that all regulations are reasonable. Even facially reasonable regulations can be taken to unreasonable lengths, or administered in ways that make them unduly burdensome. Still other regulations may be unreasonable on their face. Some communities may drastically constrain housing production through exclusionary zoning ordinances, in order to keep out "undesirables" or maximize local property tax revenues. From the standpoint of the greater regional welfare, that may be neither desirable nor legitimate. Such practices, however, reflect powerful local preferences, and are unlikely to change in the absence of fundamental property tax reform or equally fundamental changes in systems of land-use law and governance. Indeed, even in states such as New Jersey, where courts have found exclusionary zoning to be invalid, it persists even more powerfully beneath a veneer of fair share plans and affordable housing strategies than before the state supreme court's landmark *Mount Laurel* decision, a seminal case described more fully in Chapter 7.

In a nation such as the United States, where the haves outnumber the have-nots, political realities dictate that regulations that enhance the quality of life of the majority are likely to be preserved, even at the price of diminishing the minority's quality of life. Although rising prices have made it increasingly difficult for a growing share of American households to find homes they can afford—and as support for creating affordable housing has grown—the American body politic has shown little or no appetite for more than trivial deregulation. Ironically, many of the most vociferous proponents of exclusionary zoning, perhaps the most egregious form of regulation limiting housing supply, are people who in most other aspects of their lives are strongly committed to the private market and the capitalist system.

Even in those parts of the United States where regulation is modest, and where supply, in theory, should have no difficulty meeting demand, we find that the prevalence of cost burden is only slightly relieved. Table 1-4 compares cost burden by income range for renters in the three highest cost and three lowest cost states.[16] At first blush, the data suggest that the low-cost states are significantly more affordable than the high-cost states; after all, only 18 percent of Mississippi renters earning between

$20,000 and $34,999 are cost-burdened, compared to 56 percent of California's. When one looks at cost burden in the light of the income differences between the states, however, that disparity largely disappears. *Relative to the median income of the state's renters*, there is little difference between the low-cost and the high-cost states in their percentage of cost-burdened renters. Renters in the lower half of the renter population are likely to be cost-burdened, whatever the cost profile or regulatory climate of the state. In fact, the percentage of cost-burdened renters is *lower* in Massachusetts than in either Mississippi or Arkansas.[17]

This reflects two basic housing market realities. First, with rare exceptions, developers will build, owners will sell, and landlords will rent for what they can get for their product. In a high-income market, people will charge more for an immobile product like housing than in a low-income market. Second, every market sets a minimum price that must be met for the market to function, below which developers will not build houses and landlords will not rent out properties. The minimum

TABLE 1-4 PERCENTAGE OF RENTERS WITH COST BURDEN FOR SELECTED STATES, 2000

(a) By income range						
INCOME RANGE (000)	LOW-VALUE STATES			HIGH-VALUE STATES		
	Oklahoma	Mississippi	Arkansas	Massachusetts	California	Hawaii
$0–$9.9	85.1%	82.6%	83.4%	78.5%	91.3%	84.6
$10–$19.9	64.1	60.6	63.7	69.5	82.8	82.3
$20–$34.9	17.4	18.3	17.2	49.1	55.8	61.3
$35–$49.9	3.3	4.5	2.3	17.8	23.2	25.7
Median renter income	$21,807	$19,603	$21,167	$30,682	$31,912	$33,755
(b) Overall						
% of all households cost-burdened	37.5%	39.9%	39.3%	38.7%	44.9%	43.3%
Median % of income spent for rent	24.3	25.0	24.4	25.5	27.7	27.2

Source: 2000 Census

price that permits a developer to build is the price that will cover her costs—construction, site improvements, and "soft" costs—as well as the cost of land and a reasonable profit. Those costs, *excluding land and profit*, for a modest house on a small lot, in a typical suburban community in the northeastern or western states in 2006, might be in the vicinity of $150,000. Assuming a reasonable price for the land and a reasonable profit, the house could sell for slightly more than $200,000, which would be affordable—depending on a variety of assumptions—to a family with a total income of $55,000 to $70,000.[18]

Although such housing would be a great boon to struggling middle-income families in many parts of the country, it would still demand a buyer whose income is well above the levels at which housing needs are the most severe. The reality is, however, that such units rarely get built in high-demand areas, except where public sector initiatives either require it or provide incentives to make it possible. First, if the market value of that house exceeds the minimum price, a rational developer will sell the house for the market value and pocket the difference. Second, in that event, assuming the landowner is rational and conversant with market conditions, she will increase her price to reflect market value, to make the developer share the additional profit with her. Third, if the market price is indeed higher than the minimum, the market price of a larger and more luxurious house is likely to be still higher, and the profit still greater, than on a modest, no-frills house. Therefore, the developer will be motivated to build a larger house instead of the modest structure that he may have originally contemplated. As a result, economic forces work not only to push up the market price of housing, but keep it there.

Healthy market areas, where there is an ample supply of both housing and buildable land relative to demand and where regulatory impediments are modest and permit efficient high-density construction, should in theory be exceptions to this rule. While there are no perfect environments, many observers suggest that the Las Vegas area, with its miles of buildable desert, comes close. Even there, however, affordability, while greater than in New Jersey or California, is elusive. Only four out of nearly 1,600 new single-family homes on the market in the fall of 2006 were being offered for $200,000 or less, while only 87—barely five percent—were being offered for $250,000 or less.[19] With the 2005 median household income in the Las Vegas metropolitan area at roughly $50,000, virtually none of the new houses being built in one of America's most unconstrained markets were affordable to a median-income family, let alone to a lower income one.

Existing housing and filtering

Some writers who argue that the private market can meet the housing needs of lower income families acknowledge that newly built homes are likely to be outside their reach. Instead, they argue that the production of ample amounts of new housing will make the existing housing stock affordable through filtering. What that means is that that as new homes are built, more affluent families will move out of older and less desirable units into the new homes, thus reducing demand for the older units. With less demand for the older units, their cost will decline, making them available to progressively less affluent households and ultimately the poor.

As with the other propositions, this has a kernel of truth. Older houses generally cost less than new houses, but not by much. In the first quarter of 2006, the median price of existing homes sold in the United States was 88 percent of the median price of new homes. This is not a very large difference, and has more to do with the larger size and more elaborate features of new homes than with any decline inherent with age.[20] In the West, where demand is greatest, existing houses are more expensive on the average than new homes, while the price gap is greatest in the Midwest, where demand is weakest and where older homes are more likely to be found in distressed urban areas like Cleveland or Detroit.

Units do not filter down either as quickly or as sharply as would be needed to reach the nation's low-income families at prices they can afford. Price information is consistent with the data on renter cost burden. The great majority of households in the lower half of the renter income distribution consistently suffer from cost burden whether the overall housing market is strong or weak or whether housing production is booming or merely trickling along. This is partly because of the

TABLE 1-5 MEDIAN PRICES OF NEW AND EXISTING HOMES BY REGION, 1ST QUARTER 2006

	UNITED STATES	NORTHEAST	MIDWEST	SOUTH	WEST
New homes	$247,700	$339,000	$210,700	$205,000	$330,000
Existing homes	$217,900	$285,200	$158,800	$179,700	$344,000
Ratio (existing: new)	.88	.85	.75	.87	1.04

Source: New homes, U.S. Bureau of the Census; existing homes, National Association of Realtors

limits of the filtering process itself, but partly because of a phenomenon known as the "renter income/rental cost mismatch," which is immune to public-sector tinkering.

Simply stated, most households seek out the least expensive housing unit that satisfies their needs and desires. This is particularly true among renters, who are less selective because potential appreciation, which might lead one to pay more initially, is not a factor, and most renters do not intend to remain in their units for long. As a result, many affluent renters minimize their costs by seeking out houses and apartments that would otherwise be affordable to lower income households. This means those units become unavailable to lower income renters, who must seek out more expensive units, resulting in a cost burden. An analysis of this mismatch in New Jersey based on 2000 Census data found that, although nearly 400,000 renters had a cost burden, if somehow one could create a perfect fit between renter incomes and rents—if every tenant at every income level rented the most expensive unit they could afford short of the 30 percent threshold—the number of cost-burdened households would be more than cut in half.

The point is not that the government should force affluent tenants to rent more expensive apartments, which would be absurd, but that the nature of consumer preferences further limits filtering as an effective means of meeting housing needs for lower income households. While some units filter down, others will continue to be siphoned off by more affluent households, while many never filter down in the first place. In many areas these effects may be socially or demographically neutral, but in others they are compounded by the effect of race on housing opportunity, as racial steering or discrimination may give nonminority households an unfair advantage in the competition for the more desirable lower priced housing units.

This leads to a further problem with filtering, perhaps the most serious one from a policy standpoint. The uneven nature of the filtering process promotes the geographic and economic fragmentation of the housing market, leading to segregation of lower income households into the least desirable locations within each housing market area. Where housing market demand is strong, little or no filtering takes place on the basis of the *age* of the housing. A house built in 1960 and one of the same size and with similar features built in 1990 will command roughly the same price. A house built in 1890 may actually command a higher price, because of its relative rarity and historic character. In such areas, filtering takes place only when a unit becomes undesirable to more affluent families, either because of its inadequate physical features or, more often, its location.[21]

Thus, the workings of the private market lead to two particularly unfortunate outcomes for lower income households. First, while they may be more able to find housing of decent quality in low-demand regions, those are by definition the areas in which economic opportunities are fewest. They will have the hardest time finding affordable housing of decent quality in the private market in strong-demand areas such as New Jersey, Massachusetts, or California. Second, in all areas, but particularly in strong-demand areas, lower income households will typically find affordable housing, if at all, only in those locations that are least desirable from a market standpoint; that is, locations that are not only physically unattractive, but which lack job opportunities, shopping, and public services of decent quality. That is why policies designed to address the housing needs of lower income households must also address the condition of the neighborhoods in which they live.

Concentrating the poorest households, as well as those with incomes well above the poverty level, in the least desirable locations not only stigmatizes them but places them at a competitive disadvantage compared to those whose income allows them to live in areas that have better access to jobs, are safer, and offer better schools. Moreover, as suburban jurisdictions—where most of the jobs are—become increasingly unaffordable to and isolated from the region's lower income citizens, they find it increasingly difficult to recruit the workers needed to fill a host of jobs in health care, retail trade, and local government. For all of these reasons, the private sector cannot provide the United States with solutions to its affordable housing problems or fully meet the housing needs of its lower income population.

IS AFFORDABLE HOUSING A HOUSING PROBLEM OR AN INCOME PROBLEM?

While millions of American households have difficulty finding affordable housing, the great majority of those households are cost-burdened and living in housing that meets minimum standards of physical condition. That, in turn, has led many people to ask, not unreasonably, whether what is often defined as a housing problem, in the sense of an inadequacy of the housing supply, is actually an income problem, in that the real problem may not be housing, but the inadequacy of many households' incomes. From some perspectives, this distinction may not really matter; after all, the problem has the same effect on peoples' lives however it is defined. From a public policy perspective, however, it makes an important difference. It raises the critical question of whether it is better to address the problem by increasing the supply of housing lower income families can afford, or by increasing the demand for housing by raising those same families' incomes so they can afford housing that already exists in their community.

This is a very different question than that faced by policy makers in the 1930s or the 1950s, when millions of families lived in houses and apartments that lacked even the rudiments of decent housing, and a new unit in a new building was their only hope to attain sound and safe living conditions. Since the 1980s, the federal government has increasingly favored addressing the demand side of the equation through the use of the Housing Choice Voucher program, originally known as the Section 8 program.[22] For the 2007 fiscal year, HUD planned to spend nearly $22 billion on vouchers, while spending only $5 billion to build or rehabilitate affordable housing units.[23]

This is not an either-or proposition. It should be seen instead as a question: Under what circumstances, in what locations, and for which populations is it better to increase supply or to enhance demand? There are some conditions under which increasing the supply of affordable housing is clearly more appropriate, just as there are other conditions where it is less so. Increasing the supply of affordable housing is particularly appropriate in four situations:

- Areas of high housing cost and demand, where the supply of moderately priced housing is severely limited
- Low-poverty, primarily suburban areas, where affordable housing is needed in order to deconcentrate poverty and foster regional equity and opportunity
- Areas where the imbalance between jobs and housing is promoting sprawl and threatening the area's economic competitiveness
- Areas of particular housing shortage for specific groups within the larger lower income population, such as large families, the frail elderly, and individuals with special needs

Each of these four categories will be discussed briefly in this chapter. A fifth area, where affordable housing is used within the framework of urban revitalization strategies, both to foster revitalization and to preserve affordability as real estate prices rise as a result of gentrification, will be discussed in Chapter 8.

Distinguishing between high- and low-demand areas

There are many parts of the United States where it makes more sense to expand demand rather than add supply. Many regions, particularly in much of the South and Midwest, contain an ample supply or even an excess of housing relative to demand, much of it moderately priced, although often not necessarily affordable to lower income families. Housing vouchers can add enough to a household's income to allow those families to afford housing available in the private market, often at substantially lower cost to the public purse than if they were to be provided with a brand-new unit.

This is not true everywhere. In high-demand and high-cost areas such as the New York or San Francisco metropolitan areas, housing is in short supply relative to demand, and the available housing is far more expensive. As a result, the cost per household for a demand-side program will be far greater. This is illustrated in Table 1-6, which compares the cost of enabling a household earning 30 percent of the area median income to afford a median-priced rental unit in Yazoo County, Mississippi, and in Stamford, Connecticut. It is far less expensive to fill the gap between what a low-income family can afford and the cost of private market housing in Yazoo County, even though the family is far poorer than their counterpart in Stamford, because the market cost of housing is so much lower.

The table, however, illustrates another important point. In Yazoo County, the cost of enabling a large low-income family to afford a four-bedroom house in the private market is only slightly more than the cost of subsidizing a single person to afford a studio apartment. In Stamford, by contrast, the cost to enable a large low-income family to afford a four-bedroom house in the private market is nearly four times the cost of subsidizing a single person to afford a studio apartment, and represents the annualized cost of a house worth more than $250,000.

In distressed cities like Flint, Michigan, or Youngstown, Ohio, production of new affordable housing may actually be a bad idea. New housing built under the stringent regulations government imposes for affordable housing is likely to be far more expensive than existing housing. It will rent or sell for prices that may be higher than many houses in the private market, which already has a surplus of vacant houses. As a result, in such areas, construction of new affordable housing, except where it is

TABLE 1-6 COST OF ENABLING A HOUSEHOLD AT 30% AMI TO AFFORD A MEDIAN-PRICED RENTAL UNIT

NUMBER OF BEDROOMS	MEDIAN MONTHLY RENT	MEDIAN ANNUAL RENT	HOUSE-HOLD SIZE	ANNUAL INCOME AT 30% AMI	AFFORD-ABLE RENT (30% OF INCOME)	GAP (SUBSIDY COST)
Stamford, Connecticut						
0	$1137	$13,644	1	$24,150	$7,335	$6,309
1	1375	16,500	2	27,900	8,370	8,130
2	1747	20,964	3	31,400	9,420	11,544
3	2303	27,636	5	37,700	11,310	16,326
4	2993	35,916	7	43,300	12,990	22,926
Yazoo County, Mississippi						
0	$394	$4,728	1	$7,650	$2,295	$2,433
1	424	5088	2	8,750	2,625	2,463
2	475	5,700	3	9,850	2,955	2,745
3	579	6,948	5	11,850	3,555	3,393
4	655	7,860	7	13,600	4,080	3,780

Source: Analysis based on data from U.S. Department of Housing and Urban Development

part of a concerted strategy of neighborhood transformation, can actually undermine the existing housing market and contribute to further housing deterioration and abandonment.

This is not true in high-demand areas. In those areas large numbers of households at all income levels are competing for a limited supply of sound and reasonably priced dwelling units. As a result, even with financial assistance, a low-income household may not be able to find a home or apartment that meets their needs, particularly if the household is African American or Latino and potentially affected by discrimination in the housing market. Indeed, families living in such areas who receive demand-side assistance in the form of Housing Choice Vouchers [24] are often frustrated in their search for such a home, and end up returning their vouchers to the city's housing agency. A 2000 study found that only 47 percent of families receiving vouchers in Los Angeles, and 57 percent in New York City, were able to find an apartment meeting the program standards within the time permitted for their search.[25] High-demand areas need new affordable housing the most, because the available supply of housing on the private market is either too limited or too expensive for a demand-side program to be either feasible or cost-effective.

Promoting poverty deconcentration and regional equity

As America has become more suburbanized since World War II, it has also become more segregated. As a recent book put it,

> . . . . places are becoming more unequal. Economic classes are becoming more spatially separate from each other, with the rich increasingly living with other rich people and the poor with other poor. The latter are concentrated in central cities and distressed inner suburbs, and the former are in exclusive central-city neighborhoods and more distant suburbs.[26]

This has spawned a series of deeply troubling consequences both for the nation's lower income population and for America as a whole. As the middle class has fled the cities, suburban communities have become more and more the locus of jobs, resources, and opportunity. Lower income households, particularly people of color, have been prevented from moving along with those jobs and opportunities, being concentrated instead in older cities and a handful of inner suburbs largely devoid of the social, economic, or fiscal resources needed to afford their residents a minimum of opportunities and a decent quality of life.

Second, within those cities and suburbs, these households are disproportionately concentrated in high-poverty areas where they are doubly burdened by the social problems associated with the concentration of poverty. As Paul Jargowsky has written, "Concentrations of poor people lead to a concentration of the social ills that cause or are caused by poverty."[27] Among the problems strongly associated with the concentration of poverty are a lack of private-sector business activity; increased costs of goods and services for residents; limited job networks and poor access to employment; limited educational opportunity; higher levels of crime; diminished levels of physical and mental health; a reduced ability to build assets; deterioration in local government services and fiscal capacity; and increased political and societal fragmentation and division.[28]

While some economic segregation may come about through market forces and may be endemic to most industrialized societies, the economic segregation found in American metropolitan areas has historically been abetted by governmental action, from the redlining of inner city areas by the Federal Housing Administration to the exclusionary zoning practices of the nation's affluent suburbs. The widespread practice of locating affordable housing projects disproportionately in the most distressed, high-poverty areas of each metropolitan region has compounded the segregation of lower income households in the inner cities and older suburbs. Although the concentration of affordable housing in the high-poverty areas of central cities has diminished somewhat since the days of public housing, it is still strong. This subject is discussed in further detail in Chapter 8.

The deconcentration of poverty and the creation of opportunities for lower income households to share in the benefits of American society is a critically important societal goal. While it is not solely a housing issue and cannot be addressed through housing policies alone, it cannot be achieved without providing affordable housing opportunities. In most growing metropolitan areas, this goal cannot be achieved by enhancing housing demand through vouchers because of the high price and limited supply of suitable housing. In those areas, meaningful efforts to deconcentrate poverty and foster regional equity demands that new housing opportunities be created through the construction of additional affordable housing.

Fostering economic competitiveness

American metropolitan regions pay a high price for decades of policies that have dispersed employment centers into suburban areas without providing housing for the workforce needed to sustain them. Sprawl, long commuting distances, air pollution, and increasing demands on infrastructure are a few of the consequences. As these regions have become more aware of the price they are paying and of the fragility of their economic underpinnings, they have become more aware that the lack of affordable housing has a direct effect on their ability to remain competitive not only nationally but globally. As Turner and Katz write in a recent paper worth citing at length,

> When reasonably priced housing is in short supply and households have to spend large shares of incomes for housing, a region becomes a less attractive place to live and invest. High housing costs create pressures on employers to increase wages and jobs go unfilled at lower wages and as current employees demand higher wages to reflect their high costs of living. Commutes from

home to work become longer as families locate further from their jobs in order to obtain affordable housing, increasing congestion costs, reducing productivity, and possibly contributing to employee turnover. Ultimately, these trends may constrain or even destabilize a region's labor market, particularly for low- and moderate-wage labor as people quit their jobs, existing residents leave the region, and prospective residents choose not to move in the region. Some economists argue that the impacts of high housing costs on regional economies may even undermine overall national productivity.[29]

As these connections have become more widely understood, advocacy coalitions have emerged in states from Minnesota to Connecticut making the case that their states' continued economic prosperity may well depend on their ability to address their shortage of affordable housing. The At Home in Connecticut website states that "Businesses report that the availability of quality, affordable housing is an asset in attracting and retaining a quality workforce. [. . .] Housing that is affordable to a company's employees can reduce stress and financial burdens, increase productivity and improve employee satisfaction."[30]

In other jurisdictions, major employers have become involved in providing affordable housing through what has come to be known as employer-assisted housing. Illinois now offers financial incentives to employers who help their workers obtain affordable housing near their workplace.

The type of affordable housing that may have the greatest impact on economic competitiveness may not be the same as that designed to address other housing needs. The term "workforce housing" has come into widespread use to describe housing that is oriented toward individuals who will fill jobs in the local economy, such as school teachers, police officers, or nurses' aides. While there is no generally accepted definition, the term is often used in a way that is both broader and narrower, with respect to the populations it attempts to serve, than most widely used definitions of affordable housing. The National Housing Conference defines workforce housing as housing for families that contain "at least one full-time worker who earns between the minimum wage and the amount needed to afford to live in the area,"[31] a definition that includes most non-elderly lower income households as well as many households that may earn much more, but are still constrained in their ability to live near where they work, particularly in high-cost areas such as the New York or Boston suburbs. Some jurisdictions, however, may simply use the term as a seemingly less threatening synonym for affordable housing.[32]

Housing shortages for specific populations

In some regions or cities, some lower income households may be able to find affordable housing but for others it is out of reach. Table 1-6 suggests, for example, that it might be cost effective to use vouchers to meet the housing needs of single people and couples in Stamford,[33] but not the needs of large families. In such an area, it might be desirable to direct the resources for new housing production toward creating affordable homes for large lower income families.

Who should be targeted for additional housing supply will vary from area to area depending on the characteristics of the population and the availability of both market and affordable housing. While some regions have ample affordable housing for the elderly, others may need more such housing, particularly in parts of the Midwest where the number of older households is rising steadily. This may be true even in areas that are not generally lacking in moderately priced housing, but which may lack an adequate supply of housing that is appropriate for the needs of the elderly. The same is likely to be true for people with special needs, by virtue of physical or developmental disabilities. Individuals with disabilities as well as the elderly often need housing with particular features, and may need to be housed in clusters that will enable them to benefit from shared facilities and supportive services.

Other issues

The situations described above are those in which it is most appropriate to encourage the construction of new affordable housing rather than providing households with vouchers or other demand-side programs. That does not mean that they are the only circumstances under which adding to the supply of affordable housing should be entertained. There is certainly a role for building affordable housing in urban areas, even distressed areas, where it is part of a larger strategy to revitalize the neighborhood. This is particularly important in the many urban neighborhoods from Los Angeles to Boston, where market changes and gentrification have begun to price large numbers of lower income residents out of their communities.

Vouchers, moreover, are a limited resource. It is one thing to argue theoretically that it is preferable to build demand through vouchers or other demand-side assistance, but another to provide the means to do so. Federal outlays for demand-side assistance, including Housing Choice Vouchers, have not increased in constant dollars since 2002. It is not reasonable to expect a nonprofit developer or local government to refrain from building additional affordable housing if there is a need and if additional vouchers are not available and not likely to become available in the foreseeable future. This is not an abstract issue, since funds that cannot be used for demand-side assistance may be available for building affordable housing. Many public entities much prefer to provide one-time capital funds to finance additions to the affordable housing supply rather than make the long-term commitment of funds year after year needed to address the demand side.

Furthermore, by adding to the affordable housing supply at least one potentially important benefit may be gained that is not available with vouchers: permanence. Once a new affordable housing unit has been created, it can remain an affordable unit for as long as those responsible deem appropriate and desirable, up to and including forever. By contrast, demand-side assistance is not only dependent on continued annual government appropriations, it is continually at the mercy of the marketplace to ensure that units will be available to future voucher holders.

CONCLUSION

The foregoing discussion leads to a strong conclusion. If the United States is to address the housing needs of its lower income families and individuals, actions are and will continue to be needed that go beyond the workings of the private marketplace. What actions are most appropriate, however, will vary on the basis of geography, housing market conditions, and the nature of the population to be served. While solving a family's cost burden may often be addressed by providing that family with additional resources to afford housing on the private market, that strategy is least effective in high-demand areas, or as a means of fostering regional equity or creating workforce housing in areas of strong job growth. The dilemma is that the areas in which it is most important to build affordable housing to expand supply are often the areas where the highest barriers, both political and economic, potentially block its development.

The discussion that follows will answer the questions of what forms affordable housing might take, how much it will cost, and who will pay for it. These are not new questions, of course, but questions that have been asked by those concerned about housing and the needs of the less affluent in the United States since the last years of the 19th century. The manner in which those questions have been resolved by governmental officials and public bodies, philanthropists, and nonprofit organizations forms an essential backdrop to the discussion of how affordable housing works today and how it might change in the future. That backdrop is the subject of the next chapter.

NOTES

1. The Bureau of the Census, after evaluating the accuracy of the assessment of building conditions conducted for the 1960 census, which categorized all properties as sound, deteriorating, or dilapidated, concluded that the inconsistencies in the data were too great, and the feasibility of correcting them in the future too small, to continue to attempt to measure building conditions.
2. The American Housing Survey is a survey of housing conditions conducted by the Bureau of the Census. A national survey, based on a sample of 55,000 housing units, is conducted every other year, while a survey of each of the nation's major metropolitan areas is carried out every six years. It is based on a combination of visits and telephone interviews by trained enumerators, and provides data on housing conditions in far greater detail than the decennial census. Because of the sample size, however, it is not available for small areas as is the census.
3. The table presents decennial census data from 1950 through 2000, and American Community Survey data for cost burden for 2006, the most recent year available. Data on families spending 30 percent or more of gross income for rent for 1960 and 1970 was interpolated within the published range of 25 percent to 34.9 percent based on the relative distribution of households below and above that level.
4. For many years, 25 percent of gross income was generally accepted as the threshold for cost burden, and used for most official purposes by the federal government. The official federal standard used to define cost burden was changed in 1983 to 30 percent, largely as a way to reduce per-unit subsidy outlays rather than as a reflection of any material change in living conditions or costs.
5. Strangely, however, the federal government has long resisted taking the same common-sense approach to defining the poverty level, instead insisting on a single arbitrary national standard of poverty.
6. A number of states and localities use a different terminology, referring to households earning between 0 percent and 50 percent of area median income as low income, and those earning between 50 percent and 80 percent as moderate income. Anyone involved in affordable housing development needs to be very careful to make sure that their terminology is appropriate for the particular locale or circumstance.
7. Vandivere, Sharon, Megan Gallagher, Elizabeth Hair, and Richard Wertheimer. *Severe Housing Cost Burden and Hardship in Working Families*. Presentation to the 2005 Annual Meeting of the Population Association of America, online at http://paa2005.princeton.edu/download.aspx?submissionID=50752.
8. The data do not show the extent to which already cost-burdened households found their cost burden becoming even greater; for example, the household that was spending 40 percent of their income for rent in 2000, and which may be spending 45 or 50 percent of their income for rent in 2005.

9. $100 in 1950 is worth $775.18 in 2005 dollars, based on the Consumer Price Index.
10. Alexander, Frank S. 2005. *Life Together: How Housing Laws Define America's Families*. Tenth Distinguished Faculty Lecture, Emory University, 7.
11. See Myers, Dowell, William C. Baer, and Seong-Youn Choi. 1996. "The Changing Problem of Overcrowded Housing." *Journal of the American Planning Association*, 62(1) (Winter): 66–84.
12. Quoted in Nix, Crystal. 1986. "Taking Account of the Hidden Homeless. *The New York Times*, June 22.
13. This issue has been extensively studied by Myers and his colleagues, who have shown that rates of overcrowding on the part of Latino households decline far less with increased income—and the ability to buy or rent larger units—than among non-Latino Black or White households. In addition to Myers et. al, *op. cit.*, note 7 *supra*, see also Myers, Dowell, and Seong Woo Lee. 1996. "Immigration Cohorts and Residential Overcrowding in Southern California." *Demography*, 33(1) (February): 51–65.
14. A representative statement of this position is found in Husock, Howard. 2003. *America's Trillion-Dollar Housing Mistake: The Failure of American Housing Policy*. Chicago: Ivan R. Dee.
15. All of the relevant regulations appear to converge in New Jersey. The state has a strict mandatory statewide building code; exclusionary zoning provisions discouraging multifamily housing and mandated large building lots for-single family homes are widespread; multiple small jurisdictions engage in fiscal zoning; environmental regulations are rigorous; and the state has aggressive programs for both open space acquisition and farmland preservation. Between 1950 and 1969, the state typically issued about 50,000 building permits per year; since 2000, despite strong demand and an unprecedented boom in real estate values, the average year has seen only 32,000 permits.
16. Since the majority of households are home owners, we have defined cost median by house value, not rent, as a better indicator of the extent to which the larger market conditions are either keeping prices down or pushing them up.
17. One might speculate that this difference reflects the greater amount of subsidized housing offered in Massachusetts.
18. How affordability is determined, and how different assumptions about mortgage terms and other factors affect that determination, is discussed in Chapter 7.
19. Data from http://www.LVhomecenter.com/newhome.htm. Prices have declined significantly, however, in the Las Vegas metropolitan area since 2006 as a result of the massive wave of foreclosures that has engulfed the area. Given the steady economic growth taking place in the area, however, this decline is not likely to be permanent.
20. It is also likely to be affected by the irrational but widespread market preference for owning something "new" rather than "used," which permits builders—at least under strong market conditions—to charge a premium for newly constructed homes.
21. A physically inadequate unit in a desirable location is likely still to command a substantial price, although it may be discounted to some extent by the cost of renovation or expansion. In particularly attractive areas the locational premium may outweigh the discount, as the recent phenomenon of "teardowns" makes clear.
22. The Section 8 program was enacted as part of the Housing and Community Development Act of 1974. At the time, however, it was a multifaceted program that included a wide range of both demand- and supply-side programs, including (in addition to the voucher program) funding for moderate and substantial rehabilitation of existing buildings as well as new construction of affordable housing. The supply-side

programs were gradually phased out during the 1980s, leaving the voucher program as the sole remaining active element of the original legislation.
23. U.S. Office of Management and Budget, http://www.whitehouse.gov/omb/budget/fy2007/hud.html. For purpose of this discussion, tenant-based and project-based rental assistance have been combined, while the supply-side total is the sum of HOME, homeless assistance grants, HOPWA, Native American Housing Block Grant, housing for the elderly, and housing for persons with disabilities. CDBG and public housing have not been included in either category.
24. See page 43 for a discussion of Housing Choice Vouchers.
25. Finkel, Meryl, and Larry Buron. 2001. Abt Associates. *Study on Section 8 Voucher Success Rates*. Washington, D.C.: U.S. Department of Housing and Urban Development. Generally speaking, families receiving vouchers are given 60 to 120 days to find a unit meeting certain minimum conditions and maximum price standards, although the issuing agency can extend the period up to 180 days where necessary. The national average success rate in 2000 was 71 percent.
26. Dreir, Peter, John Mollenkopf, and Todd Swanstrom. 2001. *Place Matters: Metropolitics for the Twenty-First Century*. Lawrence: University Press of Kansas, 1.
27. Jargowsky, Paul. 2003. *Stunning Progress, Hidden Problems: The Dramatic Decline of Concentrated Poverty in the 1990s*. Washington, D.C.: The Brookings Institution.
28. See Berube, Alan, and Bruce Katz. 2005. *Katrina's Window: Confronting Concentrated Poverty Across America*. Washington, D.C.: The Brookings Institution. There is an extensive literature on the subject of poverty concentration. Two of the principal contributions are Wilson, William. 1987. *The Truly Disadvantaged: The Inner City, The Underclass and Public Policy*. Chicago: University of Chicago Press, and Massey, Douglas S., and Nancy A. Denton. 1993. *American Apartheid: Segregation and the Making of the Underclass*. Cambridge, Mass.: Harvard University Press.
29. Turner, Margery Austin, and Bruce Katz. 2006. "Rethinking U.S. Rental Housing Policy." Working Paper, Joint Center for Housing Studies.
30. Available at www.ct-housing.org/at_home_in_ct.html.
31. Quoted in Sullivan, Tim. 2004. "Putting the Force in Workforce Housing." *Planning*, November. A similar definition appears in a recent study conducted by the University of Georgia, which defined workforce housing as that affordable "from the minimum wage up to $60,000/year."
32. One is tempted to believe that this is an attempt to counteract the stereotype of affordable housing as "welfare" housing, and to stress the "deserving" nature of the potential beneficiaries from workforce housing.
33. This assumes, of course, that the supply of units at the rent levels shown in the table is adequate, a piece of information that is impossible to infer from the data available.

CHAPTER

2

Affordable Housing in the United States: A Short History

BEGINNINGS

The recognition of society's obligation to the poor and needy is part of the heritage of the human race, a theme of social responsibility and interdependence that mingles throughout history with darker themes of oppression and violence. It led to such gestures as the almshouses built in England as early as the 10th century as housing developments for the (usually elderly) needy, endowed by wealthy nobles and merchants with an eye to ensuring a place for themselves in heaven. A more grudging impulse led to the construction of workhouses or poorhouses, where those without means could find a roof over their heads, paying off the cost in submission and hard labor. Poorhouses emerged in England as early as the 17th century, and appeared—often as poor farms—in the United States early in the 19th century.

The modern housing movement can be said to have emerged during the second half of that century, as the United States came to recognize that it was an industrial and increasingly urban nation and began to confront the implications of its new status. A generation of reformers, of whom the writer and crusader Jacob Riis is best remembered today, brought the painful, squalid realities of life in the nation's teeming slums to the attention of America's religious, civic, and political leaders. The particular focus of the reformers was the "tenements," apartments built for the poor in America's cities. As Gwendolyn Wright describes them, the new tenements that began to appear in the 1850s were particularly oppressive:

> Larger, more crowded than earlier types of housing, the "railroad tenement" was a ninety-foot-long solid rectangular block that left only a narrow alley in the back. Of the twelve to sixteen rooms per floor, only those facing the street or the alley received direct light and air. There were no hallways, so people had to walk through every room to cross an apartment, and privacy proved difficult. The open sewers outside, usually clogged and overflowing, a single privy at best in the backyard, garbage that went uncollected, and mud and dust in alleys and streets made these environments unpleasant and unsanitary.[1]

As millions of immigrants began to arrive later in the century, the issue of tenement housing and its consequences, not only for public health but also for social order, came to be seen as a national issue; as Wright notes, "*Harper's*, the *Atlantic*, the *Arena, Municipal Affairs, Scribner's*, the *Forum* . . . and almost every local newspaper took up the issue."[2] From this point to the early years of the 20th century, reformers focused on two principal aims: the creation of tenement housing codes to ensure that future tenements would meet minimum standards of light, air, and sanitation, and the construction of "model tenements," affordably priced apartment buildings that met higher standards than those being built by speculative, profit-minded builders.

The first tenement house code was enacted in New York in 1879. This code, which required tenements to provide minimal air and light to the interior rooms of the building, created what came to be known as "dumbbell" buildings, because of the two narrow interior air shafts that were added to meet the code requirements. Significant changes to the standards for ventilation, fireproofing, and adequate sanitary facilities, however, did not take place until the new century with the enactment of the Tenement House Act of 1901, which "served, directly or indirectly, as the chief working model for most of the tenement house legislation of America since that date."[3]

Affordability as such was far less important to the reformers than the ill health and social pathology spawned by the physical conditions and overcrowding of the tenement house environment, a priority that reflected both legitimate health concerns as well as dismay over the

129 Pitt Street, a typical tenement on New York City's Lower East Side.

New York City Housing Authority Collection at the La Guardia and Wagner Archives, La Guardia Community College/The City University of New York

alien mores of the immigrant families occupying the tenements, and a desire to inculcate proper American values among them. The concept of government subsidies to wage-earning families, however poor, was unthinkable; to the extent that reformers recognized that affordability was a problem, they tended to attribute it to landlords' profiteering, and believed that by having nonprofit or limited-dividend companies build model tenements, the affordability problem would be solved along with the far more urgent problems of health and social conditions.

Affordability was definitely a factor for tenement dwellers. The extent to which affordability was a problem is reflected in the many contemporary references to families taking in boarders or lodgers, families doubling up, and families using their apartments for commercial purposes;

Abraham Cahan's famous novel *The Rise of David Levinsky* describes one 1890s family that had set up "a tiny women's wear 'factory' at home."[4]

In 1900, the rent for a three-room apartment in the most recently constructed buildings in Manhattan ranged from $7 to $15 per month, with most clustering in the $10 to $11 range.[5] What this means in modern terms is subject to interpretation. From the standpoint of the change in the Consumer Price Index since 1900, a rent of $10 per month would be seen as equivalent to a modest $240 per month in 2005. But that may not be the right frame of reference. To better reflect the impact of costs relative to a worker's earnings at the time, economists have developed an unskilled wage index, which compares the average wage for unskilled labor over time. On that basis, a $10 rent in 1900 required the same number of hours of unskilled labor as a rent of $1,123 today. These rents, however, represent the better and newer class of building; an 1894 report indicates that more than a third of New York City tenement dwellers paid $2 per month or less.[6] As is still true today, affordability was as much a problem of the lack of income as of the cost of housing.

Outside of a few progressive states like New York, and beyond the adoption of building and sanitary regulations, the housing conditions of the poor were not widely seen as a government problem. Although Congress commissioned a "special report relating to the slums of New York, Philadelphia, Baltimore and Chicago" in 1894, neither they nor President Grover Cleveland's administration took any action as a result. The first direct engagement of the federal government in housing was prompted by World War I in the form of the U.S. Housing Corporation, created in 1918 to build housing for war workers in the vicinity of ports and shipbuilding plants crucial to the war effort. Although the war ended soon after, the Corporation left a brief but distinguished legacy in a small number of well-planned and constructed developments in cities such as Camden, New Jersey, and Bridgeport, Connecticut.[7] With the end of the war it was dissolved, and the federal government withdrew from the housing field.

During the 1920s, although the conservative Republican administrations in Washington showed no interest in housing, the housing reform movement was growing and moving in new directions, powerfully influenced by the European focus on social housing. As one prominent advocate somewhat floridly put it, "The economies of Europe, painfully and slowly rising from the chaos and economic disarrangement of the World War, are leading the way, giving the challenge, accomplishing vastly, while we falter and fail to catch the great vision or clearly see the way."[8] Large-scale social housing, built with public funds in London, Vienna, and a host of German cities, gave housing advocates, or "housers" as they came to be known, a model they were eager to see reproduced in the United States. A housing agenda was waiting for the election of Franklin Delano Roosevelt and the emergence of the New Deal.

THE RISE AND FALL OF PUBLIC HOUSING

The emergence of the public housing program reflected the visionary streak of the New Deal and the determination of a staunch band of housing advocates. Rooted in the environmental determinism of the tenement house movement and the belief that the elimination of slums could rid American cities of a wide range of social ills, the program captured a historic moment in which the idea of an expansive, direct role of government in solving social problems was not merely the preserve of the radical

In the 1930s, public housing was seen as a solution to a vast array of social problems.

Library of Congress

Left, but shared by the political mainstream. Reflecting their admiration for the European models of social housing construction, advocates envisioned a future in which public housing would house "not just the working poor, but two-thirds of the American population."[9]

Even before the program was formally created with the 1937 Wagner Act, public housing was constructed by the Public Works Administration; in New York City, Mayor LaGuardia's new housing commissioner, Langdon Post, commandeered $300,000 and a gang of WPA construction workers to build First Houses on the Lower East Side in 1935. More than 70 years later, it still stands, an affordable oasis in the heart of what is now a rapidly gentrifying part of the city. All in all, even before enactment of the Wagner Act in 1937, the federal government had already built 51 housing projects containing 21,800 housing units.[10]

The financial model for public housing, as established in the Wagner Act and retained for the next 50 years, was straightforward. Local agencies created for the purpose, known as Public Housing Authorities (PHAs), would issue bonds, backed by a contract with the federal government, to construct public housing projects. The federal government would then appropriate the funds annually to make the loan payments on the bonds, so that the cost of construction would not have to be included in the project rent. The municipality in which the project was located would in turn agree to accept a modest annual payment in lieu of property taxes so that the rents would have to cover little more than the cost of operations and maintenance. Housing authorities were expected to ensure that the rents would cover costs by setting a break-even rent and accepting only working tenants whose earnings were at least five times that amount.

Although the actual production of public housing under the New Deal was modest, amounting to some 140,000 units by the time federal resources were redirected to address the urgent demands of World War II, it was widely seen as an important, and largely successful, venture in social reform. Many of the projects were architecturally distinguished, and social histories of the period are rich with accounts of the delight that new residents took in their apartments and the social fabric that developed in the projects. A long-time tenant of New York's Harlem River Houses told an interviewer that "There was a . . . *concern* might be a good word. Children here knew that if they got rambunctious somebody was going to come out of the woodwork," while another mused, "it was *beautiful* when I came."[11]

New York City Housing Authority Collection at the La Guardia and Wagner Archives, La Guardia Community College/The City University of New York

Fort Greene Houses, a public housing project in Brooklyn, New York, was used as a military barracks in 1944.

Beginning in the 1950s, however, something close to a perfect storm of well-intended but misguided policies undermined public housing and turned it into a watchword for a failed social policy. As the struggling but stable working-class families who had initially been a large part of the public housing population began to share in the postwar prosperity and move out, rules requiring housing authorities to take poorer households, coupled with other rules requiring households to vacate when their incomes grew, led to their being replaced by a far poorer, less work-oriented population.

The problem was exacerbated by other policies that used public housing as a vehicle for rehousing en masse the thousands of families being displaced from urban neighborhoods as a result of the urban renewal and highway construction programs of the 1950s and 1960s. The families that entered the public housing projects, though, were the poorest and least self-sufficient of those displaced; as Charles Abrams, perhaps the most prominent affordable housing advocate of the time, sadly wrote, "Only 3 percent of the site dwellers in one Detroit renewal project entered public housing—most preferred the slums. In a large renewal area in Los Angeles, less than 1 percent of the inhabitants were willing to occupy public housing."[12]

As the population served by public housing was becoming poorer and more problem-ridden, their environment was changing for the worse. Increased federal pressures for cost containment, often mean-spirited and draconian, meant not only that the new projects lacked even the modest amenities of their predecessors, but that they were increasingly likely to be massive, high-rise complexes often housing thousands of people in an environment devoid of stores or other amenities. Still expected to cover their costs from the rent rolls, housing authorities began to cut back on services and facilities, even basic maintenance. As families with alternatives shunned the projects, their population became poorer and more dependent. Between 1950 and 1980, the median income of public housing tenants dropped from 64 percent of the national median to 27 percent.[13]

Not until the mid-1960s did the federal government recognize that it would have to provide operating subsidies to keep public housing from drowning in red ink, but even then those subsidies tended to be too little, too late. When energy prices skyrocketed in the 1970s, housing authorities—which under the 1969 Brooke Amendment could not increase rents, including utilities, above 25 percent of tenant income[14]—lost what little operating margin they previously had. By the mid-1970s, when Congress began to appropriate significant amounts for the renovation of public housing and repealed the requirement that forced over-income tenants to vacate their units, the damage had been done. The highly publicized demolition of the Pruitt-Igoe complex in St. Louis in 1972 was a vivid lesson in the failure of a once-admirable public policy. Although construction of new public housing continued well beyond that year, the pace gradually diminished. By then, the federal government's focus had already shifted to a drastically different model for producing affordable housing, one in which the role of government was sharply reduced and superseded by private construction, ownership, and management.

Before turning to this new focus, it is important to stress that far from all public housing projects were failures, and that the routine characterization of public housing in the media as a disaster does a disservice to the many projects and housing authorities that have continued to provide decent, safe environments to many of the poorest Americans. The New York City housing authority, which accommodates more than half a million people, has an admirable record of quality and responsible

TABLE 2-1 PUBLIC HOUSING, 1949–1999

YEAR	CUMULATIVE NUMBER OF PUBLIC HOUSING UNITS	AVERAGE ANNUAL INCREASE (DECLINE) FROM PREVIOUS DECADE
1949	150,000	
1959	401,000	+25,100
1969	768,000	+36,700
1979	1,178,000	+41,000
1989	1,401,000	+22,200
1999	1,296,000	(-10,400)

Source: Listokin,[15] HUD

management, while many housing authorities in smaller towns and cities are still seen as valued parts of their community's efforts to meet the needs of their less successful residents. With a million and a quarter units still in use, public housing continues to represent an important part of the overall affordable housing inventory in the United States.

FEDERAL FUNDING, PRIVATE OWNERSHIP

The 1960s were a decade of new federal initiatives in affordable housing policy after more than two decades dominated by the increasingly troubled public housing program. Although the initial departures were small in scale, they were significant in that they reflected new ways of thinking about how affordable housing was to be provided. Early in the decade, the Section 221(d)3 program offered nonprofit organizations low-interest mortgages to build housing for moderate-income families. In 1965, a more radical approach created a new leased housing program under which housing authorities could lease privately owned homes and apartments, place low-income families in the units, paying the difference between what the tenant could afford and the rent on the lease.

In the meantime, pressures had been building for a new, large-scale housing production strategy. By 1968, the ambitions of Lyndon Johnson's Great Society, the pressure to "do something" after the urban riots of 1967, and the determined lobbying by a coalition of business, labor, and government leaders led to a massive new housing act, characterized by one advocate not long afterward as "either a bold and multidirectional onslaught against one of America's most pressing domestic problems or a vast and meaningless bureaucratic mishmash."[16] With the Housing and Urban Development Act of 1968, which established a goal of six million homes for the nation's ill-housed citizens over 10 years—600,000 per year—the government embarked on the most ambitious effort in American history to finance housing for America's lower income families.

If the idea that the government should own and operate a significant part of the nation's housing had ever had widespread support, that support had vanished with the New Deal. Under the 1968 programs, the governmental role was redefined as the provider of financial subsidies to private developers or property owners to make it economically feasible for them to house lower income residents, a role that has remained the same for all affordable housing programs enacted by the federal or state governments since. While some provision was made for nonprofit development companies, some of which had been in existence since the 1920s and 1930s, the new programs were largely devoid of a social agenda that extended beyond the provision of shelter. Profit-motivated developers whose sole expertise was housing construction were equally welcome.

The two principal programs of 1968, known from the sections of the act under which they were created, were Section 235, for affordable home ownership, and Section 236, for affordable rental housing. Section 235 represented a significant departure from past housing policy. The federal government had long since used its powers to encourage home ownership in general, creating federal mortgage insurance programs in the 1930s, and the Federal National Mortgage Association, better known as Fannie Mae, to foster a stable secondary mortgage market on Wall Street. These initiatives transformed the mortgage market and were in large part responsible for the dramatic increase in the home ownership rate in the United States from 44 percent in 1940 to 63 percent by 1970. None of these initiatives were means-tested, however, and few of the home ownership opportunities that were created benefited lower income households.

Under Section 235, the federal government subsidized the mortgages of lower income home buyers earning 95 percent or less of the area median income down to one percent. Although the buyer paid the full price for the house, the mortgage subsidy dramatically reduced the monthly payments. As Table 2-2 illustrates, based on the prevailing mortgage interest rate in 1970, the federal subsidy reduced the monthly payment by nearly 60 percent.

TABLE 2-2 EFFECT OF SECTION 235 MORTGAGE INTEREST SUBSIDY

House price (median price in 1970)	$23,400
Monthly mortgage payment at 8.5%*	$179.92
Monthly mortgage payment at 1%	$75.26
Cumulative interest costs at 8.5% for 30 years	$41,373
Cumulative interest costs at 1% for 30 years	$3,695
Cumulative subsidy cost to government	$37,678
Minimum income required (% of median) at 8.5%**	$8,636 (88% of national median income in 1970)
Minimum income required (% of median) at 1%**	$3,612 (37% of national median income in 1970)

Source: Analysis by author; median house price and median income from 1970 Census
* 30-year mortgage term; 8.5% was the prevailing 30-year mortgage interest rate in 1970
** Assumes 25% of income for mortgage payment

With the price of housing in much of the nation still modest by today's standards, the effect of this program was dramatic, putting home ownership in many parts of the United States within reach of families earning less than 40 percent of the national median income of the time. The Section 236 program worked the same way, providing mortgage interest subsidies down to one percent for developers of affordable rental housing.

Although the new programs and ambitious housing goals were enacted in the last year of the Johnson administration, they were embraced with unexpected enthusiasm by the incoming Nixon administration. "From the outset, HUD Secretary Romney," a "can-do" former automobile executive, wrote Joseph Foote, "pushed for increases in subsidized housing production."[17] Romney saw affordable housing production as little different in principle from auto making, despite its primitive technology.[18] With a liberal Congress willing to provide generous appropriations for housing programs, Romney pressed his department to ratchet up subsidized housing production to unprecedented levels. Between 1970 and 1975, when the two programs were phased out, more than 400,000 units had been produced under each of Sections 235 and 236, while an additional 320,000 units were produced under the old public housing program.[19] All in all, roughly 1.2 million units were built, more than doubling the nation's affordable housing inventory in five years. Although the nearly 250,000 units produced each year was far short of the 600,000 per year goal, that goal was not only patently unrealistic but arguably questionable as a matter of public policy. It was far more than ever before or since.

As early as 1971, however, warning clouds began to appear with respect to problems with the new housing programs. With growing numbers of abandoned houses appearing in the nation's cities, people began to question the focus on new construction, while the implications for the federal budget of a 30- or 40-year interest rate subsidy on an ever-larger number of 235 and 236 projects began to sink home. From the public's perspective, even more damning were the increasing number of revelations about poor cost controls, shoddy construction, and outright corruption and fraud in the two programs, often reflecting the extent to which the programs were run by an inadequate and often incapable bureaucracy under pressure to maximize production at all costs. This was particularly true of the Section 235 program, as one writer described matters:

> HUD relaxed inspection requirements for Section 235 housing, a fatal error when local housing authorities failed to educate prospective homeowners about the importance of maintenance. HUD's laxity proved disastrous in cities like Detroit and Philadelphia where corrupt real estate agents lured home buyers into shabbily constructed or poorly renovated housing. Having invested as little as $200 in the Section 235 housing, low-income buyers simply slammed the door and walked away when problems arose.[20]

Section 235 buyers, largely African American, were used as unwitting tools in a corrupt effort to artificially prop up a collapsing urban property market. Coupled with the White flight from the cities, this further exacerbated racial segregation and ultimately added to the abandonment already taking place. Within less than a decade after the program peaked in 1975 at 409,000 units, the number of Section 235 houses had dropped to less than half that number.

Although outright fraud and corruption were less pronounced with the rental housing program, it was subject to the same criticisms. A HUD internal report in 1971 warned that

> Instances of negligent administration, inferior projects, excessive profits and overbuilding a particular market can be expected to crop up in spite of our best efforts to prevent them, particularly since our manpower is dangerously thin in such key functions and inspections and appraising.[21]

In this climate, when the Nixon administration announced a moratorium on further funding under these programs in January 1973, few

TABLE 2-3 THE RISE AND FALL OF SECTION 235/236 SUBSIDIZED HOUSING (ANNUAL INCREASE/DECREASE IN INVENTORY)

FISCAL YEAR	SECTION 235	SECTION 236	TOTAL	CUMULATIVE TOTAL
1969	3,454		3,454	3,454
1970	62,200	5,437	67,637	71,091
1971	139,178	26,885	166,063	237,154
1972	139,531	66,377	205,908	443,062
1973	67,307	92,562	159,869	602,931
1974	7,235	102,570	109,805	712,736
1975	(-9,990)	106,529	96,519	807,255
1976	(-73,131)	46,766	(-26,365)	788,890
1977	(-37,970)	96,234	58,254	847,144
1978	(-30,950)	1,155	(-29,795)	817,349
1979	(-26,679)	(-3,055)	(-29,734)	787,616

Source: Quigley[22]

other than those developers directly involved in the programs objected more than perfunctorily. Although a trickle of Section 236 projects continued to move through the federal financing pipeline until 1978, the federal supply-side experiment with volume production of affordable housing fueled by federal interest rate subsidies was over. From this point onward, federal housing policy would tip toward demand-side measures and away from housing production.

Toward the demand side

Meeting the housing needs of lower income families by giving them allowances, vouchers, or certificates so that they could afford housing offered by the private market was not an idea new to the 1970s; in the 1930s, the National Association of Real Estate Boards had argued without success for such a scheme as an alternative to public housing. The idea took on greater relevance, however, as the quality of housing in the private market improved after World War II, and the deficiencies of the nation's production programs became apparent. Not long after authorizing the Section 235 and 236 construction programs, Congress instructed HUD to carry out a series of experiments with voucher programs. Even before the results were in, however, Nixon administration staff were already designing a new program that would make housing allowances a major element of federal housing policy.

The new program, Section 8, was enacted in the summer of 1974 and signed into law by President Gerald Ford, who had replaced Nixon only a few weeks earlier. It provided for a flexible tenant-based rental subsidy allowance, which could be used, however, either to enable a low-income family to afford a home on the private market or as the financial underpinning for production of new or substantially rehabilitated affordable housing. The Section 8 certificates, as they were initially called, could either be tenant-based, given to a low-income family so they could look for a private market rental, or project-based, where they were committed in a block to a developer. The developers built a new apartment complex and rented the apartments to income-eligible families, with HUD paying the difference between the fair-market rent determined by HUD and the amount the family could afford. Reflecting the cost of development, the fair-market rent for new construction was set at levels far higher than actual market rents in the same neighborhoods.

The federal government during the 1970s was not ready to abandon its role as financier of new affordable housing production. Not only did Congress make clear that it expected a significant part of the Section 8 funds to be spent on new construction, but, as one commentator writes,

> Carter's election in 1977 brought in an administration eager to establish an activist posture in housing and urban policy. As applied to housing, this meant going with the tide of congressional support for stepped-up production and with developers who by that time had mastered Section 8's lucrative profit potential.[23]

By the end of the 1978 fiscal year, funds had been committed for more than 500,000 units of Section 8 new construction.[24]

Construction of Section 8 housing proved to be a highly profitable proposition for developers. High fair-market rents allowed developers to construct highly expensive projects, layered with generous fees and profit margins, while generous depreciation provisions in the tax code provided substantial financial benefits to the owners far into the future. The generosity of the new construction program often benefited the tenants of the projects as well. The new Section 8 developments were generally more substantially constructed and often better maintained than either public housing or Section 236, while the flexible rental subsidy meant that no tenant was at risk of losing her apartment if her income went down, as had been true of Section 236.

Matters changed significantly with the arrival of the Reagan administration. Soon after taking office, the new president appointed a commission on housing, a distinguished body—although top-heavy with lawyers, developers and lenders—that included former HUD Secretary Carla Hills and former Senator Edward Brooke of Massachusetts. The commission, in its 1982 report, came out strongly for emphasizing vouchers, arguing that

- production programs are expensive, costing nearly twice as much as housing the same low-income households in existing housing units;
- the long-term subsidy commitments are costly and restrict the federal government's flexibility to deal with changing housing needs; and
- production programs are not the most direct way of meeting the major housing problem of lower income persons: affordability.[25]

From that point onward, Section 8 resources were increasingly redirected toward giving families the resources to gain access to private market rental housing rather than building new housing. From a high of nearly 250,000 new units in 1977, production of HUD-assisted housing dropped to less than 25,000 by 1983 and has never exceeded 50,000 in any year since then. By 2004, state and local housing authorities were administering more than two million Housing Choice Vouchers, as the program was renamed in 1998. With the exception of a trickle of funds for small production programs serving the elderly and disabled, all incremental resources administered by HUD were devoted to addressing the demand side of the affordable housing equation.

The federal government did, in fact, continue to finance affordable housing production, but in a fundamentally different fashion. The shift of federal policy from production to housing vouchers was paralleled by a gradual waning of federal leadership in American housing policy, and the devolution of decision-making power over housing development to state and local governments. This devolution coincided with a growing readiness of many state governments to fill the policy vacuum and commit both money and energy toward meeting their state's affordable housing needs. Although the federal government continued to provide some resources through two new vehicles, the HOME program and the

Low Income Housing Tax Credit, neither HUD nor any other federal agency would make decisions about the specific projects to be assisted with these funds.

THE AGE OF DEVOLUTION

State and local affordable housing programs did not begin with the devolution of federal housing activities in the 1980s. In 1923, the city of Milwaukee constructed Garden Homes, the first municipally financed public housing in the United States,[26] while in 1926, New York State enacted a law creating a State Board of Housing to partner with local governments and private companies to build affordable housing. Since the late 1950s, with New York again taking the lead, all 50 states and the District of Columbia—and many local jurisdictions—have created agencies to finance affordable housing by issuing tax-exempt bonds, known as Mortgage Revenue Bonds (MRBs). Since such bonds are exempt from federal taxes, they carry a lower interest rate than other debt, making the housing financed with the bonds more affordable. They can be used both to provide moderate- and middle-income home buyers with mortgages and to finance multifamily housing in which a percentage of the units are reserved for lower income families. MRBs are used to provide roughly 100,000 home mortgages and to finance construction of 130,000 multifamily units each year, of which a significant percentage is aimed at lower income tenants.[27]

Few states, however, used state revenues to support affordable housing until the 1980s, Connecticut being one of a handful of exceptions. During the 1970s, states leveraged federal appropriations, issuing billions in MRBs to provide the underlying financing for federally subsidized housing, first under the Section 236 program, and then under the Section 8 new construction program. As federal revenues for housing production began to dwindle, however, state governments, counties, and cities began to engage more directly with affordable housing issues. Beginning in the late 1970s, the increasingly common vehicle was a new type of financial entity, the affordable housing trust fund.

Housing trust funds are created by state or local governments to provide money for affordable housing, usually supported by a dedicated revenue source; that is, a source of funding that is devoted exclusively to that purpose and kept separate from the state's general government budget. Revenue sources vary from state to state. Arizona uses proceeds from the state's unclaimed property fund, while Minnesota uses interest on broker escrow accounts. A number of states, including Illinois, New Jersey, and South Carolina, rely on proceeds from the realty transfer tax. Although a few states created trust funds in the 1970s, most were established in the 1980s and 1990s as the flow of federal funds slowed to a trickle. New Jersey's trust fund was established in 1986, with Arizona and Washington following in 1988, and Illinois and Minnesota in 1989. By 2005, 37 states had established state housing trust funds, while the number of local housing trust funds was estimated to be around 400. State trust fund revenues in Washington and New Jersey exceed $100 million per year, while the Florida State Housing Initiatives Partnership Program, known as the Sadowski Act, generates more than $250 million per year for affordable housing. Indeed, its revenues have been so substantial that in recent years, Florida's governor has diverted increasing amounts of its revenues to other purposes, over the strenuous objections of the state's housing advocates.

In the meantime, two new federal programs provided new resources for state and local governments, which, in contrast to previous programs, were given broad discretion over their use. In 1986, as a by-product of the Tax Reform Act of that year, Congress created the Low Income Housing Tax Credit (LIHTC) program, which gives investors a tax credit in return for making an equity investment in a low-income rental development. It is a complicated program that has become by a considerable margin the largest program for construction of new affordable housing in the United States, and it is likely to remain so for the foreseeable future. Both because of its complexity and its importance, the scope of the program and the way in which it operates are discussed in detail in Chapter 8.

Since 1987, when the first LIHTC projects were approved, the tax credit program has become the largest vehicle for producing affordable housing in the United States. Through the end of 2005, nearly 1.5 million housing units in more than 24,000 separate developments have been funded through the program, outstripping public housing as the nation's largest single source of affordable housing units. The average project has nearly doubled in size over the past decade, going from an average of 42 dwelling units in 1992 to 1994 to 82 in 2002 to 2004; still, this is a far cry from the public housing behemoths of the past. In addition to funding new construction or substantial rehabilitation, tax credits have been used to upgrade or preserve older affordable housing projects, including many built under Section 236 in the 1970s.

Pyatok Architects, Inc.

Hismen Hin-Nu Terrace in Oakland, California, designed by Pyatok Architects, Inc., uses Low Income Housing Tax Credits to house families earning between 35 percent and 55 percent of the area median income.

The second federal program to provide affordable housing resources to state and local governments is the HOME[28] program, a housing block grant program created by Congress in 1990. Under HOME, states, counties, and municipalities that meet certain size and need criteria receive an annual federal block grant. They can use the grant money for a wide variety of affordable housing purposes, including not only construction or rehabilitation of affordable housing for sale or rental, but also assistance to prospective lower income home buyers and rental assistance, similar to the voucher program. During recent years, federal appropriations for the HOME program have typically run between $1.5 and $2 billion per year. While HUD's guidelines are complex, and its reporting requirements often onerous, as long as a city meets the guidelines and files timely reports, it has complete discretion over how the money is spent.

Over the 16 years the program has been in effect, nearly 800,000 families or dwelling units have been assisted through the HOME program, as shown in Table 2-4. What this actually means in terms of units added to the affordable stock, however, is far from clear. Roughly one-third of the units counted (home buyer acquisition) represent modest levels of

TABLE 2-4 HOUSING UNITS/FAMILIES ASSISTED UNDER THE HOME PROGRAM, 1990–2006

	RENTER	HOME BUYER	HOME OWNER	TOTAL
New construction	130,907	47,329	N/A	178,236
Rehabilitation	146,633	27,345	156,282	330,260
Acquisition	14,776	248,952	N/A	263,728
TOTAL	292,316	323,626	156,282	772,224

Source: HUD

assistance, usually in the form of down payment or closing cost money, to help lower income families buy houses on the private market.[29] Another large share of the funds (home owner rehabilitation) goes to provide loans or grants to help lower income home owners—usually elderly or disabled—fix up their homes. Moreover, HOME funds are often not the only money going into a new affordable housing project; indeed, many HOME dollars are used in conjunction with Low Income Housing Tax Credit projects, filling the gap between the investor's equity contribution and the total amount of funds needed to make the project fiscally sound.

Throughout most of the United States, the HOME program and the Low Income Tax Credit program are the mainstay of affordable housing production. The scope of housing trust funds and other state or local housing support activities is wildly uneven. New York City has spent billions of its money for affordable housing since the 1970s, and California has floated multibillion-dollar affordable housing bond issues, but most states, even with their housing trust funds, provide only modest amounts toward this purpose. Missouri's program provides a total of only $4 million per year, while some trust funds generate only a few hundred thousand dollars annually. All told, total housing trust fund revenues nationally have been estimated at $750 million per year. While this is not insignificant, it pales in comparison to the $6 billion or more generated by HOME and the tax credit program.

AFFORDABLE HOUSING POLICY TODAY

The most fundamental fact about American affordable housing policy today is that there is no such thing. Although the Clinton administration was not ambitious in its approach to housing policy, it nonetheless brought forth a few modest but important innovations, most notably the

Homeownership Zone and Hope VI programs. Since 2000, even that modest level of ambition has been absent from federal policy. A bipartisan Millennial Housing Commission was created by Congress in 2000 and charged with addressing the nation's housing challenges; although it produced a solid (albeit not wildly creative) body of recommendations in 2002, it was ignored both by the new Republican Congress and the Bush administration. Through the end of 2008, efforts by supporters of a federal role in affordable housing have largely concentrated on protecting existing programs from the depredations of an administration that appears to have an almost visceral contempt for domestic policy matters.

If there has been one serious housing policy thrust at the national level during the past two decades, it has been that of raising the home ownership rate in the United States, with particular respect to lower income and minority households. A focus on increasing home ownership has been reflected in marketing strategies, efforts to relax underwriting requirements, the use of public resources for down payment and closing cost assistance, and the growth of the now-notorious subprime lending industry. To the extent that the Bush administration has focused on any housing issue, it has been this one; the White House set a goal of "increasing the number of minority homeowners by 5.5 million families by the end of the decade," and has promoted a variety of largely rhetorical strategies toward that end.[30] While these efforts have had some short-term effect, they have come at a prohibitive price, particularly for many of the lower income home owners and home buyers victimized by the subprime lending industry; the problem of subprime loan foreclosures turned into a crisis of national proportions by 2007.

In the absence of national policy or federal leadership, housing policy has devolved to state and local government, as well as to a host of advocates, intermediaries, and nonprofit organizations seeking to fill the gaps and come up with solutions that make sense within their communities. The emergence of this new environment has led to both positive and negative effects. The most obvious negative effect is the dramatic decline in the overall level of financial resources available for affordable housing in comparison to earlier periods, particularly the 1970s. The growth in state and local housing trust funds, or the use of new strategies such as inclusionary zoning, has fallen far short of replacing the federal funds that were once available.

Sharp disparities in resources and legal provisions governing affordable housing have led to great variation from state to state, and sometimes from city to city within a state with respect to the opportunity to develop affordable housing. While Florida offers generous support through its Sadowski Act trust fund, and Connecticut and some other states give municipalities clear legal authority to enact inclusionary zoning ordinances and levy developer fees for affordable housing, Texas not only provides few state resources for housing, but imposes legislative restrictions on inclusionary zoning ordinances.

The other side of the coin is the increase in the number of creative local strategies that have emerged. Affordable housing developers from the 1950s through the 1970s, with rare exceptions, focused exclusively on how to comply with federal regulations. They put together applications for federal funds, fitting their ambitions into whatever mold the programs of the time demanded. Local governments either accommodated developers building under these programs or as often as not, tried to keep them out. In either case, local actors reacted to the ground rules established in Washington, D.C., rather than crafting local strategies or initiatives.

Beginning in the 1980s, that changed dramatically. The emergence of community development corporations (CDCs), locally based nonprofit organizations rooted in a particular neighborhood or city, represented a shift toward communities beginning to think through for themselves what types of affordable housing and for whom most fit their needs. With the support of national intermediary organizations such as the Local Initiatives Support Corporation (LISC) and the Enterprise Foundation, a growing number of community development corporations became not only housing developers but true community builders. By 2006, over 4,000 CDCs were active around the United States. Although varying widely in their scale and effectiveness, collectively they had produced more than 500,000 units of affordable housing, created thousands of new jobs, and provided critically needed community facilities and services.

New ways of creating affordable housing, such as inclusionary zoning, employer-assisted housing, and community land trusts, emerged in the 1970s and 1980s. In contrast to the past, the new strategies did not flow from federal dictates but from local grassroots initiatives. Such initiatives might be led in some cases by a local or county government, in others by a neighborhood-based community organization, and in still others by a major university or corporation. While these and other strategies for providing affordable housing, which will be discussed in detail in forthcoming chapters, vary widely, they had one critical feature in common: They reflected a local response to a local housing need.

As a result, the affordable housing picture today is a varied, multifaceted one. Although one can still find the looming towers of 1950s public housing here and there, they are blessedly fewer than they once were. Affordable housing developments today may be single-family subdivisions, garden apartments, or town houses. Affordable homes or apartments are often scattered around a neighborhood or tucked into a larger mixed income development in such a way that even a careful observer may have no idea which units are affordable housing and which sell or rent for far more. More than two million lower income families live in private market housing with the help of housing vouchers.

In this light, one is tempted to see the withdrawal of the federal government from the housing scene as a positive development, allowing local creativity to bloom free from the heavy hand of federal bureaucracy. That conclusion, however, would be shortsighted and misleading. In the final analysis, without both the resources and the leadership that only the federal government can offer, as well as its unique ability to counteract the schemes of the most regressive state and local governments, affordable housing programs will always fall short of reaching those in need and meeting their responsibility as a critical part of the social safety net. Should there be a revival of federal leadership in housing, however, it will have to be a different sort of leadership; not one that dictates the solution from the top down, but one that recognizes and supports the thousands of local governments, individuals, and organizations who are framing the solutions to their community's needs.

NOTES

1. Wright, Gwendolyn. 1981. *Building the Dream: A Social History of Housing in America*. Cambridge, Mass.: The MIT Press, 118.
2. Ibid., 120.
3. Ford, James, et al. 1936. *Slums and Housing: With Special Reference to New York City*, Cambridge, Mass.: Harvard University Press, Vol. 1, 217.
4. Wright, *Building the Dream*, 120.
5. Gould, R. L. Elgin. 1903. "Financial Aspects of Recent Tenement House Operations in New York." In *The Tenement House Problem*, Vol. I, 360, ed. Robert W. DeForest and Lawrence Veiller. New York: The Macmillan Company.
6. Quoted in Ford, *Slums and Housing*, Vol. 1, 184.
7. The U.S. Housing Corporation is an interesting and admirable chapter in American housing and planning history. Although its brief history limited its accomplishments, its focus on sophisticated and sensitive town planning and architecture makes it remarkable not only by the standards of its time, but of any time. Much of this can be

attributed to the work of Frederick Law Olmsted, Jr. (the son and professional heir of the designer of Central Park), who served as the manager of the Corporation's town planning division. Olmsted's 1919 essay, "Lessons from Housing Developments of the United States Housing Corporation," *Monthly Labor Review* (8), is available online at http://www.library.cornell.edu/Reps/DOCS/olm19.htm.

8. Pink, Louis H. 1928. *The New Day in Housing*. New York: The John Day Company, 14. Gov. Al Smith of New York wrote an introduction to this volume.
9. Von Hoffman, Alexander. 1996. "High Ambitions: The Past and Future of American Low-Income Housing Policy." *Housing Policy Debate* 7(3): 426.
10. Ibid., 425.
11. Mayer, Martin. 1978. *The Builders*. New York: W. W. Norton & Co., 186, 188 (italics in original).
12. Abrams, Charles. 1965. *The City is the Frontier*. New York: Harper & Row, 35.
13. *The Report of the President's Commission on Housing*. 1982. Washington, D.C., 33.
14. The percentage was increased to 30 percent in 1982.
15. Listokin, David. 1990. "Federal Housing Policy and Preservation: Historical Evolution, Patterns and Implications." *Housing Policy Debate* 2(2): 179.
16. Fried, Joseph P. 1971. *Housing Crisis U.S.A.* New York: Praeger Publishers, 107.
17. Foote, Joseph. 1995. "As They Saw It: HUD's Secretaries Reminisce About Carrying Out the Mission." *Cityscape* 1(3): 74.
18. The initiative with which Romney was most personally involved during his years at HUD was Operation Breakthrough, a highly touted, expensive, and largely unsuccessful effort to jump-start the application of advanced technologies to the housing construction field.
19. Listokin, "Federal Housing Policy," 162.
20. Biles, Roger. 2000. "Public Housing and the Postwar Urban Renaissance 1949–1973." p. 156 in *From Tenements to the Taylor Homes,* ed. John A. Bauman, Roger Biles, and Kristin M. Szylvian, eds. . University Park, Pa.: Pennsylvania State University Press.
21. Quoted in Orlebeke, Charles J. 2000. "The Evolution of Low-Income Housing Policy, 1949 to 1999." *Housing Policy Debate* 11(2): 499.
22. Table assembled from multiple government sources in Quigley, John A. 2000. "A Decent Home: Housing Policy in Perspective." Brookings-Wharton Papers on Urban Affairs.
23. Orlebeke, "The Evolution," 504.
24. New construction includes substantial rehabilitation, generally involving replacement of everything except the four walls.
25. *The Report of the President's Commission on Housing*, 17. The average outlay per unit for Section 8 new construction in Fiscal Year 1985 was $4,635, compared to $2,640 for tenant-based vouchers.
26. A description of the project can be found in Attoe, Wayne, and Mark Lattus. 1976. "The First Public Housing: Sewer Socialism's Garden City for Milwaukee." *Journal of Popular Culture*, (10)1 (Summer):142. The term "sewer socialism" was used in the 1920s and 1930s to describe Milwaukee's conservative, locally oriented brand of Socialist government, which eschewed revolutionary rhetoric in order to concentrate on infrastructure projects and good government.
27. Multifamily housing constructed with tax-exempt bonds must set aside at least 40 percent of their units for families with incomes of 60 percent of AMI or less, or 20 percent for families with incomes of 50 percent of AMI or less. As a result, a minimum of 26,000 units per year financed with tax-exempt bonds, and most probably substantially more, would meet the definition of affordable housing used in this

book. The National Council of State Housing Agencies estimates that since the program's inception, roughly one million lower income rental units have been provided through MRBs, although it is impossible to tell whether this includes units that also received federal subsidies or low income tax credits.
28. The program is sometimes referred to as the HOME Investment Partnerships program. HOME, although generally capitalized, is not an acronym or an abbreviation for anything else.
29. Although there is a real possibility of double counting, where HOME funds are used first to subsidize construction of a single-family house, and then a separate HOME grant or loan is made to provide the buyer of the house with down payment assistance.
30. Available at http://www.whitehouse.gov/infocus/homeownership. In 2002, the White House issued *A Home of Your Own: Expanding Opportunities for all Americans*, a publication promoting the administration's home ownership agenda.

CHAPTER

3

Designing Affordable Housing

WHY DESIGN MATTERS

Housing is not a commodity. It is an all-but-permanent, all-but-immovable product that affects the lives not only of those who live in it, but those who live around it, whose experience is powerfully or subtly affected by it. How a house or housing development looks, and how well it works for those who live in it or observe it from the outside, is a matter of paramount importance, whether it is designed to accommodate the neediest or the most affluent.

How a house looks and how it works are related, but are not the same. Many buildings or developments that look appealing from the outside may fail to provide, as one writer puts it, "the setting for stable, safe satisfactory family life and neighboring," for the people who live in them.[1] Similarly, however functionally sound a building's facilities may be, if it is visually unattractive or oppressive, it will not be a source of pride to its residents or comfort to its neighbors.

The quasi-permanent nature of housing is a reproach to anyone who has ever allowed poorly designed, cheaply built housing to be constructed with the excuse that it will only have a "useful life" of 10, 20, or 30 years. Despite urban renewal, abandonment, and the ravages of time and nature, three out of every five houses in America that were standing in 1950 were still in use in 2005.[2] In many cases, their value is equal to or greater than that of more recently constructed homes. That old houses have not only survived, but have remained competitive with newer houses containing far more sophisticated features, is a tribute to the quality of their often anonymous designers, and to the flexibility that they built into their designs. The majority of the houses we build today will still be standing in 2050, and many of them will still be housing our more distant descendants in 2100.

Despite the modernist architect Le Corbusier's phrase, a house is far more than a "machine for living in." A home has always meant far more than shelter from the elements or a convenient place to carry out the necessities of daily life. Individually, they provide the setting within which each family frames its domestic existence; collectively, they define their block, their neighborhood, and their community. How well they perform those tasks greatly affects the stability and health of the family and the community; as Winston Churchill is reputed to have said, "We shape our dwellings; and afterwards, our dwellings shape us."[3]

The design of houses, particularly attached and multifamily housing, is not just about the buildings themselves. As important as they are, the way in which buildings relate to one another and to their surroundings, and how the spaces between the buildings are treated, can be even more important. Many buildings of plain, functional architectural design are redeemed by the quality of their site planning or treatment, while other buildings of seemingly far more distinguished architectural quality may be less desirable environments, because of the inadequate, inappropriate manner in which they have been sited or the poor quality of their landscape treatment. It is critical to think of the two—the buildings and the site treatment—as a single, interconnected whole.

While design matters for all buildings, whether for rich or poor, residential or commercial, it has an added significance when it comes to affordable housing. Affordable housing, by its nature, is housing for people who have fewer resources and fewer options outside the home than more affluent families. As such, its residents are likely to be more dependent on their immediate environment, both the individual dwelling unit and the building or complex of which it is a part, than are the residents of more expensive housing, who are more mobile and more able to pay for entertainment and travel outside the community. The ability of the immediate environment to meet the needs of lower income families and to offer more than a minimally functional setting for their daily activities is especially important.

Another reason, unfortunate but compelling, why design is particularly important to affordable housing is the need to overcome the stigma of the history of affordable housing in the United States. Although the first examples of American affordable housing were often well designed with appropriate facilities—like the 1931 Carl Mackley Houses in Philadelphia, which included a nursery, a library, and a swimming pool—after the initial reformist zeal of the New Deal wore off, affordable housing, in architect Sam Davis's words, "became mean-spirited, the dwellings spartan."[4] By the 1940s, public housing, the only purpose-built affordable housing of the time, was, in the words of architectural historian Gwendolyn Wright, "purposely cheap and austere." As she adds, "Apartments contained no storage space for such large articles as bicycles or suitcases, as these purchases represented a more comfortable life than the tenant was supposed to enjoy. Closet doors were left off in an effort to reduce costs and encourage neatness. The parents' bedroom was purposely small so as to eliminate the practice of infants sharing the same room as the adults."[5] By the 1950s, the pressure to cut costs had become even greater and amenities had become even fewer.

The stigmatization of public housing was exacerbated by the architectural predilection, inherited from Le Corbusier, for "towers in the park," large high-rise apartment blocks surrounded by open space. High-rise projects became increasingly common and increasingly massive during the 1950s. While they reflected not only a distinctive architectural ideology and a perverse demonization of the compact, tightly integrated physical form of older neighborhoods, they also offered a concrete response to federal cost-cutting pressures by cramming ever more units on each piece of ground acquired for construction of public housing. Although much public housing, particularly in small cities and rural areas, continued to be modest in scale and often well suited to its surroundings, the looming high-rise towers of projects like Robert Taylor Homes in Chicago or Scudder Homes in Newark became the physical archetype of subsidized housing for a generation of Americans.

The perception in the American psyche of public housing—and by extension all housing for lower income families—was crystallized by the highly publicized demolition of the Pruitt-Igoe public housing project in St. Louis in the 1970s. Pruitt-Igoe, which was constructed between 1954 and 1956 to replace the city's deteriorating DeSoto-Carr neighborhood, contained nearly 3,000 apartments in 33 largely identical 11-story buildings. Designed by the famous architect Minoru Yamasaki, its rows of

Sylvia Lewis

Demolition of the Cabrini-Green public housing project in Chicago, Illinois.

long, slab-like towers were distinguished by long galleries called "sidewalks in the sky" on every third floor, and elevators that stopped only at the first, fourth, seventh, and 10th floors. "The design proved a disaster," wrote the late Oscar Newman, "because all the grounds were common and disassociated from the units, no one could identify with them. The 'river of trees' soon became a sewer of glass and garbage. The corridors, lobbies, elevators and stairs were dangerous places to walk through. They became covered in graffiti, and littered with garbage and human waste. The elevators, laundry and community rooms were vandalized and garbage was stacked high around the choked garbage chutes."[6]

As Newman pointed out, most individual apartments were neat and clean, even if modestly furnished, while those few corners where only two or three families shared a common area were safe and well tended. Families who were able to move, however, soon did so, and the occupancy rate of the project swiftly declined to the point where more than half of the apartments were vacant. After a series of unsuccessful efforts to fix its problems, the St. Louis Housing Authority began to demolish Pruitt-Igoe in 1972. Images of the project coming down, with the massive high-rise buildings crashing to the ground in a cloud of dust, were widely reproduced in newspapers and broadcast on television, becoming part of the collective American memory.[7]

While there are valuable design lessons to be learned from the failure of Pruitt-Igoe, which will be touched on below, that failure had many strands: social, economic, governmental, and racial as well as architectural. As Davis comments, "The project was the culmination of a grim public policy to warehouse the poor, to move thousands of very low income people into a single enclave that ignored the needs and aspirations of the tenants and denied them all but the most utilitarian features."[8] Its failure, however, had the effect of further stigmatizing not only the poor themselves, but future efforts to provide them with decent, affordable housing.

The experience of Pruitt-Igoe and public housing generally has not only led to important changes in how affordable housing is designed, but even more importantly, to a fundamental turning away from the practices of warehousing thousands of the poorest families and locking them into isolated ghettos of concentrated poverty. Since the 1970s, thousands of successful developments of affordable housing or containing affordable housing have been constructed, providing safe, well-maintained housing for their residents while being good neighbors to their surroundings. At the same time, however, even after three decades, affordable housing proposals are still burdened in many circles with the demand to prove that they will not become "another Pruitt-Igoe." While the response to those demands is not purely an architectural one, sensitive and high-quality design, however, is a critical element not only in creating successful affordable housing, but in ensuring its acceptance by the communities in which it is proposed.

HOUSING FOR WHOM?

Good design must work well both for the residents of the housing and for its neighbors. Before one can design housing that will work well for its residents, however, one must first ask a basic question: who will its residents be? One size does not fit all, in affordable housing as elsewhere. Potential residents of affordable housing are as diverse a body of individuals as any that may be found in the United States, so before beginning to design a development or evaluating a design that has been proposed by a developer or nonprofit organization, that question must be asked and answered.

Except for the unfortunate reality that they have less money, the universe of lower income households includes representatives of every social, economic, and demographic group making up the population of the United States. That universe, however, is not distributed in the same way as the population as a whole. It contains disproportionately more children and old people, more single-parent families, and more individuals with disabilities. In 2000, the median income for married-couple families with children was $59,500, $29,900 for single male parents with children, and only $20,300 for single female parents with children. These differences reflect the greater likelihood of married-couple families to have not one, but two, wage earners, as well as the continued disparity between the earnings of men and women.

Table 3-1 shows the distribution of families with children at different income levels by family type. In the very lowest income range, corresponding roughly to 50 percent of the national median income, roughly half of all households with children have only a single parent. In the highest range, those earning more than the median income, nearly 9 out of 10 families with children are headed by a married couple. Age is another critical factor. When one looks at how the lower income population is distributed, one finds that they are concentrated at either end of the age spectrum. Children and older individuals, particularly those over age 75, are more likely to be poor or near-poor, while adults between the ages of 35 to 64 are least likely to fall into that category.

Demographic statistics, however, can only establish a broad context for what takes place when a local organization begins planning an affordable housing development in its community. Developments are

TABLE 3-1 DISTRIBUTION OF FAMILIES WITH CHILDREN BY TYPE AND INCOME RANGE

FAMILY TYPE	$0–$24,999	$25,000–$34,999	$35,000–$49,999	$50,000+	TOTAL
Married-couple	50.7%	66.5%	75.7%	89.2%	76.3%
Male householder	8.3	9.0	7.1	4.0	6.0
Female householder	41.0	24.5	17.1	6.8	17.1
TOTAL	100%	100%	100%	100%	100%

Source: 2000 Census

designed for specific populations, reflecting the characteristics of the town or region as well as the particular needs that the town is trying to address. While some communities may perform comprehensive needs assessments, then plan a series of developments around the different needs, others may target a particular population for a particular reason. One community may seek to address the needs of disabled people or the elderly through a specific development, while another may want to provide homes for people to fill local jobs that are currently going begging because of the high cost of housing in the area. Among those communities seeking to provide workforce housing, the characteristics of the prospective residents can vary widely depending on the nature of the workers local businesses are trying to retain or the jobs they are trying to fill.

In designing an affordable housing development, it is worthwhile to identify as much as can reasonably be known about the likely population of the development. In some cases, that information can be pinned down with some specificity, as when a development is being planned for a highly specific population, like the frail elderly or a population with specific disabilities. In many other cases, one may only be able to identify general features of the likely population. Except in special cases, it is not necessarily a good idea to design a project around a prospective population that is defined in too specific or narrow terms. The characteristics of a project's population are likely to change over time, as the initial residents age and are replaced by others, or as the ethnic or demographic character of the neighborhood changes.

Key features affecting design are demographic, in terms of such characteristics as age distribution, number of children, or the likely proportion of single-parent households; and economic, in terms of the incomes, jobs, and assets of the households. Cultural features must also be taken into account, particularly where the nature of the regional or local population suggests that many of the residents of a particular development will be members of a distinct ethnic, cultural, or religious group, with distinct preferences for using interior and outdoor space.[9]

A good initial step in designing a development, once a profile of the salient characteristics of the potential resident population has been created, is to find out what they are likely to look for in terms of a home they would like to live in. This should not take place in the abstract. The residents of a proposed affordable housing development, although they may not yet be identified individually, are the architect's clients in the same sense as a wealthy couple for whom an architect is building their dream house. Just as that architect will consult regularly with the clients about their desires, the design process for affordable housing should involve, wherever possible, an ongoing process of consultation with individuals who are economically, socially, and culturally representative of the future resident population. That process can take place through focus groups, charrettes, or other ways of two-way communication between the designer and people who can be considered surrogate clients. As the design begins to take shape, and the specific features of both the site and interior layout begin to emerge, each element of the design should be tested both against the characteristics of the prospective residents, as reflected both in their profile and in the desires and perceptions of their surrogates.

HOUSING THAT WORKS FOR PEOPLE

The number of different design elements that must be addressed in order to create the best possible development is considerable. Table 3-2, adapted from the Affordable Housing Design Advisor website,[10] offers a checklist of features that are important to the design of affordable housing developments. While some of these can be considered more important than others, all of them matter and none should be overlooked in the design process. Such a seemingly minor consideration as storage, both for the residents' individual needs and for the tools, equipment, and furniture that are associated with the common open space and play areas, can have a significant effect on quality of life. Inadequate storage space not only reduces the livability of the individual homes but can lead to visual clutter and loss or damage to tools and equipment, making the outdoor spaces less usable and creating additional replacement costs for the development. While the scope of this book does not permit a detailed discussion of each of the elements in the checklist, the next few pages will explore some of the key design issues involved in creating successful affordable housing developments.

The threshold decision that must be made for any affordable housing development is what *type* of housing to build, along a continuum of housing types that runs from the detached single-family house through a variety of increasingly dense variations up to the high-rise apartment building. While the choice of housing type is affected by a variety of factors, not least local land-use regulations and economic constraints, it must also reflect an understanding of the needs and preferences of the

TABLE 3-2   DESIGN CONSIDERATIONS CHECKLIST

PARKING	LANDSCAPING	BUILDING LAYOUT
• Overall impact • Access and surveillance • Vehicle/pedestrian interaction • Car maintenance • Security PUBLIC OPEN SPACE • Outdoor rooms • Access • Boundaries • Surveillance • Play • Nighttime use PRIVATE OPEN SPACE • Space for individual dwellings • Size • Balconies • Fencing • Storage	• Plantings • Paved areas • Edges • Outdoor seating • Paths • Storage BUILDING LOCATION • Site entry and circulation • Setbacks • Climate considerations BUILDING SHAPE • Building height • Building scale and massing • Building form BUILDING APPEARANCE • Image • Visual complexity • Windows • Front doors • Facade • Roof shape • Size and rhythm of openings • Trim and details • Materials and color • Individual identity	• Entries • Central facilities and common rooms • Support and service areas • Stairs • Elevators • Access corridors • Security UNIT LAYOUT • Entry • Room relationships • Room design • Unit mix • Dining rooms • Bathrooms • Light and ventilation • Storage space • Window views • Materials • Appliances and mechanical systems

Source: Adapted from Affordable Housing Design Advisor (www.designadvisor.org)

potential residents of the housing. A basic typology of housing types is shown in Table 3-3. It does not show all building type variations, but the most common ones used for affordable housing.

At the most basic level, it is widely accepted that where alternatives are available it is not desirable to put families with children in buildings that require elevator access to the apartments; that is, buildings of five or more stories. While it is certainly *possible* to create a safe, healthy environment for lower income families with children in an elevator building, it is both more difficult as well as less cost-effective to do so because both expensive design features and greater ongoing investment in maintenance and security are needed. Except where land costs or other factors make it necessary, such choices should be avoided. Elevator buildings,

TABLE 3-3 BASIC HOUSING TYPOLOGY

HOUSING TYPE	TYPICAL DENSITY RANGE	TYPICAL NUMBER OF STORIES
Single-family detached	1–8 units/acre	1–2 stories
Single-family semidetached or two-family	5–20 units/acre	2–3 stories
Single-family attached (row)	10–25 units/acre	2–3 stories
Low-rise multifamily	15–30 units/acre	2–3 stories
Mid-rise multifamily	25–60 units/acre	4–8 stories
High-rise multifamily	40+ units/acre	9+ stories

however, can be desirable options for elderly or disabled residents because they make it possible to concentrate supportive facilities close to the apartments. A well-designed high-rise building, moreover, can be an attractive community landmark in an otherwise low-profile suburban environment. Old industrial buildings and schools also lend themselves readily to reuse as senior citizen housing.

As a general practice, it is best to provide families with children with direct access to outdoor areas from their dwelling unit without the need to reach the outdoors through a common corridor or stairwell. There are many building types that can provide such access, including detached single-family houses, semidetached houses, and row houses, as well as a variety of different multifamily configurations.

While the choice of a particular configuration will reflect economic and land-use constraints, it also has more fundamental implications. It represents a social choice and a decision about the relative weight to give to competing values of autonomy and interdependence. A detached single-family house maximizes autonomy, in the sense of the individual family's control of its physical environment. Multifamily housing maximizes interdependence, in that the environment is shared by the families in the complex, who must depend on one another for the successful functioning of the whole.

Americans, on the whole, are raised to value autonomy over interdependence, as our traditional preference for the detached single-family house demonstrates. Many lower income families are no different. A number of successful affordable single-family developments have been built, primarily in the South and Midwest, where the preference for

Alan Mallach

The Circle F factory in Trenton, New Jersey, was restored and converted to senior citizen housing by a nonprofit developer. The architect was Francis X. Moya.

that housing type is strongest and the likelihood of finding inexpensive land greater.

But in many cases that option may not be feasible, and in many it may not be desired by the potential residents. Families that may want the opportunity for greater mutual support, including many single-parent households and families from cultural backgrounds in which the preference is for greater proximity and interaction, may actively prefer an environment where they will come into greater contact with one another and where common play areas are available for their children.

With respect to the layout of the individual dwelling unit, many of the issues come down to what can be characterized as "doing more with less." American houses have steadily become larger in recent decades. The median size of new single-family houses in the United States grew from 1,520 square feet in 1982 to 2,227 square feet in 2005, an increase of 47 percent. One out of four new houses built in metropolitan areas contained 3,000 or more square feet. This allows new houses to contain a variety of special features, such as a separate dining room, a family room, and an office or study. In large single-family houses, each family member has ample private space to pursue his or her interests, often to such an extent that one can argue that the size and layout of such houses, rather than encouraging a stronger family life, actually works to undermine it.

Affordable housing developments do not have that luxury. Limited construction budgets mean that interior space is at a premium. Depending on the number of bedrooms and the size of the family to be accommodated, affordable housing units typically contain between 500 and 1,500 square feet, as illustrated in a sample of projects from northern California and the Northwest, shown in Table 3-4. The average affordable housing unit will contain about 50 to 60 percent of the interior floor space of a house or apartment with the same number of bedrooms built by the private market. With substantially less floor space to work with, but with as many or more people to house, an architect must be both creative and sensitive to come up with a floor plan that creates room for people to carry out a variety of activities and uses not that much different from those given far more space in more expensive houses.

The solution is not, as architect Tom Jones puts it, "simply shrinking the sizes of middle class rooms, or arbitrarily merging rooms." Instead, designers should go through a process of analyzing the needs of the prospective occupants, identifying their activity patterns, particularly those "which occur simultaneously, during such peak family times as after school, on weekends, and on special occasions."[11] Those activities, along with the furniture and other space requirements associated with the activity, can then be diagrammed and used to design the units, including, as Jones writes, " . . . such elements as alcoves, bays, recesses, widened halls, different wall heights and lengths, pass-through counters, changes in floor or ceiling level, or other devices which optimize

TABLE 3-4 AFFORDABLE HOUSING UNIT SIZE BY NUMBER OF BEDROOMS

	SMALLEST UNIT	LARGEST UNIT	AVERAGE SIZE
One bedroom	500 SF	850 SF	629 SF
Two bedrooms	650 SF	1019 SF	851 SF
Three bedrooms	800 SF	1340 SF	1118 SF
Four bedrooms	1188 SF	1450 SF	1289 SF

Source: *Good Neighbors: Affordable Family Housing*

the livability and flexibility of the units in the most compact and space efficient manner."[12]

The ultimate configuration should reflect the prospective occupant's cultural values and functional requirements. A kitchen, for example, can be a small, separate space used only for food preparation, or it can be the center of family life, a large room in which people cook, eat, and socialize. Both can be equally functional, but offer significantly different messages about the nature of family life and the relationship between different activities.

Function is essential, but it is not everything. The quality of the development's design is an equally important factor in determining whether a development truly works for its residents and its neighbors. The visual impact of the design powerfully influences how the residents feel about their development, the manner in which they relate to it, and the extent to which they take pride in it; whether, indeed, they consider it "theirs." In this respect, the architectural features that lead residents to take pride in their development may not be the same as those that an architect may consider important, or that may win prizes or gain notice in architectural publications. "For some architects a distinctive style is a suitable substitute for livability or amenity in housing," Davis writes.[13]

Generally speaking, lower income households are no more drawn to living in an exhibitionistic architectural statement than other Americans, particularly when it visibly stands out, aggressively calling attention to itself in the midst of a more conventional urban or suburban setting. The most successful affordable housing designs, reflected in the gallery on the Affordable Housing Design Advisor website, tend to be subtle, often elegantly proportioned adaptations of regional vernacular that meet the functional needs of their residents, usually with features that, in marked contrast to traditional public housing, use variations in massing, material, or color to individuate smaller clusters, or individual dwelling units, within the larger development.

CARS, PEOPLE, AND OPEN SPACE

The layout of the buildings on the site and their relationship to their surroundings is as important as the design of the buildings themselves. In typical suburban multifamily developments, a maximum of 25 to 30 percent of the site area is occupied by buildings, while even in urban areas, the building coverage rarely exceeds 40 to 50 percent. This means that usually half or more of the site remains open. This area must be programmed and designed as carefully as the indoor space in the project; as the Affordable Housing Design Advisor puts it, "Think of public open spaces—shared outdoor areas intended for use by all residents—as 'outdoor rooms' and design them as carefully as any other rooms in the project."

The nature of multifamily housing is such that there will usually be some outdoor areas that are part of the project as a whole, rather than belonging either legally or functionally to individual unit owners or tenants. While the typically higher densities of affordable housing developments mean that the outdoor areas are unlikely to be large, the smaller size of the dwelling units means that residents are likely to use outdoor areas more intensively.

Since developments are likely to have many different populations—small children, teenagers, and adults of all ages—who engage in different outdoor activities, particular attention must be given to organizing the outdoor space in ways that permit shared and overlapping uses of space. This allows spaces where adults can sit, socialize, or play table games while watching small children play in a playground, or that can be used some of the time for active recreation and at other times for an extended family's party or picnic.

The temptation to create more outdoor space than can actively be used by the residents must be resisted. A major failing of the "towers in the park" design principles reflected in so many housing projects of the 1950s and 1960s is that they led to the creation of large open areas with no particular use in mind and with no functional relationship between the open space and the residents' dwelling units, which were far removed, both laterally and vertically, from the open spaces. Outdoor space that performs no clear function, or bears no clear relationship to the buildings with which it shares the site, is at risk of being neglected, and may become a potential dumping ground or setting for inappropriate behavior.

Landscape design is a critical element in creating the development's "outdoor rooms," and should be incorporated from the beginning of the design process, rather than, as is too often the case, treated as a sort of green veneer to be added after the important design decisions have already been made. The right mix of spaces, materials and textures, both hardscape—concrete, brick, metal—and green landscape, and the placement of walls and fences, walkways, sitting and activity areas, planting beds, and trees and lawns, are as important to the design process as the configuration of the buildings on the site or the layout of the dwelling units themselves.

If the most important use of the space between the buildings is for common open space and recreation, the largest amount of outdoor space is often devoted not to the residents of the development, but to the parking and circulation of their cars. How to accommodate cars while keeping them under control is one of the most difficult tasks faced by architects and planners, not only in the design of affordable housing but in nearly all developments outside major urban centers. Cars and people do not mix well, and a development with a large number of small children where vehicular parking and circulation are not carefully separated from pedestrian circulation and open space can become a highly risky environment.

One solution, functional but undesirable, is to orient the buildings inward to shared open space, while placing the cars in a large parking area between the buildings and the street frontage. While it accomplishes the separation between cars and people in a cost-effective fashion, it also separates the development from the street and its neighbors in a way that tends to isolate it from the rest of the community and projects an unattractive visual impression. Even the best-designed building tends to look unprepossessing when seen from across a sea of parked cars.

Different sites may lend themselves to different solutions. In some cases, the cars can be tucked out of the way behind the development. A parking area can become part of a useful buffer if the site backs up against an incompatible use such as a highway or the back of a shopping center. In some cases, where the density of development is high enough, parking can be hidden under the buildings, a solution that has been used in a number of affordable developments in California. Such a solution is only possible where land is so expensive that the increased density, and the greater efficiency in the use of the land, offsets the considerable added cost of the parking structure. In low-density single-family or town house developments, each family's cars can often be placed behind their dwelling unit, in a separate driveway. They can also be placed in *front* of the unit, a solution, again, that is functional but far less attractive.

Outdoor play and carefully controlled vehicle access coexist in the auto court in the Gateway Commons development in Emeryville, California, designed by Pyatok Architects, Inc.

The central court at Sara Conner Court in Hayward, California, designed by Pyatok Architects, Inc., offers a mixture of different types of open space and levels of privacy within a single area.

Pyatok Architects, Inc.

The interior court at Via del Mar in Watsonville, California, offers privacy and intimacy and opportunities for interaction among the tenants. The architects were Pyatok Architects, Inc.

SAFE SPACES

A development that works ensures the security of the occupants and accommodates their activities. How this can be accomplished varies greatly from one development to another, depending as much on the setting in which the development is placed as on the development itself. When an affordable housing development is constructed in an area where crime and drugs are a significant neighborhood presence, the ability to create a secure environment within the development becomes a critical issue. Failure to do so, as the experience of Pruitt-Igoe showed, can make a development literally uninhabitable. While security issues may be less pressing in areas with less crime, the importance of ensuring a high comfort level, particularly for parents of small children and for vulnerable populations such as the elderly and disabled, cannot be underestimated. While the only ultimate guarantee of security is the safety of the larger environment, design features can affect the security level of the residents of affordable housing developments, even in the most difficult of settings.

Two basic principles of designing for security that have emerged over the past decades are surveillance and defensible space, the latter defined and analyzed by Oscar Newman in his seminal work beginning in the 1970s. Surveillance is simply visual control of the environment; the ability of residents to *see* what is happening around them—who is coming up the steps to their door and watching their children play outdoors from the kitchen window. Video technology and security personnel can enhance their ability to monitor their surroundings, but, as Newman observed, "The after-the-fact employment of fences, alarms, hardware, and security personnel . . . is akin to the shoring up of inadequately designed building structures after they have been occupied—a circumstance most professionals would find intolerable and would view as a demonstration of poor initial design."[14]

This is not to suggest that there is no role for alarms and security personnel. Exclusive apartment buildings employ doormen and utilize video surveillance and many gated communities employ security personnel not only to keep out unwanted visitors but to monitor resident behavior. The critical point is that good design can minimize the need for such measures, while bad design can exacerbate it to the point where no realistically available measures can compensate for the inherent failure of the building layout.

While defensible space begins with visual surveillance, the concept as articulated by Newman is richer and more complex; as he described it, it is the creation of an interrelated collection of physical elements in the development that " . . . release the latent sense of territoriality and community among inhabitants so as to allow those traits to be translated into inhabitants' assumption of responsibility for preserving a safe and well-maintained living environment."[15] The relationship of indoor to outdoor spaces, the use of materials, the clear delineation of areas for particular functions, and the creation of a strong hierarchy of spaces—from the individual dwelling to the public street—are all means by which an individual in a development "is able to conceptualize that an area is within his realm of concern and control and that he has the right to monitor behavior in it in a critical and questioning fashion."[16]

Central to this concept is the use of design to inculcate attitudes and behaviors into the residents of multifamily rental housing that tend to be more common, for both architectural and cultural reasons, among owner-occupants of detached single-family houses. The institution of the private yard surrounding the single-family house and the separation of that house from its neighbors fosters a sense of territoriality that, although problematic in some larger societal respects, nonetheless promotes a strong sense of the individual home owner's responsibility for her property and her family's security. The physical configuration of multifamily housing, which makes up a large part of the affordable housing inventory, tends to promote an intrinsically weaker sense of territoriality on the part of its residents.

The essence of successful multifamily housing, as Newman recognized, is that territoriality must be connected to community. No individual family in an apartment complex can take responsibility for the security of the complex; indeed, without the cooperation of their neighbors, they cannot exert effective control over any area much beyond the door of their apartment. Newman's particular contribution was to show that by creating a hierarchy of spaces from private to public one could create a setting in which a spatially territorial community could be more readily created. This hierarchy begins with the corridor or landing shared by a small number of households on each floor and extends to the common entry or entries to the building; from there it moves to the development's open spaces as defined by the building configuration, and finally to the interface between the development and the public realm. At each stage in the hierarchy, the number of different individuals who must cooperate grows, but the framework for their cooperation has been created by their engagement at earlier stages involving smaller numbers of individuals and families.

At the time Newman wrote, the pendulum had only begun to move away from the practice of building large-scale, isolated high-rise projects for the poor. Today, not only is construction of such projects all but unthinkable, but many of the large public housing projects of the 1950s and 1960s have been demolished, replaced in some cases by more modest row houses and garden apartments that often house an economically diverse population. While this is on the whole a positive development, it encourages the fallacy that, by ridding ourselves of the "towers in the park" projects and by building at more modest scale we have somehow solved the problems of security and community that Newman wrote about without needing to address these concerns explicitly in the design process.

Building form and scale, however important, are not enough in themselves. A badly designed two-story apartment building that fails to address the issues raised above, while less overwhelming than a badly designed 20-story building, is neither a blessing to its residents nor an asset to the community in which it is located. Davis chronicles in detail the collapse of Acorn, a 1960s low-rise development in Oakland, California, describing how "Certain planning decisions that had been lauded as humane, socially responsive and architecturally clever [had] disastrous consequences."[17]

DESIGNING HOUSING THAT FITS IN

The goal of all development is to add both economic and psychological value to the built environment. This is particularly important with affordable housing, in light of the historical stigma attached to it and the fear and hostility that so often emerge whenever proposals for building affordable housing are put forward. While abundant research evidence has accumulated to demonstrate that the presence of affordable housing in itself does not lower property values of nearby private housing, the better and more compatible the housing, the more likely it is to enhance rather than undermine the quality of its surroundings and win acceptance by the larger community.

In most cases, this is best accomplished by making the housing fit into—or at times subtly shifting for the better—its neighborhood context and streetscape. Affordable housing, like most housing, is background architecture, forming a part of the neighborhood fabric rather than seeking to dominate it, whether its setting is urban or suburban. Sometimes it is relatively easy to define that fabric and design housing to complement it; in other cases the fabric is elusive, or arguably nonexistent, and the architect's task becomes a matter of reframing a broken fabric or trying to establish a prototype that may become the basis for a future neighborhood. This is particularly true when a site is being developed in a particularly devastated innercity area, or in a suburban "no-man's land," such as a highway commercial strip or a transitional area between residential and industrial uses.

Much of the affordable housing built in urban areas, and some in suburban settings, is sited within areas that have a clearly defined character. In many urban neighborhoods, affordable housing takes place through infill development, in which small numbers of dwelling units are constructed on scattered vacant lots interspersed within a small area, generally a few blocks. The existing houses in such neighborhoods are typically based on a distinct prototype, which can be 19th century brick row houses in Philadelphia, 1920s single-family houses with large front porches in many parts of Detroit, or single-story "shotgun" houses in Houston's Third Ward. Even then, there is often considerable variation in detail from one neighborhood to the next or even one block to another. One Philadelphia block may have three-story and another, two-story, row houses, with their widths varying from 12 to 20 feet; in Detroit, there can be considerable variation in the width of houses and lots, and the spacing between houses, from one block to the next.

Compatibility between new and existing housing can often be eased by straightforward design guidelines that address such features as maintaining a consistent setback line or a consistent pattern of variation in setbacks; maintaining a consistent ratio between the building volumes and the space between the buildings; maintaining a consistent pattern of building height; and replicating key design features, such as porches, stoops or gables.[18] The goal is not to slavishly recreate the look of houses built 80 or 100 years ago, but to make the new housing fit in so that it seamlessly fills the holes in the neighborhood, rather than flaunting its incompatibility with the rest of the block. The buildings designed by the design firm The Narrow Gate in Boston achieve this goal brilliantly.

The architect has greater flexibility when the development occupies a larger site within an area of distinct character, but it is still critical to respect the local vernacular. The Boston architectural firm Goody Clancy reinterpreted the 19th century Boston vernacular in two high-density developments, Langham Court and Tent City; their compatriot William Rawn reinterpreted the traditional row house in the Charleston Navy Yards project and used the New England farmhouse vernacular in a suburban development in affluent Lincoln, Massachusetts. These are all examples where a high level of creativity led to construction of affordable housing projects that are architecturally rewarding and not only fit with, but enhance, their surroundings.

Tent City occupies a block-long site that abuts the high-density Copley Square commercial complex at one end and the South End, a historic 19th century row house neighborhood, at the other. The development steps down from 12 stories to four stories; large family units are in stacked two-story town houses, each with their own exterior entry and private outdoor space, while the units in the high-rise part of the complex are one- and two-bedroom apartments, all sharing access to a common interior courtyard. At the opposite end of the urban intensity spectrum, the principal housing type in Rawn's Battle Road Farm project in Lincoln was a four-unit structure "articulated to recall the New England farmhouse: a formal building on the street with a gable roof and generous porch linked by two smaller connecting units and ending with a barn-like building at the back."[19]

In both cases, the site bore a relationship to an established architectural framework, although in the latter case the framework was more aspirational than literal, in that Rawn's design responded to the suburban Massachusetts ideal of what housing should look like, rather than to any specific buildings that abutted the Battle Road Farm project. In both cases, moreover, the housing was being integrated into a high-value environment. In contrast, other affordable housing developments may be sited in low-value or ambiguous settings, where the development itself must either enhance its surroundings or create a new shape in an amorphous setting.

Photo © Lucy Chen

In Battle Road Farm in Lincoln, Massachusetts, the architectural firm William Rawn Associates captured the feeling of the New England vernacular without being imitative.

The problem of creating an architectural fit in an ambiguous setting often arises from the common practice of siting affordable housing in mixed use or transitional locations, in which the fabric of the neighborhood is either unclear or broken. This reflects the difficulty of finding sites for affordable housing projects, and their frequent relegation to sites considered marginal by other developers. The Hismen Hin-nu Terrace project in Oakland, California, was built along a heavily disinvested commercial street as a part of a strategy to "mend a deteriorating neighborhood by restoring its main boulevard with housing over shops." In this case, the once-strong commercial streetscape had been compromised since the 1950s with a mix of suburban strip development and underutilized lots interspersed with surviving multistory mixed use buildings. The East Bay Asian Local Development Corporation, the developer of the project, and architects Pyatok Associates wanted to "recreate the older, denser pattern of mixed use as an example of better planning for future developers."[20]

In the case of Hismen Hin-nu Terrace, the architect could find a model in a historic, albeit diminished, development pattern. In some cases, where there may be quite literally no framework, the architect is unconstrained by context. An extreme case is The Beach, a multifamily development designed by Antoine Predock in Albuquerque, New Mexico, on a narrow, isolated site adjacent to Highway 66, "a dissonant mishmash of undistinguished strip commercial centers and uncoordinated signage." In the absence of a local frame of reference, the architect took his model from the mountainous natural landscape and, although he incorporated references both to traditional Native American architecture and the neon landscape of Highway 66, created a unique "mock-mountain" of apartments.[21]

The Beach, however, is the rare exception among affordable housing projects, where a gifted architect was able to impose a personal vision and distinctive imagery on a site that was, from a contextual standpoint, a *tabula rasa*. Although unusual, it does illustrate a solution to a problem that is far from rare; that is, how to create successful affordable housing on sites that are difficult to develop, by virtue of their configuration, terrain, incompatible adjacent uses, or other constraints, particularly when, for economic or other reasons, more desirable sites are not available. This issue will be further addressed in the next chapter, which discusses issues of site selection and approval for affordable housing developments.

NOTES

1. Jones, Tom, William Pettus, and Michael Pyatok. 1997. *Good Neighbors: Affordable Family Housing*. New York: McGraw-Hill, 10. This book provides an excellent catalogue of first-rate affordable housing developments. The catalogue is also available online at http://www.designadvisor.org.
2. In 1950 there were 46.1 million housing units in the United States. The 2005 Annual Housing Survey reported that there were 28.6 units in the national housing inventory constructed prior to 1950. Although some of these units were undoubtedly created after 1950 using pre-1950 nonresidential structures, the overwhelming majority was already in residential use in 1950.
3. Delivered in a speech to the House of Commons, October 28, 1944, on the subject of the rebuilding of the Houses of Parliament.
4. Davis, Sam. 1995. *The Architecture of Affordable Housing*. Berkeley: University of California Press, 13. This book, both descriptive and analytical and infused with the author's personal observations and philosophy, is the best single book available on design issues and affordable housing.
5. Wright, Gwendolyn. 1983. *Building the Dream: A Social History of Housing in America*. Cambridge, Mass.: The MIT Press, 229, 231–232.
6. Newman, Oscar. 1996. *Creating Defensible Space*. Washington, D.C.: U.S. Department of Housing and Urban Development, 10.
7. Those images continue to reverberate. They appear prominently in Gregory Reggio's well-received 1982 documentary film, *Koyaanisquatsi*, and continue to show up in planning and design publications. A music group named Pruitt-Igoe, whose work has been described as "spoken-word quasi-opera art-rock" is popular on the West Coast.
8. Davis, *Architecture of Affordable Housing*, 16.
9. The way in which space is both used and perceived in different cultures was explored by Edward T. Hall in the 1950s and 1960s; see *The Hidden Dimension*. 1966. New York: Doubleday & Co.
10. The Affordable Housing Design Advisor (http://www.designadvisor.org) is an invaluable website created by the Center for Architecture and Building Science Research at the New Jersey Institute of Technology under contract with the U.S. Department of Housing and Urban Development. It provides a wealth of information, both general and project-specific, that can assist lay people thinking about architectural issues and architects who design affordable housing projects. A second valuable web-based resource for design of affordable housing is Design Matters, a site established by the City Design Center at the University of Illinois at Chicago, and available at http://www.uic.edu/aa/cdc/AHDC/website.
11. Jones, Tom. "Activity-based Design for Living, Dining, Kitchen and Work Areas," available at http://www.designadvisor.org.
12. Ibid.
13. Ibid., 111.
14. Newman, Oscar. 1976. *Design Guidelines for Creating Defensible Space*. Washington, D.C.: National Institute of Law Enforcement and Criminal Justice, 1
15. Ibid., 4.
16. Ibid., 5.
17. Davis, *Architecture of Affordable Housing*, 121.

18. The author's *Bringing Buildings Back: From Abandoned Properties to Community Assets*. 2006. Montclair N.J.: National Housing Institute, from which this is adapted, contains a more extensive discussion of infill development in urban neighborhoods on pages 266 to 282.
19. Jones, Pettus, and Pyatok, *Good Neighbors*, 166.
20. Ibid., 100. The name means "sungate" in a local Native American language.
21. Davis, *Architecture of Affordable Housing*, 180.

CHAPTER

4

Finding Sites and Gaining Approval for Affordable Housing

No housing can be built without a site to put it on, and no site, once acquired, can be developed without receiving the approvals imposed by state and local government bodies. While these statements are seemingly straightforward, separately and in combination they represent the single greatest obstacle to the development of affordable housing in many parts of the United States, particularly in the areas of greatest need in major metropolitan areas and in the more heavily developed coastal states. This chapter will first address the criteria that are used to determine whether a site is suitable for affordable housing and how sites may be obtained for that purpose. This will be followed by a look at the project approval process and the manner in which affordable housing developments either move forward or fall by the wayside as a result of site unsuitability, poor planning, or community opposition.

CRITERIA FOR SELECTING SITES

Most criteria for selecting sites for affordable housing are no different than they would be for a housing development of similar physical type that might be built for the marketplace. They flow from the features of the land and their relationship to the use being proposed, including the size and configuration of the site, the availability of infrastructure, and the absence of significant environmental constraints. Although not inherent to the site itself, the consistency of the proposed use with local zoning and land-use regulations is also a consideration that applies for any development. All of these criteria are indifferent, at least in principle, to how the development is going to be financed, or the demographic or social characteristics of its residents. At the same time, additional site or location criteria may be triggered by a proposed affordable housing development, depending on who is to be accommodated. Such considerations can include the accessibility of the site to services that residents may need, such as public transportation or child care.

The most important site selection criteria, including some that are specific to affordable housing developments, are summarized in Table 4-1. These criteria cannot be applied in an absolute or dogmatic fashion. No county or municipality can reasonably require that every development's use be fully consistent with local land-use regulations, or that infrastructure is always fully available in advance and that environmental constraints are entirely absent. Indeed, if those criteria had to be met routinely by development proposals, few would ever see the light of day. The critical threshold, for affordable housing projects as well as any other proposed development, is that to the extent necessary, the developer be able to obtain necessary changes to land-use regulations, extend or provide necessary infrastructure, and mitigate environmental constraints in a responsible fashion so that the development can proceed.

Any proposal for affordable housing development should be given the same opportunity as any other development to demonstrate that the deviations from the land-use regulations are reasonable, that infrastructure can be provided, and that environmental constraints can be mitigated. Affordable housing projects, however, may be disadvantaged in this respect relative to other developments, in that they are often subject to more severe scrutiny than other projects and often operate under severe cost constraints. While a developer of luxury housing may be able to expend substantial funds to extend a sewer line for a considerable distance, as well as to pay carrying costs on the land while pursuing the time-consuming land-use and environmental review processes that may be necessary, a developer of affordable housing may not be able to do so. As a result, a site that may theoretically be suitable for affordable housing may not realistically be put to that particular use.

TABLE 4-1   PRINCIPAL SITE SELECTION CRITERIA

CATEGORY	ELEMENTS	KEY QUESTIONS
Size and configuration	• Size • Depth • Regularity or eccentricity	Is the size and shape of the site adequate to accommodate the proposed use?
Zoning and land-use regulations	• Use • Height, floor area, coverage, setback, or other restrictions • Parking • Open space dedication • Special permits, design review, or other discretionary requirements	Is proposed development consistent with land-use regulations? IF NOT, is there a sound argument for seeking variances or exceptions, and are such potentially available?
Infrastructure	• Sewer treatment • Water supply • Vehicular access	Is infrastructure available at the site? IF NOT, can facilities be brought to the site? IF NOT, can facilities be provided on-site?
Environmental constraints	• Wetlands • Flood plains • Steep slopes • Natural resource preservation • Environmental contamination • Geotechnical issues • Other	Is all or part of the site affected by environmental constraints? IF YES, is the nature and extent of the constraints such that they can reasonably be mitigated?
Suitability for prospective residents	• Access to public transportation • Access to jobs and services • Access to supportive services, such as child care • Access to open space and recreational facilities	Is site accessibility adequate to meet prospective resident needs? IF NOT, can access be improved or services provided on-site?
Compatibility with surrounding uses	• Proximity of uses that are incompatible with housing • Proximity to areas that would perceive affordable housing as incompatible	Is site adjacent or proximate to potentially incompatible uses? IF YES, can effects of proximity to incompatible uses be mitigated through design or other strategies?
Special considerations or constraints	• Historic districts • Farmland preservation • Easements or rights of way • Regional planning conditions • Specific affordable housing funding program criteria	Is site or proposed use subject to any special considerations or constraints? IF YES, can they be addressed in ways that do not impair the feasibility of the proposed development?

Land-use regulations, which will be discussed in more detail in the following section, can be equally problematic. While in theory local zoning boards and governing bodies should entertain variances and other deviations from the ordinance purely on their effect on the physical configuration of the project, in practice many towns hold affordable housing developments to more stringent standards, or refuse to offer the same variance or rezoning options that they routinely grant developers of more expensive housing. A Dayton, Ohio, planner testified, years ago, that "Many, many times a rezoning application will be treated differently if it is for a luxury apartment than if it is for a 236 project."[1] In one Long Island town, the planning board recommended against a rezoning application for a subsidized housing development in part because it was unsatisfied with the applicant's plans for supervising the children of single-parent families who might live in the development, an issue that one doubts was raised with respect to pending applications for expensive condominiums.[2]

Two criteria, those dealing with the site's suitability for prospective residents and its compatibility with proximate land uses, operate somewhat differently with respect to affordable housing. The lower incomes of residents of affordable housing dictate that their mobility will be less than that of more affluent families to some extent, so that sites that provide for either pedestrian or public transportation access to key services and facilities, such as schools, shopping, parks, and playgrounds, are particularly desirable. At the same time, lack of public transportation should not rule out a site, particularly where most of the occupants of the housing are likely to be moderate-income working families. Car ownership is widely diffused among lower income households, and carless families are rare outside of high-density urban areas. In 2001, according to the U.S. Department of Transportation, all but eight percent of American households owned at least one car, and nearly 80 percent of households earning less than $25,000 per year (roughly 60 percent of the national median income) owned at least one. Households without cars are heavily concentrated in higher density urban areas, among the elderly, and among people with disabilities.

Access to public transportation, as well as pedestrian access to a wide range of services and facilities, is relatively common—although far from universal—in urban areas. Although the quality and frequency of the service is often inadequate, it is not difficult to find urban sites that meet reasonable standards of access to public transportation. The same is not true of many suburbs, particularly the outer suburbs that have been developed since World War II. Public transportation in those communities may be entirely absent, or at best no more than a bus route along a major arterial highway or a single train station.[3] In such a setting, a rigid policy demanding that affordable housing sites have convenient access to an all-but-nonexistent public transportation network is likely to be little more than a superficially plausible cover for exclusionary practices.

That notwithstanding, *relative* accessibility is an important consideration. A site that is truly isolated, particularly if it is likely to contain a large number of particularly transit-dependent households, such as the elderly or low-income, single-parent families, can become a trap for its residents, segregating them as thoroughly as if they were housed in the most heavily poverty-concentrated neighborhood. A good approach is embodied in the "access to services checklist" offered by the Affordable Housing Design Advisor, which provides a planner with the ability to describe the proximity of 25 different services and facilities that might be important to the prospective residents of an affordable housing development, such as a bank, bus line, clinic, or supermarket, and then to assess whether the proximity or distance of that service is "negative, neutral, or positive" for the residents, and why.[4] By working through such a checklist with a group of individuals representative of future users, planners can thoughtfully evaluate whether the location of the site is likely to be truly problematic for its residents, or—even if less than optimal—no more than moderately inconvenient This is true of suburban living for most people, whatever their income may be.

Even if a site lacks important access features or facilities, it may not necessarily be a permanent condition. Some deficiencies of access or facilities can be mitigated, either by taking specific actions or by the passage of time. If the development is large enough, it may be possible to locate desirable facilities such as a child care center within the development, or—if the development brings enough consumer demand to the area—to encourage the development of a convenience store, such as a CVS or Rite-Aid drugstore, on a nearby parcel or even within the development itself. Similarly, the local transit agency may be willing to accommodate a new population of potential users by adjusting its routes or adding a stop close to a new development. Finally, a property that is distant from services and facilities today may gain access to convenient facilities a few years later as the surrounding area grows, and as nearby properties, which may already be zoned for commercial or institutional uses, are developed or redeveloped. Planners must recognize that change is a constant, and that the particular configuration of land uses that exists today may change in the future in ways that benefit the residents of the development.

The question of compatibility with adjacent or nearby land uses cuts two ways. On the one hand, sound planning, not to mention common sense, dictates that housing, whether affordable or market-driven, should not be located too close to noxious or unpleasant uses such as heavy industrial plants or heavily utilized high-speed highways (although some communities have indeed sited affordable housing in such areas, in some cases as a buffer between noxious uses and more "desirable" residential areas).

While such sites are not optimal, those bordering attractive and compatible uses on at least one side, such as other residential neighborhoods or open space, need not be rejected out of hand. If the site is deep enough to permit an adequately deep buffer between the housing and the adjacent incompatible uses, with solid fencing and plantings, it may still be appropriately considered suitable for affordable—or market-rate—housing development. To some extent the question of suitability may hinge on whether the incompatibility can truly be resolved by buffering, as is the case if the adjacent use is merely visually unattractive, or is inherently incompatible, which is the case if there are long-term environmental hazards associated with that use.

At the same time, painful reality suggests that prospective affordable housing developers also avoid sites where particularly strong opposition can be expected from nearby residents and property owners. The home owners in an upscale suburban area of expensive single-family houses are not only likely to strongly oppose the siting of a nearby affordable housing development—with the possible exception of one for senior citizens—but are likely to have the means and influence to block its approval or subject the development to potentially ruinous delays. Although there are a few cases in which such sites have been developed for affordable housing, particularly in towns with a strong social justice ethos such as Princeton, New Jersey, or Palo Alto, California, most affordable housing developers instinctively give such sites a wide berth.

At the opposite end, there are sites that are inappropriate for affordable housing developments because the area is too badly deteriorated or already too heavily concentrated with poor and near-poor households. Not only do such areas rarely offer a safe or healthy environment for the residents of the development, but the construction of affordable housing with public subsidies can further undermine what little private market activity exists, increasing the risk of further abandonment and disinvestment. Finally, if publicly subsidized housing becomes too large a share of the total housing stock in a neighborhood, it can have the effect of discouraging much-needed market investment in the area. These issues, and the contrasting circumstances under which it is appropriate, even desirable, to build affordable housing in distressed inner-city areas, are discussed further in Chapter 8.

GOOD SITES ARE HARD TO FIND

Finding suitable sites for affordable housing can be a difficult proposition. Where the local housing market is healthy, developers of affordable housing will have difficulty competing financially with market-rate developers for sites that are both physically appropriate and suitably zoned. The added site suitability considerations that come into play with respect to affordable housing developments, moreover, as well as the constant risk of community opposition, mean that many available sites may not be truly suitable, or if they are, may be incapable of winning the necessary approvals. As a result, many worthwhile efforts to create much-needed affordable housing founder even before truly getting under way because of the difficulty of finding sites that are suitable, approvable, and affordable.

This is not true everywhere. The most significant exceptions to this rule are found in distressed urban areas. In large parts of cities such as Detroit or Philadelphia, property values are low and there is little or no demand for land from private market developers. As a result, developers of affordable housing face little competition for available sites. Moreover, such areas, although once fully built up, have undergone widespread abandonment in recent decades, so that large numbers of vacant sites and buildings are potentially available. As a result of tax foreclosures, much of this land may belong to the city or county. Many cities in this situation are willing to sell these properties to affordable housing developers, often at nominal cost, as are many private owners. As a result, inexpensive land is often available in such areas to be developed for affordable housing. Many of these areas, however, may be marginal or even inappropriate locations for building additional affordable housing.

This picture can change dramatically, sometimes seemingly overnight, as market conditions change in urban neighborhoods. When the market gets stronger, competition from private developers increases while the availability of land diminishes. Property owners hold onto their properties, paying their taxes more regularly to avoid foreclosure. At the same time, local governments who were content to give away land to nonprofit developers of affordable housing when they were the only option may develop a strong preference for selling their land to developers of private market housing at full market value once they appear on the scene. Such a transformation took place in northern New Jersey cities like Newark and Paterson after 2000; within less than five years, CDCs that had once found it relatively easy to obtain land for affordable housing in these cities at modest cost discovered that it was all but impossible to do so without great expense and effort.

Limited availability and private market competition can make it difficult for developers to find sites for affordable housing in urban areas, but many of the other constraints one finds in suburbia are lacking. By and large, urban sites are zoned in ways that make possible at least some affordable housing options, while opposition to zoning changes is rarely as intense as it can be in suburban areas. Moreover, urban sites generally have access to infrastructure, and—with the exception of brownfield sites—tend to have relatively few environmental constraints. As a result, if an affordable housing developer has the resources to compete effectively for available sites, it is likely to ultimately obtain the necessary approvals to move forward.

The suburban environment is more difficult to navigate. Few sites of any kind in most developing suburbs are already zoned as of right in a way that makes them suitable for affordable housing development. Those few sites are likely to be just as attractive to developers of upscale apartments or condominiums. Where a market exists for either market-rate or affordable housing, any site on which either one can be built as of right will command a higher price for market-rate housing. The would-be affordable housing developer will invariably be outbid.

As a result, almost any affordable housing developer's options will be limited to sites that will require rezoning or some other form of discretionary action by a local planning commission or zoning appeals board. While sites already zoned for multifamily housing are likely to have adequate sewer and water infrastructure, other potentially suitable sites may not; they may require approval either to extend sewer and water lines or to construct a well and a sewerage treatment plant on-site. Even where a rezoning is needed, affordable housing developers may also be in competition with market developers, who not only may have an easier time getting discretionary approvals, but can more easily afford to pay for the additional infrastructure costs involved.

In many cases, unless the town is willing to step in and use its powers to help overcome the inherent economic imbalance between affordable housing and other competing uses, few opportunities may become available for affordable housing development. Those properties that are potentially available are more likely to be borderline sites located in areas that are less attractive to the market, such as mixed commercial or industrial areas, or sites which have some other problem—such as an environmental constraint or difficulty of access—rendering them harder to develop. Recognizing this reality, some communities have provided municipally owned land to affordable housing developers, while others have attempted to use their land-use powers to level the playing field and make affordable housing development feasible.

Simply zoning more land for higher density development is not likely to foster affordable housing, because most communities are experiencing strong demand for higher density living from the market as well. A few communities have created special affordable housing zones. Santa Cruz County, in California, created an affordable housing zone with a number of unusual features. Within the zone, developments that are 100 percent affordable housing receive priority processing. If a developer proposes any other type of permitted development for a site within the zone, the county has 12 months to acquire the property for affordable housing; if the county chooses not to acquire the property, the developer can build, but must set aside 35 percent of the residential units in the development as affordable housing.[5]

Exclusive affordable housing zones, which permit no use other than affordable housing, are rarely used; indeed, such zones, which classify uses by their economic rather than their physical character, may be outside the permissible scope of zoning regulations under some state laws.[6] As an alternative, municipalities have made it easier to develop affordable housing by creating "floating zones" and "overlay zones" for affordable housing. A floating zone is a zoning district that does not actually appear on the zoning map, but exists solely in the text of the zoning ordinance until it is triggered by an application for a project on a site meeting the criteria set forth in the zone, at which point it lands on that site. An overlay zone is a mapped zone, which typically provides for higher density or other more advantageous standards for affordable housing compared to the other uses permitted in the zone. The provisions of floating or overlay zones may apply solely to developments that are made up entirely of affordable housing, or may be available to mixed income developments in which some minimum percentage of the units are affordable, while the rest are sold or rented at market rates. The latter is sometimes used as an incentive within an inclusionary zoning program, a subject that is discussed further in Chapter 12.

In addition to using their land-use powers, municipalities have used a variety of other strategies to encourage use of suitable sites for affordable housing. Some towns have donated or sold at below-market prices surplus municipal property for affordable housing, as have churches, philanthropic organizations, or socially motivated individuals. Cranbury Township, an affluent central New Jersey suburb, required a developer of expensive single-family homes to convey a portion of his site to the municipality, which passed it on to a local nonprofit developer. The nonprofit developer then constructed an affordable housing development on the site whose buildings, although containing two to five dwelling units in each, were similar in appearance to the adjacent upscale single-family homes.

Alan Mallach

Affordable multifamily housing in Cranbury, New Jersey, an upscale suburban community, designed by J. Stevens and Associates to look like large, single-family homes.

Fort Collins, a rapidly growing suburban city in Colorado, adopted a long-term strategy by creating a land bank that would buy sites for affordable housing well in advance of immediate needs. Starting in 2001 with a municipal appropriation of $925,000, the city began to purchase property in the unincorporated portion of the county, to be retained for five or more years and sold at a discount for affordable housing development as the areas become ripe for development. By 2006, the city had assembled 30 acres in its land bank, which will result in at least 300 to 360 future affordable housing units.[7]

Ultimately, municipal or county cooperation is critical. Local officials should recognize the importance of affordable housing in their community, assist qualified developers to find suitable sites, and provide those developers with the same level of regulatory flexibility that they would offer an equally qualified legitimate developer of a luxury housing development or upscale shopping center. While a few states provide machinery for a frustrated developer of affordable housing to gain redress from the courts, such as the Massachusetts 40B process described in Chapter 7, these are the exceptions rather than the rule.

GETTING PROJECTS APPROVED

The process by which development proposals are reviewed, and sometimes—but not always—approved is often time-consuming and almost Byzantine in its complexity. The technical demands of project approval are often exceeded by the political controversies spawned by development proposals; as one lawyer-architect has written, "the approval process is only about 10% design and 90% regulation but is 100% political."[8] How a piece of land should be developed, and often, whether it should be developed at all, have become subjects that can be all but guaranteed to bring out vocal opposition in almost any community, particularly in growing suburban jurisdictions, reflecting the powerful role zoning is seen to play in defining the quality of life and preserving the suburban social order.[9] In the course of many such controversies, thoughtful consideration of the merits of the proposal is often at risk of being lost.

This is not the case everywhere in the United States. There are many areas, particularly unincorporated areas in the South or Midwest, where regulations are less stringent and opposition to development less passionate, and a few, even today, where little is required of the developer beyond recording the subdivision plan in the county courthouse. The approval process is usually quite onerous, however, in almost any jurisdiction in any of the major coastal states and in most major metropolitan areas. In many coastal states, including New Jersey and California, multiple layers of local land-use and state environmental regulation make the process particularly difficult and time-consuming.

The developer of affordable housing is at a particular disadvantage in all of this. First, she rarely has the deep pockets of most other developers. Massive sums may be needed not only to hire the experts, commission the studies demanded by the many regulatory agencies, and pay expensive lawyers to sit through interminable planning commission hearings, but also to hold the property for the years that may be necessary from initial application to approval.[10] Second, the fact that a proposal is for affordable housing, rather than McMansions or a big box shopping center, can be counted upon in many jurisdictions to bring out an additional layer of public opposition from those who fear that the presence of affordable housing in their community will reduce their property values or undermine their schools, or who simply object to the idea of subsidizing housing for the poor. Before discussing the specific issues associated with approval of affordable housing, a short overview of the approval process in general is appropriate.

The development approval process in brief

A greenfields development of reasonable size in a growing suburban jurisdiction may have to obtain 10 or more separate approvals before construction can begin. A representative—but far from exhaustive—list is given in Table 4-2. While some approvals are triggered by specific conditions, such as when the site contains wetlands or abuts a floodplain, the presence of one or more such conditions is common rather than rare. Adding to the complexity of the process is the likelihood that more than one jurisdiction will be involved in the approval process. Land-use regulations—comprehensive plan, zoning, site plan review, and subdivision review—are likely to be centralized in a single jurisdiction, typically the municipality or in unincorporated areas, the county. However, the process for approving others will vary from state to state and on the basis of the nature of the approval needed. Approval for an on-site sewerage treatment system might take place at the county level, but approval to extend a regional sewerage treatment area to the site might require action by the state environmental agency.

The critical forum for development approvals, particularly for affordable housing developments, is generally the municipality. Ultimately, most environmental permits, however cumbersome the process and

TABLE 4-2 TYPICAL APPROVALS NEEDED FOR NEW DEVELOPMENTS

CATEGORY	DESCRIPTION	LEVEL OF GOVERNMENT
Approvals required of all (or nearly all) developments		
General (or comprehensive) plan	Proposed development is consistent with general or comprehensive plan	Municipality or County
Zoning	Land-use regulations must permit the use and bulk (height, setback, etc.) standards of the proposed development	Municipality or County
Site plan	Site plan meets objective (location of curb cuts, number of trees planted) and subjective standards of site plan ordinance	Municipality or County
Subdivision	Subdivision of property into separate lots (if any) meets legal standards	Municipality or County
Sewerage	Site can be connected into public sewer system OR on-site treatment (septic or package plant) meets legal and technical standards	Municipality, County, or State
Water supply	Site can be connected into public water system OR on-site water supply (well) meets legal and technical standards	Municipality, County, State, or private water purveyor
Traffic	No undue impacts on traffic flow OR road improvements are made to mitigate impacts	Municipality, County, or State
Storm drainage	Site will not generate downstream runoff OR runoff can be retained on-site	Municipality, County, or State
Soil erosion and sedimentation control	Construction activity will not trigger undue soil erosion or stream sedimentation	County or State
Approvals triggered by particular site or location features		
Wetlands (property contains or abuts wetlands)	No construction takes place in wetlands and adequate buffer areas are provided OR wetlands mitigation is provided	County or State
Floodplain (property is located within delineated floodplain)	No construction takes place in floodplains OR floor elevations are above flood levels	County or State
Natural resources protection (property contains woodlands or valuable habitats)	Mature trees are preserved OR no endangered species habitats are destroyed	Municipality, County, or State
Stream encroachment (property contains or abuts a stream)	No negative impact on stream flow or water quality	County or State
Historic preservation (property is located within a historic district)	Design is consistent with standards for historic district	Municipality or County
Brownfields (property is a former industrial site, or has other form of environmental contamination)	Environmental remediation will render site safe to use for residential development	State

extended the delays, are granted or denied on the technical issues involved. The most intense battles, and those in which the most wide-ranging issues are likely to arise, are at the local level, and most often revolve around zoning changes. While some municipalities make provision for affordable housing in their zoning ordinances, as noted earlier, a disproportionate number of proposals for development of affordable housing require zoning changes.

The procedures by which zoning ordinances can be changed, as well as the standards governing such changes, vary widely from state to state. Most states permit the use of a property to be changed through a use variance, which is typically granted by a quasi-judicial board known as the Zoning Board of Appeals or Zoning Board of Adjustment. Under nearly all such state laws, however, the circumstances under which a use variance can be granted are limited to those in which there is "no reasonable use" (Wisconsin) or "no viable use" (Ohio) of the property, or in similar vein, that the applicant must demonstrate that she "cannot realize a reasonable return, provided that lack of return is substantial as demonstrated by competent financial evidence" under the existing zoning provisions, as set forth in New York State law.[11] Clearly, under such a standard, the likelihood of an affordable housing developer obtaining suitable zoning through a use variance is remote.

The principal exception to this rule is New Jersey, which permits zoning boards to grant use variances "in particular cases for special reasons," without requiring a finding of hardship or lack of an alternative viable use, as is the case in other states. As a result of court decisions over the years, a doctrine has evolved under which certain uses are considered "inherently beneficial" and can be approved through use variances as long as the applicant shows that the use can be approved "without substantial detriment to the public good and will not substantially impair the intent and the purpose of the zone plan and zoning ordinance."[12] In an important 1970 case, the New Jersey Supreme Court upheld the Town of Englewood's grant of a use variance for an affordable housing development, finding that the provision of housing for low- and moderate-income households was an inherently beneficial use serving the public good.[13] Under this standard, use variances have been used to approve a number of affordable housing developments in New Jersey towns and cities.

In most states, however, applicants for approval of affordable housing projects will have to seek a rezoning of their property, a legislative matter at the discretion of the municipal or county governing body.[14] This is usually a far more complicated matter because it often involves an application first to the local planning commission, then a second application to the governing body. This may require duplicate public hearings, presentations by experts, and the like, all adding to the time and expense involved. In states that require strict conformity between the comprehensive plan[15] and the zoning ordinance, such as California, if the effect of the zoning change is to render the ordinance out of conformity, a general plan amendment must be simultaneously prepared and submitted to the planning commission and governing body for their approval.

Navigating the approval process

Navigating this process is difficult enough for any development, but particularly difficult for affordable housing proposals because of the large number of issues, many unrelated to the use of the land, that such proposals trigger. As Danielson wrote, "in the wake of disclosure that subsidized housing is planned for a site, opponents usually turn out in force, dominating hearings and other public proceedings."[16] The objections—over and above any issues common to all developments—typically fall into two broad categories: the effect of the proposed development on nearby property values, either directly or as a result of increased property taxes, and the deleterious social effect that the presence of lower income households will have on the community.

Although it is almost an article of faith on the part of suburban opponents of affordable housing that such a development in their midst will lower their property values, there is little evidence in support of that proposition, although, in light of the complexities of extracting the impact of a single factor on something as complex as property values, a simple answer is not always available. A meta-analysis of studies of the effect of affordable housing on property values prepared in 1996 for Habitat for Humanity, after reviewing 11 separate studies, concluded that

> The assumption that property values will decline with the location of affordable housing is based on the idea that one facility can affect a whole neighborhood, and that such facilities will be conspicuous, unattractive, poorly maintained and poorly managed. The studies show that these assumptions are incorrect.[17]

Many of the studies they looked at were for group homes rather than affordable housing developments, and the methodology of some of the studies was not always completely reliable. A more rigorous analysis by George Galster in 2002 found that the picture was more complicated. He concluded that "assisted (or subsidized) housing had positive or insignificant effects on residential property values nearby *in higher value, less vulnerable neighborhoods*, unless the assisted housing exceeds the thresholds of spatial concentration or scale (emphasis added)."[18] Galster also found, however, that positive effects were less likely in lower value, more vulnerable neighborhoods, and that the concentration of disproportionate numbers of subsidized units in large-scale projects could lead to negative effects.

The risk of negative effects, therefore, is far greater in more vulnerable urban neighborhoods, where current residents are likely to have—at most—moderate incomes, and where property values are already low relative to the regional norm. In more affluent suburban areas, however, the evidence is strong that well-designed and well-maintained affordable housing, built at a scale that is reasonable in light of the size and character of the area, is unlikely in the extreme to have any negative effect on the property values of nearby homes.

Of course, citing the studies themselves is not likely to convince any doubters. Similarly, while attractive renderings of the proposed development are an important part of any presentation, they are also likely to be dismissed as no more than "pretty pictures" by many of those not predisposed in favor of the project. Supporters of affordable housing proposals have found two other strategies to often be more effective: first, establishing the track record or credibility of the entity developing the housing, and second, organizing visits to attractive, well-maintained affordable housing projects in similar communities elsewhere, especially projects of a similar physical character and housing a similar population to those who are most likely to live in the proposed development.

The most credible development entities are those that have already built attractive, well-maintained affordable housing, either in the same community or in similar ones nearby. A newly established entity cannot demonstrate such a track record. One approach in that situation is to involve credible community leaders or representatives of well-respected community institutions in the organization, a step that sends the message to the community that the organization will be driven by concern for the community rather than either a quick financial return or abstract ideological principles. When Princeton Community Housing, Inc., a nonprofit developer of affordable housing, was organized in the late 1960s, it created a board made up of representatives of a wide spectrum of community institutions, including Princeton University and a number of churches and service organizations. Today, with a number of large and highly successful developments under its belt, its track record is more than adequate to give the nonprofit credibility.

Community opposition may not be entirely based on economic concerns. Many residents may fear the introduction of people of lower social or economic status into their midst, and worry about their effect on the community's quality of life. These fears are often associated with suburbanites' negative perceptions of urban areas, and their association of lower income individuals and families with the mean streets of inner city neighborhoods. These sentiments can be particularly strong in suburban areas where large numbers of the residents are themselves former urban residents, who see themselves as having "escaped" the city to the cleaner, safer world of suburbia. While some of this opposition may be driven by racial prejudice and stereotyping, it is not only unfair but unproductive to dismiss it, or the people voicing their fears, on those grounds. Strictly speaking, there is no way to prove or disprove such allegations; the best response is to be able to point to successful affordable housing developments in similar settings, and show that such fears have turned out to be without foundation.

Advocates also try to educate people about the nature and variety of people who need affordable housing, particularly in affluent suburban communities where large parts of the area's working population has been priced out of the market. As the Columbus, Ohio, Board of Realtors' website puts it,

> **The Faces of Affordable Housing** ... conjures up all kinds of stereotypes, doesn't it? But, truth be known, these faces touch us all daily. They belong to our school administrators and teachers, our computer programmers and store clerks, our police and firemen. These are the faces of a single parent seeking a reputable school district, a grandparent wanting to purchase a retirement home close to their remaining family, a divorcee reentering the work place, a blended family beginning anew and young couples looking for a safe environment to raise their small children.[19]

Many of the people who cannot afford to live in a community perform essential roles there; as Ashland, Oregon's website points out,

"Our quality of life is directly related to our ability to provide affordable housing."[20]

Despite determined efforts, it may not always be possible to win over enough opponents to get a project approved. And in the absence of clear community support for the project, local officials may not be brave or responsible enough to approve the project in the face of determined opposition. The town supervisor (mayor) of Brookhaven, New York, stated at a public hearing: "There is a need for this housing desperately in the Town of Brookhaven. But until it has the support of the community where it is located, I don't feel you are going to get a town board that is going to approve it."[21] Success in such cases is likely to depend on the ability of advocates to mobilize enough support to demonstrate to a planning board or town council that there is an affirmative constituency in the community, not just a negative one.

An affordable housing proposal may be given unusually rigorous scrutiny with respect to facially legitimate planning or environmental issues such as storm drainage or traffic impacts. While the line between legitimate concerns and those that are excessive or spurious is not always a hard and fast one, there have been many cases where concerns have been raised as a way of giving seeming legitimacy to an opposition that was actually grounded in social or economic concerns. A similar strategy is for opponents to cloak themselves in concern for the putative low-income occupants of the development, by claiming that the project is not suitable for the potential residents by virtue of such factors as inadequate public transportation or incompatible adjacent land uses.

As is the case with any development proposal, some affordable housing projects do raise legitimate planning and environmental questions and should properly be turned down. Similarly, some sites are indeed inappropriate for a particular population and should not be used to house them. It is essential to put this into perspective. The likelihood is substantial that a proposed site for affordable housing will be less than ideal, given the severe difficulty of finding *any* sites for affordable housing in many parts of the United States. Recognizing that, prospective developers must avoid selecting sites that truly are inappropriate. Having chosen the best available site, they must be candid about its constraints and the potential impacts of developing it, and ensure that their plans address the constraints and mitigate the impacts as much as possible. No more can reasonably be expected. For a municipality or county to demand of an affordable housing site that it be ideal in every respect—a standard to which other developments are rarely, if ever, held—is not good planning. It is exclusion and discrimination by another name.

Litigation as a last resort

As with any other development, the developer of an affordable housing project that has been turned down by the municipality or county has the right to appeal the denial to the courts. Litigation, however, is not only a last resort, but often beyond the means of many affordable housing developers. Not only is the cost of litigation itself considerable, but except in those unusual cases where the developer owns the property outright, it may be difficult if not impossible to hold onto the property for the years that litigation may require. If the developer loses control of the property, a court victory will be a Pyrrhic one.

The likelihood that an affordable housing developer can overturn a municipal denial in court varies greatly from state to state. In some states, such a developer will fare no differently from a developer of luxury housing, shopping centers, or industrial parks. In others, legislation or court decisions have given affordable housing special status reflecting its importance for the public welfare, as described in Chapter 7.

Under some circumstances, an affordable housing developer can bring and win a suit against an unreasonable denial in federal court under the Fair Housing Act. Since affordable housing *as such* is not protected under the Fair Housing Act, success requires proof that the denial had a discriminatory effect on a protected class under the law. In *Huntington Branch NAACP v. Town of Huntington*,[22] the Second Circuit overturned a municipal denial of approval for a subsidized housing development in an almost entirely White section of a large town on Long Island. The court found that racial minorities—and all existing subsidized housing—were limited to one small portion of the town, and that by denying a project that would have had a significant integrative effect, the town's action had a racially discriminatory impact. The court did not require proof of racially discriminatory *intent*, which is often extremely hard to prove; as the leader of the opposition to one Long Island affordable housing development told a reporter, "We're a middle class community here—we're too smart for that."[23]

Florida, however, has gone one step further and incorporated affordable housing *as such* as a protected class under the state's Fair Housing Act, which reads: "It is unlawful to discriminate in land use decisions or in the permitting of development based on race, color, national origin, sex, disability, familial status, religion, or, except as otherwise permitted by law, *the source of financing of a development or proposed development* (emphasis added)."[24] If the developer can show that the development was rejected because it was affordable housing, or was treated differently than a development of more expensive homes, under the Florida law they are likely to prevail.

The Florida law grew out of a struggle by affordable housing advocates to build affordable housing for farm workers in Lee County, on the state's Gulf Coast. A faith-based nonprofit organization's request to rezone a 26-acre site zoned for mobile homes to permit duplex units faced vocal opposition: "The planning department [was] deluged with letters decrying the horrors which they associated with the type of people who would be living in the development. Substantial pressure was brought to bear on the County Commission; protests were held with signs promising to oust in the next election those Commissioners who would permit the development to go forward. The County Commission gave way and denied the rezoning request."[25]

The nonprofit developer brought suit under Florida property rights law, while the U.S. Department of Justice moved to intervene under the federal Fair Housing Act. In the end, the County Commission settled the case, largely to avoid the risk that—if they lost a Fair Housing Act case—they could be liable for damages. The development was built and has been a great success, warmly accepted by its neighbors.

The Connecticut Affordable Housing Appeals Act also provides strong support for developers who have been denied local approvals; under the Act, the court will affirm the denial only if the municipality can show that its decision was based on "substantial public interests in health, safety or other matters which the [municipality] may legally consider."[26] Between 1991 and 2004, the Connecticut courts issued 128 decisions in appeals from a town's denial, of which developers prevailed in slightly more than two-thirds. Where the issues involved substantive planning and environmental issues such as inadequate water supply or sewerage disposal, the town prevailed. Where the town had denied projects on more subjective grounds, or on matters outside the scope of land-use regulation—such as preservation of community character, excessive school enrollment, fiscal impact, or adverse aesthetic impact—the developer prevailed.[27]

In the final analysis, however, hardly anyone, with the exception of trial lawyers, actually likes litigation. It is time-consuming, expensive, and unpredictable. While some towns turn down projects knowing that their action will be overturned, hoping to gain some political advantage, such behavior is both bad policy and irresponsible governance. Towns should plan for affordable housing as an integral part of their land-use regulations and treat affordable housing proposals as they would any other development proposal. Recognizing the political pressures that work against this, professional staff and consultants—planners, lawyers, engineers, administrators—working for towns have a particular obligation to do their best to see that the public officials for whom they work live up to this standard.

NOTES

1. Quoted in Danielson, Michael. 1976. *The Politics of Exclusion*. New York: Columbia University Press, 97.
2. See Mallach, Alan. 1986. "The Tortured Reality of Suburban Exclusion: Zoning, Economics and the Future of the Berenson Doctrine." *Pace Environmental Law Review* 4(1): 97.
3. Train access in most suburban communities in the United States, even where it exists, is usually of little value for lower income residents, because typical train route patterns tend to be oriented to taking white-collar suburban commuters into urban jobs (not to mention relatively high costs compared to buses).
4. Available at http://www.designadvisor.org/pdfs/svces.pdf. Design Advisor includes a completed checklist for a hypothetical site.
5. Santa Cruz County Code, Chapter 13.10.433.
6. The legal question would hinge on the scope of the municipal zoning power, and the extent to which state law recognizes affordable housing as a distinct category and whether affirmative use of the police power is appropriate. In New Jersey and California, exclusive affordable housing zones would most probably pass muster, unless the property owner could claim—perhaps by showing that public subsidies were not adequately available to make development of the site possible—that the zoning constituted a taking of the property.
7. Available at http://www.ci.fort-collins.co.us/affordablehousing/land-bank.php.
8. Charles H. Place, quoted in http://www.aiaarchitect.net/site/news/04/8.04/negotiate_land_approval.htm.
9. For an excellent discussion of this issue from the perspective of a scholar who is both an anthropologist and city planner, see Perrin, Constance. 1977. *Everything in its Place: Social Order and Land Use in America*. Princeton, N.J.: Princeton University Press.
10. A by-product of the market-based developer's deep pockets is their ability to obtain political influence by making substantial campaign contributions. This is another advantage affordable housing developers rarely have.
11. New York State Town Law, Sec. 267-b(2)(b).
12. N.J. Stats. Ann. 40:55D-70(d).
13. *De Simone v. Greater Englewood Housing Corporation*, 56 NJ 428, 267 A.2d 431 (1970).
14. A small number of jurisdictions, including Stamford, Connecticut, for obscure historical reasons permit changes to the zoning ordinance to be made by an administrative body, such as a zoning board, rather than the legislative body.

15. Different states refer to the overall guide plan adopted by the municipality by different names. In California it is called a general plan, in New Jersey a master plan, and in Wisconsin a comprehensive plan. It is the same thing in all cases, although its legal authority and weight vary widely from state to state.
16. Danielson, *The Politics of Exclusion*, 97.
17. "Why Affordable Housing Does Not Lower Property Values," prepared by HomeBase/The Center for Common Concerns for Habitat for Humanity, available at http://www.habitat.org/how/propertyvalues.aspx.
18. Galster, George C. 2002. *A Review of Existing Research on the Effects of Federally Assisted Housing Programs on Neighboring Residential Property Values*. Washington, D.C.: National Association of Realtors, 26.
19. Available at http://www.columbusrealtors.com/880.cfm.
20. Available at http://www.ashland.or.us/page.asp?NavID=526.
21. Mallach, "Tortured Reality," 98.
22. 844 F.2d 926, affd. per curiam, 488 US 15 (1988). The author was an expert witness for the plaintiffs in this case.
23. "Rental Plan Stirs Three Villages." 1982. *New York Times*, December 19.
24. Florida Statutes, Sec. 760.26, added 2000. The "except as otherwise permitted by law" language was added to make clear that statutes that provide for affirmative steps to further affordable housing, such as existing state laws requiring expediting permits, remained lawful.
25. 1000 Friends of Florida. 2005. *Creating Inclusive Communities in Florida: A Guidebook for Local Elected Officials and Staff on Avoiding and Overcoming the Not in My Backyard Syndrome*, 44.
26. Conn. Gen. Stats, Sec. 8_30g(c.)
27. Town of Washington, Ct. 2005. "Affordable Housing Appeal Statistics." Available at http://www.washingtonct.org/ahstats.html.

CHAPTER

5

Making the Numbers Work: Financing Affordable Housing

The most fundamental condition of affordable housing is that it must be *affordable*. That means that the families or individuals to whom it is aimed must be able to afford to live there without paying an undue or disproportionate share of their income for shelter. Affordable housing, moreover, must be built and financed in ways so that it can be afforded by families who typically do not have enough income to afford housing being produced by the market. That can mean different things, depending on the income of the families being targeted and the cost of producing the housing. In some cases, it may be possible to produce affordable housing without financial assistance, simply by building as inexpensively as possible and getting local governments to relax some of their development standards.

Those situations are the rare exceptions. They only work where the developer is targeting families whose incomes are relatively high—by the standards of what are considered lower incomes—and where land and other building costs are relatively modest. In most cases, particularly where the families being targeted are very low-income families, or where land may be scarce and housing costs high, the ability to put together not just mortgage loans, but subsidies, tax abatements, housing vouchers, and other forms of financial assistance become a necessary condition to making the housing happen.

This chapter will provide an overview of the many ways in which different financial mechanisms, many of which have already been mentioned in these pages, can be used separately or in combination to make various types of housing affordable to populations in need. Before turning directly to those mechanisms, it is important to make clear what the term "affordable" means, and how it translates into how much can be charged in rent or for the sales price of a house.

DEFINING AFFORDABILITY

Affordability, like many similar terms, cannot be defined scientifically. What represents an undue or disproportionate share of a particular family's income to spend for shelter, making it unduly burdened by housing costs, is to some extent a subjective matter and will vary from family to family based on their means, their preferences, and the other demands on their income. At the same time, certain standards are adopted by government, developers, and lenders to guide both housing policy in general and specific decisions about who is eligible to rent or buy a particular dwelling, based on reasonable rules of thumb. The most common standard is that a family should not be required to spend more than 30 percent of its gross income for shelter. Nearly two-thirds of very low-income families and one-third of low-income families in the United States exceed that threshold.

This standard is not immutable. When the public housing program was created in the 1930s, the government set the affordability threshold at 20, not 30 percent. In order to qualify for the program, a family needed to have an income at least five times the base rent, including utilities, of the apartment. As housing costs increased, and the cost of other staples such as food and clothing declined in relative terms during the 1960s and 1970s, the threshold was raised first to 25 percent, and then in 1982 to 30 percent.

When it comes to lower income rental housing, public agencies and developers continue to use the 30 percent threshold as the standard for who can afford to rent an apartment in a subsidized development, or how much subsidy to give a family in the form of a housing voucher so they can afford an apartment that would otherwise be beyond their means. The standard is less clear with respect to affordable home ownership, where standards tend to vary from place to place or from lender to lender. For many years, the most widely used threshold was that a family should spend no more than 28 percent of its gross income for what is commonly abbreviated as PITI—principal, interest, taxes, and insurance—and, where applicable, condo fees. Today, the threshold is often set at 33 percent of gross income, and sometimes higher. Many subprime lenders approved loans where the home buyers were going to spend 40 percent or more of their income for PITI.

In determining whether a particular unit is affordable, the appropriate income share, however defined, is converted into a rent level or a purchase price. In the case of rental housing, the process is straightforward. If a family has an income of $25,000 per year, 30 percent of that income is $7,500 per year, or $625 per month, which becomes that family's affordable rent. If, as is common today, utilities are paid directly by the tenant rather than the building owner, it is customary to adjust the rent by a "utility allowance" reflecting the average family's expenditure on heat, hot water, gas, and electricity for a unit of the size the family occupies. Thus, if the utility allowance is $75 per month, the family will pay the landlord a net, or contract, rent of $550 per month.

Where dealing with affordable housing for owner-occupancy, one must work backward from the monthly carrying cost or PITI to establish an affordable house price. In order to do so, however, one needs to plug in different numbers, which require either factual information or assumptions, including the following:

- What is the mortgage interest rate?
- How much is the down payment (what is the ratio between the mortgage and the total price)?
- How much will property taxes be?
- How much will insurance be?
- If the unit is part of a condominium, how much will the condo fees be?

Each of these assumptions will contribute to defining what is considered an affordable selling price. The lower the interest rate of the mortgage, or the larger the down payment, the more house one can afford at a given monthly cost.

By juggling these variables, developers can push the affordable price up a good deal, but only at the cost of potentially imposing unsustainable future burdens on the home buyer. For example, large numbers of houses were built in the 1980s and 1990s and sold to low- or moderate-income buyers in Midwestern cities such as Cleveland and Flint, Michigan, with a tax abatement program that meant that the home owner paid no property taxes for the first 10 or 12 years. Since the cost of taxes that were factored into the amount the family could carry was zero, they could carry a larger mortgage and a higher purchase price. All good things, however, come to an end. At the end of the abatement period, the properties went on the tax rolls, and home owners suddenly became responsible for an additional $200 to $300 in monthly payments. Many could no longer afford their homes, and others, when the time came to sell, discovered that their homes were worth less than the amount they had paid 10 years earlier.

The fundamental principle in setting affordable house prices is that the price should be sustainable; in other words, the relationship between price and carrying cost should be based on realistic assumptions that provide as much cost stability over the long term as is reasonably feasible. The most reasonable assumptions, as well as unreasonable or tendentious ones, are shown in Table 5-1. Any situation where any of the unreasonable assumptions are used can create future difficulties for the home buyer. Using reasonable assumptions, and plugging in values representative of cities in the Northeast in 2007, Table 5-2 shows the income

TABLE 5-1 REASONABLE AND UNREASONABLE ASSUMPTIONS FOR CONVERTING CARRYING COSTS INTO AFFORDABLE HOUSE PRICES

CATEGORY	REASONABLE ASSUMPTIONS	UNREASONABLE ASSUMPTIONS
Interest rate	Current widely available interest rate for 30-year fixed-rate mortgage	Any interest rate that is either not widely available or is based on an adjustable rate or other "exotic" mortgage with initially low monthly payments
Down payment	No more than 5 percent	Any down payment level greater than 5 percent
Property taxes	Full taxes, or if property is receiving tax abatement, one should still plug in a figure that is equal to or greater than half of the difference between the abatement and full taxes	Full tax abatement, or a figure less than half of the difference between full and abated taxes
Insurance	Normal industry standard in light of unit type and location	"Low-balling" normal industry standard
Condominium fees	A full, sustainable fee adequate to cover both ongoing costs and maintenance of reserves	"Low-balling" initial condo fees or creating low condo fees for affordable units that do not permit residents of those units access to all condo facilities

TABLE 5-2   INCOME NEEDED TO CARRY A $150,000 HOUSE

CATEGORY	ASSUMPTION	COST/FEE SIMPLE	COST/CONDO
Annual mortgage payment	6.5% interest rate 5% down payment	$10,808	$10,808
Annual property taxes	2% of house value	$3,000	$3,000
Insurance	0.25% of house value	$375	$375
Condo fees	$100/month	$0	$1200
TOTAL		$14,183	$15,383
MINIMUM INCOME NEEDED	33% of gross income for PITI and condo fees	$42,549	$46,149
	28% of gross income for PITI and condo fees	$50,653	$54,939

that is needed to afford a $150,000 house. Where property taxes are lower, as in much of South and in California, the minimum income needed might be lower. Conversely, many condominiums impose fees that are substantially higher than the figure used in the table. The table also illustrates the impact of underwriting on the basis of the family spending 28 percent versus 33 percent of their income for PITI. In the former case, the family can afford three times their income in house price; in the latter, that increases to 3.5 times their income. Similar calculations can define, for a household of any given income level, what they can afford to pay in rent or what they can afford to spend to buy a home.

The financing of affordable housing comes down to how to bring the cost of a home within a lower income family's financial reach, filling the gap between what they can afford and what the house would cost or what the monthly rent would be without assistance. Whether the home is to be rented or sold, there are two ways in which that can be done: by defraying some part of the capital cost of the home or development (capital cost assistance), or by covering some part of the monthly cost that the home owner or tenant pays, or that the owner of a rental building must raise from the rent roll (carrying cost assistance). All of the many different financial mechanisms that are used to make affordable housing possible fall into one or the other category. In many cases, developers of affordable housing will combine some of both forms of assistance into a project to make it affordable. An affordable home ownership project might include a capital grant to reduce the cost of the housing in the first place, coupled with tax abatement to reduce the home owner's monthly payment.

The next section will provide an overview of the different mechanisms that are available to reduce the initial capital cost or the ongoing carrying cost in affordable housing, followed by a section in which the most important capital subsidy programs currently available are described. The closing section of this chapter will describe how developers combine or layer multiple sources of financial assistance in order to make possible successful development of affordable housing, including illustrations of how the financing might be assembled for a hypothetical Low Income Housing Tax Credit development.

FILLING THE GAP

Capital cost assistance

Table 5-3 illustrates the various ways in which the capital cost of an affordable housing development can be defrayed. While some of these actually reduce the cost of developing the project, such as a waiver of a fee or a donation of land, the most significant ones—grants and equity investments—don't actually change the cost of building the development, but work by reducing the amount of debt the building must subsequently carry. Since they are provided to the project up front as a capital contribution to the cost of development, they are considered to be a form of capital, rather than carrying cost, assistance. Ultimately, all capital subsidies are designed to reduce the amount of debt that the house or project must carry, in some cases eliminating it entirely.

The two most substantial forms of capital assistance are grants and equity investments. Capital grants are generally provided by government (although occasionally by philanthropic or institutional supporters), and can be paid into the project on completion of construction or simultaneously with the developer's construction loan during the construction period, a method known as *pari passu* financing.[1] Developers typically try to receive the grant money as early as possible, since the earlier the grant money goes into the project, the less construction financing has to be borrowed, and the less construction interest ultimately must be repaid. Many public agencies providing grants, however, prefer to provide it only after the project has been completed, in order to reduce their risk and exposure. *Pari passu* financing represents a compromise between the developer and the financing agency.

TABLE 5-3   CAPITAL COST ASSISTANCE FOR AFFORDABLE HOUSING DEVELOPMENTS

CATEGORY	DESCRIPTION	EXAMPLES
Capital grant	Direct cash contribution toward cost of development that does not need to be repaid, or only repaid when funds are available (cash flow loan)	• Federal HOME program • Home Loan Bank Affordable Housing Program (AHP) • State housing trust fund programs
Equity	Equity investment where investor gets return from tax or other benefits rather than requiring cash return from project	• Low Income Housing Tax Credit program • Historic preservation tax credit programs
Land donation	Sale of land for affordable housing projects for nominal cost or at below market project	• Chicago sells vacant lots for $1 as part of city's New Homes for Chicago program • King County, Washington, prioritizes county-owned land for sale or lease for affordable housing
Fee waivers	Waiver of fees associated with development process, such as review fees, building permit fees, sewer hookup fees, etc.	• Austin, Texas, SMART Housing Initiative provides for waiver of many city fees for affordable housing
Tax waivers	Waiver of taxes such as property taxes during construction period, or sales taxes on building materials	• New York Sec. 421a program exempts properties from taxation during construction
Reduced site planning or building standards	Reduction in cost-generating standards such as minimum parking requirements, unit square footage requirements, etc.	

Donation or below-market sale of publicly owned land, particularly in areas like Chicago or the Seattle area, where land tends to be expensive, can significantly reduce the ultimate development cost of a project without a direct cash outlay by the government. The other forms of assistance shown in the table, such as fee or tax waivers, are useful but rarely if ever make an affordable housing project feasible by themselves. Their great virtue, however, is twofold. By reducing the total project cost, they may enable the project to qualify for certain programs or resources that would otherwise not be available, and by reducing the amount of scarce capital grant subsidy needed, they increase the likelihood that the project will get the money it needs, while permitting the limited funding available to go further.

Carrying cost assistance

Even where capital costs have been significantly reduced, the monthly carrying costs that an owner or tenant must pay can still be a factor pushing the price of housing above the reach of some families, particularly those of very low income. As the managers of public housing programs learned in the 1960s and 1970s, even if 100 percent of the capital cost is defrayed by federal grants, and the property taxes are abated by the municipality, many poor families may not even be able to afford to pay enough rent to cover the project's operating costs. While public housing may be an extreme case, the problem is a recurrent one—to make housing affordable to low-income households, operating and capital cost assistance are both likely to be needed.

Housing choice vouchers (Section 8)

The largest source of carrying cost assistance to low-income tenants is the federal Section 8 or Housing Choice Voucher program. This program provides a monthly payment to the landlord for the difference between

TABLE 5-4   CARRYING COST ASSISTANCE FOR AFFORDABLE HOUSING DEVELOPMENTS

CATEGORY	DESCRIPTION	EXAMPLES
Vouchers or other forms of rental assistance	Payments directly to tenants to cover the difference between the monthly cost and what the tenant can afford to pay	• Federal Housing Choice Voucher program • New Jersey State Rental Assistance program
Tax abatement	Reduction or exemption from property taxes otherwise due	• New York City J-51 and 421a programs
Low-interest financing	Mortgage financing, either for a rental project or individual home owners, at interest rates below generally available rates	• Tax-exempt bond mortgage financing provided through state housing finance agencies
Operating subsidies	Grants to operators of affordable housing to defray part of ongoing operating cost	• Public housing operating subsidies provided by federal government to local housing authorities
Operating cost savings	Reductions in operating costs through cost-saving activities	• Bulk purchasing of supplies • Insurance buying pools

the actual rent of the home and 30 percent of the voucher recipient's gross income.[2] The dwelling unit must meet reasonable quality standards, and the actual rent must not exceed a level established by HUD and known as the Fair Market Rent, which is based on the location and size of the unit. As of the beginning of 2007, nearly two million households had received assistance under this program. While the majority of voucher recipients live in private market housing, a significant percentage live in affordable housing developments where without the voucher the rent would otherwise be too high for them to afford. Under federal law, the state or local housing agencies that administer the voucher program (usually, but not always, the local public housing authority) may designate up to 20 percent of their vouchers as project-based vouchers and allocate them to a specific affordable housing project. In contrast to other vouchers, which are portable and follow the family that holds the voucher, project-based vouchers are tied to units in the particular project.

In recent years, as waiting lists for vouchers have risen along with housing costs and the federal government has provided little money for additional vouchers, a number of states have enacted their own rental assistance programs to supplement the federal program. The largest is in Illinois, where the state assists roughly 4,000 families with rental assistance, supported by a $10 surcharge on real estate document recordings. Other substantial rental assistance programs have been established in New Jersey and Connecticut.

While vouchers are a major part of the American effort to house its low-income families, they play a smaller role in the process of *developing* affordable housing. Although many voucher holders live in subsidized housing, including housing built with low income tax credits, except in cases where the voucher is project-based, the entity operating the project cannot count on the additional revenue on an ongoing basis. The benefit of the voucher goes to the tenant, who is thereby enabled to live in a high-quality house or apartment they otherwise could not afford.

Tax abatement
Tax abatement programs for affordable housing are widely used throughout the United States. In some cases, a city or town will exempt a development entirely from local property taxes, while in others it will reduce or abate some part of the taxes. Where rental projects are exempt from property taxes, they are often required to make a payment in lieu of taxes, often referred to as a PILOT, instead. Public housing authorities, whose

projects are exempt from local property taxes, pay an annual PILOT to the city equal to 10 percent of their modest gross rent collections. In New Jersey, a municipality can negotiate a PILOT with the developer of affordable rental housing. The amount can vary from as little as one percent to as much as 15 percent of the rent roll.

Tax abatements on owner-occupied housing are sometimes used to reduce the carrying cost to make the homes affordable to lower income households, and sometimes to enable the house to be sold at a higher price to a household of a given income level. For example, using the assumptions in Table 5-2, if a household earning $50,000 must pay full property taxes, it can afford a house priced at $148,000 while paying 28 percent of its income in carrying costs. If the entire property tax bill were abated, the same household could afford to spend $187,000 for the house and keep its monthly carrying costs the same. In that way, every dollar in annual tax abatement offsets roughly $13 in capital cost subsidies.

Tax abatements raise two important issues. First, they reduce local government revenues relative to what projects would pay in full taxes or what the project's service costs may be, and second, they are invariably time-limited. The first is a matter of trade-offs. Many projects are not feasible without tax abatements; moreover, many state housing agencies will require municipal tax abatement as a condition of approving grant applications or tax credit equity allocations. Thus, the trade-off is not really between getting the same project with or without tax abatement, but between granting the tax abatement or not getting the project at all. In comparing the benefits of gaining the project with the costs of providing services to it, municipalities should take into account the likelihood that many if not most of the residents of affordable housing projects will already live in the municipality, so that many costs—such as educating their children—will not represent an incremental cost to the city or school district.

The time-limited nature of tax abatements raises a different problem. Tax abatements on owner-occupied homes typically run for five to 15 years from the date the first occupant moves into the home. At the end of the abatement period, under many state laws the taxes jump immediately to the full property tax rate based on the value of the house at that point. Even if the family's income has risen in parallel with their house value, this can impose a severe burden. In the case described above, the family's monthly costs would go from 28 percent to 35 percent of their gross income overnight. If the family income has not risen at that pace, which is a more likely scenario, the impact on the family's financial picture and their ability to continue to carry the costs of owning the home could be even more devastating.

Low-interest mortgages

Low-interest mortgage financing is a widely used vehicle to lower carrying costs for both lower income home buyers and for affordable housing rental projects. In 1954, the federal tax code was amended to permit what are known as "private activity" bonds, permitting government agencies to issue bonds to be used by private entities for purposes that benefit the public, and providing that the interest on those bonds would be exempt from federal income tax. Because the interest is exempt from income tax, investors are willing to accept a lower interest rate on the bonds, thus making it possible for the agency to pass on the savings in the form of a lower interest rate to a home buyer or affordable housing developer.

In 1960, New York State established the New York State Housing Finance Agency for the purpose of issuing tax-exempt bonds for affordable housing projects. Today, every state in the United States has a state agency or authority, generically known as housing finance agencies, with the power to issue tax-exempt bonds for this purpose. States, and where authorized by state government, localities can issue Mortgage Revenue Bonds to make home mortgages to moderate-income buyers, and Multifamily Bonds to make mortgages and construction loans for affordable or mixed income rental developments. Both are tightly regulated by the IRS, and the amount that each state can issue is capped by a formula established in the federal Tax Reform Act of 1986.[3]

Over the years, state housing finance agencies have provided over 3.5 million lower income households with home purchase mortgages, and created nearly one million affordable rental housing units. In today's tax and interest rate climate, however, the advantage of tax-exempt bond financing for home owners is often modest; as of January 2008, the California Housing Finance Agency was offering a 30-year, fixed-rate mortgage at six percent, while the New Jersey Housing & Mortgage Finance Agency offered the same product at 6.125 percent, not markedly different from market rates. CalHFA was, however, offering a number of special mortgage products, including loans to low-income borrowers at 5.375 percent, loans to disabled buyers at four percent, and a special program for low-income self-help projects at three percent, all for 30-year fixed-rate mortgages.

Other means of reducing carrying costs tend to be rare, or modest in their effects. While the federal government provides operating support for public housing agencies, a necessary outcome of the policies that targeted public housing for the poorest families, public grants to provide operating support for other affordable housing projects are all but unknown. Similarly, reducing operating costs through bulk purchasing and similar means, while helpful, tends to have no more than a limited effect on a project's bottom line. It is far more cost-effective in the long run to build projects that are energy efficient and use high-quality, durable materials and systems, so that energy costs and the costs of ongoing maintenance, repair, and replacement are kept as low as possible. That, of course, means that the project will be more expensive to build and will require more initial capital subsidy. In the long run, however, the savings will vastly exceed the added costs.

CAPITAL GRANTS AND TAX CREDIT EQUITY

There are two principal ways by which developers of affordable housing bridge the affordability gap. One is by obtaining capital grants, often from multiple sources, and the second is by selling the equity in a rental project to investors who gain tax benefits rather than cash flow from their investment. Nearly all housing developments designed to be affordable to low- and moderate-income households will use either or both means of making the development feasible and affordable.

Capital grants

Through the early 1980s, most developers of affordable housing would typically go to the federal government for a single package of financial assistance that would make the project feasible, but those days are over. Today, a developer will typically look for a variety of forms of assistance from different sources, including not only the federal government, but also state and local housing funds as well as private or quasi-private sources such as the network of federal Home Loan Banks. Table 5-5 illustrates the different sources that developers can use to support affordable housing projects. This table does not include programs that offer investors tax credits in return for their equity investments, which are discussed in the next part of this section.

As the table shows, the federal government is but one of many possible sources that a developer can draw upon. This is somewhat misleading, however, because the availability of nonfederal sources varies widely

TABLE 5-5 PRINCIPAL SOURCES OF CAPITAL SUBSIDY FOR AFFORDABLE HOUSING

SOURCE	PROGRAMS
Federal government	• HOME program • Community Development Block Grant (CDBG) program (limited to certain uses) • HUD discretionary programs, such as HOPE VI • U.S. Department of Agriculture Rural Housing Service
State government	• Housing trust funds (dedicated revenue sources) • Housing bond issues • Housing program appropriations
Local government	• Housing trust funds (dedicated revenue sources) • Housing bond issues • Housing program appropriations • Tax increment financing • Developer contributions (linkage)
Private	• Federal Home Loan Bank Affordable Housing Program • Foundation grants • Individual philanthropic grants • Institutional grants • Corporate or institutional employer-assisted housing programs

around the United States. In states such as California, Massachusetts, or New Jersey, which have historically provided financing for affordable housing and also have an extensive institutional and corporate infrastructure, nonfederal funding is widely available. In many other parts of the United States, the trickle of federal funds from the HOME and CDBG programs may be the only housing subsidy money available.

HOME and CDBG

These two federal subsidy programs have been in existence since 1990 and 1974, respectively, and still represent the bread and butter of local affordable housing efforts in many parts of the nation. While the HOME program can only be used for affordable housing activities, CDBG can be used for almost anything that either helps lower income families or removes slums and blight from a community; moreover, CDBG funds cannot be used to subsidize new construction directly. They can be used to fund rehabilitation, and can assist new construction indirectly by picking up ancillary but necessary costs such as site acquisition, utility hookups, or street improvements needed for the project. Still, with stiff competition for that money from innumerable different directions, little CDBG money is used in ways that lead to new affordable housing production.

In the 2007 fiscal year, Congress appropriated $3.772 billion for CDBG and $1.733 billion for HOME. Although these are not insignificant amounts, they are distributed among 1,200 separate states, counties, municipalities, and territories, so that the amount many individual communities have available is quite small. In Ohio, for example, $162 million in CDBG funds were distributed among 35 separate cities, eight counties, and the state. The HOME program, for which eligibility criteria are somewhat more restrictive, allocated a total of $63 million to 15 cities, along with the same eight counties and the state. After the state of Ohio, which received the largest single amount, the city of Cleveland received $25 million in CDBG funds and $6 million in HOME funds. Other cities received varying amounts of HOME funds, from nearly $5 million in Columbus down to $368,000 in Mansfield. Of the 23 Ohio cities and counties that qualified to receive HOME allocations, 14 received less than $1 million.

These numbers make it easy to understand why so many communities use their HOME funds for low-cost activities such as down payment assistance or fix-up grants to elderly home owners, where an expenditure of $5,000 per unit or even less can make a difference. With the cost of subsidizing a new affordable unit usually in excess of $50,000, and far more in high-cost areas, a small city's HOME allocation does not go very far when applied to new production or substantial rehab of affordable housing, unless it can be leveraged with nonfederal sources of subsidy.

State and local government resources
Most states provide at least some money to developers building affordable housing. By 2007, 38 states and the District of Columbia had created housing trust funds, dedicating some source of public revenue to the "express and limited purpose of providing affordable housing."[4] The resources available from these funds vary widely; some generate more than $100 million per year, while others still exist only on paper. The largest state funds are in Florida (known as the Sadowski Act), New Jersey, Illinois, Ohio, and Washington. More than 500 cities and counties around the country also have their own trust funds, with the largest being in New York City, San Francisco, Los Angeles, and Washington, D.C. All together, these trust funds generate approximately $1.6 billion per year for affordable housing, an amount roughly equivalent to the annual federal appropriation for the HOME program.

In some towns and cities, trust funds are created by levying a fee on developers, in many cases developers of nonresidential projects such as shopping centers or office towers, who are required to pay an affordable housing fee known as a linkage fee that reflects the extent to which their projects add to the demand for affordable housing in the community. Two long-standing programs are in San Francisco and in Boston, which enacted its linkage fee ordinance in 1983. By 2004, the city had allocated a total of $81 million in linkage revenues, which it used to assist in the construction or preservation of 6,159 affordable housing units. Boston requires developers to pay $7.18 per square foot to the affordable housing fund, and an additional $1 per square foot for job training programs.

Although trust funds typically have a dedicated revenue source behind them, it does not necessarily mean that their revenues are secure or predictable. In Florida, recent governors have regularly raided the Sadowski Act fund, which is financed by a documentary stamp tax on real estate transfers, taking part of the "dedicated" revenues for the state's general fund. Many of the trust funds, moreover, are funded by sources that are heavily dependent on the strength of the real estate market. Not only Florida's Sadowski Act fund, but trust funds in Hawaii, Illinois, Maine, Nevada, New Jersey, and other states find that their revenues rise when the market is strong, only to plummet when, as is currently the case, the market slows down and the number of transactions drops. Even with these limitations, housing trust funds are still a major resource for developers of affordable housing in many parts of the country.

Trust funds with dedicated revenue sources are not the only way by which states and localities support affordable housing. Some states, led by California, have floated bond issues for affordable housing. In contrast to housing finance agency bonds, which are not considered subsidies since they must be repaid by project revenues, these bond issues are general obligation bonds, paid back through the state's general revenues. Since 1988, California has authorized $5.45 billion for affordable housing through a series of bond issues, with $2.8 billion being authorized in a single issue in 2006. In addition to this amount, which substantially exceeds the state's share of federal HOME funds during this period, California also earmarks large amounts of money for affordable housing through a mechanism known as tax increment financing.

Tax increment financing, or TIF, is a method widely used throughout the United States to finance redevelopment activities. Under a TIF program, the tax increment—the net increase in property or other tax revenues in a specified area resulting from the redevelopment of that area—is dedicated to financing redevelopment activities rather than going into the city's general fund. For example, if the properties on a block generated $100,000 per year in property taxes before the redevelopment project was initiated, and $500,000 per year afterward, $400,000 per year is dedicated to finance redevelopment activities. In most cases, this money is used to pay off bonds that are floated by the local redevelopment agency, which can be used both to pay for public improvements as well as help finance private development activities. Once the bond issues are paid off, future tax revenues go into the city's general fund. In California, TIF and redevelopment are all but inseparable. Where there is redevelopment, there is tax increment financing.

Since 1976, California law has required city and county redevelopment agencies to set aside not less than 20 percent of all TIF funds collected for low- and moderate-income housing, and deposit them in a special fund known as a Tax Increment Set-Aside (TISA) fund. These funds must be spent for low- and moderate-income housing. They do not have to be spent within the redevelopment area, but can be spent anywhere in the city, and even, under certain conditions, outside the city where the funds were collected. During the fiscal year ending June 30, 2006, nearly $668 million in TIF proceeds were deposited by California redevelopment agencies into TISA funds for low- and moderate-income housing, by which date the total balance of all funds held in TISA accounts statewide had reached $3.3 billion.[5] The magnitude of that figure reflects not only the productivity of this revenue source, but the difficulty that some redevelopment agencies have in spending their TISA funds.

Finally, some states, counties, or cities will simply appropriate funds from time to time to assist affordable housing development, or utilize other revenue sources they have available. Many long-established state housing finance agencies, for example, have accumulated large amounts of reserves, often the product of the fees or premiums that they have charged for issuing bonds over the years. In New Jersey, the state Housing & Mortgage Finance Agency has taken a portion of these funds and used them to establish a creative program to subsidize mixed income home ownership in distressed urban neighborhoods. Under the program, half of the homes must be reserved for low- and moderate-income households, but half are sold at low prices but without income restrictions, as a way of encouraging middle-income households to move into these neighborhoods.

Private revenue sources

Governmental funds are the most significant and most predictable source of money for affordable housing development, but not always the only source. One major nongovernmental, or perhaps quasi-governmental, source comes from the network of federal Home Loan Banks, a network of federally chartered private entities that was initially created to ensure a flow of capital to savings and loan institutions. Today they continue to fulfill that function, although rather than being limited to savings and loans, they are open to any federally chartered banking institution that pays the fees necessary to become a member of the system. Although they are technically private entities, Home Loan Banks have both special privileges and special obligations under their charter.

One obligation, imposed in 1991 in the wake of the savings and loan crisis, is to provide funds for affordable housing. Each bank is required to set aside 10 percent of each year's net income to fund an Affordable Housing Program, through which they make grants to affordable housing developments. Although these grants are typically small, running between $5,000 and $15,000 per unit, they are often valuable as the additional piece that, combined with HOME or state funds, can make a project a reality. In 2006, the nation's 12 Home Loan Banks provided a total of $295 million in grants under the Affordable Housing Program. An unusual feature of this program is that would-be developers of affordable housing cannot apply directly to the Home Loan Bank in their region, but must find a local bank that is a member of that bank to apply on their behalf. In an age where local banks have become an endangered species in much of the country, a bank sponsor is not always easy to find.

Other private resources tend to be idiosyncratic, often "one-shot" contributions arising from particular circumstances or relationships. A few examples will illustrate this. In Albany, New York, a local philanthropist builds houses in the city's distressed Arbor Hill neighborhood, selling them at affordable prices by personally absorbing the difference between the cost and the selling price. In Boston's Allston-Brighton neighborhood, Harvard University gave the local CDC $3.5 million, which enabled it to complete the financing for an affordable housing development. Harvard's motives, however, were not purely altruistic. The university was eager to develop major new facilities on land it had acquired in the neighborhood, and was facing widespread resident concern and uncertainty.

A number of foundations have also supported affordable housing development, both through grants and through program-related investments where they allocate a portion of their endowment to be invested in areas that complement their grant-making activities, often at below-market interest rates. While large national foundations rarely provide project-specific assistance, local foundations will often consider the possibility of doing so. The MacArthur Foundation, a Chicago-based national organization with a strong institutional commitment to housing as well as to its home city, has used both methods to support affordable rental housing in Chicago.

In areas of particularly high housing cost, such as California's Silicon Valley, corporations eager to retain or attract a labor force often undertake what are known as employer-assisted housing programs. While in most cases these programs are carried out by the employers giving money to their workers to assist them to buy housing in the area, in a growing number of cases employers are finding it both more cost-effective and more productive to provide funds to nonprofit developers, to enable them to create affordable or "workforce" housing within reasonable commuting distance of the company's offices.

In the final analysis, private resources are hardly ever the principal means by which a particular development is made possible, a role that remains firmly within the public sector. Still, many CDCs and other nonprofit developers of affordable housing have discovered, usually on a case-by-case basis, that private resources *can* be found, often in unlikely places.

Tax credit equity

The second way to generate cash to cover the capital cost of affordable housing projects is to raise what is known as tax credit equity. While investors typically expect a cash return when they make an equity investment in a conventional real estate venture, in a tax credit equity investment the investor receives credits against its federal or state tax obligations in lieu of a cash return. Since the federal Low Income Housing Tax Credit was created in the Tax Reform Act of 1986, tax credit equity investment has become by far the largest single source of funds for affordable housing in the United States.

A tax credit is different from a tax deduction. A tax deduction is taken off the taxpayer's income before taxes are calculated. As a result, if a taxpayer has a deduction of $100 and her tax bracket is 25 percent, the actual cash value of the deduction is $25, not $100. A tax credit, however, is taken directly off the tax liability, reducing that liability by the amount of the credit. Thus, a tax credit of $100 is worth $100 to the taxpayer.

The Low Income Housing Tax Credit (LIHTC) gives investors a credit on their federal income tax in return for making equity investments in low income rental housing projects.[6] The LIHTC program is complex, but its importance demands that it be well understood not only by affordable housing developers, but by those whose work connects them in some fashion with the development of affordable housing. Although there are actually two separate LIHTC programs, widely but somewhat inaccurately known as the "nine percent credit" and "four percent credit" programs, the former is by far the most important, and will be the principal focus of this discussion.

Under the nine percent credit program, the investor is entitled to a tax credit that, taken in annual installments over the course of a 10-year period beginning with the year the project is initially occupied, translates to an amount that has a present value equal to 70 percent of the project basis.[7] The actual annual tax credit percentage, which was nine percent in 1987 when the program was first established, is adjusted monthly on the basis of changes in certain federal rates. As of January 2008, the annual rate was 7.93 percent. In so-called "difficult to develop" or "qualified" census tracts, which are principally high-poverty areas, the investor is eligible for a 30 percent increase in the tax credit, so that over the 10 years, the investor actually receives credits equal to 103 percent (79.3 percent × 1.3) of the project basis. The term "project basis" refers to that percentage of the total project cost that can be counted toward the tax credit. In practice, this includes all of the significant elements of project cost except for certain fees, and, depending on certain conditions, may or may not include the cost of acquiring the land or buildings for the project.[8]

On a 100-unit rental project, which might have a total development cost of $20 million and a project basis of $18 million put into service in January 2008, an investor will receive $14,274,000 in tax credits in 10 annual installments over 10 years. If the project is in a qualified census tract, the investor will receive $18,556,200. These are considerable sums, making this a very attractive proposition for investors, particularly corporations with substantial federal tax liabilities. The amount the investor will put into the project as its equity investment will not be the full amount of the tax credits it will receive, for a number of reasons. First, the investor takes the tax credits over 10 years, so they are worth less in present value than their face value. Second, the investor is looking for some return on investment; and third, as will be discussed further, the investor is incurring certain potential risks with respect to the project. While the first two considerations are dictated by the market, and are roughly similar for all projects and all investors, the third varies from project to project. In practice, the amount of the investor's equity investment tends to range from 70 to 85 percent of the face value of the tax credits.

By making the investment, the investor takes the principal interest in a partnership that is created to own the project. The typical partnership will have two partners—the investor, known as the limited partner, who owns 99 percent of the project but is not directly involved in managing the project, and the managing partner, usually the developer, who retains a one percent interest and actually runs the project. By buying the tax credits, the investor is obligated to remain the owner of the project for a minimum of 15 years, during which period it is legally responsible for ensuring that the project is operated successfully as low-income rental housing. If the project is abandoned, or fails to comply with the requirements of the LIHTC program, the investor's tax credits are potentially subject to recapture by the IRS. As a result, investors will typically not only carefully evaluate the qualifications of the developer that is going to become the managing partner, but will assess the relative risk associated with the project, based on its location and likely occupancy characteristics. A project for senior citizens located in a stable area will typically draw a higher equity investment relative to its project basis than a project for large families located in a distressed urban neighborhood.

To be eligible for a tax credit investment, a rental project must be rented to households earning under 60 percent of the Area Median Income, with the rents set so that eligible households pay no more than 30 percent of their income for their house or apartment. When the tax credit is used in a mixed income development, at least 40 percent of the units must be affordable to households at 60 percent of AMI, or 25 percent at 50 percent of AMI. In a mixed income project, the investor only receives the tax credit on the low-income units, not on the project as a whole. In practice, the financial structure of the program makes it difficult to use the tax credit for mixed income development, and over 80 percent of all LIHTC projects are entirely devoted to low-income occupancy, despite efforts by some states to encourage mixed income development.

Although the tax credit is on the investor's federal tax obligation, administration of the program is delegated by the federal government to the states. Each state is given a certain dollar amount of tax credits that it can allocate each year, and must designate a state agency—almost always the state housing finance agency—to allocate the credits among prospective developers.[9] In light of the demand for low-income rental housing in most communities, there tends to be considerable competition for the credits, and most state agencies receive applications from developers for substantially more than they have available to hand out. In order to ensure that the process is fair, and that the allocation of credits is based on objective criteria, each state allocating agency must adopt an annual Qualified Allocation Plan (QAP), setting forth precisely what criteria will be used to determine how the state will allocate its pool of tax credits. Once a developer has received an allocation from the state, it then sells the allocation to an investor in return for the equity investment in the project.

The state agency has broad discretion to use the QAP as a vehicle for pursuing a wide range of objectives. In addition to making sure that projects are financially sound, and that the developer controls the site on which the project will be built, state agencies may give preference to projects that meet various policy criteria, such as fostering mixed income development, extending the duration that they remain affordable to low-income families, or providing social and educational services to their tenants. The state agency then has the responsibility to monitor the recipients of the tax credit allocations, to make sure that the projects are built in timely fashion, and that their operation—how rents are set, how tenants are qualified, and the like—meets the requirements established by the IRS.

Since its creation in 1986, the Low Income Housing Tax Credit has created a total of 1,530,000 low-income rental units in 27,410 separate developments around the United States. At present it provides state agencies with authority to allocate nearly $5 billion in tax credits each year, a figure that is adjusted annually for inflation. These funds make possible the production of roughly 1,400 developments, containing 100,000 units of housing, each year. The Danter Company, a market research firm, has estimated that roughly one out of every six multifamily units built in the United States since 1987 is a LIHTC unit, including 25 percent of multifamily housing in Massachusetts, 33 percent in Delaware, and 72 percent in West Virginia. Although this total is much less than that of earlier production programs such as Section 236 during their brief heyday, it is far greater than any other affordable housing program being provided in the United States today.

From an economic standpoint, the tax credit program is less efficient than if the government were simply to appropriate the money and use it to make capital grants to projects. Because investors put into the project 70 to 85 percent of the amount of the tax credits they receive, for every dollar invested in a low-income rental project, the federal government loses between $1.18 and $1.43 in tax revenues. Moreover, the complicated nature of the investment and the limited partnership structure that must be created adds thousands of dollars in legal and accounting fees to the cost of each project. From a political standpoint, however, matters are very different. Tax credits are all but invisible. They do not appear in the federal budget, and fly under the radar of the contentious appropriations process. At the same time that HOME and other HUD programs are the subject of annual battles, and see their appropriations rise and fall unpredictably, the low income tax credit not only survives, but—since the amount allocated to the states has been indexed to inflation since 2003—grows.

While the federal low income housing tax credit is by far the most important one, it is not the only tax credit with some relevance to affordable housing development. A number of states, for example, have enacted their own low income tax credits that permit the developers of LIHTC projects to generate a larger equity investment by offering investors credits against state as well as federal taxes. Similarly, the federal government and a number of states offer tax credits for rehabilitation of historic properties. When a historic property is rehabilitated for low-income rental housing, the developer can piggy-back the two credits in order to generate a greater equity investment. Finally, some states offer tax credits to induce corporations to invest in upgrading lower income communities generally, including affordable housing. The New Jersey Neighborhood Revitalization State Tax Credit, enacted in 2003, gives corporations a 100 percent credit against their state tax obligations if they contribute money to a nonprofit corporation to implement a comprehensive neighborhood revitalization strategy; under the law, 60 percent of the money the nonprofit receives must be spent on bricks and mortar housing and economic development activities.[10]

PUTTING THE PIECES TOGETHER: SUBSIDY LAYERING AND THE DEVELOPMENT PRO FORMA

In figuring out how to make an affordable housing development work financially, the developer begins with three fundamental questions to define the project's parameters:

1. What type of housing am I going to build (sales or rental, housing type)?
2. Who is my target population (by income, household size, special needs, or demographics)?
3. How many units of what type and size am I going to build?

The first question will begin to define the cost parameters of the project, while the second will work similarly to define the revenue parameters, in the sense of defining what the target population will be able to pay in rent or purchase price. It will also affect the costs, because different demographic characteristics will dictate different features that must be incorporated into the housing. Finally, the third question allows the developer to begin translating the parameters into real numbers.

Development and operating costs

Based on the answers to these three questions, the developer will put together what is known as a development pro forma, or a statement of "sources and uses" for the project. In this document, which is in its initial stages highly generalized and gradually becomes firmer and more detailed as project planning moves forward, the developer lays out the breakdown of the costs for which funds must be raised (uses), and where the money to cover those costs will come from (sources), so that at the end of the day the project is both financially sound and affordable to its target population. If the project is going to be sold to home buyers, the developer needs only to prepare a development or capital pro forma. If the project is to be a rental project, the developer must prepare an operating pro forma as well, in order to establish that the projected operating costs, along with taxes and debt service on the project mortgage, will not exceed the projected rent collections and other ongoing revenues.

Tables 5-6 and 5-7, respectively, show the breakdown of the major costs that go into a development budget and those that go into an operating budget for an affordable housing project, or for that matter, any housing development. As the former illustrates, far more goes into the cost of developing housing than the "bricks and mortar" of the buildings themselves, which are rarely more than 70 percent and often less than half of total development cost. Not all of the costs shown in Table 5-6 apply to all developments. An urban project, particularly if it involves reuse of existing buildings, may require environmental remediation, demolition, and sometimes relocation of existing residents or businesses. That project, however, is unlikely to require off-site costs such as widening a road or extending a sewer line, which may be needed for a project on a suburban or rural greenfield site.

The long list of items under the category "soft costs" can easily amount to 20 to 30 percent of the development budget. In LIHTC projects, the cost of the extensive legal, accounting, and due diligence work needed to meet the conditions of that program can easily add a few hundred

TABLE 5-6   ELEMENTS OF A HOUSING DEVELOPMENT BUDGET

CATEGORY	BREAKDOWN
Land	• Cost of land acquisition • Holding costs
Hard costs	• Site grading and preparation • Demolition • Environmental remediation • On-site utilities • Off-site utilities and hookups • Parking areas, driveways, and other pavement • Street and sidewalk improvements • Landscaping • Building construction • General contractor or construction manager fee
Soft costs	• Interest on construction loan • Property taxes during holding and construction • Relocation • Municipal fees • Financing fees • Architectural, environmental, and engineering services • Legal, appraisal, survey, title, and related services • Accounting services • Security and insurance during construction • Marketing and advertising, including rent-up allowance (for rental projects) • Office expenses during holding and construction
Other	• Developer profit • Development fee (for nonprofit developer) • Contingency

TABLE 5-7 ELEMENTS OF A RENTAL HOUSING OPERATING BUDGET

CATEGORY	BREAKDOWN
Management	• Administrative payroll • Legal and accounting • Marketing and advertising • Office costs • Management fee
Operations and maintenance	• Operating payroll • Security • Maintenance of mechanical equipment • Painting, repairs, and supplies • Extermination • Lawn and landscape maintenance, snow removal • Trash removal • Resident services
Utilities paid by project (where applicable)	• Water and sewer • Heat and hot water • Gas and electricity
Taxes and insurance	• Property taxes or payment in lieu of taxes • Other state and local taxes and license fees • Insurance
Reserves	• Operating reserve • Replacement reserve
Debt service	• Mortgage payments • Debt service coverage

thousand dollars to the cost of the project. Architectural fees are often in the area of six percent of project cost.

An equally long list of potential costs applies to the ongoing operation of a large rental project. The number of separate tasks that must be carried out on an ongoing basis to ensure a well-managed and well-maintained housing development is considerable, from collecting rent to making repairs, removing trash, repairing and repainting apartments as families move in and out, mowing lawns, and screening new tenants. The project must also create and maintain adequate reserves for the future, not only for the inevitable replacement of the many different parts of a building that wear out over time, but for the unanticipated costs that inevitably arise sooner or later.

Putting together the pro forma

Using the information that has already been pinned down about the project and its target population, the pro forma for a rental project must cover three areas of information:

- How much will it cost to develop the project?
- How much will it cost to operate the project, including the cost of taxes and reserves, each year?
- How much income will the project receive from rents each year?

By comparing the total rental income to the operating cost, one can calculate how much money will be available to pay debt service on a mortgage for the project. Knowing the likely terms and interest rate of the mortgage, it is a simple matter to compute how large a mortgage the project can carry from that information. By comparing that figure to the total cost of the project, one then can determine how much additional money is needed, in the form of grants, tax credits, or other assistance, to make the project feasible. The analysis presented in the following pages will provide a general overview of each of these areas, rather than get into the details of all of the specific costs shown in the tables above. All of the figures are, of course, purely hypothetical.

This process will be illustrated with a proposed 100-unit low income tax credit garden apartment development to be built in a healthy neighborhood in the Peoria, Illinois, area, containing a mixture of one-, two-, and three-bedroom apartments. Starting with that information, the developer calculates the rental income from the project as shown in Table 5-8. The projected rents involve subtracting a percentage from the gross rental income known as "vacancy and collection loss" to reflect the reality that even the best-managed developments can never expect all of their apartments to be full every month, or every tenant to pay her rent religiously.

The next step is to estimate operating costs, which are shown in summary form in Table 5-9. The developer cannot use the entire difference between the operating costs and the rental income for mortgage payments. A responsible lender will insist on the developer factoring in a margin, known as debt service coverage, in the event that operating costs increase or rents decrease relative to the developer's projections. As a result, it appears that the project will have roughly $200,000 per year in net income to apply to debt service payments.

TABLE 5-8 RENTAL INCOME PROJECTION FOR HYPOTHETICAL LIHTC PROJECT

UNIT TYPE	NUMBER	HOUSEHOLD SIZE TARGET	INCOME TARGET	MONTHLY GROSS RENT	UTILITY ALLOWANCE	MONTHLY NET RENT	TOTAL NET RENT
1 bedroom	30	2 persons	$24,950	$624	($60)	$564	$16,920
2 bedroom	50	3 persons	$28,100	$701	($75)	$626	$31,300
3 bedroom	20	5 persons	$33,700	$841	($100)	$741	$14,820
Total monthly rent roll							$63,040
							× 12
Total annual gross rent roll							$756,480
Less 5% vacancy and collection loss							(37,824)
Annual rental income							$718,556

TABLE 5-9 FIRST-YEAR OPERATING COST PROJECTION FOR HYPOTHETICAL LIHTC PROJECT

CATEGORY	ASSUMPTION	PROJECTED ANNUAL COST
All operating costs (including reserves)	$350/dwelling unit/month	$420,000
Payment in lieu of taxes	10% of rent collections	$71,856
TOTAL OPERATING COSTS		$491,856
Rental income (from Table 5-8)		$718,556
NET INCOME (rental income less operating costs)		$226,700
Less debt service coverage (15% of debt service)		(29,570)
AVAILABLE FOR DEBT SERVICE ON MORTGAGE		$197,130

The developer will simultaneously project the development costs for the project, using the actual land costs and the best available figures for construction and soft costs from its own experience and that of others building similar projects in the same market area. In this case, for purposes of the hypothetical example, the project was fortunate to be able to obtain a site at a significantly below-market price from a local religious institution.

Having estimated the total development cost, the developer then takes the annual debt service figure from Table 5-9 to calculate the maximum mortgage the project can carry, based on rates offered by a local lender or the state housing finance agency. As Table 5-10 shows, that amount is roughly $2.5 million, or $25,000 per unit, far from the amount needed to build the project. The difference between that figure and the total development cost represents the amount of "soft" money, either from grants or tax credits, that the project will need to be feasible. The hypothetical project reflects the reality of developing low-income rental housing, in that the mortgage that its rents can carry represents only a tiny share of the total development cost.

TABLE 5-10   DEVELOPMENT COST PROJECTION FOR HYPOTHETICAL LIHTC PROJECT

CATEGORY (USES)	ASSUMPTION	PROJECTED COST
Land	Acquired at below-market price	$100,000
Construction	90,000 gross square feet at $100/square foot, including contractor's fee	$9,000,000
Other hard costs	$10,000/dwelling unit	$1,000,000
Soft costs	25% of total project cost	$3,367,000
TOTAL DEVLOPMENT COST		$13,467,000
Maximum mortgage amount to carry with available debt service amount	7% interest rate with 30-year amortization	$2,469,200
GRANT/TAX CREDIT FUNDS NEEDED		$10,997,800

TABLE 5-11   TAX CREDIT EQUITY INVESTMENT FOR HYPOTHETICAL LIHTC PROJECT

CATEGORY	ASSUMPTION	AMOUNT
Total development cost	From Table 5-10	$13,467,000
Project basis	Includes all hard costs, 80% of soft costs, but excludes land	$12,593,600
Tax credit value to investor	Project basis × 7.93% × 10	$9,986,725
Purchase price of tax credits (percentage of total value to investor)		× .80
TOTAL PROJECTED EQUITY INVESTMENT		$7,989,380

The lion's share of the missing funds will come from an equity investment under the low income housing tax credit program. The amount the project can expect to receive in equity from an investor, as shown in Table 5-11, is roughly $8 million. Since the project is not in a difficult to develop area or a qualified census tract, it is not entitled to the 30 percent bonus tax credit. Comparing that amount to the shortfall shown in Table 5-10, one finds that without any additional subsidies, the project is roughly $3 million short of the funds it needs to be financially feasible. If the project had been located in a qualified census tract, it might have been able to raise an additional $2.4 million from tax credit equity, reducing the shortfall to a modest $600,000.

The next step is often the most difficult and time-consuming element of the period preceding construction, which determines whether there will indeed be a project to be constructed. The developer must cobble together, or layer, enough different capital subsidies from various sources to fill the shortfall, recognizing that it will usually not be possible to find a single source to cover the entire shortfall. This process is often frustrating, as the developer must apply to multiple agencies with different guidelines, procedures, and timetables. During this period, which can easily take a year or more, the developer must make sure that critical aspects of the project, in particular control of the site and local approvals, are not lost. Site control is particularly risky, because many landowners are reluctant to give an affordable housing developer an option for the length of time it may take the developer to line up all of the funding needed to be able to close on the property.

In the end, the developer may be able to close the gap. A hypothetical solution might resemble the breakdown of sources in Table 5-12. All of the sources shown in the table, and the amounts projected for each, are at least *plausible* for a project of this nature built in the state of Illinois today. Whether they would *actually* be available for this project at the point when the project was actively seeking the funds would depend on the amount of money available in each fund, the specific criteria being used by the fund managers, and the amount of competition for the money available. As a result, a developer of affordable housing must work for years, spending thousands of dollars on plans, architects, land options, and other predevelopment costs, all the while operating in conditions of total uncertainty.

As noted previously, the process for developing an economically feasible affordable housing project for home ownership is much simpler

TABLE 5-12   SOURCES FOR HYPOTHETICAL LIHTC PROJECT

SOURCE	AMOUNT
Mortgage	$2,469,200
Tax credit equity investment	$7,989,380
Illinois Housing Trust Fund	$1,500,000
Illinois Energy Efficient Affordable Housing Construction Program	$202,500
State or local HOME funds	$750,000
Home Loan Bank of Chicago Affordable Housing Program	$555,920
TOTAL SOURCES	$13,467,000

in concept. Since the units will be sold to home buyers, there is no need to address rental incomes or operating costs. It simply involves finding enough capital subsidy funding to lower the sales price of the unit to the level that families at the target income for the project can afford.

However simple that may be in concept, it is often very difficult in practice to find enough capital subsidy for owner-occupied housing to reach low-income families. While the low income housing tax credit provides in one piece the great majority of the subsidy needed to make a rental project work, it has no counterpart on the home ownership side of the ledger.[11] To make a home ownership project designed to reach families earning $30,000 to $40,000 work, the homes must be able to sell for $100,00 to $120,000. In many areas, if the land for the project is acquired on the private market, reaching that target may require a capital subsidy of $100,000 to $150,000 per home. That figure, if reachable at all, will require layering of multiple subsidy sources, and may be achievable only for a handful of units at a time even in a large community.

Along with finding suitable sites and obtaining necessary local approvals, finding the money to make affordable housing developments feasible is the hardest task facing the developer of affordable housing. With limited federal resources available for this purpose, developers are increasingly driven to seek out state, local, and private resources. Opportunities to find those resources, however, are uneven. While some areas, including states like California, Illinois, or New Jersey, or the city of New York, have been generous in their support of affordable housing, developers in many other parts of the country are still heavily dependent on the low income housing tax credit and the federal HOME and CDBG programs.

The limited resources available, and the difficulty of putting them together project by project, places a heavy obligation on any locality that recognizes its need for affordable housing to do what it reasonably can to facilitate developers' efforts to gain access to scarce subsidy resources. Localities must complement those efforts by providing fee waivers, tax abatements, reasonable development standards, and other forms of assistance, and if local resources and legal authority permit, creating local housing trust funds to add to the pool of funds available.

NOTES

1. *Pari passu* is a Latin phrase meaning "hand-in-hand" or "at the same time."
2. In 1998, Congress amended the law governing the Housing Choice Voucher program to permit it to be used to help defray the cost of eligible households becoming home buyers, as well as for tenants. HUD adopted rules to govern the program in 2000. Only a handful of vouchers are being used for home ownership, however, so that the program can still be reasonably characterized as a rental program.
3. The act created what is known as a unified volume cap, which combines into a single cap all tax-exempt bonds issued for private users, known as "private activity" bonds. These include bonds for economic development and other activities as well as housing. This has led to disputes in some states over how much of the cap to allocate to affordable housing versus other competing uses.
4. This language is from the *Housing Trust Fund Progress Report 2007*, prepared by Mary Brooks for the Center for Community Change. This report, as well as the quarterly reports issued by the Center's Trust Fund Project, is a valuable resource to understanding how states and cities around the United States earmark financial resources in different ways for affordable housing.
5. California State Controller. 2007. *Community Redevelopment Agencies Annual Report for the Fiscal Year Ending July 30, 2006*. There are 422 redevelopment agencies (27 inactive) and 759 separate currently ongoing redevelopment projects in California.
6. Regulations governing the LIHTC program are found in Chapter 42 of the Internal Revenue Code.
7. Present value is the value today of a series of payments over time, where the dollar amount of the payments is discounted on the basis of a specified interest rate. It is based on the principle that since money typically loses value over time because of inflation, and because cash in hand can earn money for the holder, the later money is received, the less value it has today.
8. The principal consideration is how long the property was in the hands of the seller before she sold it to the entity developing the rental housing project. As a general rule, if it was held for 10 years or more, the price can be included in project basis.
9. New York City and Chicago also allocate low-income housing tax credits directly.
10. N.J. Stats. Ann. 52:27D-490 et seq.
11. A home ownership tax credit paralleling the Low Income Housing Tax Credit has been proposed since the 1990s, and was supported, albeit without much conviction, by the Bush administration. The tax credit would go to a developer of an affordable ownership unit, to be taken over the five years following sale of the unit to a qualified home buyer.

CHAPTER

6

Developing Affordable Housing, Step-by-Step

Preceding chapters have looked at the different issues associated with developing affordable housing, including assessing needs, evaluating development sites, gaining approvals, and putting together the financing for a project. All of those issues, however, are elements in an integrated development process that must be pursued—from initial concept to ultimate sales or rent-up—by the developer of the housing. While much of the process is little different from that followed by any developer, it has many distinctive features unique to the development of affordable housing. In order to show how the process works, and how its different elements relate to one another, this chapter will describe the process as it might be pursued by a nonprofit developer seeking to build an affordable housing development in an affluent suburban town. While the development described is a purely hypothetical one, not modeled on any specific real-life example, the description draws extensively on the author's experience over the years. As the process unfolds, it will attempt not only to describe the steps that the developer will be following, but the reasoning or critical decisions involved in those steps. A flowchart illustrating the process up to the point of construction, albeit in much simplified form, is presented as Figure 6-1.

While for-profit developers of affordable housing usually look for development opportunities throughout a state or region, most nonprofit affordable housing developers tend to be more locally oriented, and

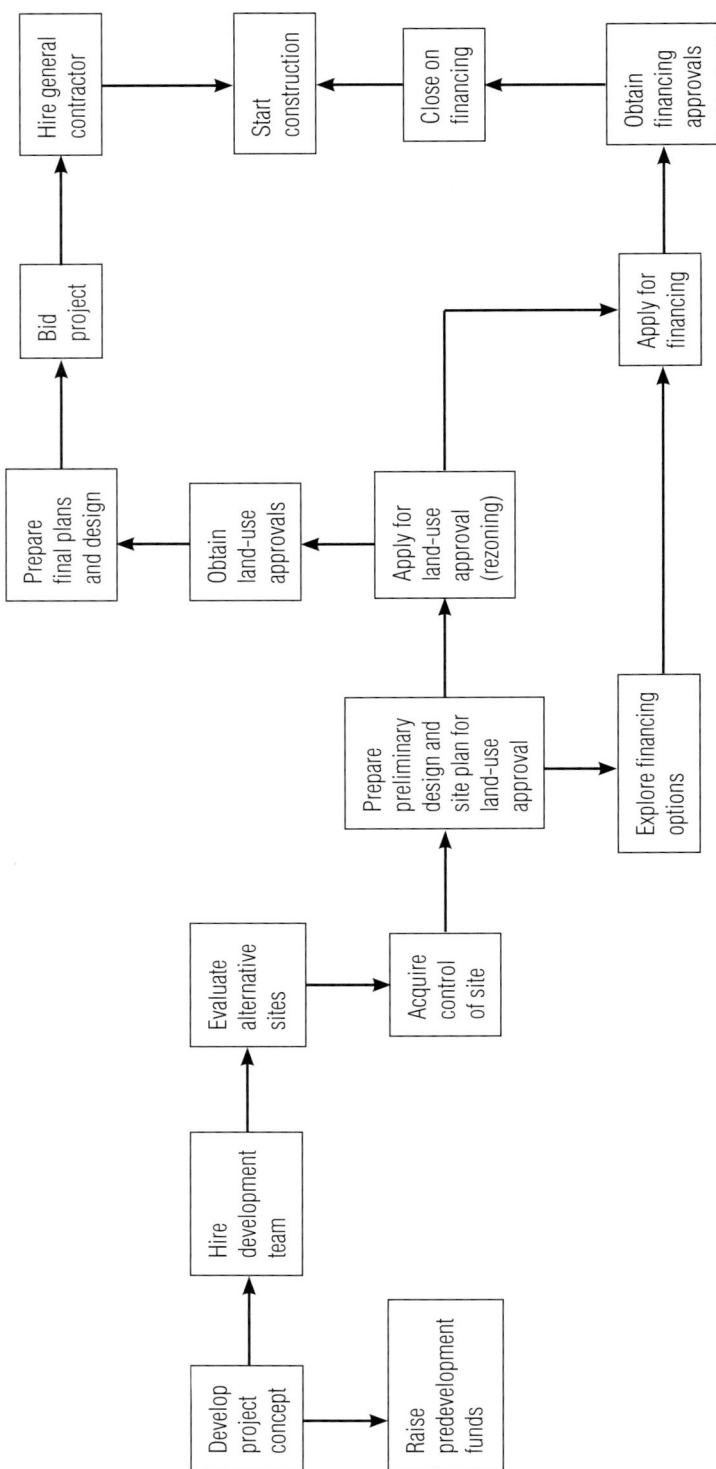

Figure 6-1 Simplified Flowchart of Affordable Housing Predevelopment Process

focus less on development opportunities as such as on opportunities to meet their community's housing needs. For this description, we have invented a hypothetical developer of a sort often found in suburban communities, a nonprofit entity called Our Neighbors, Inc. or ONI, created some years earlier by a number of local churches and synagogues as a vehicle to help meet the housing needs of the town's low-income residents and workers. After some 10 years of existence, and the development of a few small-scale projects, ONI has decided it is time to embark on a more ambitious effort.

THINKING THE PROJECT THROUGH

While the ideal development process should begin with an assessment of the most urgent housing needs in the community and the conceptualization of one or more projects of the nature and scale to meet those needs, in practice the process is more complicated, and involves from the beginning the balancing of a series of different factors. While need is a fundamental threshold concern, in framing its project ONI must balance its mission to meet housing needs against its understanding of what alternatives are likely to be most welcomed by the community, what sites might potentially be available within the town, and what funding resources—whether federal, state or local—are likely to be available. All of these factors, to varying extents, are on the table from the first moment in which a potential development is given consideration.

Funding is a threshold issue. Without it, no plan, however worthy, will come into being. Funding and scale are interwoven. If the organization is seeking to develop 15 or 20 housing units, it may be able to pursue an affordable home ownership development. Both the amount of capital subsidy needed for each unit, and the limited resources that are available in most housing trust funds, may make 50 units of owner-occupied housing unfeasible. By contrast, a 50-unit or larger low income tax credit project may be not only more financially feasible, but better positioned to compete for an allocation from the state housing finance agency and a sounder long-term management proposition than one with only 15 or 20 units.

Siting alternatives are also a factor that can drive development choices. If, after meeting early in the process with the mayor and council, ONI were offered a four-acre town-owned site, with the possibility of having it rezoned to a density of 10 units per acre, it is likely to accept the offer and scale its plans accordingly, even if it had initially planned to build

100 units. The advantages of being able to lock in a site at low cost, along with support from local officials for the necessary rezoning application, are likely to outweigh the advantages of trying to find and negotiate the acquisition and subsequent rezoning of a larger privately owned site. While it is not unusual for local officials to offer publicly owned sites to nonprofit affordable housing developers when they are available, such opportunities do not often arise. It is more likely that ONI will have to find a site on the private market and secure an option or other agreement with the owner.

A locally based nonprofit developer will be painfully aware that there may be community opposition to any affordable housing proposal presented. From the beginning, ONI is already likely to be thinking of how it will best counter and defuse potential opposition, how it will reach out to the community, and how it will "spin" the project. Their project is likely to be presented as a means of meeting the housing needs of people who already live in the town, or who work in the town but cannot afford to live there. An effort may be made to put faces on the housing need, either by describing the kinds of people who would live in the housing, such as teacher's aides, home health aides, or senior citizens, or even recruiting a few such people to participate in community meetings or kaffeeklatsches in civic leaders' living rooms. In the end, assuming that community sentiment is at least moderately supportive, it is likely that the project design will reflect a compromise between a focus on the most urgent needs and on those needs to which the community is most sensitive, such as senior citizens.[1]

In a number of states, state fair share laws are a further consideration that will strongly weigh on local officials, and to some extent on community sentiment. To the extent that the town has a fair share obligation, as is the case in New Jersey, California, Massachusetts, and some other states, ONI can make the point that it can help the town meet that obligation in a way that is sensitive to community concerns. This may also affect the nature of the needs addressed by ONI's project, because under some state fair share regulations, towns are limited in the extent of their obligation that can be met through construction of senior citizen housing.

Ultimately, the balancing of the four factors—need, community sentiment, site availability, and funding availability—will enable ONI to frame a project that not only addresses community housing needs, but has a realistic possibility of coming to fruition. At this point, however, the uncertainties are still considerable. No site has been found, and no assurance exists that once found, ONI will be able to obtain the necessary land-use approvals. No financing is in place, and there is no assurance that it will be forthcoming, even if and when a site has been found and a development approved. The nonprofit, at this point, must embark on a time-consuming and expensive process with no assurance that it will be successful in the end.

FORMING THE DEVELOPMENT TEAM—FINDING A SITE

Our Neighbors, Inc. has set a goal of developing a 100-unit affordable rental housing development and obtaining a Low Income Housing Tax Credit allocation from the state housing finance agency. The size of the development was based on a number of considerations. Their conversations with realtors and property owners found that a variety of 10- to 20-acre sites with access to sewer service were potentially available in the town. Each site could accommodate 100 units at densities of five to 10 units per acre, efficient enough for a multifamily rental development but still compatible with the town's suburban character. By developing 100 units, ONI felt that they would be able to create two viable clusters of 50 units each within a single development, one for senior citizens and the other for families with children, thus both meeting two distinct needs and responding to two distinct community concerns.

Up to this point, ONI has operated with limited professional support. Such an organization may have a full-time director—perhaps the organization's only full-time employee—or may have an ongoing relationship with a consultant or other individual knowledgeable about housing development who has helped its board, made up of local religious and civic leaders, think through the project's initial issues. At this stage, ONI needs to assemble the professionals that will carry the project through to completion, a group of people known as the development team. The composition of the development team for a project of this nature is shown in Table 6-1.

Different members of the team are recruited at different times during the course of the process. While the architect is needed from the beginning, the property management firm is only recruited at the point where the developer is both reasonably confident that the project will be built and has a fairly firm timetable for its completion. Primary team members are those hired directly by the developer and who will interact directly with the developer, while secondary members are those who

TABLE 6-1 COMPOSITION OF HOUSING PROJECT DEVELOPMENT TEAM

	STAGE AT WHICH TEAM MEMBER IS RETAINED		
	Predevelopment	Preconstruction	Preoperation
PRIMARY	Attorney Architect Loan consultant*	General contractor	Property management company*
SECONDARY	Realtor Appraiser Engineer Planner Environmental consultant Tax credit attorney Tax credit accountant Market analyst	Subcontractors Vendors	Subcontractors Vendors

* Where nonprofit developer does not have in-house staff to perform this function.

are usually hired by the primary members, such as the engineers who are retained by the architect, and paid out of her fee, or the tax credit attorney and accountant hired by the loan consultant and paid as part of the transaction. In a large, experienced nonprofit developer, management of the process will usually be in the hands of a full-time member of its staff. Smaller organizations will hire an individual known as a loan consultant or "packager" to manage the process on their behalf. Under the guidance of the staff member or consultant, the developer then hires the two key initial members of the team, the attorney and the architect. Their first mission will be to find a site for the project.

ONI will look for an attorney who has expertise in two critical areas—real estate and land-use law—or alternatively, a firm with individual attorneys with the requisite expertise. The attorney will be called upon to assist ONI in negotiating the acquisition of the site, negotiating contracts with other professional team members, and above all, representing ONI in its effort to obtain the necessary rezoning from the town. These are specialized skills and experience that most lawyers do not have. An organization that hires an attorney without that experience will be paying for an expensive form of on-the-job training that could end up costing far more than the legal fees it would pay a more experienced attorney.

The same is true of architects. Most architects have never designed an affordable housing project, and may not be familiar with either the financial and design constraints imposed by government funding programs, or the many human and social issues that need to be taken into account in order to design a project that will fit within those constraints yet be both a visual asset to the community and a safe, healthy environment for its residents.[2] Many architects are uncomfortable or unfamiliar with the experience of sitting down with laypeople—other than conventional architectural clients—and working with them to frame the design program for a development that will achieve those goals.

If the would-be developer is faced with a choice between a variety of different sites, the services of a planner are essential to bring a body of skills to bear on evaluating both the suitability of the different sites as well as identifying particular issues that would need to be addressed in developing each site. Some loan consultants are trained as planners, as are some architects. Many architects, however, tend to look at sites with respect only to the physical constraints or opportunities they offer for the placement of buildings, and may be less sensitive to broader issues of environmental impacts, access, and community fit. It may be difficult, however, to justify hiring another independent professional for this task. If the town has an adequately staffed planning office, a member of the town's staff may assist ONI in site evaluation, bringing relevant information from local and regional comprehensive plans and environmental studies to bear on the process.

With its professional help, ONI selects a site. While the site selection process may begin in a seemingly systematic fashion, with the planner or loan consultant preparing a matrix of potential sites evaluated on the basis of a variety of criteria, in the end it is likely to be a matter of finding the site that meets threshold planning criteria as well as a three-part reality test:

1. Is the owner willing to sell?
2. Is the price within realistic parameters for a project of this type?
3. Will the owner enter into an option or similar agreement that will give ONI control of the site for long enough to work through the rest of the process?

Positive answers to the first two questions are absolute conditions for site selection. The third is an equally absolute requirement, except in those rare cases that the nonprofit has a well-heeled benefactor willing to put up the acquisition cost of the site up front. In most cases, the nonprofit will not have the funds to pay the full amount up front, particularly in light of the uncertainties that still remain in the process.

As was discussed in Chapter 4, in many cases the only sites that meet these reality tests will not only require rezoning or other discretionary municipal action, but will have one or more features that make the site less than ideal for its proposed use as affordable housing. The site that is both perfect for the purpose and realistically available rarely, if ever, exists. The mission of the development team is to find the best *available* site, and then for the architect to design the project in such a way that the site's constraints are mitigated and its advantages fully utilized. At the same time, ONI will have to marshal its arguments in favor of the site against those opponents of the project who will attempt to derail it by pointing out the site's inevitable limitations, although—while claiming that they are not opposed to affordable housing as such—offering no alternative sites for consideration.

THE PREDEVELOPMENT PROCESS

The critical stage in development of an affordable housing project is the predevelopment phase, which takes place up to the point where ground is broken for construction. The ultimate goals of the predevelopment process are twofold: to obtain the different land-use approvals required from the town, county, and state governments, and to obtain the combination of loans and grants needed to finance construction of the project, once approved.

The predevelopment phase usually lasts as long or longer than the construction phase, and contributes substantially more to the overall aggravation and stress level of all those concerned. Things invariably go wrong during construction; they are usually corrected and rarely cause the project to founder. But any of the many things that can go wrong during the predevelopment phase can result in the project failing and having to be abandoned.

Before ONI can move forward to obtain the approvals it will need, however, it must address a more immediate issue, which is how to pay for the costs associated with the predevelopment phase before any of the loans and grants that will ultimately pay for the project have been obtained. Although many professionals will require only part of their ultimate fee at this stage, and defer the balance to the point where more funds are available, few responsible professionals will work over an extended period without a fee, nor is it necessarily in the interest of an organization like ONI to ask them to do so.[3] For a project of the scale and type planned by ONI, the predevelopment work, from the point at which the professionals begin work until the construction closing, is likely to cost between $200,000 and $500,000. The most unpredictable factor, in addition to the cost of carrying the land, is the land-use approval process, including the number of hearings that will have to be scheduled and the number of changes in plans and designs that will have to be made in the course of obtaining the approvals. The more complicated the site, particularly in terms of environmental issues, the more expensive will be the necessary analyses and development of mitigation plans. In some cases, of course, environmental due diligence may lead to a decision not to pursue development on a particular site, and to seek another in its place.

Although from time to time a nonprofit may be able to obtain a loan to cover predevelopment costs as a community-minded gesture from one of the few surviving community banks, or from a well-endowed local institution such as a university, ONI cannot expect to borrow money for this purpose on a conventional basis, since the likelihood of success—and therefore the ability to repay the loan—is too uncertain. As a result, predevelopment funds must come from other sources. Some well-established nonprofits may be able to cover these costs out of funds that they have accumulated from developer fees realized on earlier projects, while others may do fund-raising from local individuals, businesses, and religious institutions.

Recognizing the difficulties of raising predevelopment funds, a number of organizations have created loan programs specially designed to help nonprofit developers with this need. National support organizations such as the Local Initiatives Support Corporation or Enterprise Community Partners provide predevelopment assistance to nonprofits in the cities where they are active, as do some state community affairs or housing finance agencies. One excellent program is the New Jersey Predevelopment Loan and Acquisition for Nonprofits (NJ-PLAN) Fund, a partnership of the Housing and Community Development Network of New Jersey, a statewide association of nonprofit developers, and the state Housing & Mortgage Finance Agency, which is administered by The Reinvestment Fund, a Philadelphia-based community development investment and policy advocacy organization.

Under NJ-PLAN, nonprofit developers can obtain three types of predevelopment assistance: (1) zero percent loans for preliminary costs, prior to obtaining site control, up to a maximum of $50,000; (2) low-interest loans for predevelopment costs once site control has been established, up to a maximum of $250,000; and (3) site acquisition loans, up to a maximum of $500,000. The funds are largely put up by banks as part of their commitment to lower income communities under the provisions of the Community Reinvestment Act. Half of their investment is at risk and the other half is guaranteed by the Housing & Mortgage Finance Agency.

Once funds are in hand, ONI will proceed to spend them in a variety of ways to obtain the land-use approvals it needs to build the project. As Table 4-2 has shown, many potential approvals may be needed, and the cost of obtaining them can be considerable. If sewer lines have to be brought to the site even a moderate distance, that will not only trigger substantial engineering costs, but may require time-consuming and expensive applications to regional or state environmental bodies.[4] Environmental features on the site, such as wetlands, streams, or floodplains, will trigger still other requirements.

While preparing its site plans, architectural plans, and engineering drawings for its land-use application, ONI will continue to meet with community residents to build their support for the project. At this stage, with a particular site in hand, they will be making a particular effort to win the support—or at least the neutrality—of the residents in the areas abutting the site for the proposed development. They know from the history of similar efforts in nearby communities that where neighbors are strongly opposed to affordable housing projects, hundreds of angry citizens can show up at local planning or zoning commission meetings, creating overwhelming pressure on local officials to find reasons to turn down the project.

The rezoning process is discretionary with the town's zoning commission, and ONI is aware that if the project is turned down, they will have to spend still more time, effort, and money in an attempt to have the denial reversed in court, with an uncertain outcome.[5] As a result, the process of obtaining approvals is planned rigorously by ONI's consultant, attorney, planner, and architect, making sure that every issue that may arise is addressed in their presentation. In addition to the architect and planner, the presentation may have to include reports and testimony from the engineer, addressing sewer and water issues as well as site constraints, environmental consultants dealing with other site issues, a traffic consultant to testify that the project will not have a negative effect on the area's roads and streets, and various individuals to establish that in fact there is a need for the project and for the particular types of accommodation it will provide. Table 6-2 outlines the scope of a typical presentation by a nonprofit developer in support of rezoning for a large-scale affordable housing development proposal.

The whole application preparation process is likely to take six to nine months, starting from the point at which ONI instructs its various consultants to begin preparing the approval to the point where the application is submitted to the zoning commission and other local, county, or state agencies. Once it is submitted and found by the town planner to be complete, it is likely to take a few months before it can be scheduled for a

TABLE 6-2 SCOPE OF REZONING PRESENTATION FOR AFFORDABLE HOUSING PROJECT

SUBJECT	PURPOSE OF PRESENTATION	PRESENTER(S)	WRITTEN SUBMISSION
Mission of organization	Establish nonprofit community-serving role of organization and history in community	Board chair Local civic leaders	None
Housing need	Establish need in community for housing project	Planner Market analyst Individuals with housing needs Firms with workforce needs	Planning report Market demand report
Site plan and design	Describe project and use of site	Planner Architect Engineer	Site plan Schematic architectural drawings[6]
Utility service	Document that site has access to necessary utilities or how utilities will be brought to site	Engineer	Letters from utility service providers Plans for extending utilities
Environmental	Document that site has no environmental constraints or how project will mitigate or address constraints	Planner Environmental consultant Engineer	Environmental conditions and mitigation report
Traffic	Document that site will create no traffic impacts or how project will mitigate impacts	Planner Traffic consultant	Traffic report
Legal	Document how project meets legal standards for rezoning or if applicable, how it will address municipal fair share obligation under state law	Lawyer	Legal memorandum

hearing, during which time the town's staff and consultants will review the application. Since zoning commissions are made up of volunteers and meet only in the evenings, if a large number of individuals want to testify on the application, the hearing may be extended to three or more evenings over the course of two months or more. In the ONI application, testimony will be presented by ONI's development team, by the town's planner and consultants, by professional consultants retained by objectors to the proposal, and finally by interested citizens, both for and against the proposal.[7]

As Figure 6-1 indicates, ONI can only submit formal applications for project financing once it has obtained the critical land-use approvals. While lenders may provide a conditional mortgage commitment subject to obtaining approvals, before they are in hand, applications for grants or, most importantly, applications for a Low Income Housing Tax Credit allocation, require proof that approvals have been obtained. The application to the Affordable Housing Program of the Home Loan Bank of New York requires evidence of approvals as follows:

> . . . copies of building permits, an *executed* municipal resolution or planning board ordinance, a letter from an authorized representative of the appropriate review agency, a letter from the sponsor's attorney or other similar evidence. A letter from the sponsor's attorney is acceptable only if the letter affirmatively states that the Project conforms to local permitted use ordinances and, as such, no approvals are necessary; or details the necessary approvals and that the Project has successfully obtained such approvals.

In addition to evidence of site control and approvals, the LIHTC application may also require ONI to have in place a commitment from an investor to buy the project's tax credit equity in the event it obtains an allocation.

Thus, after spending what could easily be a year or more obtaining approvals, ONI's project must enter into a second time-consuming process that can take a year or more to complete, assuming—which is not always the case—that it is successful. With LIHTC applications in many states substantially exceeding the volume of tax credit allocations that the state housing finance agency can distribute, the possibility is always present that the project will not receive an allocation and will have to reapply the following year.

The length of time and cost involved in seeking project financing will depend on the nature of the financing being sought and the number of different applications that have to be put together. In the simplest case, the project may only need two types of financing—a tax credit allocation and a mortgage from a lender to cover the share of project cost not covered by the tax credit buyer's equity investment. More often than not, however, the project will need additional capital subsidies to supplement the tax credit equity, so that applications will have to be submitted to a variety of different agencies, each with its own particular application requirements, eligibility criteria, and timetables.

Once the project has received its approvals, the architect and engineers begin to develop the working drawings for the project. These drawings will serve as the basis on which prospective contractors will bid on the project. In all likelihood, ONI's consultants will begin talking to the larger residential contractors in the area even before the working drawings are complete, finding out which firms are likely to be available at the time construction is likely to take place and which might be interested in bidding on the project.[8] Once the working drawings are complete, ONI's architect will assemble them into a bid package, and solicit firm bid proposals from those qualified contractors that have expressed an interest in the project. Since it is a private entity, ONI is not obligated to go through a formal "all-comers" bidding process as would a public agency undertaking a construction project.

Once all of the financing pieces are in place, ONI is finally in a position to set the stage for construction. That takes place by a series of closings and contract signings that take place more or less simultaneously, including

- closing on (taking title to) the property;
- closing on the bank construction loan;
- executing the partnership and other agreements with the tax equity investor;
- closing on any other subordinated loans secured to finance the project[9];
- executing contracts on any grants secured to finance the project; and
- executing the contract with the general contractor.

At the point that ONI closes on the construction loan, it also uses part of the proceeds of that loan to pay any of the consultants who have deferred part of their fees up to this point and repay any loans previously obtained to cover predevelopment costs. The contractor is now ready to obtain building permits for the project and to begin construction.

Assuming things have gone smoothly, it is likely at this point to be more than three years since the ONI board first met and decided to build an affordable rental project. One of the most frustrating aspects of the predevelopment process, however, is the extent to which a would-be developer can spend months pursuing a particular course of action, only to be forced to return almost to the beginning. The developer can spend months negotiating with a landowner, only to discover at the last minute that the owner has decided not to sell, or to sell to another party. Similarly, after a denial of land-use approvals, it may be necessary to extensively redesign the project and resubmit the application; or, in the worst case, give up on the particular property and seek another site that may not raise the same difficulties. Finally, as noted earlier, applications for tax credit allocations or capital grants may be rejected because the project was not competitive with other projects competing for the same limited funds, requiring that the project be resubmitted for the next funding cycle—which may not be for another year. In the final analysis, it is likely to require a great deal of both faith and determination from ONI's board, staff, and supporters to get to the point where they are ready to break ground for the project.

CONSTRUCTION, MARKETING, AND RENT-UP

Construction is a messy process but it generally comes to a satisfactory conclusion. That does not mean that projects can routinely be expected to be completed in line with the initially projected budget and timetable; if anything, the opposite is true. Delays and change orders are the rule rather than the exception in large construction projects. In the final analysis, however, it is rare that a construction problem results in anything more than a modest disruption to the process. Since the construction process is no different than for most other residential projects, it need only be described briefly.

In broad outline, a construction project has four stages, beginning with site work and foundations, followed by framing, interior work, and finishing. A highly efficient contractor is likely to be at work on the site within days after obtaining initial building permits. In some cases, to save time, the contractor may take out building permits for the initial stages of work even before the completion of all of the drawings that will be necessary to take out permits for later stages.

Before work can begin on the buildings, the site must be prepared. It must be graded so that level foundations can be poured, trenches dug and utilities installed, and roads, driveways, and parking areas constructed. If the site was previously used for a nonresidential use, particularly if it was used for a factory, service station, or similar facility, it is likely to need environmental remediation, a process which, depending on the nature of the environmental contamination, can be speedy and inexpensive, time consuming and costly, or somewhere in between.[10] Given the cost constraints involved in an affordable rental project, if the initial environmental investigation had identified major problems that would be expensive to remediate, ONI would not have pursued the site. Even the most diligent investigation, however, cannot always find everything. Surprises are still possible once the contractor's earthmoving equipment has begun to dig up the site.

Once the site work has been completed and the foundations have been poured, the buildings are framed and the walls and roof assembled. ONI's development, a cluster of two-story buildings, is likely to be a wood frame structure—not markedly different from a single-family house. This is true of the great majority of affordable housing projects, except for multistory buildings in high-density urban areas. Today, even buildings that appear to have been constructed from brick are more often than not wood frame buildings onto which a thin brick veneer, known as brickface, has been attached. After years of technological change in other areas, wood frame continues to be a cost-effective, and when properly done, highly durable means of building.[11]

Framing usually takes place relatively quickly, followed by the far more labor-intensive and time-consuming process of completing the building's interior. In today's buildings, whether single-family or multifamily, by far the greater part of both the cost and time of construction takes place inside the building frame, weaving together the many different electrical and mechanical systems and floor, wall, and ceiling finishes that make up the modern house or apartment. As standards and requirements for building systems become more demanding, the cost of those systems continues to rise; in recent years, growing demand for "green" buildings, as well as safety requirements such as hardwired smoke detectors, carbon monoxide detectors, and sprinkler systems, have all added to the cost of building new housing.

Finishing work is the final stage. Once the construction has been completed and the procession of trucks and people moving in and out of the property has come to an end, the contractor can put the final details on the building, install the landscaping, and prepare the property for occupancy. At this point, ONI staff, the architect, the contractor, and the firm selected to manage the property on completion will walk through the property to prepare a punch list of items that need to be fixed, replaced, or finished before the project is truly complete. Once the punch list items have been addressed, and the town has issued a certificate of occupancy, the contractor's work is finished. ONI accepts the project, and the tenants can begin to move in. This point is likely to be reached between nine months and a year after the contractor first began to work on the site.

In order to make sure that everything is ready for occupancy of the project at the moment the contractor is finished, ONI and their consultants have been busily at work for some time. Even before construction begins, ONI has began to look into which firms in the area are qualified to act as their property managers, to take day-to-day responsibility for the project once it is completed. While a nonprofit corporation with a large inventory of projects adding up to at least a few hundred units is likely to develop the capacity to manage its projects in-house, it does not make sense for ONI, with only one project, to do so. Within the region they are likely to find a number of different companies with experience managing multifamily housing projects.

Managing affordable housing, particularly LIHTC rental housing, is something of a specialty within the world of property management. In addition to the tasks involved in management of any residential property, the manager has to be able to carry out a variety of procedures mandated by different federal and state regulations, including certifying tenant incomes and meeting the reporting requirements imposed by the IRS. Moreover, where the project is designed to house senior citizens or other populations with special needs, the property manager needs to understand those needs and be able to provide the appropriate services and activities. While some commercial property management firms have these skills, ONI may well turn to a large nonprofit development corporation in a nearby town or city, which has already built up enough expertise and staff capacity to manage its project under contract.

The most urgent task for the property management firm as soon as it is brought on board is to prepare the project for rent-up. While the market study done during the predevelopment phase established that the need was there, a major effort must be made to find qualified tenants, particularly those whose incomes are neither too high nor too low for the project. The nature of LIHTC projects is that tenants' incomes must not only fall below a particular level in order to be eligible to live in the project, but that they must also be above the minimum amount needed to cover the project's operating cost and debt service requirements. While ONI has tried to plan its project so that there will be a fairly wide band between the maximum and minimum, it nonetheless means, ironically, that many families in the community may be too poor to qualify for affordable housing. It also means that the number of families who are realistic potential tenants will be much smaller than the total number of families in need. Other families may not be interested in the particular project for any of many different reasons, or may not qualify by virtue of serious credit problems or criminal histories.

In order to make sure that there will be enough families to fill the units, ONI and its management company will have to undertake an extensive marketing effort, not only by placing newspaper ads, but by reaching out to churches, social organizations, employers, social service agencies, and senior citizen centers in order to create a pool of prospective tenants. They have another compelling reason to make a major outreach effort. In the absence of systematic outreach and marketing, prospective tenants are likely to emerge through word of mouth, a process that unduly favors those who have connections to people involved with the project or others, such as local officials, with advance knowledge. Moreover, in a predominately nonminority community, that process tends to favor White applicants and works to the disadvantage of prospective minority tenants. In order to make sure that the process is fair, ONI is expected to carry out what is known as "affirmative marketing," a process that consciously seeks to connect with people who, by virtue of their location and racial or ethnic background would not otherwise know about the project and be less likely to seek access to it. Affirmative marketing is required by most federal and state agencies funding affordable housing projects, although the standards vary widely both in how they are defined and how strictly they are enforced.

In the meantime, ONI and the management company have set up an office and begun to hand out application forms and interview prospective tenants. By the time the development is near completion, they will be well along in selecting the tenants and executing leases, and the first group of tenants will be eagerly waiting to move in. Before the tenants move in, the property management company will have taken over control of the property. From this point, they will be dealing with the day-to-day matters involved in operating a complex of buildings occupied by 200 to 300 people of all ages, backgrounds, and temperaments. The company will manage an annual budget of at least $750,000, maintain the buildings and grounds, collect rent, and recertify tenant incomes annually.

Although ONI will not be involved in the day-to-day management of the project, their responsibility is not at an end. As a part of the transaction that brought them the tax credit equity to build the project, ONI became the managing partner in a partnership created to own the project, with a 15-year fiduciary obligation to the tax credit investor to make sure that the project is operated properly, both in general and with specific regard to the legal conditions imposed by the IRS for LIHTC projects. They must set overall policy for operating the project and monitor the work of the management company to make sure not only that the project is safe, clean, fully occupied, and well maintained, but also that the tenants meet the LIHTC selection criteria, that the necessary documentation is being maintained, and that the necessary reports are provided on a regular basis to the state housing finance agency and the investors. If ONI concludes that the property management company is not carrying out its obligations, it will have to take corrective action, up to and including removal of the company and replacing it with another firm in order to live up to its obligations to its investors and tenants.

Development of affordable housing is a long-term commitment. The four to five years from initial planning to the point where families first move into the development and the 15-year fiduciary commitment to the tax credit investors are merely the beginning of ONI's commitment. The project just completed will remain affordable housing for far longer than the 15-year holding period. At the end of that time, ONI will acquire the partners' interest in order to ensure that the project remains affordable housing. If ONI is unable to do that, it will arrange to transfer its interest to another entity so the project's future is not jeopardized. ONI's goal, however, is to remain a viable organization and over that period to develop additional affordable housing to address needs of the community's residents.

Many similar nonprofit development corporations around the United States have demonstrated both long-term staying power and a continued commitment to develop housing and build an inventory of affordable housing in their communities. The Palo Alto Housing Corporation (PAHC) was created in 1970 in the Silicon Valley city of Palo Alto, California, through the initiative of community leaders with the assistance of the city council. Thirty-seven years later, PAHC owns and operates nearly 600 units of affordable housing, including 133 units of single-room-occupancy housing. The units are located in 20 separate developments, ranging from a restored downtown hotel to small infill units tucked into single-family residential neighborhoods. In addition, PAHC handles sales and rentals for the affordable units created through the city's inclusionary housing program, which includes 225 owner-occupied units and additional units in five mixed income developments. Through its subsidiary, PAHC Management and Services Corporation, it manages its housing inventory and provides a wide range of support services to its residents.

Palo Alto is a largely developed city, and PAHC has had to confront many delicate issues in finding sites for its affordable housing developments. For its most recent development, PAHC obtained a site of less than an acre in the city's older University South neighborhood "marked by quiet streets, mature trees, and classic single-family Craftsman homes with a median price of $1.5 million."[12] It hired Pyatok Associates, an architectural firm with a track record not only for good design but for engaging residents and neighbors in the design process, and developed their plans for the site with community input gathered during a series of meetings. Oak Court Apartments, which opened in 2005 with 53 units made up of one-, two-, and three-bedroom apartments, won a Builder's Choice award from *Builder* magazine. Twelve hundred applicants competed for a chance to move into the new development.

Across the country, Princeton Community Housing, Inc. (PCH) was established in 1967 in Princeton, New Jersey, by a coalition of religious institutions with the strong support of Princeton University. Although the local governments[13] were not involved in its creation, they have strongly supported PCH ever since. Today, PCH has 18 sponsoring organizations, including 12 religious institutions and six other groups, among them the university, the Institute for Advanced Study, and the Princeton YWCA. Over its 40 years of existence, PCH has developed four projects containing a total of 534 affordable housing units, of which 70 are under resale-restricted owner-occupancy with the balance rentals. Like the Palo Alto Housing Corporation, PCH manages its properties directly.

PCH's most ambitious development project was Griggs Farm, completed in 1989 on a 26.5-acre site in a low-density part of Princeton Township. Developed in close partnership with the township, for which the project represented a significant part of the township's fair share

Pyatok Architects, Inc.

Pyatok Architects, Inc.

Oak Court was designed by architect Michael Pyatok to blend into an expensive neighborhood of classic Craftsman homes in Palo Alto, California.

obligation under New Jersey law, it contains 280 apartments and town houses, of which 140 are affordable housing and 140 market housing. Of the affordable units, 70 are owner-occupied and 70 are rented. PCH manages the rental housing, while resales of the owner-occupied units, along with other affordable units developed under the township's inclusionary housing program, are handled by the township's housing board. Designed by Robert Geddes, a distinguished local architect, in a style that reflects the area's 19th century vernacular architecture, Griggs Court is a thriving community, demonstrating the viability of its unusual 50–50 mix of affordable and market housing.

Not every nonprofit housing development corporation has either the track record or the staying power of the Palo Alto Housing Corporation or Princeton Community Housing. Some have fallen by the wayside, while others, after successfully developing one or two projects, have lapsed into inactivity, relying on outside firms to manage their projects and having no interest or ability in creating more housing. One can argue that neither PAHC nor PCH are entirely typical. Both are located

Princeton Community Housing, Inc.

Griggs Farm in Princeton, New Jersey, designed by architect Robert Geddes, contains half affordable housing and half market-rate housing.

in affluent university towns with strong traditions of committed civic engagement and social responsibility. Still, these two organizations are not unique. They demonstrate what can be accomplished and sustained over decades through dedicated locally based leadership.

NOTES

1. This issue does not always arise. While the mission of the hypothetical ONI is to house those in need in the community generally, many locally based nonprofit developers have narrower missions, targeting the needs of senior citizens or the developmentally disabled, or in other cases seeking to build vaguely defined "workforce housing" for struggling middle-income households. These missions tend to some extent to have been "prescreened" to meet a threshold level of community acceptability.
2. The author, in his consulting days, had the experience of being hired in midstream by a nonprofit developer that owned a series of buildings it wanted to rehabilitate for affordable rental housing. The nonprofit had hired—and already paid a substantial part of the fee to—a young, inexperienced architect who was related to one of the board members and totally unfamiliar with the techniques of creating cost-effective and well-functioning apartments through substantial rehabilitation. Her plans were all but unbuildable, and in the end—at considerable expense—the developer had to hire a new architect to design the project from scratch.
3. Experience dictates that if a professional is doing work of a complex, ongoing nature without a fee, the client is constantly at risk that the professional will defer the client's work or give it less priority than work simultaneously demanded by paying clients.
4. If the sewer extension will ultimately benefit other properties, the developer may be legally entitled to reimbursement of part of its cost by the owners of those properties, but in most cases, that reimbursement will only be provided at such time in the future that the properties are developed and need to connect to the sewer line.
5. The likelihood of a court reversing the local decision will vary significantly by state, and by municipality within many states. In states with zoning appeal laws, such as Massachusetts, Connecticut, and Rhode Island, if the municipality's existing share of affordable housing is below the state-mandated level, ONI would have a good chance of having a denial overturned unless there is a compelling environmental or planning reason for the denial. In some other states, such as Florida, although the process would be more uncertain, ONI could use the general language in state statutes in support of an appeal. In many other states, however, they would be required to meet a heavy burden of showing that the town's action was arbitrary and unreasonable. Even where the likely outcome of a court case would be favorable, the time and money involved in pursuing it is likely to discourage all but the most determined advocates.
6. Schematic drawings typically refer to a package that includes, in addition to the site plan, elevations and floor plans of the buildings. They do not include engineered or working drawings, which are generally prepared after land-use approval has been obtained.
7. State laws vary with respect to the legal principle known as "standing"—that is, which parties have the right to participate in legal proceedings such as rezoning applications. In practice, many local zoning and planning commissions tend to err on the side of inclusivity in order to enable residents to participate in the process.

8. There are alternatives to the conventional structure of owner, architect, and general contractor, including a design-build contract, where ONI would contract with a single entity to both design and build the project, and a construction management contract, where ONI would contract with a construction management firm to supervise the project on its behalf. Although there are arguments in favor of both alternatives, they are rarely used in residential projects of the scale contemplated by ONI.
9. Many government agencies provide capital grants to affordable housing projects in the form of subordinated loans that typically do not have to be repaid unless there is excess cash flow, or if the project ceases to be affordable housing for some reason. Although they have the financial effect of a grant, from a legal standpoint they are treated as loans.
10. For example, removal of old underground gasoline tanks at a former service station is a speedy and inexpensive process. If, however, the tanks have cracked or broken, and gasoline has spilled from them into the adjacent soils, or even worse, leached into the groundwater, the remediation can be highly time-consuming and expensive.
11. There have been a variety of technological improvements, although of a low-tech nature, in wood frame construction over recent decades. Standardized materials, pre-hung doors and windows, panelized wall sections, and preconstructed roof trusses, have all helped keep wood frame construction cost effective and efficient. Modular housing, for the most part, is another form of wood frame construction, except that the framing takes place in a factory rather than on the site.
12. "Good Neighbors." 2005. *Builder Magazine*, June.
13. There are actually two "Princetons," a situation that is not unusual under New Jersey's municipal government structure. The central part of the community is Princeton Borough, which is completely surrounded by Princeton Township. Although the two municipalities share a variety of joint services, including a joint planning board, they are two distinct and separate incorporated municipalities. Both municipalities support the work of PCH, but land availability has dictated that all of PCH's developments are located in the township (although one sits on a site that straddles the boundary between the two).

CHAPTER

7

Concentration and Opportunity: Undoing the Exclusion of Affordable Housing

Lower income Americans are disproportionately concentrated in the nation's urban areas and older inner ring suburbs, often within areas of concentrated poverty within those communities. Despite periodic attempts to address the issue, the great majority of affordable housing has been constructed in those locations, reinforcing the relegation of low-income households to areas that lack access to jobs and educational opportunities and are also often unsafe and unhealthy. Today, it is widely recognized that this is a problem not only for the lower income households trapped in conditions that fail to offer a decent quality of life, but for the society and economy of the United States as a whole. Many of the most important affordable housing initiatives of recent years, including the Hope VI program, inclusionary housing programs, and suburban fair share plans, have grown out of a desire to frame affordable housing strategies that foster social inclusion rather than isolation.

This situation arose neither by chance nor as the pure product of the working of neutral economic forces. The suburbanization of the United States, particularly after the end of the World War II, was furthered by an interlocking system of governmental regulations and financial subsidies, all working to institutionalize patterns of economic and racial segregation into the form of America's metropolitan areas. Although the postwar move to the suburbs was driven by strong consumer desires, public policies played an important role in defining the nature of the new suburban environment. Federal Housing Administration underwriting policies that directed investment away from existing houses and older neighborhoods to new houses in the growing suburbs, transportation and land use policies that meant that newly built communities would be dependent on cars, and official tolerance for racially discriminatory real estate and lending practices, all played a part in creating that environment.[1] Even as those practices began to give way to change in the 1960s and 1970s, however, conditions did not change significantly. Exclusion of lower income households and affordable housing had already been institutionalized into the very fabric of local government zoning and building regulation, reinforced by a behavioral pattern that had come to be seen as characteristic of suburbia known as NIMBY, or "not in my back yard."[2]

This chapter will first provide an overview of exclusionary practices and regulations and how they emerged, followed by a discussion of the different ways in which these practices have been challenged since the 1970s and the effect of these challenges, including court decisions and state laws that have significantly changed the suburban exclusion ground rules in states across the United States. This is important not only as a reflection of the way values and attitudes have changed in recent decades, but as a practical matter, in that these laws and decisions form a key part of the legal framework for affordable housing development today. Statutory or case law that specifically affects the ways in which local government can regulate the development of affordable housing exists in most of the larger states of the nation. Anyone building affordable housing, reviewing affordable housing proposals, or helping to design a housing strategy for their county or city needs to be familiar with these laws.

THE PRACTICE OF SUBURBAN EXCLUSION

The origins of suburban exclusion lie in the highly decentralized manner in which American local governments are organized. In contrast to many other nations, where the role of local governments tends to be constrained by more powerful provincial or national bodies, the United States, from its earliest years, tended to foster the creation of separate local governmental units, which during the course of the 19th and 20th centuries came to play a growing role in managing matters of concern to their citizens. Although the Constitution makes no provision for local government, and state courts have ruled that local governments have no inherent powers other than those granted them by the state,[3] a combination of legislative action, tradition, and inertia have fostered a proliferation of local governments throughout most of the United States whose exercise of a wide range of powers under the legal or rhetorical rubric of "home rule" is largely sacrosanct.[4]

Small municipalities proliferated in many American metropolitan areas during the latter years of the 19th century in the nation's first wave of suburbanization, driven by the industrialization of central cities, the growth of the immigrant population, and the new accessibility of former open country resulting from the construction of rail and streetcar lines. The Cleveland area, for example, began to fragment at the end of the century; today, Cuyahoga County, which forms the heart of the metropolitan area, contains 38 separate cities, 19 villages, and two townships within a land area of only 458 square miles. The proliferation of towns, villages, and cities, often driven by motives of social or economic exclusion to begin with, tended to foster an increasingly narrow and often defensive perspective characterized by Robert Wood as the division of the metropolitan population into "clusters homogeneous in their skills and outlook which have achieved municipal status and erected social and political barriers against invasion."[5] In the small suburban municipality, politics and civic life turned inward, focusing on preserving the values and features that are perceived as offering the justification for the community's existence. Those values were often social or economic, and the preservation of property values and the perpetuation of economic or racial homogeneity were often seen as much the same thing. Within this fragmented suburban political system, consideration of the social and economic health of the larger metropolitan area received little attention.

It was inevitable that suburban towns would focus on the use of undeveloped land within their boundaries as the single most important factor in preserving the social and economic character of the community and the value of the homes already built and occupied.[6] Although towns had made different efforts to direct the course of development before zoning came into being, the emergence of zoning as a powerful legal tool to control land use was to become the critical element in determining the future of American suburban growth and development.

Zoning can be defined as a body of regulations that divides a municipality into separate districts (zones), specifies the use or uses permitted in each zone, and establishes standards to govern the manner in which the land in each zone can be developed for each use. Zoning regulations may define permitted uses broadly—such as "residential" or "industrial"—or may divide those categories into subcategories, such as single-family detached residential, town houses, or apartments. The regulations may further refine those subcategories by such features as density—the amount of land area required for each dwelling unit—the height of the building, the number of feet the building must be set back from the street, and so forth, all of which can lead to a patchwork of dozens of separate zoning districts within a medium-sized town or city.

Zoning, which appears to have originated in late 19th century Germany, became the subject of considerable attention among early 20th century town planners in the United States, particularly after New York City adopted a comprehensive zoning ordinance in 1916. The use of zoning did not become widespread, however, until the 1920s, when its growth was furthered by two critical steps. The first was the active promotion of zoning by the U.S. Department of Commerce under Herbert Hoover, which published a Standard Zoning Enabling Act for use by state governments in 1926; the second was the decision by the Supreme Court that upheld the legality of zoning ordinances in the 1926 *Euclid v. Ambler* case. In that decision, involving a suburb of Cleveland, the Court not only upheld the validity of zoning ordinances generally, but specifically held that a municipality could exclude apartment buildings from its residential zones; as Justice Sutherland wrote, reflecting a sentiment that is still widespread 80 years later, that "the development of detached house sections is greatly retarded by the coming of apartment houses, which has sometimes resulted in destroying the entire section for private house purposes; that in such sections very often the apartment house is a mere parasite . . . Moreover, the coming of one apartment house is followed by others [. . . .] until finally, the residential character of the neighborhood and its desirability as a place of detached residents are utterly destroyed."[7] With the imprimatur of both the federal government and the Supreme Court, zoning spread quickly. By 1930, 35 states had passed enabling statutes patterned after Hoover's model legislation, giving local governments the power to enact zoning ordinances.[8]

That zoning would and could be used as a vehicle for social exclusion was recognized early by the trial judge in the *Euclid* case, who wrote presciently that "in the last analysis, the result to be accomplished is to classify the population and segregate them according to their income or situation in life."[9] By the 1960s, the extent of that practice as a vehicle for excluding the less affluent from the greater part of suburban America had become widespread. While explicit racial and economic zoning—including ordinances that banned specified ethnic groups from residence or required that houses sell for a minimum cost—had been outlawed by that point,[10] local governments had found that economic exclusion could be achieved through ordinance provisions that maintained at least some connection to the use of the land. While some provisions that had an exclusionary effect might have a legitimate land-use purpose under some circumstances, such as minimum lot sizes, others, such as prohibitions on multifamily housing or minimum house size requirements, were clearly economic in nature; as Norman Williams stated forthrightly in his famous treatise on American land-use law: "The purpose of minimum-building-size zoning ordinances is to force up the cost of housing."[11]

In addition to minimum building size and minimum lot size ordinances, many suburban zoning ordinances either banned multifamily housing outright or limited it through other means. In contrast to single-family development, which can typically be developed as of right[12] in nearly all suburban jurisdictions, most such towns permit multifamily housing only as a product of a discretionary approval by the municipal governing body, often after an extensive and tortuous review process during which the town may impose conditions—such as requiring that the project be sold as condominiums rather than rented—that would be illegal if included in a zoning ordinance. Similarly, many communities have limited the number of children in multifamily housing by imposing limitations on the number of bedrooms. A common provision in New Jersey ordinances in the 1960s was known as the 80/20 rule. At least 80 percent of the apartments could contain only one bedroom, no more than 20 percent could contain two bedrooms, and none could contain more than two bedrooms.

While exclusionary zoning in its most generalized form affects all housing, many suburban municipalities used their zoning regulations as a vehicle to bar housing projects built under government subsidy programs, particularly after 1968. With large amounts of federal subsidy funds available for the first time to private developers seeking to build affordable housing under the Section 235 and Section 236 programs, and without any requirement that the municipality take affirmative steps to facilitate the housing, "land use controls became the key suburban weapon to check the construction of subsidized housing."[13] In one notorious case, the residents of an unincorporated area not far from St. Louis incorporated themselves as a village for the purpose of gaining the legal authority to enact a zoning ordinance that would bar construction of an affordable rental development. Although the developer was able to have the new village's action reversed in the courts, the villagers ultimately won; by the time the litigation had been resolved, funds were no longer available for the project.[14]

Exclusionary zoning has never been universal. In the 1960s, as is still true although to a far lesser degree today, large parts of many southern and western states had no zoning regulations, while even in heavily zoned states like New Jersey and California, one could find an occasional suburb whose zoning might permit an occasional subsidized housing development. In the nation's major metropolitan areas, however, exclusionary zoning, if not quite universal, was pervasive. As the racial conflicts of the 1960s fueled a greater awareness of America's patterns of racial and economic segregation, many observers singled out the role of exclusionary zoning in perpetuating those patterns, a relationship documented by the National Commission on Urban Problems (the Douglas Commission) in 1968.[15] Their work led to a series of challenges to exclusionary zoning practices, which led directly to the legal framework governing the land-use regulation of affordable housing in many states today.

CHALLENGING EXCLUSION IN THE COURTS

During the 1960s, a growing number of civil rights and other organizations, including the NAACP, the League of Women Voters, and the National Committee against Discrimination in Housing, began to turn their attention to exclusionary zoning and its implications for housing opportunities and the future of America's metropolitan areas. The Suburban Action Institute, which led the challenge to suburban exclusion under Paul Davidoff's dynamic leadership, was founded in 1969. At the same time, the first state legislative efforts to rein in suburban exclusion were being made.

Although Suburban Action, the League of Women Voters, and others attempted to gain support from suburban political leaders, residents, and businesses to break down land-use barriers to affordable housing, these efforts were largely unsuccessful in the face of staunch—sometimes intense—suburban hostility. Their efforts to challenge exclusionary zoning in the courts were more, although not always, successful. These challenges typically took one of two forms. They were either public interest-based challenges to a zoning ordinance, grounded in its exclusion of inexpensive housing and lower income residents, or challenges brought by a developer or civil rights organization to reverse a local decision barring construction of a particular affordable housing development.

Suburban Action was particularly active in the former arena. Focusing largely on New Jersey, they brought a flurry of cases against suburban towns in that state's courts beginning in 1970, often selecting towns that combined large-scale employment and exclusionary zoning in particularly egregious fashion.[16] Examples were Mahwah, on New Jersey's northern border, which contained a massive Ford assembly plant alongside exclusionary practices in the town's residential areas; and Bedminster, a town in which virtually no development was permitted other than single-family houses on five-acre lots, where AT&T was building an office complex to accommodate 5,000 workers being relocated from New York City.

The case that turned out to be the defining one, however, was not brought by Suburban Action or any of the other national organizations, but by a group of lower income African American residents of Mt. Laurel, a southern New Jersey suburb of Philadelphia. Faced with a municipal government that was using a combination of restrictive land-use regulations and code enforcement efforts to force them out of town, they enlisted the support of the local NAACP chapter and Camden Regional Legal Services to bring a lawsuit against the township. It was that lawsuit, *Southern Burlington NAACP et al. v. Township of Mt. Laurel*, decided by the New Jersey Supreme Court in 1975, that became the seminal case in the challenge to exclusionary practices.[17] Reminding local officials in uncompromising terms that the power to zone comes from the state and is not inherent in local government, the court ruled that every "developing municipality" must afford the opportunity for low- and moderate-income housing "at least to the extent of the municipality's fair share of the present and prospective regional need therefor."[18]

The court, however, offered no direction with respect to *how* that need was to be either determined or accommodated. In the wave of litigation that followed, lower court decisions reflected confusion, inconsistency, and in a few cases, a patent unwillingness of some judges to follow the state high court's lead. As a result, in 1980 the court took six cases for review—including its remand of the original *Mt. Laurel* case—which led to its 1983 decision, known as *Mt. Laurel II*.[19] The *Mt. Laurel II* decision, while making clear that the court meant what it had said eight years earlier, enunciated a body of policies and procedures to turn the principles of the earlier decision into a reality.

While setting down a variety of measures in the hopes of fostering affirmative compliance by New Jersey's towns and villages with the fair share principle initially espoused in 1975, the *Mt. Laurel II* court added a new twist, reflecting its frustration with the widespread failure of municipalities to comply with its 1975 ruling. In order to ensure compliance with the *Mt. Laurel* doctrine and make the constitutional principle that it represented a reality, the court held that where a municipality had failed to address that obligation, lower courts should overturn the municipal denial of permission to build and grant a builder's remedy, "where a developer prevails in *Mt. Laurel II* litigation and proposes a project providing a substantial amount of lower income housing."[20] The controversial principle that the courts could and should overturn local zoning regulations where needed to further the goal of providing affordable housing has become a part of land-use law, and not only in New Jersey. In 1991, the New Hampshire Supreme Court adopted the *Mt. Laurel* principles largely in their entirety, albeit on statutory rather than constitutional grounds.[21]

New Jersey was not the only state in which exclusionary zoning litigation was taking place, although it was the only one in which the litigation was driven by public interest or low-income plaintiffs and not developers. It was also the one that led to the most far-reaching legislative action. Courts in other states, however, were establishing similar principles. The New York Court of Appeals (the highest state court), in a case involving the affluent Westchester County town of New Castle, ruled in 1975 that the town's zoning must reflect regional needs, including the needs of "residents of Westchester County, as well as the larger New York City metropolitan region [who] may be searching for multiple-family housing in the area to be near their employment or for a variety of other social and economic reasons."[22] The New York courts, however, have been slow to apply this standard, and only in the past few years does a clear legal standard for inclusion of either multifamily housing in general or affordable housing in particular in New York State appear to be emerging.

A series of Pennsylvania cases beginning in 1970 led to a different approach to the same issue. Rather than overturn exclusionary zoning on the grounds that lower income households were excluded, the courts in that state have held that local ordinances are exclusionary where inadequate amounts of land are zoned as of right for the diverse residential land uses that might accommodate a diverse body of people; i.e., apartments, town houses, and mobile homes.[23] While the Pennsylvania approach does not appear to have brought about as much low- or moderate-income housing as in New Jersey, it well may have prompted more overall housing production of moderately priced housing by the private market.[24]

All of the cases described above took place in state courts. Also notable from the same period are federal cases that overturned local zoning regulations barring construction of subsidized affordable housing. While the federal courts do not consider discrimination based on economic status to be barred either by the U.S. Constitution or any federal laws, discrimination based on race is clearly prohibited both by the Constitution and by the federal Fair Housing Act. Federal courts have held that in the context of racially segregated housing patterns within a town or metropolitan area, municipal use of zoning to prevent construction of racially integrated subsidized housing may constitute a violation of the Fair Housing Act because of its racially discriminatory *effect*, even without overt evidence of discriminatory *intent*.[25]

The effect of these cases is that in many states frustrated developers of affordable housing—or mixed income housing developments that contain some percentage of affordable housing—may have access to the courts to overturn municipal action barring their project. The judicial process is, however, both slow and uncertain. As a result, many states have adopted statutes and regulations designed to further affordable housing, in some cases creating administrative procedures through which municipal actions may be reversed. These statutes have become increasingly important vehicles for creating opportunities for affordable housing development, particularly in suburban communities where opposition to such housing remains widespread.

STATE PLANNING LAWS AND AFFORDABLE HOUSING MANDATES

Since 1969, when Massachusetts enacted Chapter 40B, the Comprehensive Permit Law, more than a dozen states have enacted laws designed to encourage or require their municipalities to provide affordable housing. Along with states like New York and Pennsylvania, which established affordable housing obligations through the courts, states containing nearly half of the population of the United States offer some legal standard, although not always an enforceable one, for inclusion of affordable housing by the state's towns, cities, or counties.

State law provisions for affordable housing generally fall into two categories. States may require that municipal comprehensive plans take affordable housing needs into account, or may establish enforcement mechanisms to require municipalities to approve affordable housing developments or provide adequate amounts of affordable housing through other means. Some states, like New Jersey and Illinois, do both by providing for enforcement where the municipality fails to adopt a plan or to carry out the provisions of the plan they have adopted. While many state statutes do not contain similar teeth, a town's failure to carry out the provisions of the law could potentially lead to a lawsuit by an unhappy developer or group of housing advocates.

Housing planning requirements

Roughly half of the states contain some reference to housing in the state statutes which authorize, and in some cases require, municipalities to prepare a comprehensive or master plan. In some cases, it is an optional feature of the plan, and in others, while it may be required, the statute does not spell out specifically how the plan must address housing needs and further the provision of affordable housing. A number of state planning laws, however, are quite clear on what a town, city, or county must do in its comprehensive plan to address both local and regional affordable housing needs.

Under Vermont law, regional planning commissions must identify "the need for housing for all economic groups in the region and in communities." The municipal plan must then include "a recommended program for addressing low and moderate income persons' housing needs as identified by the regional planning commission."[26] The Maine statute is even more specific. Municipal comprehensive plans must ensure that their land-use policies and ordinances encourage the siting and construction of affordable housing, while the municipality's land-use regulations "must seek to provide at least 10% of new residential development as affordable housing."[27]

California has the most elaborate requirements for municipal and county planning for affordable housing. Following guidelines prepared by the state, each regional council of government must adopt fair share goals for each city or county in the region; each local jurisdiction must then incorporate those goals as targets for their housing element. The housing element, which must be updated every five years, must contain a detailed needs assessment, site inventory and analysis, analysis of governmental constraints on housing development, and specific programs that the city or county will carry out to accommodate its share of regional housing need. All plans must be submitted to the state Department of Housing and Community Development for review and for a determination that the plan is in compliance with the state statute and the department's regulations.

Despite the strong language contained in some housing element statutes, their substance is often modest. One longtime Vermont housing advocate commented to the author regarding that state's law that "there is no expert review by the state, no rewards or incentives for creating an adequate plan, and no penalties for producing a pitiful one." Housing elements in California are taken somewhat more seriously, since state law requires local land-use regulations to be consistent with the general plan, including the housing element. Since the state has no power to impose sanctions on a city or county whose plan is not in compliance with state regulations, the only route to compel a reluctant city to adopt a compliant housing element is through the courts. At that point, a determination of noncompliance by the state can play an important role in the success of a lawsuit.

In one case against a town in affluent Marin County, the court enjoined the city from issuing any land-use approvals except for affordable housing until the town adopted a housing element that met state standards.[28] Such outcomes are rare, however, and the level and severity of state housing element compliance review has fluctuated with the political winds over the years. One veteran commentator on the California scene has summed up the picture as follows: "the housing element law does not require local governments to build affordable housing. The result has been a paper chase that 'focuses on the question of whether the housing element complies with state law, rather than the question of whether enough housing is being constructed.'"[29]

Enforcing housing outcomes

While most states have focused on housing plans, others have tried to promote affordable housing construction by creating legal procedures under which the state can override municipal land-use decisions and approve affordable housing developments rejected by the municipality.

Such laws exist in Connecticut, Illinois, Massachusetts, New Jersey, and Rhode Island. Although the laws vary in important ways, they share the common feature that the state's ability to override local decisions is triggered *only* if the municipality has failed to comply with state requirements or failed to achieve certain affordable housing goals.

The first such statute was enacted by Massachusetts in 1969 after a vociferous legislative debate, and it subsequently became the model for legislation in Connecticut and Rhode Island. Under the Comprehensive Permit Law (Chapter 40B), known informally as the "anti-snob zoning law," if a housing development in which at least 25 percent of the units are low- or moderate-income housing (as defined by federal or state statute) is rejected by the local authorities, or approved with conditions the developer considers unreasonable, the developer has the right to appeal to the State Housing Appeals Committee, which can overrule the local decision unless the proposed development presents serious health or safety concerns that cannot be mitigated. The right of appeal exists only in communities where less than 10 percent of the year-round housing meets the state definition of low- and moderate-income housing, or where such housing occupies less than 1.5 percent of the municipality's land area.

Chapter 40B has been both effective and controversial. Since its enactment, approximately 43,000 units in 736 developments have been created, of which 23,000 are affordable to families earning less than 80 percent of area median income. Between 2000 and 2005, 82 percent of all new affordable housing production in Massachusetts was the direct result of the law.[30] At the same time, local officials still find it problematic, regarding it "as a blunt instrument, leaving them with no control over where development goes and putting a big strain on schools and municipal services."[31] Others, including some housing advocates, have attacked it as a "developer's dream" rather than an effective vehicle for production of affordable housing.[32] Despite the production it has triggered, after over 30 years only 47 out of 351 Massachusetts cities, towns, and villages have reached the 10 percent level. While this is a modest number, it is, nonetheless, a notable improvement from 23 in 1997. Another 30 towns and villages have passed the eight percent mark.

Perhaps the most telling criticism of Chapter 40B and its counterparts in Rhode Island and Connecticut, as initially enacted, is that they provide no real incentive for local governments to act affirmatively to foster affordable housing. Under the statutes, a town that is actively working to create affordable housing opportunities, but is still below the 10 percent threshold, is treated no differently from one that is sitting on the sidelines or actively blocking efforts to produce affordable housing. Both Massachusetts and Rhode Island have made changes in recent years to address this concern. Massachusetts adopted regulations in 2004 to give credit to municipalities that are making progress. For towns with approved plans, a 0.75 percent increase in their affordable housing stock grants them a one-year moratorium on Chapter 40B applications, while a 1.5 percent increase grants them a two-year moratorium. In Rhode Island, a 2004 amendment provided that where a municipality's affordable housing plan has been approved by the state Housing Resources Commission, the state Housing Appeals Board must use the local housing plan as the standard against which proposals must be evaluated.

In contrast, New Jersey's Fair Housing Act, enacted in 1985 as a legislative response to the *Mt. Laurel II* decision, created an elaborate planning edifice in which the process risks overwhelming the product. The Act created the Council on Affordable Housing (COAH), a state agency with the authority to set fair share goals for the state's municipalities and certify local affordable housing plans. Although participation in the COAH program is voluntary, towns and villages that receive certification are protected from the imposition of a builder's remedy for the duration of the certification, initially six years and subsequently increased to 10 years by legislative amendment. As a result, by the 1990s, the great majority of those municipalities experiencing development pressure, or with substantial inventories of undeveloped land, had entered the COAH program.

In contrast to many states' housing element laws, under the New Jersey law municipalities must take affirmative steps to see that the housing units that make up their fair share obligation are actually produced. Despite considerable foot-dragging on the part of some townships, the results, as reported by COAH, are not insubstantial. Between 1986 and 2004, 34,900 new units of affordable housing were constructed (or were under construction as of January 1, 2004), 13,900 units have been rehabilitated, and—under a controversial program known as Regional Contribution Agreements under which municipalities pay other municipalities to accept a portion of their fair share obligation—8,650 units transferred to other municipalities, generally older urban centers.[33] Still, all of this represents only slightly more than 3,000 units per year in a state where affordable housing needs are generally held to be in the hundreds of thousands of units.

One of the most contentious issues in the New Jersey program has been the determination of fair share, which until the most recent cycle of certifications was done on the basis of a complex formula that generated a specific number for each municipality, a number which might bear little relationship to the actual growth taking place or the amount to which affordable housing already existed in the town. In 2004, COAH shifted gears sharply, adopting a "growth share" approach, under which future fair share goals were set as a percentage of each township's growth. Under the new regulations, each municipality was required to provide one affordable housing unit for every eight market units approved, and one affordable housing unit for every 25 jobs added through new construction. It remains to be seen, however, whether this change will lead to more or less affordable housing than the previous approach. A revision to the rules prompted by a scathing decision by a state court led to the ratios being increased to one affordable housing unit for every five market units, and one unit for every 16 jobs added through new construction, in 2008.[34]

The Illinois Affordable Housing Planning and Appeal Act is the most recent of these laws, having been enacted only in 2004. It combines planning requirements with a state appeals procedure. Municipalities over 1,000 population with less than 10 percent affordable housing are required to adopt a housing plan containing specific affordable housing goals. A state Housing Appeals Board, which does not go into effect until 2009, can hear appeals from aggrieved developers, but only against those municipalities that are *either* below the 10 percent threshold or fail to meet the goals of their housing plan.

The outcome of the Illinois law is uncertain at this time. The Illinois Housing Development Authority has determined that only 49 out of the state's more than 1,200 municipalities are subject to the law. With these municipalities just beginning the process of implementing their plans, and with the Housing Appeals Board not slated to go into effect until 2009, it remains to be seen whether the law will in fact be a significant force for affordable housing production in Illinois.

Table 7-1 summarizes the statutes that either mandate planning for affordable housing planning, or provide mechanisms through which local governments are obligated to provide affordable housing for selected states.

TABLE 7-1 SELECTED STATE STATUTES ENCOURAGING OR REQUIRING PROVISION OF AFFORDABLE HOUSING

STATE	PLANNING REQUIREMENT	ENFORCEMENT	COMMENTS
California	All city or county general plans must contain a housing element that must be updated every five years and must address the jurisdiction's share of regional affordable housing need as determined by the state or a regional council of governments. Housing element must include specific programs by which need will be addressed. Housing elements must be submitted to state Department of Housing & Community Development for review and determination of compliance. (CA Govt. Code Sec. 65580-65589.8)	Contents of housing elements can be challenged through litigation. Courts can enjoin a municipality from enforcing land-use regulations or granting land-use approvals pending adoption of compliant housing element.	Only those cities and counties with compliant housing elements are eligible for funding under certain state housing programs.
Connecticut	Comprehensive plan must "make provision for the development of housing opportunities, including opportunities for multifamily dwellings, consistent with soil types, terrain and infrastructure capacity, for all residents of the municipality and the planning region in which the municipality is located." (Chapter 126, Sec. 8-23(d))	The Affordable Housing Land Use Appeals Law provides that if town has not met fair share standard (10% of town's housing is affordable), developer proposing development in which 30% of units are affordable at 80% AMI may appeal denial to courts, which may overturn municipal action and grant permits. (Chapter 126a, Sec. 8-30g)	
Florida	Comprehensive plan must include a housing element that includes "the provision of adequate sites for future housing, including affordable workforce housing [...] housing for low-income, very low-income, and moderate-income families, mobile homes, and group home facilities and foster care facilities, with supporting infrastructure and public facilities." Counties in high-cost areas must develop a plan for providing affordable workforce housing. (Sec. 163.3177(6)(f))	The Florida Fair Housing Law prohibits a municipality from discriminating in land-use or permitting decisions on the basis of the source of financing of a proposed development. (Sec. 760.26)	After July 1, 2008, counties subject to the affordable workforce housing requirement are not eligible for any state housing grants until requirement is met.

TABLE 7-1 SELECTED STATE STATUTES ENCOURAGING OR REQUIRING PROVISION OF AFFORDABLE HOUSING (CONTINUED)

STATE	PLANNING REQUIREMENT	ENFORCEMENT	COMMENTS
Illinois	Affordable Housing Planning and Appeal Act requires all municipalities with less than 10% affordable housing to adopt a plan to reach a goal of 10% affordable housing, with specific goals that must be included in the plan. (Public Act 93-0595 and 93-0678)	Effective 2009, a Housing Appeals Board will be able to reverse municipal denials of affordable housing developments in municipalities subject to the act.	The Illinois Housing Development Authority has determined that 49 municipalities in state (out of more than 1,200) are noncompliant and subject to the requirements of the law.
Maine	Comprehensive plan must ensure that land-use policies and ordinances "encourage the siting and construction of affordable housing." Municipalities must seek to provide at least 10% of new residential development as affordable housing." (Title 30-A, Sec. 4326, 3-A(G))		
Massachusetts	Master plans must include a housing element that analyzes housing needs and provides programs to preserve and develop "a balance of local housing opportunities for all citizens." (Chapter 41, Sec.81D)	The Comprehensive Permit Law provides that if town has not met fair share standard (10% of town's housing is affordable), a developer proposing development in which 25% of units are affordable at 80% AMI may appeal denial to state Housing Appeals Committee, which may overturn municipal action and grant permits. (Chapter 40B)	Chapter 40B was enacted in 1969. Since then, over 25,000 units of affordable housing have been approved in 173 municipalities.
Minnesota	Comprehensive plans must include (1) a housing element "containing standards, plans and programs for providing adequate housing opportunities to meet existing and projected local and regional housing needs" and (2) a housing implementation program "which will provide sufficient existing and new housing to meet the local unit's share of the metropolitan area need for low and moderate income housing." (Minn. Statutes 475.859)		A separate statute, the Livable Communities Act, creates a program of incentives for affordable housing development within the Minneapolis–St. Paul metropolitan area. (Minn. Stats. 475.25)

New Jersey	Master plans must include a housing element "designed to achieve the goal of access to affordable housing to meet present and prospective housing needs, with particular attention to low and moderate income housing." (N.J.S.A. 52:27D-310)	New Jersey Fair Housing Act establishes procedure through which municipalities can obtain state certification of their housing element and fair share plan. Municipalities that do not obtain certification, or do not carry out their obligations under their certified plan, are potentially subject to builder's remedy. (N.J.S.A.52:27D-301 et seq.)	Fair Housing Act was enacted in 1985 as a result of the Supreme Court's *Mt. Laurel II* decision. Through January 1, 2004, 35,000 new affordable housing units have been constructed (or were under construction at that time) under the provisions of the act.
Rhode Island	Comprehensive plans must include a housing element "recognizing local, regional and statewide needs for all income levels and for all age groups." (R.I.G.S. Sec.45-22.2-6)	The Low and Moderate-Income Housing Act was closely modeled on Massachusetts Chapter 40B, offering developers the right to appeal municipal denials to the state Housing Appeals Board. (R.I.G.S. Sec.45-53)	The Low and Moderate-Income Housing Act was amended in 2004 to build in planning incentives.
Vermont	Municipal plans must include a housing element that includes "a recommended program for addressing low and moderate income persons' housing needs as identified by the regional planning commission." RPC plan must identify "the need for housing for all economic groups in the region and in communities." (Title 24, Sec. 4382(a)(10) and Sec. 4348A(a)(9))		
Washington	Comprehensive plans prepared by cities and counties subject to the Growth Management Act must "encourage the availability of affordable housing to all economic segments of the population of this state" and include a housing element that, *inter alia*, "identifies sufficient land for housing, including but not limited to . . . housing for low-income families." (RCW 36.70A.070(2)	State can impose sanctions for municipal failure to comply with provisions of Growth Management, including withholding of state revenues collected on behalf of municipality and rescission of municipal authority to collect real estate excise taxes. (RCW 36.70A.330)	
Wisconsin	Comprehensive plans must include a housing element that identifies "specific policies and programs that . . . provide a range of housing choices that meet the needs of persons of all income levels and all age groups. . ." Local land-use regulations must be consistent with comprehensive plan. (Wis. Statutes Chapter 66.1001(2)(b))		

CONCLUSION

It would be vastly unrealistic to suggest that suburban exclusion of affordable housing is a thing of the past. Exclusionary land-use regulations are still commonplace, and even in those states that have housing appeals or fair share statutes, the process of overcoming local regulations is often slow and expensive. This is particularly true in Connecticut, where appeal from a municipal denial goes to the courts rather than to an administrative board as in Massachusetts. Land-use regulations, moreover, are far from the only obstacle that suburban developers of affordable housing face. Sites are hard to find, infrastructure—roads and sewer and water lines—often hard to obtain, and local opposition remains widespread.

Just the same, the ground rules have changed significantly over the decades since Suburban Action and others began to challenge the practice of exclusionary zoning. Some municipalities are taking affirmative steps to accommodate affordable housing in their plans, including a growing use of inclusionary housing strategies, while others are identifying suitable sites and eliminating regulatory barriers that obstruct housing production. In others, developers have recourse to the legal system and to state appeals boards to overcome the opposition of suburban officialdom. As a result of these efforts, large numbers of affordable housing units have been constructed in locations that offer important opportunities to lower income families in terms of access to jobs, quality education, and public services.

NOTES

1. An extensive literature exists documenting these practices and their effects; see in particular Jackson, Kenneth. 1985. *Crabgrass Frontier: The Suburbanization of the United States*. New York: Oxford University Press (especially chapter 11); Beauregard, Robert. 2006. *When America Became Suburban*. Minneapolis: Minnesota University Press; and Dreier, Peter, John Mollenkopf, and Todd Swanstrom. 2001. *Place Matters: Metropolitics for the Twenty-First Century*. Lawrence: University Press of Kansas (especially chapter 9).
2. The term NIMBY is arguably too flip and dismissive to use to characterize a wide range of behaviors that range from the rational, even admirable, to the irrational and deplorable, but has clearly entered the English language. According to one source, it was coined about 1980, presumably with deliberate intent to be dismissive, by the head of the American Nuclear Society. See http://www.word-detective.com/042702.html.
3. This formulation is most often known as "Dillon's Rule," after Iowa Supreme Court Justice John Forrest Dillon, who famously wrote in an 1868 decision that "municipal corporations owe their origin to, and derive their powers and rights wholly from, the

legislature. It breathes into them the breath of life, without which they cannot exist. As it creates, so may it destroy. If it may destroy, it may abridge and control." *Clinton v. Cedar Rapids and the Missouri River Railroad*, 24 Iowa 455.

4. According to the 2002 Census of Government, there are 87,549 separate units of local government in the United States, of which 38,971 are general purpose local governments and the balance school districts and special purpose districts, like water, sewer, or drainage districts. This represents an average of nearly 800 general purpose local government entities per state. The effects of the proliferation of governments in the New York area were analyzed in detail nearly 50 years ago in Wood, Robert C. 1961. *1400 Governments: The Political Economy of the New York Metropolitan Region*. Cambridge, Mass.: Harvard University Press.
5. Quoted in Danielson, Michael N. 1976. *The Politics of Exclusion*. New York: Columbia University Press, 27. This book provides an excellent overview of the historical roots and dynamics of suburban exclusion through the mid-1970s.
6. Efforts to control the characteristics of the people who were moving into homes in suburban areas formed a parallel regulatory track during the first half of the 20th century, in particular the use of religious and racial covenants barring sale of properties to Jews, African Americans, and other "undesirable groups," and subsequent to their abolition, practices of racial steering and discrimination. Such activities, however, rarely reflected the overt use of governmental powers.
7. *Village of Euclid v. Ambler Realty Co.*, 272 US 365, 47 S. Ct. 114, cited in Ellickson, Robert C., and A. Dan Tarlock. 1981. *Land-Use Controls*. Boston: Little, Brown & Co., 48.
8. Ibid., 39–41.
9. 297 F. 307 (N.D. Ohio 1924), in ibid., 49.
10. A detailed discussion of the use of explicitly racial and economic criteria in zoning regulations can be found in Williams, Norman Jr., and John M. Taylor. 1987. *American Land Planning Law*. Wilmette, Ill.: Callaghan & Co., 731–788.
11. Ibid., 789.
12. The term "as of right" is used in land-use practice to refer to circumstances where an ordinance grants the landowner the *right* to develop property for a particular use, as long as she meets explicit technical or procedural standards set forth in the town's ordinances. This is in contrast to those circumstances under which the town retains the discretion to approve or reject the use, such as when a variance or special permit is required for approval.
13. Danielson, *op. cit.*, 96.
14. Ibid., 166–167.
15. See Williams and Taylor, *op. cit.*, 351–352.
16. While exclusionary zoning was widespread in New Jersey, it was no different in that respect from other states in the Northeast. The decision by SAI and others to concentrate on that state reflected a number of opportunistic factors, including the history of land-use case law in New Jersey, with its strong public interest orientation, an activist state supreme court, and the presence on that court of Justice Frederick Hall, who was widely known as an articulate and passionate opponent of exclusionary zoning.
17. An excellent account of the *Mt. Laurel* story and its aftermath is Kirp, David L., John P. Dwyer, and Larry R. Rosenthal. 1995. *Our Town: Race, Housing and the Soul of Suburbia*. New Brunswick, N.J.: Rutgers University Press.
18. 67 NJ 151, 336 A.2d 713, at 724.
19. 92 NJ 158, 456 A.2d 390.

20. Ibid., at 452. The court made clear that, in addition to providing affordable housing, the development must meet reasonable site suitability standards.
21. *Wayne Britton v. Town of Chester*, 134 NH 434, 595 A.2d 492.
22. *Berenson v. Town of New Castle*, 38 NY.2d 102, 341 NE.2d 236, at 242.
23. The leading Pennsylvania case is *Surrick v. Zoning Hearing Board of Township of Upper Providence*, 476 Pa. 182, 382 A.2d 105 (1977).
24. See Mitchell, James L. 2004. "Will Empowering Developers to Challenge Exclusionary Zoning Increase Suburban Housing Choice?" *Journal of Policy Analysis and Management* 23(1): 119, for a comparison between outcomes in Pennsylvania and New Jersey.
25. The leading cases are *Metropolitan Housing Development Corp. v. Village of Arlington Heights*, 558 F.2d 1283 (1977), and *Huntington Branch NAACP v. Town of Huntington, New York*, 689 F.2d 291 (1982).
26. Title 24, Sec. 4348A(a)(9) and Sec. 4382(a)(10).
27. Title 30-A, Sec. 4326, 3-A(G)
28. *Marin Family Action, et al., v. Town of Corte Madera*, Marin County Superior Court No. 174793 (1998). The town subsequently settled the litigation.
29. Calavita, Nico, Kenneth Grimes, and Alan Mallach. 1997. "Inclusionary Housing in California and New Jersey—A Comparative Analysis." *Housing Policy Debate* 8(1): 118, quoting in part Fulton, William. 1991. *A Guide to California Planning*. Point Arena, Calif.: Solano Press.
30. "Fact Sheet on Chapter 40B: The State's Affordable Housing Zoning Law." 2006. Boston: Citizens' Housing and Planning Association.
31. Flint, Anthony. 2004. "Massachusetts Law Still Evolving," *Planning*, November.
32. Belkis, John. "Chapter 40B: Overview of a Failed Policy." Massachusetts Coalition for Healthy Communities.
33. In July 2008, the New Jersey Fair Housing Act was amended to abolish Regional Contribution Agreements, a goal long sought by the powerful speaker of the State Assembly.
34. The COAH regulations provide in Appendix D a detailed table of coefficients for municipalities to use to convert approved square footage to jobs, depending on the nature of the development. Available at http://www.state.nj.us/dca/coah/597.pdf.

CHAPTER

8

Affordable Housing, Community Development Corporations, and Neighborhood Revitalization

The discussion in the two preceding chapters has largely focused on development of affordable housing in suburban settings, typically on greenfield sites, and the issues particular to those settings. Both historically and today, however, most affordable housing has been built in urban areas, particularly in the older central cities of the nation's Northeast and Midwest. Because of this history of urban concentration, along with the distressed condition of many urban centers and their efforts to rebuild their physical and economic fabric, the issues affecting planning and building affordable housing are very different in the cities than in their surrounding suburbs.

In the growing suburban ring of each metropolitan area, the most powerful issue driving affordable housing is the need to provide affordable units for people who are priced out of decent accommodations by the high cost of housing in those communities, particularly since the dramatic run-up in prices during the past decade. By contrast, in urban settings, affordable housing is driven by a complex series of concerns, reflecting not only the desire to improve individual families' lives but also to eliminate blighting conditions and upgrade the quality of life in the city's neighborhoods. The combination of these two concerns raises important questions not only about how to design affordable housing in urban areas, but about where it should be located, recognizing that in the past, low-income housing developments have not always contributed to a better quality of life in their surroundings and in some cases contributed to its deterioration. The harm done by Chicago's massive public housing projects, for all the good intentions that may have driven their construction, still reverberate through many parts of that city.

It is important, however, not to look at urban America through a "one-size-fits-all" perspective and lump all urban centers into a single undifferentiated category called "the cities." Cities vary greatly one from the other with respect to both their physical character and their economic conditions. From an economic standpoint, the extremes are defined by cities such as San Francisco, where housing affordability issues are as severe as in the most affluent suburb, to Flint, Michigan, where most of the city's lower income families can find affordable housing in the private market. Other cities, such as Newark, New Jersey, or Providence, Rhode Island, fit somewhere in between. Although historically relatively affordable, they have become less so in recent years as a result of market pressures, demand-supply imbalances, and the beginnings of gentrification. Moreover, in almost every city, individual neighborhoods vary widely; even in Flint, with a deeply depressed housing market, some neighborhoods are healthy and well maintained, even though the houses in those neighborhoods can be bought for prices well below comparable homes in nearby suburbs.

These variations in economic condition and neighborhood character all call for different approaches to the provision of affordable housing. Affordable housing, looked at in the context of urban neighborhoods, cannot simply be about creating housing units and addressing housing needs. It must take into account the relationship between the housing and the particular dynamics of the neighborhood, and the way in which the key affordable housing development choices—where to build, what types of housing to build, and in some cases, whether to build at all—will affect the future health and vitality of the neighborhood.

This chapter begins by taking up the themes of concentration and deconcentration of affordable housing already touched upon earlier, followed by a discussion of the larger issues associated with the rebuilding of urban neighborhoods as healthy communities, an issue of paramount importance to the future of American cities, and the critical role played in that process by community development corporations. The final section of the chapter directly addresses the role of affordable housing in neighborhood revitalization, and the ways in which it can ensure that it will both further sustained neighborhood change and offer lower income households the opportunity to benefit from that change.

AFFORDABLE HOUSING AND POVERTY CONCENTRATION

Since the publication of William Julius Wilson's *The Truly Disadvantaged: The Inner City, The Underclass and Public Policy*, in 1987, considerable research and policy concern has focused on the phenomenon known as the concentration of poverty and its negative effects. As various authors have established, areas with high concentrations of the poor suffer from a long list of social and economic ills, ranging from breakdowns in social institutions, poor health conditions, low school completion rates, low labor force participation and high unemployment, family disruption, teen pregnancy, and high levels of crime and drug abuse. While the reasons for these conditions are complex, and the causal relationships between them subject to considerable disagreement, there is little doubt that they exist, and that they lead to millions of Americans living lives of social isolation and lack of opportunity.

The decisions made about where to build affordable housing have tended to increase concentrations of poverty and social isolation, rather than reduce them. This pattern was most notable with the public housing program. Public housing projects, whose residents are often the poorest members of their communities, are located in the poorest sections of a city and metropolitan area. In 20 out of 46 metropolitan areas studied by the Harvard School of Public Health, over half of the region's public housing was located in the most extreme poverty neighborhoods, those in which over 40 percent of the neighborhood's population was in poverty, as shown in Table 8-1.[1] Nationally, less than three percent of the population lived in extreme poverty neighborhoods.

While the spatial concentration of public housing is more extreme than that of more recent affordable housing programs, the overall tendency of subsidized housing to concentrate the poor or near-poor has continued. Table 8-2 compares the effects of three different affordable housing programs for the nation's 10 largest metropolitan areas, looking at the concentration of each in high (20 percent or higher) poverty areas. For purposes of comparison, the percentage of the nation's population in poverty in 2000 was 11 percent. Generally speaking, the movement

TABLE 8-1 PERCENTAGE OF PUBLIC HOUSING UNITS IN EXTREME POVERTY AREAS (OVER 40% POVERTY) BY METROPOLITAN AREA, 2000

METRO AREA	PERCENTAGE	METRO AREA	PERCENTAGE
Ft. Worth, Texas	86%	Baltimore	59%
New Orleans*	83%	Tampa	58%
Dallas	83%	Phoenix	57%
Kansas City	80%	Cleveland	56%
San Antonio	71%	Cincinnati	55%
Chicago	69%	Houston	54%
St Louis	66%	Atlanta	54%
Norfolk, Virginia	63%	Minneapolis–St. Paul	52%
Buffalo, New York	62%	New York	51%
Nashville	59%	Philadelphia	51%

Source: Diversity Data Project, Harvard School of Public Health
* Before Katrina

TABLE 8-2 PERCENTAGE OF AFFORDABLE HOUSING BY CATEGORY IN HIGH POVERTY AREAS (OVER 20% POVERTY) FOR 10 LARGEST METROPOLITAN AREAS, 2000

METRO AREA	PUBLIC HOUSING	PROJECT-BASED SECTION 8 HOUSING	HOUSING VOUCHERS
New York	82.4%	89.6%	71.5%
Los Angeles	89.7%	53.6%	45.3%
Chicago	88.3%	73.2%	46.8%
Philadelphia	79.0%	51.6%	45.0%
Detroit	87.7%	59.5%	49.0%
Boston	64.7%	61.0%	30.4%
Miami	67.4%	66.1%	44.7%
Dallas	89.2%	68.9%	22.1%
Houston	60.9%	73.3%	46.1%
San Francisco	69.8%	61.9%	25.1%

Source: Diversity Data Project, Harvard School of Public Health

during the 1970s and 1980s from public housing to new construction and rehabilitation using project-based Section 8 subsidies and Low Income Housing Tax Credits (LIHTC) resulted in only modest change in the overall relationship between affordable housing and high poverty areas, although new Section 8 projects were more likely to be sited in areas that, while still high-poverty areas, were not the areas of extreme poverty concentration where most public housing was to be found. Still, concentration continued to be the norm; in one notable example, 17 separate Section 8 projects were constructed in one small part of Washington, D.C., in an area of little more than 30 city blocks bounded by 13th Street NW, Florida Avenue NW, 15th Street NW, and Spring Road NW.[2]

Housing voucher holders are highly concentrated in New York City, but far less so in some other cities, including Boston, Dallas, and San Francisco. The citywide data, however, masks significant racial variation. As Table 8-3 illustrates, in the same 10 metropolitan areas, Black voucher holders were substantially more likely to end up living in high-poverty areas than non-Hispanic White voucher holders, and in most metro areas, slightly more than Hispanic voucher holders. Only in New York City and Houston was there no racial disparity in the concentration

TABLE 8-3 PERCENTAGE OF VOUCHER HOLDERS IN HIGH-POVERTY AREAS BY RACE/ETHNICITY FOR SELECTED METROPOLITAN AREAS, 2000

METRO AREA	BLACK	HISPANIC	NON-HISPANIC WHITE
New York	68.8%	72.1%	68.3%
Los Angeles	48.9%	42.7%	28.6%
Chicago	50.6%	47.7%	5.9%
Philadelphia	50.7%	42.7%	12.7%
Detroit	69.0%	61.6%	22.0%
Boston	46.8%	44.7%	7.3%
Miami	50.2%	36.0%	42.2%
Dallas	28.2%	20.4%	15.0%
Houston	46.1%	41.4%	49.0%
San Francisco	33.5%	15.9%	32.3%

Source: Diversity Data Project, Harvard School of Public Health

of voucher holders. In New York, the overall tightness of the city's housing markets appears to force the great majority of all voucher holders, whatever their race or ethnicity, into high-poverty areas.

Affordable housing policy at the national level has been ambivalent about the goal of deconcentrating affordable housing and low-income tenants. This has been true since the 1980s, when the production side of the Section 8 program was phased out in favor of what came to be known as the Housing Choice Voucher program, under which individual families received vouchers to move into privately owned houses and apartments, which for the most part they found on their own. While the voucher program can be considered at least moderately deconcentrating on the whole, its effects are highly uneven, as can be expected from a program that places the onus on finding apartments on individual tenants, and tends not to monitor landlord behavior closely. While the New York City pattern of concentration may be extreme, studies in cities as diverse as Columbus, Ohio, and Omaha, Nebraska, have shown similar concentrations of voucher holders in both high-poverty and high-minority areas.

At the same time, the ambivalence of federal policy toward deconcentration is reflected in the fact that, as the vouchers were becoming the largest federal housing subsidy program, the rules governing the principal housing production program—the Low Income Housing Tax Credit—*favored* locating projects in areas of concentrated poverty. The program gave investors a significant boost in the value of their tax credits for building projects in Qualified Census Tracts, areas in which more than half of the population had incomes below 60 percent of the area median income, roughly corresponding to the high-poverty areas described above.[3] During the first 15 years of the LIHTC program, every single tax credit project built in the Cincinnati, 91 percent of those built in Miami, and 84 percent of those built in Chicago and Washington, D.C., were built in Qualified Census Tracts.[4] A study for HUD by Abt Associates of a sample of 39 LIHTC projects in five metropolitan areas found that 46 percent of the projects were in high-poverty areas (defined in this case as areas with 30 percent or more of the population in poverty), and 63 percent were in urban majority-minority areas.[5] In an extreme case, in a small, largely low-income majority-minority neighborhood in Trenton, New Jersey, by 2001 over two-thirds of all of the housing units in the neighborhood were low-income rental housing as a result of a large Section 8 rehabilitation project in the 1980s and three separate LIHTC projects in the 1990s. Challenges to practices in the LIHTC program that tend to perpetuate both economic and racial segregation under fair housing laws, including lawsuits in Connecticut and New Jersey, have been mounted, but have been so far unsuccessful.[6]

The HOPE VI program, designed to replace the most severely distressed public housing projects in ways that would "provide housing that will avoid or decrease the concentration of very low-income families and build sustainable communities,"[7] was a more focused strategy of deconcentration mounted by the federal government during the 1990s. Under the program, public housing authorities received grants from HUD to cover a substantial part of the cost of demolishing distressed public housing projects and replacing them with mixed income developments, building measures into the physical rebuilding program to foster the economic self-sufficiency of the families affected by the projects. Since, as a rule, the proposed replacement developments contain fewer very low-income units than the public housing projects they replaced, far from all residents will have the opportunity to return to the new housing being built. Although in theory a substantial percentage of the initial residents were expected to return, in practice this number appears to be small, since many years often ensue between relocation and the availability of the replacement units. More than half of the displaced families were placed in other public housing projects, while the remaining families received vouchers in order to find housing elsewhere.

From the 1993 inception of the HOPE VI program through 2005, HUD issued a total of 239 grants to 126 separate public housing authorities, totaling $5.8 billion. The largest recipients were Chicago, with eight separate projects, Atlanta with seven, and Baltimore and the District of Columbia with six each. Through the end of 2002, 63,100 public housing units had been demolished, and another 20,300 were slated for redevelopment. The HUD funds were not designed to cover the entire cost of the projects, so the housing authorities and the developers they hired had to fill the gap with a complicated combination of Low Income Housing Tax Credits, other public subsidy funds, and private debt. As a result of these complex financing structures, along with time-consuming property acquisition, relocation, and other features of the program, HOPE VI projects have moved slowly. By 2002, nearly 10 years after the program began, only 15 projects had been completed.

It is hard to generalize about the effects of the HOPE VI program. The variation in the nature of the projects chosen for removal is considerable,

North Beach Place, a 341-unit HOPE VI development in the heart of San Francisco, fronts on a busy urban street while providing a secluded private space for residents in the development's interior. The architects were Barnhart Associates.

Photos by Bob Canfield, courtesy of BRIDGE Housing

while the variation in the features of the replacement projects is even greater, ranging from those that in effect replace one public housing project with another—generally smaller and presumably better designed—to those that incorporate significant diversity of incomes, housing types, and tenures. An assessment by the Urban Institute suggests both positive and negative features. While many HOPE VI projects have replaced distressed housing with well-designed and economically mixed housing that has helped to turn around conditions in many of the neighborhoods, major issues remain, particularly with respect to the outcomes for the families displaced as a result of the HOPE VI projects. As the study notes, "some of the original residents of these developments may live in equally or even more precarious circumstances today."[8]

The idea of deconcentration as a major theme of affordable housing policy and the importance of embedding future affordable housing in more economically diverse environments appears to have become widely accepted, in principle if not always in practice. The HOPE VI program and the increasing use of the LIHTC program in suburban areas[9] have changed the norms for publicly subsidized development, while the increasing popularity of inclusionary zoning as a tool for providing affordable housing and the effects of state-level actions such as the Massachusetts Comprehensive Permit Law and the New Jersey *Mt. Laurel* decision have had an effect that, although hard to quantify, is nonetheless significant.

At the same time, this shift raises a troubling question about the course of affordable housing policy. Along with the move toward deconcentration, it reflects an upward bias in the direction of many affordable housing efforts away from the neediest and most impoverished households toward those who, although in need, have higher incomes, are more likely to have stable employment, and are closer in their demographic and social features to mainstream middle America. While this eases the acceptance of affordable housing by more diverse communities, it increasingly leaves out those who may need it most. With the number of public housing units steadily being reduced, and the number of vouchers available increasing slowly, if at all, many households who live in the worst housing and are most heavily cost-burdened may be offered little opportunity in coming years to escape their increasingly difficult housing conditions.

THE ROLE OF COMMUNITY DEVELOPMENT CORPORATIONS

The adage that a particular city is a "city of neighborhoods" applies to most older cities.[10] Ultimately, whether an older city can be a healthy and sustainable entity depends even more heavily on its ability to restore vitality to its neighborhoods than on its ability to regenerate its downtown center, a task that is often more easily accomplished. As a result, rebuilding a city's distressed and at-risk neighborhoods is a critical issue for older cities, and often looms larger than affordable housing in the eyes of many local officials and decision makers. Since the late 1960s, a major role in the effort to rebuild urban neighborhoods has been played by community development corporations or CDCs, a distinctive and important player in the world of both affordable housing and community revitalization.

While CDCs take many forms, the term is generally used to describe nonprofit entities created to carry out activities and provide services to enhance and rebuild a specific lower income or distressed neighborhood, cluster of neighborhoods, or small town or city. CDCs are accountable to the residents of the communities where they work, and are often directly governed by residents, in some cases through community elections. Many, perhaps most, CDCs are engaged in developing affordable housing, but many are involved in other areas, including economic development, social services, and community greening, as well as community-building and organizing efforts.

The first CDCs, such as the Bedford-Stuyvesant Restoration Corporation in Brooklyn, New York, were founded in the 1960s, but CDCs as a field—or perhaps a movement—emerged in American cities during the 1970s and 1980s. They grew out of an amalgam of community organizing efforts such as Saul Alinsky's Industrial Areas Foundation, some surviving community action agencies from President Johnson's War on Poverty, and a variety of social service agencies, religious institutions, and grassroots organizations, all of which began to focus during those years on changing their neighborhoods. With strong support from a number of philanthropic individuals and organizations, the number of CDCs, as well as a strong support system for their efforts, grew steadily. By 1998, according to a national survey, there were 3,600 CDCs active across the United States.[11]

In contrast to many earlier community-based efforts, which focused either on delivering services to individuals, organizing people to block unwanted investments, or to demand services from local government, the focus of the CDC was on the neighborhood as a whole, and on a different approach; as Paul Grogan and Tony Proscio put it, one of " . . . seeking investments, developing or renovating property, building on assets, and generally drawing power and capital in to the community, rather than scaring it away."[12] By leveraging public and private funds—which increased notably after enactment of the Community Reinvestment Act in 1977, which required banks and thrift institutions to offer credit throughout their service areas, particularly to underserved lower income areas—CDCs built and rehabilitated affordable housing, assisted small businesses, and developed commercial corridors and shopping centers. By 1998, CDCs had created more than half a million units of affordable housing.

An important part of the success of the CDC movement over the years, and particularly since 1990, has been the emergence of networks of CDCs, at the local, state, and national levels, and the growth of a support system grounded in organizations known as *intermediaries*. The two principal national intermediaries are the Local Initiatives Support Corporation (LISC), founded through the leadership of Mitchell Sviridoff of the Ford Foundation in 1980, and Enterprise Community Partners (formerly the Enterprise Foundation), established by developer James Rouse and his wife Patty in 1982. LISC, which defines its mission as helping "resident-led, community-based development organizations transform distressed communities and neighborhoods into healthy ones—good places to live, do business, work and raise families,"[14] raises capital nationally to support the work of CDCs locally, providing them with both financial and technical assistance and ensuring that the voice of the movement is heard at the national level. LISC and Enterprise are both local and national organizations. Each has established programs in selected cities, metropolitan areas, or states around the United States, to which they direct a major part of their energy while still providing a variety of resources to the CDC movement nationally.

Along with the creation of local intermediaries such as Neighborhood Progress, Inc., in Cleveland and Neighborhoods Now in Philadelphia, a process generally driven by local funders, CDCs have also organized themselves into networks, particularly at the state and local level. This not only improves their own work, but builds power in ways that would be impossible for individual organizations. Statewide organizations such as the Housing and Community Development Network of New Jersey, founded in 1989, and the Massachusetts Association of Community Development Corporations, founded in 1982, have become more than advocates for their members at the state level; they are leaders in fostering creative state-level policies and practices in support of affordable housing, community development, and urban revitalization. Local organizations such as the Chicago Rehab Network and the Philadelphia Association of Community Development Corporations have played similar roles, bringing about important changes to housing policy in their cities. A national organization to bring these networks together, the National Alliance of Community Economic Development Associations, was established in 2007.

An example of an effective CDC that has sustained a coherent vision for its neighborhood over time is Bethel New Life in the West Garfield Park section of Chicago, an area devastated by violence, White flight, and disinvestment in the 1960s and 1970s. Organized by a small Lutheran church in the neighborhood, Bethel New Life was established in 1979 with the mission of "realiz[ing] God's vision of a restored society by empowering individuals, strengthening families, and building neighborhoods through community-driven, solution-oriented, and value-centered approaches"[14] in West Garfield Park and the adjacent East Garfield Park and Austin neighborhoods, collectively known as the West Side. Since that time, the organization has developed more than 1,000 units of housing, from single-family homes to large-scale multi-family development; it provides home ownership counseling to more than 250 individuals annually, serves nearly 400 preschool children with child development programs and more than 2,000 school-age children with after school programs, and provides 3,000 people with job training or career development support each year. These activities are integrated into a strategic plan (Table 8-4), organized around three themes—quality education for all, sustainable wealth creation, and affordable housing for all. Although the West Side is still a distressed area in many respects, it is an improving one. Crime and unemployment have steadily declined, while the graduation rate in the local high schools has increased.

Not all CDCs are as capable of sustained effort and productivity as Bethel New Life. Of the thousands of CDCs around the United States, the great majority are small-scale organizations that in all likelihood have a modest, although most probably positive, effect on their communities. Bethel New Life, however, is not unique. A large number of CDCs in cities from Boston to Atlanta and Philadelphia to San Francisco have mounted sustained, effective strategies of change. The work of organizations such as the Dudley Street Neighborhood Initiative in Boston, or the Reynoldstown Revitalization Corporation in Atlanta, has had a significant impact on their communities. A 2005 study by the Urban Institute concluded that "econometric analysis shows that CDC investments in affordable housing and commercial retail facilities have led to increases in property values—the single-best measure of neighborhood improvement—that are sometimes as great as 69 percent higher than they would have been in the absence of the investment."[15]

As organizations devoted to addressing the concerns of their largely lower income constituents, CDCs have traditionally devoted a substantial part of their resources to low-income housing. During the course of the 1990s, however, how they approached that mission began to take a sharply different direction. During the early years of CDC efforts, in the 1970s and 1980s, affordable housing was often "the only game in town" in their neighborhoods. Deeply disinvested, with house values well below replacement cost and little or no private market interest, affordable housing was the only vehicle for physical regeneration of many areas. By the

The Narrow Gate Architects

The Border Falcon Condominiums were developed by NOAH (Neighborhood of Affordable Housing), a community development corporation in East Boston, Massachusetts, and designed by The Narrow Gate Architecture.

TABLE 8-4 BETHEL NEW LIFE'S STRATEGIC PLAN

AREAS OF WORK	EMPLOY (model workforce)	INVEST (resources and products)	BUILD (family assets)	RETAIN (retain and renew)
QUALITY EDUCATION	• Develop skills-based models • Improve school performance • Find quality placements	• Foster high financial IQs among residents • Include elders and youth • Use of investment products to help	• Support a financial education network • Foster a 24/7 learning culture • Grow parent capacity	• Cultivate schools of choice • Retain intellectual capital • Grow postsecondary opportunities
SUSTAINABLE WEALTH	• Encourage retention of employees • Accelerate wage progression • Develop career paths	• Connect with mainstream • Create new products • Develop entrepreneurial infrastructure	• Develop a wealth community • Increase matched savings • Incubate and promote	• Introduce broader investments • Grow community hires • Increase messaging
AFFORDABLE HOUSING	• Deliver jobs with living wages • Develop housing models • Deliver transit-oriented jobs	• Encourage use of green technologies • Engage leveraged finance to create affordability • Encourage location efficient housing	• Increase ownership • Leverage resources through partners • Create a path toward earned income	• Train to keep assets • Ensure special needs are met • Preserve diversity and stock

Source: *Bethel New Life Key Indicators Report, 2007*

1990s, reflecting in some cases the effects of CDC activities, but more often the way in which the market had begun to perceive many American cities, that situation had begun to change. Coupled with a greater awareness of the importance of the marketplace, CDCs and other entities began to formulate new ways of looking at urban neighborhoods and a new place for affordable housing to preserve opportunities for lower income families in the midst of market-driven neighborhood change.

TOWARD COMMUNITIES OF CHOICE

In recent years, as the relationship between the social and economic vitality of a neighborhood and the strength of its real estate market became more apparent, the phrase "community of choice" came into use as a shorthand term to describe a healthy neighborhood.[16] The term reflects the importance of consumer choice in the growth or decline of a neighborhood. Simply stated, if consumers—home buyers, renters, and other investors—choose to move into or stay in a neighborhood, it will thrive. If they do not, and the only people in an area are those who perceive their own neighborhood as undesirable but have no other choices, and who would prefer to live elsewhere but cannot afford to do so, it will decline. Communities of choice are neighborhoods where people *choose* to live, because of the location, quality of life, or value the neighborhood offers. Ideally, communities of choice will make room for people of all income levels; as Bruce Katz describes them, they are "communities in which people of lower incomes can both find a place to start and, as their incomes rise, a place to stay. They are also communities to which people of higher incomes can move, for their distinctiveness or amenities or location."[17]

If enough people with the income to choose between neighborhoods choose a particular area, their decisions will be reflected in the strength of its real estate market. Properties will rent or sell readily at prices that exceed the replacement or rehabilitation cost of the property, and property values will rise at a level equal to or greater than the increase in the region as a whole. A vital real estate market will result in behavioral changes on the part of property owners in the area, including a greater propensity to invest in their property, a greater likelihood of new infill construction and rehabilitation of vacant properties, and a reduction in tax delinquencies and foreclosures. Upwardly mobile home owners in the neighborhood are more likely to stay in their present homes—or buy homes in the same neighborhood—than to move out.

Conversely, a decline in a neighborhood real estate market, reflected in prices below replacement or rehabilitation cost and stagnation or decline in property values over time, will translate into a variety of negative trends. Maintenance will deteriorate, as owners see no return from investing in their properties. Disinvestment, if the decline is protracted or substantial enough, will lead to abandonment. No housing other than subsidized housing will be built, tax delinquencies and foreclosures will increase, and upwardly mobile households will move out rather than remaining in the neighborhood. The population will become poorer and more isolated. While these negative trends may be mitigated in some cases by strong neighborhood cohesion, perhaps arising from a shared racial or ethnic identity, it is likely that over time—as those cohesive forces weaken—they will assert themselves.

From the perspective of any local government, neighborhood association, or CDC seeking to revive a distressed neighborhood showing strong symptoms of disinvestment and decline, the message is clear. Revitalization must be built around a strategy to build the market; that is, to convince people with enough means to choose to live elsewhere to *want* to move into, or stay in, the neighborhood. Strategies that can be employed to that end tend to fall into three broad categories:

1. Increase desirability of the housing stock, either through physical improvements, financial incentives, or marketing strategies.

2. Increase the stability of the neighborhood by reducing abandonment, fighting crime and drug activity, or improving schools.

3. Increase amenities, such as visual appearance, open space, shopping, transportation, or schools.

Effective strategies are likely to be multidimensional, designed to bring about change across a wide spectrum of neighborhood conditions.

Better schools, although difficult to bring about, play a dual role in how residents and potential movers assess neighborhood conditions. To families with school-age children, good schools are an important amenity from which they benefit directly; to others who may have no direct stake in them, they nonetheless represent a major indicator of the stability and quality of the neighborhood.[18] At the same time, given the predominance of households without school children in the demographic makeup of the United States in general, and its cities in particular, many neighborhoods have made significant strides toward revitalization even in the absence of meaningful improvement in the local public schools.

There are many different ways these strategies can be pursued, reflecting the distinctive characteristics of different neighborhoods and the market dynamics of the cities and regions within which they are located. San Diego's Azalea Park, a neighborhood of charming but small bungalows, marketed itself successfully to the area's gay community; Both Pawtucket, Rhode Island, and Peekskill, New York, created a market for their distinctive historic buildings, including 19th century mill buildings, among the region's artists. The Patterson Park CDC in Baltimore used the restoration of Patterson Park, a historic landmark park in the heart of the neighborhood, as the centerpiece of their strategy to rebuild the area's housing market at the same time as they embarked on a systematic effort to gain control over and restore the neighborhood's abandoned houses.

Fall Creek Place in Indianapolis built on its historic houses and proximity to a riverbank to build a highly successful new neighborhood, into which some 400 economically diverse families moved between 2000 and 2006.[19] Fall Creek Place was one of a handful of communities that was able to take advantage of the Homeownership Zone program, a short-lived but effective HUD program. Under this program, which ran for only two years during the 1990s, a small number of cities received grants to carry out comprehensive, locally designed strategies to transform distressed neighborhoods through increasing the number of home owners. Under the program's rules, at least half of the new or rehabilitated homes were sold to home buyers earning 80 percent or less of the area median income, and the other half to more affluent buyers.[20]

Those focused on rehabilitating distressed neighborhoods must maintain a delicate balance to create sustainable economic diversity, a process with powerful implications for affordable housing development. Too great a concentration of low-income households, particularly in highly visible subsidized housing projects, and the opportunity for neighborhood revitalization may be diminished or even permanently forestalled. As Tony Downs wrote over three decades ago, "both the upgrading desired by low- and moderate-income households and the protection of neighborhood quality desired by middle- and upper-income households can be achieved simultaneously in the same neighborhoods if a significant number of low and moderate-income households live there, *providing that middle-class dominance is maintained* (emphasis added)."[21] Families must be assured that the neighborhood offers them the amenities associated with middle-class communities, in particular personal and financial security, if they are to remain in a neighborhood or move in from the outside. At the same time, too little affordable housing will create hardships for residents of an area undergoing price appreciation and potential destabilization of neighborhoods elsewhere.

What percentage of lower income households is consistent with a sustainably healthy neighborhood is clearly not a matter of hard science; Downs suggests that the middle- and upper-income percentage should be "well over 50 percent, so that middle-class mores and behavior remain prevalent."[22] In the early stages of neighborhood change, the middle- and upper-income percentage is likely to be much less; at that stage people investing in the neighborhood are buying not the reality but the expectation that middle-class dominance can be anticipated in the foreseeable future. If too much of the neighborhood's housing is public or subsidized housing, which is likely to remain low-income housing indefinitely, those expectations can never be realized. Under those circumstances, most middle-income families will not move in, or if already in the area, will move out.

It is important to remember, however, that lower income households, who make up 40 percent of the American population, cannot be characterized in uniform terms. The middle class that Downs speaks of can easily include a large number of lower income households. In Stamford, Connecticut, and other high-income, high-cost areas, a family of four may have an income of $75,000 or $80,000 and still be considered "lower income." Most people would appropriately consider most such families—which will probably include two employed wage earners—to be middle class by any reasonable definition. As Fall Creek Place demonstrated, a neighborhood heavily oriented toward home ownership can succeed in which half or more of the home owners are lower income. The affordable housing in Fall Creek Place, moreover, is scattered throughout the community in single-family houses and a few small multifamily buildings rather than concentrated in one or more distinct developments; houses selling for $75,000 abut other houses selling for $250,000, with little or no visible difference between the two.

If too little affordable housing is available, it can be as serious a problem. In a typical low-income neighborhood the great majority of households own or rent private market housing rather than occupying affordable housing that is price or rent controlled. As a result, too little affordable housing in the face of rising prices can mean that large numbers of households are faced with sharp increases in rents or property taxes, which may ultimately lead to displacement of the lion's share of the area's lower income population. That, in turn, is likely to mean severe hardship for many of the families and individuals affected. That is not only a problem for them, but it defeats the goal of a stable and economically diverse neighborhood and potentially adds to concentrations of poverty and destabilized neighborhoods elsewhere in the city or region. How to address the need for affordable housing in ways that integrate it with the goal of neighborhood revitalization is one of the most complex tasks facing local governments and CDCs in urban neighborhoods across the country.

BALANCING AFFORDABLE HOUSING AND NEIGHBORHOOD REVITALIZATION

Affordable housing can play an important role in any neighborhood strategy, whatever the current economic or market conditions of the neighborhood. In a deeply distressed neighborhood, a well-designed affordable housing development, particularly if it is sited and designed in a way that removes or restores blighted problem properties and provides the block with a strong visual anchor, can contribute to the neighborhood's revitalization. At the same time, great care must be taken with respect to both the type and quantity of affordable housing added to a neighborhood where market demand is weak and rents and property values are low.

In many weak-market-demand urban neighborhoods, rents and sales prices in the private market are affordable to a large part of the lower income population. In Flint, Michigan, for example, the median private market rent in 2000 was affordable—depending on unit size—to very low-income families earning between 38 and 41 percent of the area median income, and the rental vacancy rate was an astronomical 13 percent.[23] In such a market environment, one could question the need for additional Low Income Housing Tax Credit developments, which are designed to be affordable to households earning 50 percent of the area median income. Such a development could easily end up cannibalizing demand from adequate older private market housing, further destabilizing an already severely distressed market.

Even in Flint, however, one cannot say that *no* tax credit housing should be developed. Given that unsubsidized private market investment is unlikely for the foreseeable future, it might be an appropriate way to preserve an architecturally or historically valuable building at risk of demolition, or to strengthen the fabric of a target revitalization area. In such cases, however, those developing the housing need to be aware of the potential impact of their activities on the city's private rental housing market.

The issues are very different in neighborhoods experiencing market-driven change. The question of how to balance fostering that change with the provision or preservation of affordable housing is a difficult one. In the past decade, as the revival of housing demand has pushed up real estate prices in urban neighborhoods across the United States, this question has become a burning concern for CDCs, housing advocates, and neighborhood organizations. The task is how to manage forces of change that once set in motion take on a life of their own.

Precisely how lower income families and affordable housing will be affected by market-driven change[24] will vary from neighborhood to neighborhood depending on the intensity and characteristics of the market pressures working there. In an area where the market demand is coming from families seeking to buy large Victorian houses, its effect on rents in nearby multifamily buildings may be, at least at first, quite modest. On the other hand, that demand may reduce the affordable private market rental stock as young families buy absentee-owned houses for their own use, or restore to single-family use houses that had been converted to two- or three-family occupancy. Where market demand is driven by young single people and couples, modest apartments in older buildings may be in greatest demand. Once-inexpensive apartments in five-story walk-up tenements in Hoboken, New Jersey, have been spruced up and converted into condominiums, selling today for upwards of $500,000.

While some lower income families, particularly home owners, may benefit from appreciation, and others may be relatively unaffected in the short run, it will inevitably put pressure on at least some families and individuals while setting in motion a long-term process that may ultimately lead to the displacement of much of the area's lower income population. Confronting these pressures demands that two quite different—although related—affordable housing issues be addressed. One is preventing, or at least minimizing, involuntary and untimely displacement of lower income families as a result of higher housing costs; the other is preserving a stock of affordable housing in the area so that the neighborhood will remain economically diverse on a long-term, not just transitional, basis, even if the price of private market housing rises to the point where it is no longer affordable by lower income households. Each of these requires different, although overlapping, strategies. While the former is perhaps somewhat removed from the central themes of this book than the latter, it raises important issues and calls for some exploration.

Minimizing involuntary displacement in appreciating areas

The idea that the current residents of any neighborhood or their descendants will remain there forever is an unrealistic one, grounded in a romantic image of the stable, unchanging neighborhoods that disappeared long ago—if indeed they ever existed. People in modern America move. The average urban renter occupies her house or apartment for less than three years, while even home owners rarely stay in the same house for the majority of their adult lives. Many, if not most, of the residents of an appreciating neighborhood will move sooner or later, including many home owners who will want to take advantage of the higher sales prices that neighborhood change has made possible. Similarly, no neighborhood can be said to "belong" indefinitely to any racial, ethnic, or cultural group, however defined. As long as there have been neighborhoods in American cities, populations have succeeded one another in those neighborhoods, a process that is going on today and likely to continue for the foreseeable future.

Just the same, people should not be forced to move against their will. The tenant's right to "quiet enjoyment" of her dwelling, in the phrase made familiar from lease agreements, creates a strong ethical argument against involuntary displacement as long as she pays her rent and refrains from damaging the property or offending her neighbors. That a landlord should be permitted to force such a tenant out because market conditions in the area have made it possible for him to charge a rent that she cannot afford may be legal, but raises ethical questions. If that is true for tenants, it should arguably be even more so for a home owner who may be at risk of losing his home because property taxes—reflecting the greater market value of the house—have risen beyond his ability to pay.

In contrast to actions taken to develop or preserve affordable housing, preventing or mitigating displacement is more likely to involve regulatory changes such as imposing rent control, strengthening anti-eviction laws, or requiring property owners to provide relocation assistance. A strong tool to prevent displacement has been pioneered by Washington, D.C., which enacted the Tenant Opportunity to Purchase Act (TOPA) in the 1980s.[25] Under TOPA, if the owner of any rental property has an offer to buy from a third party, the owner must notify the tenants and give them the opportunity to match the price. In one dramatic example, the tenants of 1330 7th Street, NW, a 136-unit affordable multifamily building that was on the verge of being converted to market-rate housing, partnered with a local nonprofit corporation to buy their building. Using Low Income Housing Tax Credits and financial assistance from the local Housing Finance Agency, the tenants and the nonprofit were able not only to buy the building, but provide the long-postponed and urgently needed repairs the building needed while keeping rents affordable to lower income tenants.

Their experience points out, however, that without the ability to gain access to financing for acquisition and repair, the right to purchase is meaningless. The package that made it possible was complex and could never have been put together without the involvement of the Community Preservation and Development Corporation, a sophisticated nonprofit developer that partnered with the tenant association. In light of the rapid gentrification of large parts of the District, and the importance of preserving affordable rental housing, Washington CDCs and support organizations have given high priority to putting together financial resources to support future TOPA purchases.

These and similar steps are designed either to prevent outright actions by property owners that lead to displacement, or to discourage them by making them more difficult or expensive while still allowing owners a reasonable return on the value of their property. TOPA does not require the owner to sell the property at a discount, only to give the tenants or their representatives an opportunity to buy it at the same price.

While TOPA appears to be financially neutral, except for a modest level of inconvenience to the landlord,[26] other regulations such as rent control may not be. In such cases, the effect of the regulation on the owner as well as on the overall climate of neighborhood investment must be given consideration. Rent control laws affect investment in rental housing, although it is uncertain whether an ordinance that exempts buildings constructed after a certain date would necessarily have that effect. At the same time, the benefits of rent control to the neighborhood's sitting tenants in an appreciating climate may more than offset its negative effects, particularly if, as is customary in most contemporary rent control laws, the owner can obtain rent increases on grounds of hardship or to recoup the cost of major repairs or capital investments.[27]

Other measures to mitigate displacement can involve incentives. A landlord could be offered a low-interest rehabilitation loan or partial abatement of property taxes in return for agreeing to maintain affordable rents for some period. Similarly, lower income home owners may stay in their homes longer if they have affordable financing for home repairs, if they can create accessory apartments in their homes in order to provide an additional source of income, or if property tax "circuit-breakers" cap tax rates at a set percentage of the household's income. Ultimately, however, the home owners that benefit from these various supports are likely to sell their homes at prices reflecting the appreciation in the neighborhood. The new buyers are unlikely themselves to be lower income households.

Preserving and expanding the affordable housing stock

While the rationale for minimizing involuntary displacement is grounded in simple fairness, the argument for a long-term goal of preserving and even expanding the dedicated affordable housing stock in an appreciating neighborhood is more complicated. At least three different arguments support that goal. First and foremost, the benefit of living in an economically diverse community is obviously lost if lower income households can no longer afford to live in a neighborhood that has become desirable to more affluent residents. Second, the greater the number of lower income housing units that are lost and not replaced within any given area, the more likely poverty concentrations will increase in other parts of the city or region.[28] Third, if there is a clear societal benefit to economic integration, as suggested by the literature on poverty and social change, that benefit is undone if the effect of revitalization of one neighborhood is to perpetuate or exacerbate economic segregation, only changing the pattern by which it is distributed across the region's geography.

The inevitable outcome of significant appreciation in neighborhood housing prices is that the private market housing stock will become, with rare and scattered exceptions, too expensive for most lower income families in the area. As a result, those seeking to preserve the neighborhood as an economically diverse community have a twofold mission: First, to preserve as much as possible of the affordable housing that was already in the area prior to the beginning of market-driven change, and second, to add to that stock in order to replace at least some part of the private housing that was hitherto affordable.

In some neighborhoods that contain large amounts of subsidized housing, preserving the existing housing may be enough to achieve reasonable economic diversity goals. In others, such as some of the HOPE VI target areas, the amount of subsidized housing could arguably be reduced in the interest of making diversity possible. Those areas tend to be few, even in the most distressed urban centers. More often than not, maintaining a neighborhood's economic diversity will require the creation of additional affordable housing to add to the existing inventory. That can be accomplished not only through construction of new affordable housing, but through converting some part of the existing housing stock into housing that will remain affordable on a long-term basis. Table 8-5 illustrates some of the programs that may be used to preserve and create affordable housing in appreciating neighborhoods, organized around three distinct strategy areas.

TABLE 8-5 STRATEGIES AND PROGRAMS TO PRESERVE AND EXPAND AFFORDABLE HOUSING IN APPRECIATING AREAS

STRATEGY	PROGRAMS
Preserve existing subsidized or affordability controlled housing	• Upgrade the quality and appearance of existing subsidized housing stock through high-level maintenance and repair programs • Facilitate retention of subsidized projects subject to expiring use restrictions as permanent or long-term affordable housing
Convert private market housing into dedicated affordable housing	• Enact ordinance giving tenants right of first refusal, and create financing program to enable tenants to purchase properties and maintain as affordable housing • Provide incentives such as rehab grants/loans or tax abatements to landlords in return for their maintaining affordability • Acquire and rehabilitate privately owned properties to be maintained as affordable housing
Create new dedicated affordable housing	• Create a land bank of vacant publicly owned land to be held in reserve for future construction of affordable housing • Enact inclusionary zoning ordinance requiring that a percentage of units in future market-rate developments be affordable housing units and ensuring that units created remain affordable on a long-term basis • Enact an affordable housing replacement ordinance, requiring replacement of affordable units lost through demolition, condominium conversion or conversion to nonresidential use or housing trust fund contributions in lieu of providing replacement units • Use vacant property receivership to restore properties held vacant for speculative purposes

Some of the programs in Table 8-5 are likely to have broader application than others. An inclusionary zoning ordinance, which requires private developers to set aside a percentage of new units built in the area as affordable housing, is one of the most widely applicable. This strategy, which is being adopted increasingly in urban and suburban areas, is discussed further in Chapter 12. Vacant property receivership, on the other hand, under which a municipality or nonprofit entity is given control of a vacant property by the courts for the purpose of restoring it to productive use, does not exist in the legal systems of most states. Still, where it does exist, it has been a productive tool, particularly in Baltimore, where a determined effort to use this power led to some 300 houses being restored during the past decade.[29]

Preservation of existing affordable housing is critically important, because producing new affordable housing is not only intrinsically more expensive than preservation, but can be expected to become progressively more difficult and more expensive as the prices of land and buildings rise and the competition for available properties from market-rate developers increases. With the sole exception of public housing, virtually all subsidized housing built in the United States over the past 40 years has been designed to remain affordable only for a fixed period, rather than in perpetuity. The legal controls, generally referred to as "use restrictions," requiring that the project be rented at affordable prices can vary from as little as 10 years to as much as 50 years, will all come to an end sooner or later. This issue first became of widespread concern in the early 1990s, when the use restrictions controlling the first wave of projects built under the old Section 236 program in the early 1970s—subject to 20 year restrictions—began to expire. Today, expiring use restrictions are affecting hundreds of thousands of affordable housing units, not only from the Section 236 program, but from the Section 8 construction programs of the late 1970s and early 1980s, the low income tax credit projects built from the late 1980s on, and the growing number of units constructed under inclusionary housing programs. This subject is discussed further in chapter 10.[30]

Not all subsidized housing projects are at risk of being lost through expiring use restrictions. Community-serving nonprofit entities that own subsidized housing are generally committed to preserving them as affordable housing indefinitely. Where a project is located in an area where market demand is not strong, and the rents available on the open market may be no greater than the subsidized rents, the owner has no economic motive to change the status quo and may be receptive to financial incentives offered in return for an agreement to enter into a new, extended period of affordability controls. Where projects have been built in strong market areas, or where the market has materially improved in recent years—particularly in urban neighborhoods undergoing market-driven change—the owner may be strongly motivated to take the project to market. Ensuring that such projects, many of which have suffered from inadequate and deferred maintenance and repair over the years, are preserved must be a high priority for local governments and CDCs working in those neighborhoods.

The other side of the coin is the construction of new affordable housing to replace the units being lost from the private market, as well as others potentially lost through expiring use restrictions on subsidized housing. Here, timing is everything. The more the area appreciates, the harder it will become to create new affordable housing. At the same time, if too much affordable housing is built too soon, it might potentially slow down or choke off the market demand that is essential to the area's revitalization. The likelihood is small that upper-income buyers or market developers will seek out the remaining housing units in the Trenton neighborhood cited earlier, despite the architectural distinction of many of its structures and its proximity to the city's downtown.

Similarly, while land banking of sites for future affordable housing production is a good strategy in principle, the practice can be complicated. The presence of too many vacant lots, unless well maintained or used for productive interim uses such as miniparks or community gardens, can be a source of neighborhood blight. The more attractive and desirable the interim uses, however, the greater the likelihood that residents will become attached to those facilities. As a result, they may object strongly if at some future date the city or a CDC proposes to use the site for the purpose for which it was held.

The same timing issue affects the use of inclusionary housing even more strongly. The existence of private market demand for housing is a *sine qua non* for a successful inclusionary housing program but it may not be enough, particularly when the demand is new and relatively fragile. Imposing an inclusionary requirement in the form of a set-aside of affordable housing units too early in the emergence of the market could undermine it, while waiting too long could mean the loss of an opportunity for large numbers of badly needed affordable housing units. One possible approach might involve using public subsidies to help write down the cost of the affordable units at first, reducing and ultimately removing the subsidies once the market has become strong enough to sustain the inclusionary requirement on its own.

The greatest difficulty in coming up with an effective strategy is that the market moves quickly and often unpredictably. By its nature, a market is far more nimble in its movements and its response to stimuli than are nonmarket entities such as municipal governments or community development corporations, which tend to be more risk averse and operate with more convoluted and time-consuming decision-making procedures. As a result, it is easy for a city government or a CDC to find itself caught behind the curve, still acting and making decisions on the basis of conditions that are already obsolete.

There is no simple solution to this problem. It is clearly not enough to come out with hortatory statements that cities or CDCs must act more like entrepreneurs, even though there is some merit to that argument. The real issue is how to enable cities and CDCs to act effectively within the constraints imposed by public and nonprofit missions and fiduciary responsibilities in an environment where the rules are being set by entrepreneurs. New tools are emerging for this purpose through the efforts of a number of organizations working at the state and national level. These tools include lending pools offering financial resources that can be accessed quickly enough so that CDCs can compete effectively with speculators and other private investors for properties, and tracking systems that enable local governments and neighborhood organizations to monitor market change on an all but real-time basis in order to build strategies for today's reality rather than the reality of one, two, or five years ago.

NOTES

1. Depending on the size of the public housing project or projects in a given tract, the concentration may reflect the character of the surrounding neighborhood, may be triggered by the projects themselves, or be a combination of the two factors. Since in many cities the residents of public housing projects are predominately poor, their numbers could easily "tip" a surrounding area in which poverty was less concentrated.
2. Analysis by Rob Goodspeed, posted on http://goodspeedupdate.com.
3. The number of Qualified Census Tracts is capped by law at no more than 20 percent of the population of any metropolitan area. Where the number of tracts meeting the definition exceeds that level, tracts are ordered by highest percentage of eligible households to lowest, and the lowest ones are deleted until the population of the remaining tracts is below 20 percent of the area.

4. Analysis of HUD data by Jewell, Kevin. 2005. "The Poverty Concentration Implications of Housing Subsidies: A Cellular Automata Thought Experiment." Unpublished paper, McComb School of Business, University of Texas at Austin.
5. Buron, Larry, et al. 2000. *Assessment of Economic and Social Characteristics of LIHTC Residents and Neighborhoods: Final Report*. Boston: Abt Associates.
6. See Roisman, Florence Wagman. 1998. "Mandates Unsatisfied: The Low Income Housing Tax Credit Program and the Civil Rights Law." *University of Miami Law Review* 52(4): 1011. The Internal Revenue Service, which is responsible for administering the LIHTC program, has taken the position that it is not subject to the same civil rights mandates that govern other housing programs under the jurisdiction of the Department of Housing and Urban Development.
7. Section 24 of the United States Housing Act of 1937 as amended by Section 535 of the Quality Housing and Work Responsibility Act of 1998, P.L.105-276.
8. Popkin, Susan J., et al. 2004. *A Decade of Hope VI: Research Findings and Policy Challenges*. Washington, D.C.: The Urban Institute/The Brookings Institution, 4.
9. See McClure, Kirk. 2006. "The Low Income Tax Credit Goes Mainstream and Moves to the Suburbs." *Housing Policy Debate* 17(3): 419.
10. It is rare, when being shown around a city, that one is not told that the city is a "city of neighborhoods." The drive to identify and give some form of distinction to smaller spatial units within cities appears to be all but universal, or at least was during the period in which most American cities took their shape. Even in the absence of distinct boundaries between areas—such as rivers, railroad lines, and the like—people tend to give their immediate area a distinct identity, even if its boundaries may be somewhat fuzzy. Although western cities, including those largely developed since World War II, are not without their distinct neighborhoods, they are not always as pervasive—or as significant as social and political entities—as in the older industrial cities of the Northeast and Midwest.
11. The census was conducted by the National Congress for Community Economic Development, a now-defunct organization that represented the CDC field. The National Alliance of Community and Economic Development Associations (NACEDA) conducted a new census of CDCs in 2008.
12. Grogan, Paul S., and Tony Proscio. 2000. *Comeback Cities*. Boulder, Colo.: Westview Press, 67.
13. Available at http://www.lisc.org/section/aboutus.
14. Available at http://www.bethelnewlife.org/about.asp?id=01~Mission_and_Vision.
15. Galster, George, Diane Levy, Noah Sawyer, Kenneth Temkin, and Christopher Walker. 2005. *The Impact of Community Development Corporations on Urban Neighborhoods*. Washington, D.C.: The Urban Institute.
16. It is not clear when this term first came into use in this context, but it is now widely used, both in a general descriptive sense as well as a phrase used to market neighborhoods and housing developments. A typical example can be cited from the Greensboro, North Carolina, website, which describes how "the $76 million Willow Oaks Revitalization Project, a public-private partnership sponsored by the Greensboro Housing Authority and the City of Greensboro, is transforming the obsolete Morningside Homes and the surrounding Lincoln Grove area into a vibrant, mixed-income, mixed tenure, mixed-use community of choice." Available at http://www.greensboronc.gov/departments/hcd/planning/revitalization/willowoaks.htm.
17. Katz, Bruce. 2004. *Neighborhoods of Choice and Connection: The Evolution of American Neighborhood Policy and What it Means for the United Kingdom*. Washington, D.C.: The Brookings Institution, 17.

18. For a discussion of school-related issues in the context of the marketing of urban areas, see Varady, David P., and Jeffrey A. Raffel. 1995. *Selling Cities: Attracting Homebuyers Through Schools and Housing Programs*. Albany: State University of New York Press.
19. See Palladino, Chris. 2003. "If revitalization can occur on the Near North Side of Indianapolis, it can occur anywhere." *Planning*, March.
20. This program, which never received an appropriation of its own and was funded through recaptured funds from other programs, was in place only during the 1996 and 1997 fiscal years, during which time 12 cities received a total of $50 million in grants (one city subsequently withdrew from the program). An interim evaluation of the program's effect in the 11 remaining cities was commissioned by HUD in 2005. As of Spring 2008, the full report had not yet been released by HUD, an executive summary is available online at http://www.hud.gov/offices/cpd/affordable housing/programs/hoz/hozoutcomes.cfm.
21. Downs, Anthony. 2003. *Opening Up the Suburbs: An Urban Strategy for America*. New Haven, Conn.: Yale University Press, 87. This extraordinarily prescient book is still worth reading.
22. Ibid., 87.
23. Given economic trends since then, the affordability level of rents in Flint today is likely to be similar or even greater; that is, affordable to even lower income households.
24. In this section the terms "market-driven change" and "appreciation" are used rather than the commonly used term "gentrification" for two reasons. First, gentrification has come to be associated with a particular subset of market-driven change; namely, the radical transformation of an area, generally within a short period, as a result of an influx of households that are significantly different both economically and demographically from the neighborhood's population base. Second, the term has become highly value laden and difficult to use in a framework that is seeking to promote a thoughtful discussion of the issues associated with change. The issue is not that market-driven change is an inherently bad thing; indeed, its benefits are considerable and important. The issue is how to protect the residents of a neighborhood undergoing change from being victimized by the effects of that change.
25. D.C. Code §§ 42-3401.01-42.3405.13. A detailed study, *An Analysis of the Strengths and Deficiencies of Washington D.C.'s Tenant Opportunity to Purchase Act*, prepared by the Harrison Institute for Public Law at the Georgetown University Law Center, can be accessed online at http://www.knowledgeplex.org.
26. Although, to be fair, some landlords would dispute whether the inconvenience level is in fact modest. If the delay results in an owner losing a buyer, and in the end the tenants do not exercise their right to buy the property, the harm may be more than negligible.
27. The economist Richard Arnott has cast significant doubt on the analytical justification underlying the seeming consensus of economists in opposition to rent control in "Time for Revisionism on Rent Control?" 1995. *Journal of Economic Perspectives* 9:1. The effectiveness of rent controls as a means of reducing displacement, however, is strongly affected by its interaction with other landlord-tenant laws, particularly those governing eviction. In a state such as New Jersey, with strong protections for sitting tenants, rent control is likely to be more effective in this respect than in states that permit landlords to vacate units at the end of lease periods without cause.
28. It is important to remember that by definition the percentage of lower income households (defined as a percentage of the area median income) within a region remains the same or nearly so over time. As a result, to the extent that that percentage is reduced in one neighborhood, or one part of the region, it *must* increase elsewhere.

29. For a discussion of vacant property receivership, see the author's *Bringing Buildings Back*, 157–165. For a detailed description of the Baltimore experience, see Kelly, James J., Jr. 2004. "Refreshing the Heart of the City: Vacant Building Receivership as a Tool for Neighborhood Revitalization and Community Empowerment." *Journal of Affordable Housing and Community Development Law* 13(Winter): 210.
30. A good overview of the issue is Atlas, John, and Ellen Shoshkes. 1996. "Saving Affordable Housing: What Community Groups Can Do and What Government Should Do." Published as a special issue of *Shelterforce* 90(November–December). Available online at http://www.nhi.org/online/issues/sf90.html.

CHAPTER

9

The Risks and Rewards of Affordable Home Ownership

HOME OWNERSHIP—THE AMERICAN DREAM

In recent decades, the goal of owning one's own home has become part and parcel of the American vision of the good life, seen as all but inseparable from the much-heralded American Dream. In 2003, the Bush administration's barely noticeable initiative to provide lower income home buyers with down payment assistance was grandiosely labeled the "American Dream Down Payment Assistance Act." Home ownership has been promoted as not only a way for individuals to build stability and control their social and domestic environment, but as an investment, a favored path toward building wealth and improving one's economic condition; as two prominent commentators write, "home ownership . . . is valued and promoted by government; it is considered good for the buyers, good for their communities, and good for the country. It is not far behind motherhood and apple pie as an American symbol."[1] This is not unique to the United States; contrary to the impression many Americans have, home ownership—although perhaps not treated to the same extent as an ideological imperative—is common elsewhere, with home ownership rates actually higher in most European countries than in the United States.[2]

For most of the nation's history, home ownership was the exception rather than the rule. In 1910, little more than a third of nonfarm households owned their own homes, with urban areas—including row house cities like Philadelphia—having far lower rates of home ownership than today. Many homes were bought for cash; mortgages were typically loans of three to five years with down payments of 50 percent or more, often negotiated informally between home buyers and small locally owned banks and savings associations. Government, with the exception of limited state regulation of savings banks, played no role beyond intermittently "using its bully pulpit to spur home ownership."[3] Contrary to what is widely believed today, the home mortgage interest and real estate tax deductions, which today heavily subsidize American home owners, were not intended as a spur to home ownership, but were an inadvertent byproduct of the interest deduction inserted into the first Internal Revenue Code in 1913 "without any thought to their effect on housing purchases."[4]

The federal role in home ownership began with the Depression, less as a means of fostering greater home ownership than as an emergency response to the devastating wave of foreclosures that led to more than 250,000 families losing their homes in 1932. President Franklin Roosevelt, in one of the first major actions of the New Deal, established the Home Owners' Loan Corporation (HOLC) to buy mortgages from their holders and refinance them over longer terms and lower interest rates. It was a

Photo courtesy of *Philly*history.org, a project of the Philadelphia Department of Records

A group of typical Philadelphia row houses, circa 1916.

spectacular success and played a major role in preventing a collapse of the real estate market. As Arthur Schlesinger writes, "By enabling thousands of Americans to save their homes, it strengthened their stake both in the existing order and in the New Deal. Probably no single measure consolidated so much middle-class support for the administration."[5] The success of the HOLC led to the 1934 National Housing Act, which created the Federal Housing Administration. The FHA in turn established the Federal National Mortgage Association, known today as Fannie Mae, to create a national secondary market in home mortgages. By the end of the 1930s, a standardized national mortgage system had been established based on the principle of low down payments and long-term, fully amortizing mortgages at an interest rate fixed for the duration of the loan.

The impact of this system was felt most fully after World War II. Coupled with the new Veterans Administration home mortgage guarantee program for returning war veterans, it made possible an explosion in home ownership. Between 1945 and 1950, the number of home owners in the United States increased by over eight million families, an increase of 55 percent.[6] The transformation of the United States into a nation of home owners largely took place between 1945 and 1960, the years it also first became a suburban nation. During those years, the number of home owners more than doubled, while the home ownership rate (the owner-occupied share of all occupied housing units) went from under 44 percent to nearly 62 percent, as shown in Table 9-1. The continued increase in home ownership over the nearly half century since 1960, although still significant, has been more modest. Indeed, while the number of home owners increased during the 1980s, the number increased less than the overall increase in the nation's households, and the rate of home ownership declined. With a stronger economy and public policy increasingly fixated on expanding home ownership, the rate rebounded in the 1990s and continued to rise until a few years ago, peaking in 2004.

The home ownership boom that characterized postwar America was uneven, with its benefits directed far more at certain sectors of the nation's population than at others. Those benefits were aimed at the growing middle class, and in particular, at the White middle class. Black home ownership rates had been historically far lower than those of White households. Their numbers did grow after World War II, though at a slower pace than those of White home owners. Blacks were hindered not only by lower incomes but by discriminatory practices, both in the real estate market and in the lending industry. Racial covenants

TABLE 9-1 HOME OWNERSHIP TRENDS IN THE UNITED STATES, 1930–2000

YEAR	NUMBER OF HOME OWNERS	INCREASE OVER PRECEDING DECADE		HOME OWNERSHIP RATE
		Number	Percentage	
1930	14,280,000			47.8%
1940	15,196,000	916,000	6.4%	43.6%
1950	23,560,000	8,364,000	55.0%	55.0%
1960	32,706,000	7,146,000	30.3%	61.9%
1970	39,886,000	7,180,000	22.0%	62.9%
1980	52,223,000	12,337,000	30.9%	64.4%
1990	60,248,000	8,025,000	13.3%	64.2%
2000	71,250,000	11,002,000	18.3%	66.2%

Source: U.S. Census

restricting the sale of houses in newly developed subdivisions were widely used during the 1940s and 1950s, while "redlining"—the denial of mortgage credit for buyers in areas considered undesirable and often disproportionately occupied by racial and ethnic minorities—was even more widespread. Initiated by the HOLC in the 1930s, it continued to be practiced by mortgage lenders until enactment of the Community Reinvestment Act (CRA) in 1977.

These patterns began to change significantly during the 1990s. The effect of the CRA, the changing structure and practices of the lending industry, and a deliberate public policy focus on minority and lower income home ownership led to a marked increase in home ownership among lower income households generally and African Americans and Latinos in particular. From 1994 to 2000, "Loans to black home buyers soared 89 percent, loans to Hispanic buyers rose by 138 percent, but loans to whites grew by only 25 percent."[7] No one would argue that racial discrimination had been eliminated from the American housing market, but the remaining disparities between White and minority home ownership rates were largely attributable to economic factors—household income and, perhaps more important, family assets or wealth—in itself a reflection of historic discrimination.

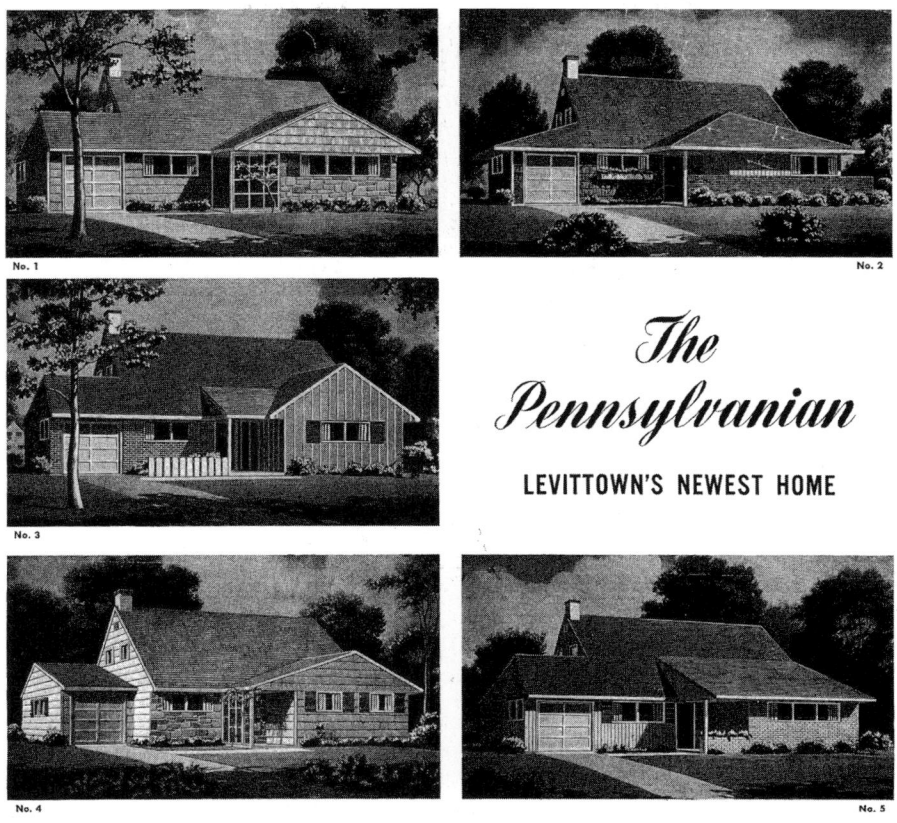

The homes of William Levitt's developments in New York, New Jersey, and Pennsylvania were the prototypes for thousands of suburban tract developments built during the 1950s and 1960s.

At the same time that opportunities were growing in some areas, rising housing costs were closing off opportunities in others. Particularly after 2000, house prices in strong market areas, including much of the Pacific coast and the Northeast, began to rise to the point where middle-class families that had historically had access to home ownership were being frozen out of the market along with lower income buyers. That trend, with its implications for local and regional economic growth, has led to a new focus on so-called "workforce housing"—housing for families whose incomes may be higher than those officially designated low or moderate-income under existing programs, but who are nonetheless unable to find affordable housing in the communities where they were raised or where they work.

Today, affordable home ownership, whether for lower income inner city families or struggling middle-class workers in high-cost areas, is a major theme, perhaps even the dominant element, in American public policy regarding affordable housing. Significant amounts of public funds are used to foster low-income home ownership. These include capital subsidies to reduce the price of the home and funds to assist first-time home buyers with their down payments and closing costs and overcome the wealth gap standing between many buyers and home ownership. At the same time, doubts have grown about some of the ways lower income home ownership has been encouraged and whether all of those efforts are actually in the best interests of the borrowers or their communities. The increasingly notorious subprime lending industry has come under particular scrutiny. Actively fostered by powerful interests in government and Wall Street, it offered mortgages designed to reach people of lower income with fewer assets and with poorer credit histories in the mid-1990s. By 2007, as foreclosures were reaching crisis levels in many of America's towns and cities, a growing number of voices questioned the means being used to increase lower income home ownership, as well as the extent to which it was appropriate to do so at all.

Home ownership has benefits, but they must be balanced against risks and costs. The following section will explore both aspects of owning a home, and how the balance of costs and benefits often shifts when low-income families become home owners. That is followed by a discussion of the strategies public agencies and private organizations use to help lower income families to become home owners and an exploration of subprime lending and the effect of its growth and subsequent collapse on lower income home ownership.

The final chapter of this book will return to this theme to explore future policy directions for affordable home ownership in the wake of the subprime debacle, including the use of emerging "shared-equity" models of ownership such as community land trusts and limited-equity cooperatives, which have the added value of preserving the benefit of the initial public subsidy used to create the dwelling unit for future generations.

THE COSTS AND BENEFITS OF HOME OWNERSHIP

The benefits of home ownership

Few people would argue against the premise that home ownership, as a general proposition, confers benefits on both the home owner and the

TABLE 9-2 POTENTIAL BENEFITS OF HOME OWNERSHIP

	INDIVIDUAL BENEFIT	COMMUNITY BENEFIT
Social	• Residential satisfaction • Psychological health and self-esteem • Physical health	• Neighborhood stability • Civic participation and social involvement • Youth behavior
Economic	• Housing quality • Neighborhood quality • Housing cost • Wealth accumulation • Access to credit	• House value appreciation

community. Those benefits, real or potential, tend to fall into three distinct categories:

- Intangible social or psychological benefits to the home owner
- Economic benefits to the owner, particularly in accumulation of personal and family wealth
- Neighborhood benefits arising from a greater share of home owners, or the conversion of households in the neighborhood from renters to owners

These benefits, which can be divided into individual benefits and community benefits, are further broken down in Table 9-2.

Studies over the past decades show that each of these areas have some foundation, although the evidence is not always as strong or as consistent as advocates of home ownership tend to claim. Research studies have found positive relationships between home ownership and resident satisfaction as well as between home ownership and physical health, but no more than ambiguous relationships between home ownership and general measures of psychological health such as self-esteem. Research studies have also provided support for the proposition that home ownership benefits communities by increasing neighborhood stability and increasing civic participation, as reflected in familiarity with local political leaders, voting, and organizational participation. It may also have an effect on positive youth behavior, including greater educational attainment, lower drop-out rates, and lower rates of teen pregnancy.

The most common reasons given for promoting home ownership, however, tend to be economic. Home ownership is widely seen as a way of simultaneously improving housing quality for the home buyer;

stabilizing, if not actually lowering, housing costs relative to the cost of renting; and, above all, as a way of building wealth and increasing family assets. As the National Association of Realtors claims, "Home owners accumulate wealth for the future while enjoying the benefits of a shelter that they have can use, improve and sell. Their home is a safe haven for investment." For most prospective home buyers, the social and neighborhood benefits are secondary; it is unlikely that those benefits would in themselves convince them to become home owners if they did not feel strongly that they would benefit economically.

This is particularly important because there is a very real question about whether some of the social and community benefits mentioned above derive from home ownership as such, or whether they are actually the product of the household's stability or the length of time they stay in the same place. While home ownership is associated with residential stability,[8] the two are not the same. A study carried out for the National Association of Realtors noted, "One consistent difficulty of many research studies is to separate the impact of home ownership from that of stable housing." Ultimately, the study concluded, "If it is in fact the case that housing stability matters more than home ownership in bringing social benefits, then the policy implication is not necessarily to promote home ownership but to assist in residential stability."[9] In that respect, although most renters remain in their homes for much shorter periods than home owners, that is not necessarily true of many affordable rental developments, which are often far more stable in their occupancy than private market rentals.

Although it is all but universally assumed that home ownership builds wealth, it is far from a sure thing—as people began to realize once again as housing prices began to fall in 2006 and 2007. Indeed, historically, housing appreciation is a highly uncertain proposition. Table 9-3, using the authoritative Case-Schiller index of house prices, illustrates the return for a home buyer in the Los Angeles metropolitan area who bought between 1987 and 1997 and sold the home after living in it for 10 years. The table shows that during most of the two decades covered by the index, a house was not a particularly good investment. Only after 2003 did the return from house price appreciation become better than alternative investments. Between 1990 and 1996, house prices declined and did not return to 1990 levels until 2000; someone buying a house in Los Angeles in 1990 and selling it at any time prior to 2000 was more likely to lose money that make it. For much of the period, a

TABLE 9-3 AVERAGE RETURN FROM 10-YEAR HOME SALES IN LOS ANGELES METROPOLITAN AREA, 1987–2007

YEAR PURCHASED	YEAR SOLD	YEAR PURCHASED INDEX	YEAR SOLD INDEX	TOTAL 10-YEAR APPRECIATION	ANNUAL APPRECIATION
1987	1997	60.81	74.82	23.0%	2.1%
1988	1998	70.83	83.96	18.5	1.7
1989	1999	92.11	93.95	2.0	<1
1990	2000	99.99	103.70	3.7	<1
1991	2001	92.83	114.12	22.9	2.1
1992	2002	90.58	126.23	39.4	3.4
1993	2003	82.05	149.65	82.4	6.2
1994	2004	76.44	193.22	152.8	9.7
1995	2005	74.78	231.59	210.1	12.0
1996	2006	73.35	270.44	268.7	13.9
1997	2007	74.82	263.36	252.0	13.4

Data is for April of each year. The index is calibrated so that January 2000 = 100

home owner might well have been better off putting his money under the mattress.

How income affects the costs and benefits of home ownership

In addition to benefits, home ownership carries costs. For lower income households, particularly those living in distressed cities and neighborhoods, the cost of home ownership can be higher, and the value of its benefits less, than for more affluent home owners. Lower income buyers can only purchase the least expensive units available within a region's housing market. These units will more often be older and subject to inadequate maintenance over the years. They are more likely to be located in distressed areas, typically in inner city neighborhoods, and have less access to jobs, poorer services, and higher crime rates. One researcher, after studying the neighborhood effects of home ownership for lower income and minority households, concluded, "Lower income buyers can purchase homes only in neighborhoods that are more distressed than the ones in which they are renting."[10]

The fact that lower income buyers have limited choices has serious consequences. Property taxes and insurance costs are typically higher, as a percentage of house value, in distressed urban areas than in their more affluent surrounding communities. Maintenance and repair costs are also likely to be high for older, poorly maintained houses, further burdening households who typically have little savings and little disposable income. Over and above the cost to buy the property, continued home ownership is likely to impose a disproportionate financial drain on a lower income home owner.

While being disproportionately burdened with the costs of home ownership, a lower income or minority owner is also less likely to gain the economic benefits of ownership. Because their incomes are lower and they are less likely to itemize their deductions, they realize fewer of the tax benefits associated with ownership,[11] while the characteristics of the neighborhoods where they can afford to buy mean that they are less likely to see their homes appreciate. A study that looked in detail at the return from the sales by low-income home owners of homes in Philadelphia, Boston, Chicago, and Denver found that when sales prices were adjusted for transaction costs and inflation, more than half of the owners lost value in the first three cities, while 41 percent lost value in Denver.[12] In the final analysis, while some lower income buyers do gain some appreciation, and a few gained spectacular windfalls recently as their neighborhoods became "hot" in the boom of the early years of the 21st century, on the whole their homes appreciate less than those of more affluent home buyers, and in many cases not at all.

If their housing costs were lower, that might compensate for the lack of appreciation. The housing costs of lower income home owners as a percentage of income, however, are considerably higher than those of more affluent owners. In 2005, roughly 70 percent of all home owners earning less than $20,000 per year spent more than 30 percent of their gross household income for housing costs—of those who had mortgages on their homes, 97 percent spent more than 30 percent of their gross income for housing.

The benefit of home ownership to lower income households is further reduced by the fact that they are at much greater risk of losing their homes and being forced back into the rental market. More than half of low-income buyers no longer own their own homes only five years later, something that is also true for African American buyers.[13] In fact, researchers have found that their shorter tenure accounts for more of the disparity in home ownership rates between White and African American households than do differences in the frequency with which they became home owners in the first place. This finding, which is fraught with important policy implications, has been largely ignored by public policy makers.

The higher cost and shorter duration of ownership reduces both the social and economic benefits associated with home ownership. The greater frequency with which home ownership is lost carries powerful negative effects, particularly when the loss is involuntary as a result of foreclosure or a forced sale. Shorter tenure reduces the likelihood that the household will realize significant appreciation from the sale of the home, while the loss of a home is not only a significant economic loss—involving the loss of cash, assets, and future credit—but also a social and psychological one, including "the emotional and physical stress of managing the foreclosure process; the psychological effects of a dramatic and public 'failure' at one of life's key milestones and simultaneous reduction in socioeconomic status; and negative effects on children in households forced to move as a result of foreclosure."[14]

The ways in which having a low income affects the benefits of home ownership are summarized in Table 9-4. These differences do not mean that there is no value to lower income home ownership. What they do mean is that if one wants to ensure that lower income families truly benefit from home ownership, that goal must be pursued with great care. The strategies employed to foster lower income home ownership must go well beyond simply putting people in houses, and must make the home ownership experience affordable and stable, rather than expensive and transitory. Over the past decade, a variety of programs and initiatives, with varying degrees of success, have been pursued to that end.

PUBLIC AND NONPROFIT STRATEGIES TO FOSTER LOWER INCOME HOME OWNERSHIP

From the end of the 19th century through the 1960s, and to a large extent even beyond then, affordable housing was largely synonymous with rental housing in the United States. This was not a function of economic conditions, but a matter of ideology; indeed, throughout this period many lower income families became home owners without benefit of governmental assistance, buying modest row houses in Philadelphia

TABLE 9-4 INCOME DISPARITIES IN THE BENEFITS OF HOME OWNERSHIP

POTENTIAL BENEFIT (FROM TABLE 9-2)	DIFFERENCE IN BENEFIT FOR LOW-INCOME HOME OWNERS
Residential satisfaction	Satisfaction may be lower because of lower satisfaction with neighborhood conditions
Psychological health and self-esteem	Effect on psychological health and self-esteem may be lower because of shorter ownership tenure, lower satisfaction with neighborhood conditions, and greater risk of negative psychological effects from difficulty making payments or foreclosure
Community benefits	Community benefits may be less because shorter spells of home ownership reduce residential stability
Physical health	Not known
Housing quality	Housing quality may be lower because homes bought by lower income buyers are more likely to be in poor condition and in need of repair
Neighborhood quality	Neighborhood quality may decline because lower income home buyers may only be able to afford to buy homes in neighborhoods of similar or lower quality than those in which they rent
Housing cost	Housing cost benefits are less because lower income buyers spend a higher percentage of income for housing costs and benefit less from tax advantages
Wealth accumulation	Wealth accumulation is less because homes bought by lower income buyers are more likely to be in neighborhoods with below-average rates of appreciation, and families are likely to remain in the home a shorter time
Access to credit	Credit access to lower income buyers is likely to be less because of higher current costs and reduced wealth accumulation, as well as greater risk of losing the home

or Baltimore or frame "shotgun" cottages in the South. Low-income housing, however, as it was generally known at that time, was seen as a thing apart. It was the product of the public or the philanthropic sector, not to be confused with the private market in which home builders, developers, and contractors operated. Today, the picture has changed significantly. Public funds are now used to build affordable homes to sell to lower income occupants and to assist lower income families to buy homes on the private market, while public and philanthropic funds are used to prepare buyers for the responsibilities of home ownership and to protect them when they find themselves at risk of foreclosure. Proponents of workforce housing are trying to break down the barriers to building homes that struggling middle-class families can afford, with or without public subsidy.

The federal government first provided public funds to help lower income families buy homes in 1968 under the Section 235 program.[15] The collapse of that program amid controversies and indictments in the mid-1970s led to years during which public officials and housing advocates looked with reservations upon subsidized home ownership. By the 1990s, however, subsidized home ownership had returned, through a host of tailored state and local efforts reflecting differences in resources, priorities, and local conditions. While the federal government provides some funds for affordable home ownership, mainly through the HOME program but also through smaller efforts such as Hope VI and the short-lived Homeownership Zone program, these funds are widely supplemented with money from state and local trust funds, tax increment financing, and other local resources, and used in ways determined by local officials, developers, and CDCs.

Subsidizing affordable home ownership

There are two distinct ways in which the public sector subsidizes affordable home ownership. Some programs use public funds to subsidize the cost of building new homes, which are then sold at a reduced price to income-qualified buyers; others use funds to enable similarly income-qualified buyers to purchase homes on the private market by helping buyers with down payments and closing costs, or by filling the gap between what the house costs and what buyers can afford.

Subsidizing new construction or gut rehabilitation of vacant houses for affordable home ownership tends to be very expensive, particularly if the target households are lower income families earning less than 80 percent of the area median income. If the cost of building a new house is $250,000 and the maximum income for an eligible household is $40,000, and the rule of thumb is applied that the family can afford a house priced at three times their income, that means that $130,000 in public funds will be needed to subsidize that house. That is a huge sum in light of the limited funds that a town or city has to spend on affordable housing. As a result, subsidized home ownership construction programs tend to be small in scale, targeted to people at the upper reaches of the low-income range or to moderate-income households with incomes between 80 and 120 percent of the area median income. Wherever possible, cities try to use "off-the-books" subsidies such as tax abatements or discounted land sales to reduce the size of the direct, visible cash outlay needed.

The New Homes for Chicago program operated by the city of Chicago is a good example. Under this program, the city combines a variety of different forms of assistance to the developer of the houses, including sale of vacant lots for $1, waiver of fees, city-provided site improvements, state tax credits to project donors,[16] and state energy efficiency assistance to lower the cost of the unit. On top of that, the city provides each buyer with a capital subsidy that can vary from $10,000 to $80,000 depending on the buyer's income, the location of the property, and whether it is a one- or a two-family house, along with access to below-market mortgage financing and tax benefits. It would be difficult to disentangle and price out all of the elements in Chicago's subsidy program, but the total public cost for each house is probably between $150,000 and $200,000.

Subsidizing the construction of new houses to be purpose-built for affordable home ownership, particularly when looked at in the context of the cost of existing houses on the private market, is not always an appropriate or cost-effective use of public funds. Where large numbers of existing houses are priced below replacement cost, which is typical of many cities in the Northeast and Midwest, it is usually preferable to help families buy houses on the private market, except where building new houses serves a separate purpose by revitalizing a block or neighborhood or stimulating a neighborhood housing market. Even where existing houses are more expensive, it may still be more cost-effective to help families buy houses on the private market, unless the market is so tight that few homes are available or if developers or CDCs can build new houses for less than the cost of existing homes on the private market.

State and local governments help low- and moderate-income households buy homes on the private market through a variety of mechanisms. Most widely known are programs that provide buyers with down payment or closing cost assistance, an activity which consumes a significant amount of the federal funding available for affordable housing. The American Dream Down Payment Initiative, enacted late in 2003, provides block grants to states and selected cities[17] to provide assistance to first-time home buyers for down payments, closing costs, or rehabilitation expenses of $10,000 or six percent of the house price, whichever is greater. Its scope is modest, both for the individual home buyer and overall. The FY 2007 appropriation for the program was $24.75 million. At the rate of $10,000 for each home buyer, this means only 2,475 home

Infill housing for affordable home ownership developed by the Jamaica Plain Neighborhood Development Corporation in Boston, designed by The Narrow Gate Architecture.

The Narrow Gate Architecture

buyers across the United States can receive assistance. That is less than one-sixth of one percent of the low-income families buying homes that year. States and cities spend much more than that to help home buyers, using federal HOME funds as well as their own money. Since the HOME program's inception in 1990, nearly a third of all the households that have benefited from that program have been home buyers receiving down payment or related assistance.

This emphasis on down payment assistance raises the question of whether the barrier to lower income home ownership is the cost of the house or the access to enough cash to cover the transaction costs associated with buying the house. Historically, lack of cash has been an impediment. For many years, banks required down payments of at least 20 percent.[18] Although private mortgage insurance (PMI) that enabled buyers to reduce their down payments became widely available in the 1960s, even with PMI a buyer might still have to come up with a five percent down payment as well as closing costs that could add as much as two or three percent. For low-income home buyers without well-to-do parents or in-laws, these costs could be prohibitive. Since the 1990s, however, an increasing number of mortgage programs, created by banks as a result of pressure under the Community Reinvestment Act or offered through the subprime mortgage market, were available with smaller down payments or none at all, often allowing buyers to roll even their closing costs into the mortgage.

A second question that arises is whether, even if lack of down payment money is an impediment for some households, reducing down payments below some threshold is really a good idea as a matter of public policy. One national down payment assistance program boasts: "If you are a qualified home buyer using an eligible loan program, such as an FHA loan, you may be able to move into your new home with zero cash out of pocket!"[19] This practice may not do these buyers a service. There is considerable evidence that foreclosures are significantly higher among home buyers who make no down payment, whether because of the lack of a financial stake or psychological commitment to the property, or the likelihood that such buyers are simply less likely to have the resources to deal with the uncertainties of home ownership. The haste of many policy makers to promote home ownership runs the risk of pushing people into situations that in the end work to their disadvantage.

Public officials find down payment assistance programs such as the American Dream Down Payment Initiative attractive because they are very inexpensive and offer exceptional opportunities both to generate impressive numbers and create photo-ops more than nearly any other kind of housing assistance. In the end, however, they put people into houses without necessarily addressing either the affordability or stability issues that plague lower income home owners. Programs that go at least some way to filling the affordability gap are likely to make more of a difference, but the more they do so, the more expensive they are. Los Angeles offers a Low Income Purchase Assistance Program, under which a lower income first-time home buyer can receive a deferred loan of up to $125,000 toward the purchase of a home in the city. The magnitude of the loan reflects the reality that the median priced house in Los Angeles today costs roughly double what a median income household can afford. Not surprisingly, the program is over-subscribed and maintains an extensive waiting list.

Lowering affordable housing costs by reducing barriers[20]

As housing prices have skyrocketed in many of America's metropolitan areas, growing numbers of families have been priced out of home ownership. In the Boston area, for example, the median house price is $345,000, for which a family needs an income of over $120,000 to afford. Yet the average social worker earns $47,000 per year and the average librarian $58,000. In Los Angeles, the median house price at the beginning of 2007 was $525,000, although it has dropped sharply since then.[21] In many of these areas, however, the cost of housing is being driven up not only by market demand pressures, but also by constraints on housing production, in particular the limited availability of land for development and regulatory barriers such as exclusionary zoning or high impact fees.

Removing regulatory barriers and increasing land supply will not in themselves reduce the price of housing to where it becomes affordable to low-income families. If, however, the households who are targeted for assistance are moderate-income families, those earning 80 to 120 percent of area median income—which can mean families earning up to $100,000 or more in many high-cost market areas—the picture becomes a different one. If it were possible to build modest-sized houses efficiently in such areas, with manageable land costs, the price of housing could be brought down so that many such families could afford to buy. Furthermore, if the price of housing is brought down enough, then relatively inexpensive forms of financial assistance, such as tax abatements or lower interest mortgages, might further expand the range of families to whom the housing would be affordable.

In a number of cases public land has been made available for development subject to a condition that it include a percentage of affordable housing, such as the former site of Stapleton Airport in Denver, where developers were required to build 10 percent of the units as moderately priced housing. King County, Washington, has adopted a broader policy that prioritizes suitable surplus county-owned land to be sold or leased for affordable housing. Where public land is unavailable or in short supply, rezoning land for higher density development can have an impact on housing costs, particularly where high costs stem at least in part from an inadequate supply of land to meet market demand. To be most effective, the higher density should be for the purpose of providing affordable housing, as in the Santa Cruz, California, ordinance mentioned earlier, or should require a affordable set-aside under an inclusionary ordinance. Increasing land availability and rezoning, particularly use of inclusionary zoning strategies, can be further leveraged with other steps that reduce costs, such as expedited or "fast track" permitting, reduction in impact fees or other charges such as utility hookup fees, and elimination of cost-generating elements in zoning and site plan ordinances. When a community is serious about trying to increase the affordability of its housing stock, local planners have a major responsibility in figuring out how to use these tools in ways that are consistent with the community's overall goals without placing undue burdens on other developments or on the taxpayers.

Austin's S.M.A.R.T. Housing Initiative uses expedited reviews and fee waivers to stimulate the production of affordable homes in transit-oriented (thus the S.M.A.R.T. acronym) locations that also meet Austin's green building standards. Developers of qualifying projects receive an expedited review that averages about half the time of conventional projects, as well as waivers of the city's capital recovery fee, development review and inspection fee, and certain construction inspection fees. They typically save $600 per unit for multifamily homes and $2,000 per single-family home from the fee waivers, as well as reduced carrying costs from the expedited review process.

Massachusetts adopted a creative approach in 2004 when the legislature passed Chapter 40R, which provides incentives for towns to create "smart growth zoning districts," rezoning land for as of right development of higher density housing.[22] Under Chapter 40R, towns that change their zoning to create smart growth zoning districts in suitable locations, such as areas near transit stations or located close to existing centers, receive a first incentive payment from the state for rezoning the land and another after building permits are issued. Under companion legislation passed the following year, local school districts get supplementary aid to the extent that the higher density development increases the number of schoolchildren in the district. In 2007, Connecticut enacted legislation closely modeled on the Massachusetts law.

Ultimately, though, most efforts to remove regulatory barriers, particularly in highly regulated and heavily developed settings such as Massachusetts or Connecticut, will not in themselves lead to dramatic change in the affordability of housing. That is one reason the Massachusetts law specifically requires that 20 percent of all of the housing units built in a smart growth zoning district be priced so that they are affordable to households earning less than 80 percent of the area median income. In addition to using inclusionary ordinances, many communities provide various forms of financial assistance to further increase affordability once land availability measures or zoning changes bring the cost of the units within striking distance of the target population. These are rarely direct cash subsidies, but usually take the form of the sort of "off-the-books" assistance described earlier, or involve short-term forms of assistance such predevelopment or acquisition loans that are repaid as the development moves forward.

In some communities, employers have provided financial support to their workers through employer-assisted housing programs. Under the REACH Illinois (Regional Employer Assisted Collaboration for Housing–Illinois) program enacted in 2000, the state of Illinois provides tax credits to participating employers, and match employer contributions up to $5,000 when the beneficiary is a low-income household earning 80 percent or less of the area median. Yale University provides a grant of up to $30,000 for its employees to buy homes in target neighborhoods in the city of New Haven, a program that both increases home ownership and helps revitalize neighborhoods. Eighty percent of the participants are first-time buyers, and 50 percent are members of minority groups.[23]

Tax abatements, particularly in towns with high property tax rates, can be an effective way to reduce the monthly carrying cost of a home and make it more affordable. A reduction of $3,000 per year in annual property taxes can allow a home buyer at a given income level to afford as much as $40,000 more in the price of the house. The danger of tax abatement, aside from the loss of local government revenues, is the shock when it ends and full taxes suddenly become due after five, 10, or 12 years. Some tax abatement programs provide for a gradual phase-in of full taxes over a number of years, so that home owners are not confronted with a sudden jump in their housing costs.

In the final analysis, removal of barriers is more of a starting point for a workforce housing strategy than a strategy in itself. By increasing production, however, and at least marginally reducing the cost of the units, it creates a framework in which limited forms of assistance such as tax abatements and low-interest mortgages can often make up the difference and provide housing for at least some struggling working families, if not those of very low income.

Counseling and education programs

Home ownership education and counseling (HEC) programs play an important role in public and nonprofit programs to foster lower income home ownership. While most of these programs exist to help people become more successful home buyers and owners in the first place, more and more programs are being set up to help people deal with the vicissitudes of home ownership and avoid foreclosure, particularly since the explosion in subprime foreclosures since 2007.

The purpose of prepurchase education and counseling before the family has made a commitment to buy a home is primarily to help the prospective buyer make an informed, rational decision and also to provide the buyer skills and knowledge so they will be able to remain in and properly maintain a home they do buy. It is predicated on the assumption that prospective home buyers who have had little or no prior family experience with home ownership and limited formal education and financial resources will benefit from assistance as they take this important step in their lives. There is research evidence that, if properly carried out, counseling does make a difference.[24]

Although local groups had been advising prospective home buyers for decades, HEC became part of the national housing scene during the 1970s, when the federal government began to provide funds for public and nonprofit counseling agencies and helped create the Neighborhood Reinvestment Corporation and its network of local Neighborhood Housing Services programs. Further impetus for counseling programs emerged from the Community Reinvestment Act and from special mortgage programs created in the 1990s by Fannie Mae and Freddie Mac, which required prepurchase counseling as a condition of eligibility. The

Neighborhood Reinvestment Corporation, since renamed NeighborWorks America, has continued to play a major role in this area, and in recent years has led an effort to develop national industry standards for HEC, a matter of considerable importance in light of the great variation in the quality of counseling offered by different practitioners.

Potential home buyers participate in a HEC program over the course of a number of weeks or months that ideally covers the following topics:

- Assessing home ownership readiness
- Budgeting and credit
- Financing a home
- Shopping for a home
- Maintaining a home and finances

In addition to classroom instruction, it includes one-on-one counseling sessions, during the course of which the counselor reviews the prospective buyer's financial information, and, if appropriate, helps to develop a formal "action plan" for buying a home.

NeighborWorks America and other nonprofit counseling providers consider it essential for the counseling to take place in person, and at least in part on a one-on-one basis. Personalized counseling can be expensive, however, and during the 1990s, as lenders expanded mortgage programs for underserved populations, many of them began to use a shorthand approach to meeting counseling requirements. The prospective buyer would receive a workbook, read it through at home, and then take a short quiz over the telephone. Assuming the buyer passed the quiz, she was certified as having received counseling, a certification that met the requirements of the Fannie Mae and Freddie Mac programs, as well as those of most of the CRA lending programs.

It is doubtful that this type of experience significantly improves the quality of most buyers' decisions, and research has shown that, in contrast to more intensive in-person counseling, it has no measurable impact on the likelihood of future default or foreclosure. Moreover, it typically comes after the would-be buyer has already made the decision to buy rather than before, when counseling is most critical. NeighborWorks America points out that less than one out of five families counseled by their affiliates actually becomes a home owner. They believe that discouraging unsuited people from buying is as important a function of counseling as helping people buy a house that is appropriate to their needs and resources.

HEC, properly conducted, can improve the outcomes of the home-buying decision for many lower income families. At the same time, it is not a panacea. Low-income home buyers are inherently vulnerable to financial and other stresses. As a result, many counseling agencies have begun to provide postpurchase counseling as part of an ongoing support system for lower income home owners and, particularly during the past two years, have turned to providing foreclosure prevention counseling in light of the surge in demand resulting from the subprime lending crisis. NeighborWorks America has redirected much of its energy toward efforts to mitigate the impacts of foreclosures by setting up the National Center for Foreclosure Solutions to coordinate local efforts to address the crisis. At the end of 2007, it received a special $180 million congressional appropriation to provide counseling assistance to prevent foreclosure, help home owners refinance, or resolve the situation in some other beneficial manner for the home owner.

Elsewhere, public agencies have established emergency assistance programs to help home owners in temporary financial difficulty. Pennsylvania's Homeowners Emergency Mortgage Assistance Program, or HEMAP, is a notable example. Under HEMAP, a home owner is eligible to receive a loan of up to $60,000 or 24 months of mortgage payments, whichever comes first. Since its enactment in 1983, HEMAP has helped more than 38,000 of the state's home owners avoid foreclosure. Such assistance can be a godsend to those who are experiencing temporary difficulties that can right themselves over time. It does not address, however, the growing problem of home owners holding subprime mortgages that they literally cannot afford to carry. Addressing that issue, if it is to be addressed at all, will require more far-reaching measures.

LOW-INCOME HOME OWNERSHIP AND THE SUBPRIME MELTDOWN

During 2006, observers noticed a disturbing increase in the number of new mortgage loan defaults and foreclosure filings. By 2007, the growth in defaults and foreclosures had become a tidal wave, nearly doubling from 2006 and sweeping across America's towns and cities; 2008 was even worse than 2007, as house prices and sales activity continued to drop. Nationally, the home ownership rate is slipping, while more than a million American families have already lost their homes to foreclosure. Towns and cities across the country are seeing empty, boarded-up houses appear on once-stable neighborhood streets.

This crisis did not emerge out of nowhere. It is the outcome, in retrospect all but inevitable, of a series of policy choices and private decisions that lend to the creation of what is known as the subprime lending industry. That industry, however, came about as a result of a series of changes in the financial world that came together during the 1990s. For that reason, it is appropriate to begin with a brief overview of how the crisis came into being.

The rise and fall of the subprime lending industry

The idea behind subprime lending is a simple one. Traditionally, lenders have required good credit before providing home buyers with mortgages, which were typically provided at a single or "prime" interest rate, varying slightly depending on the loan term or other conditions. The subprime lending industry emerged to provide loans to borrowers with poor credit who would not qualify for prime loans. Based on the proposition that higher risks are associated with those borrowers, subprime loans carry higher interest rates than loans in the prime market. This industry would not have emerged, however, were it not for dramatic changes in the financial world that uncoupled mortgage-making from the traditional banking sector, and turned it into a worldwide investment opportunity for high-net-worth individuals and institutions.

A mortgage broker, who might have few assets other than an office and a bank of telephones, made the mortgages on behalf of a financial institution that provided the funds. That institution then packaged many mortgages together, and sold them to an investment banking firm like Bear Stearns or Lehman Brothers, which bundled them into a marketable security, and sold them to investors.[25] The investment banker also hired a firm, known as a servicer, to manage the mortgage pool for the investors.

In theory, this seemed to be a rational system. In practice, there was a great deal wrong with it. The notion that instead of avoiding risk one could simply increase the cost on the basis of the risk involved, coupled with the seemingly insatiable demand for high-yield investment paper from investors around the world, set off a race among mortgage brokers and lenders to make the greatest number of mortgages at the highest possible interest rates. This was aided and abetted by lender policies called Yield Spread Premiums, which gave brokers bigger commissions for making higher interest, riskier loans.

There were, however, only a limited number of home buyers with poor credit who could truly afford these loans. As a result, brokers and lenders began to come up with increasingly ingenious ways to make more loans by qualifying more buyers, particularly lower income borrowers. One way was by offering adjustable rate mortgages (ARMs) with "exploding" interest rates, which started out with a low introductory or teaser rate that skyrocketed, usually after two years. Another was by offering so-called "no-doc" loans, where in return for not requiring the borrower to document her income or other obligations, a lender would give her a mortgage at an even higher interest rate. Other "exotic" mortgages included negative amortization mortgages and mortgages with balloons at the end of 10 or 15 years. All of them carried interest rates far above what conventional lenders were charging customers with better credit. As time went on, more and more of the subprime loans were either ARMs, no-doc loans, or other exotic loans.

A second approach to generating more business was to get existing home owners, of whom there were many more than new buyers, to refinance. Aggressively marketing their products to unsophisticated elderly or lower income home owners in urban areas, subprime lenders made millions of refinancing loans. Some subprime lenders steered certain borrowers, often African American or Latino families, into high-cost mortgages when they could have qualified for less expensive loans. More than two-thirds of all subprime mortgages are refinancings rather than home purchase loans.

Under the guise of "democratizing" credit, subprime lenders saddled millions of lower income home owners and home buyers with loans that sooner or later they would be unable to repay. As long as house prices in most parts of the United States kept rising steadily, as was the case through 2005, the effects of these loans seemed manageable. As house prices rose, most borrowers gained enough equity so that if they were unable to make their loan payments, they could sell the house or refinance. Meanwhile, the number of subprime loan originations kept growing, until by 2006 they represented more than one out of every four new mortgage loans.

In 2006, when the housing market bubble began to burst in one metropolitan area after another, more than seven million home owners were holding subprime mortgages. Millions of these were ARMs, whose low introductory interest rates were beginning to reset to much higher rates that many borrowers could not afford to pay. With house prices falling, they could no longer extricate themselves from unaffordable loans. The resulting foreclosure wave was all but inevitable.

While many factors contributed to the foreclosure crisis, including abusive or fraudulent behavior by some mortgage brokers, and deceptive or irresponsible behavior by some borrowers, the brief discussion above should make it clear that the roots of the problem lie not in a handful of bad apples, but in the subprime industry itself, and the internal dynamic of that industry that pushed everyone involved to make ever-riskier mortgages at ever-higher interest rates. When thinking about how to address the crisis, it is important to bear that point in mind.

The impact of the foreclosure crisis

The effect of the subprime foreclosure crisis has sent ripples throughout the world economy. As foreclosures have risen and the housing market declines, hundreds of mortgage brokers and lenders have gone into bankruptcy. The survivors are tightening credit, further pushing the housing market downward and affecting credit markets worldwide. The greatest and most devastating impacts of the crisis, however, are not on the international bankers, hedge funds, and mortgage lenders. They are the impacts on the home owners who borrowed from subprime lenders, and on the neighborhoods where those home owners live, or used to live.

The statistics are daunting. In 2006, there were 1.2 million foreclosure filings across the United States; that number increased to 2.2 million filings on 1.3 million properties in 2007.[26] The great majority of foreclosure filings lead to foreclosures. These filings are not only concentrated in the subprime market generally, but in subprime ARMs in particular. In the third quarter of 2007 alone, foreclosures were filed against almost one in 20 outstanding subprime ARM mortgages. The Center for Responsible Lending estimated at the end of 2006 that 2.2 million families have lost, or will lose, their homes to foreclosure of subprime mortgages made between 1998 and 2006. Over one million subprime mortgages are currently in default.

The foreclosure crisis is heavily concentrated among low- and moderate-income households and people of color—African Americans and Latinos—and in those urban neighborhoods and modest suburbs where struggling working class families were most likely to own homes or buy them. In the Cleveland suburb of Maple Heights, a town of modest postwar bungalows and Cape Cods, nearly one out of every 10 houses has been seized by lenders since the beginning of 2006.[27]

Almost from the beginning, subprime lenders targeted minority and lower income communities for their products. In 2006, more than half of all the mortgages made to African Americans and 40 percent of the mortgages made to Latinos were subprime, compared to only 22 percent of the mortgages made to non-Latino White borrowers. In many heavily minority urban neighborhoods, 60 to 70 percent of the mortgage loans—including refinancings—in recent years have been subprime loans. This lending pattern may be reflected in the fact that home ownership in the nation's African American population has been dropping steadily since 2004, when it peaked at just under 50 percent of all African American households. By the third quarter of 2007, that number had dropped to less than 47 percent.[28]

The effects of foreclosure on the individuals and families who lose their homes can be shattering, but the potential impact on neighborhoods may be as great a problem. The impact of foreclosures on neighborhoods or small towns such as Maple Heights is a function the number of foreclosures as a share of total housing in the area, and how the foreclosure affects the property. When a foreclosure takes place in a wealthy suburb, the creditor—recognizing the value of the property—makes sure that the property is well maintained and quickly resold, usually to a new home owner. As a result, the foreclosure is likely to have little impact on the neighbors or on the community as a whole.

The situation can be very different in a neighborhood of modest single-family houses in Cleveland or Philadelphia. In such neighborhoods, housing demand is limited. Even before foreclosures became a major problem, it was often difficult to sell houses coming on the market through normal turnover in those neighborhoods. When large numbers of houses are foreclosed, there may not be enough market demand to absorb them. In this situation the neighborhood impact is likely to be dire. The property will have little value, and is more likely to be abandoned—or at best, bought by a speculator—than sold to a new home buyer. The creditor, usually the servicer who represents the investors, will have little interest in spending money to foreclose and maintain the property.

Where foreclosures lead to abandonment, they soon destabilize the neighborhood around them. Abandoned properties add to crime, fire hazards, and environmental health risk, as well as diminishing the property values of surrounding houses. Even a single abandoned house on a block, as a Philadelphia study found, can reduce the value of nearly all the other properties on the block by 15 percent.[29] In addition to devaluing the neighborhood, the increase in abandoned properties places growing demands on services, which financially strapped older cities are hard-pressed to provide.

The intimate relationship between foreclosures and abandonment in inner city areas is confirmed by a growing body of accounts. Describing Cleveland's Slavic Village neighborhood, Cuyahoga County Treasurer Jim Rokakis writes, "The neighborhood wasn't always a haven for criminals—not until hundreds of foreclosures destabilized the community. Houses (800 at last count) and then entire streets were abandoned. Crime increased as vacant properties offered shelter to people who had a reason to hide." At some point, the cumulative effect of abandonment can make the neighborhood real estate market effectively grind to a halt. As Rokakis comments about the home owners in Slavic Village, "Even if they wanted to sell their homes, they wouldn't be able to find buyers. Who wants to live in a sea of foreclosures?"[30] A real estate agent recently quoted in an article on a middle-class Detroit neighborhood impacted by subprime foreclosures says, "Nobody's going to want to buy into a neighborhood with 20 percent foreclosures. You end up with no neighborhood."[31]

It is these neighborhoods, most often found in America's older cities and their inner-ring suburbs, that represent ground zero in the foreclosure crisis. They are not, for the most part, the most severely distressed neighborhoods of those cities and suburbs. Instead, they are typically areas a notch higher on the socioeconomic scale, the neighborhoods that during the past decade thousands of striving lower income families have seen as the next step up, the place where they could find a house they could afford and begin their pursuit of the American Dream.

What is to be done?

A crisis of this magnitude has many different dimensions and many points of attack. From the standpoint of those faced with having to deal with it, either at the local or state level, it requires them to focus on three separate issues:

- Protecting the interests of households already in the foreclosure process or at risk of future foreclosure
- Preserving the stability of neighborhoods and communities potentially impacted by foreclosures
- Eliminating the practices that led to the current crisis, in order to prevent a future recurrence of the crisis, including greater regulation of the mortgage brokerage industry

Each of these issues can be addressed through any number of different approaches, although the painful reality is that, notwithstanding the best efforts of state and local government and as local nonprofit and philanthropic organizations, many home owners and their neighborhoods will suffer badly before the crisis runs its course.

Housing agencies are trying to protect households who are in the foreclosure process by giving them access to foreclosure counseling, helping them to refinance their mortgages, or offering them short-term emergency assistance, similar to Pennsylvania's HEMAP program. In California, Gov. Arnold Schwarzenegger has "jawboned" a number of major servicers into agreeing to modify many outstanding loans, while at the national level, the Bush administration has negotiated an agreement under which interest rates on some borrowers' outstanding ARMs will be frozen for up to five years. HR 3221, the Housing and Economic Recovery Act of 2008, which was passed by Congress and reluctantly signed by President Bush in July of that year, establishes a major program for refinancing problem loans through the Federal Housing Administration. Its success depends on cooperation by lenders and servicers, however, and it is uncertain whether that cooperation will indeed be forthcoming.

It is equally important to make sure subprime industry practices do not make a comeback now that we clearly understand how destructive they are. While brokers and lenders have for the moment cut back markedly on the number of questionable mortgages they make, memories are short in the financial world. Teaser rates, yield spread premiums, no-doc loans, and other loans made without consideration of the borrower's ability to repay should simply be banned as a matter of fairness and common sense. The Federal Reserve System, which regulates national banks, has proposed rules to address some of these practices, while a number of states, including Massachusetts, Ohio, and North Carolina, have already taken action in this direction. State action is as necessary as federal action, since mortgage brokers are not subject to federal regulation.

Even more far-reaching measures may be needed to address the ways foreclosures are creating, in Barry Zigas's words, "a tidal wave of abandoned homes, particularly concentrated in minority and low- and moderate-income neighborhoods." Zigas, among others, has called for federal action along the lines of the Depression-era Home Owners' Loan Corporation, which had a dramatic impact on halting the wave of foreclosures that threatened to engulf the United States in the 1930s, or the Resolution Trust Corporation, that was created to resolve the Savings and Loan crisis of the late 1980s.[32] In the meantime, states, communities, and private nonprofit organizations are exploring local solutions. Without access to large capital resources, however, and without vehicles capable of taking title to and recycling properties in an efficient, timely fashion, a solution will be hard to find.

Finally, a larger issue remains: how to foster lower income and minority home ownership in a way that will be both more effective and more ethical than the subprime market. Many people who gained no direct benefit from the subprime industry gave it their support because they believed that it was opening the doors to greater home ownership by people who had been barred from achieving that dream. In reality, it has accomplished the opposite. That does not mean the goal is not worth pursuing. Once the urgency of the crisis has abated, new and creative approaches to lower income home ownership could be a fruitful field for state policy intervention. This subject will be explored further in the closing chapter of this book.

NOTES

1. Retsinas, Nicolas P., and Eric S. Belsky. 2002. "Examining the Unexamined Goal." p. 3 in *Low-Income Homeownership*, ed. Nicolas P. Retsinas and Eric S. Belsky. Cambridge, Mass.: Joint Center for Housing Studies and Washington D.C.: Brookings Institution Press.
2. Fourteen of the 25 countries in the European Community have home ownership rates that are higher than the current U.S. rate of 68 percent, including countries as diverse as Estonia, Hungary, Spain, Italy, and the United Kingdom.
3. Retsinas and Belsky, "Examining the Unexamined Goal," 2.
4. Bourassa, Steven C., and William G. Grigsby. 2005. "Income Tax Concessions for Owner-Occupied Housing." *Housing Policy Debate* 11(3): 525.
5. Schlesinger, Arthur C. 1958. *The Coming of the New Deal*. Boston: Houghton Mifflin Co., 298. For a detailed description of the work of the HOLC, see Pollock, Alex J. 2007. *Crisis Intervention in Housing Finance: The Home Owners' Loan Corporation*. Washington, D.C.: American Enterprise Institute for Public Policy.
6. Strictly speaking, this increase covers the years 1940 to 1950; although there is no solid data for the number of home owners between census years, observers agree that there was little or no net increase in home ownership during the war years.
7. Retsinas and Belsky, "Examining the Unexamined Goal," 4.
8. As of 2000, the median length of residence for home owners in the United States was nine years, compared to two years for renters. Between 2002 and 2003, only 7.4 percent of owner-occupants changed their place of residence, compared to nearly one-third of renters.
9. National Association of Realtors. 2006. *Social Benefits of Homeownership and Stable Housing*. Washington, D.C.: National Association of Realtors Research Division.
10. Van Zandt, Shannon. 2007. "Racial/Ethnic Differences in Housing Outcomes for First-Time, Low-Income Home Buyers: Findings From a National Homeownership Education Program." *Housing Policy Debate* 18(2).

11. Even if they do itemize, their benefits will be less because their marginal tax rates are lower than those of more affluent households.
12. Belsky, Eric S., and Mark Duda. 2002. "Asset Appreciation, Timing of Purchases and Sales, and Returns to Low-Income Homeownership." In *Low-Income Homeownership*, ed. Retsinas and Belsky.
13. Reid, Caroline Katz. 2004. *Achieving the American Dream: A Longitudinal Analysis of the Homeownership Experiences of Low-Income Households*. Dissertation Discussion Paper, University of Washington, and Donald R. Haurin and Stuart S. Rosenthal. 2004. *The Sustainability of Homeownership: Factors Affecting the Duration of Homeownership and Rental Spells*. Washington, D.C.: U.S. Department of Housing and Urban Development.
14. Apgar, William C., Mark Duda, and Rochelle Nawrocki Gorey. 2005. *The Municipal Cost of Foreclosures: A Chicago Case Study*. Minneapolis: Homeownership Preservation Foundation.
15. A similar program was established at the same time for rural areas by the Department of Agriculture, through that department's Farmers Home Administration (now renamed the Rural Housing Service), known as the Section 502 Single Family Direct Loan Program. Largely scandal-free, in contrast to the Section 235 program, it currently assists about 550,000 households.
16. Illinois offers a state income tax credit to individuals and corporations who donate funds to nonprofit developers to build affordable housing.
17. Eligible cities are those cities that are participating jurisdictions under the HOME program *and* have a population greater than 150,000.
18. Reflecting the fallout from both the collapse of the housing bubble and the credit crunch triggered by the subprime mortgage crisis, by 2008 many mortgage lenders were again demanding 20 percent down payments. Moreover, providers of private mortgage insurance "have already flagged nearly a quarter of the nation's ZIP codes where they refuse to insure some home loans." "Insurers Tighten Reins on Risky Loans." 2008. *The Star-Ledger*, March 21.
19. From the Nehemiah Program website. Available at http://www.getdownpayment.com/buyers.
20. A detailed guidebook to strategies that can be used to expand workforce housing opportunities, *Increasing the Availability of Affordable Homes: An Analysis of High-Impact State and Local Solutions* is available from Homes for Working Families. Homes for Working Families is a national coalition led by financial and development interests that promotes state and local efforts to increase housing for households earning between 60 and 120 percent of the area median income.
21. This data comes from Homes for Working Families.
22. To qualify as a "smart growth zoning district," the zoning must provide for a minimum density of eight units per acre for single-family houses, 12 units per acre for two- and three-family houses, and 20 units per acre for multifamily housing.
23. The program at present provides an initial grant of $5,000 and additional annual grants of $2,500 for the next 10 years, as long as the buyer remains in the home. Since the inception of the program in 1994, the university has committed $21 million to 835 home buyers. See http://www.yale.edu/hronline/hbuyer.
24. See Hirad, Abdighani, and Peter M. Zorn. 2002. "Prepurchase Homeownership Counseling: A Little Knowledge is a Good Thing." In *Low-Income Homeownership*, ed. Retsinas and Belsky.
25. A critical group of players in this scheme were Standard & Poors and Moody's, the supposedly independent agencies that issue credit rating for Wall Street securities.

They developed complicated models to justify giving these securities high-level credit ratings, thereby making them marketable to a wide range of investors, including pension funds and public bodies. Since the collapse of these securities, the firms' methods, as well as the fact that they gained substantial fees from the issuers of the securities, has come under considerable scrutiny.

26. RealtyTrac. "U.S. Foreclosure Activity Up 75 Percent in 2007." Press Release, January 29, 2008.
27. Schwartz, Nelson D. 2007. "Can the Mortgage Crisis Swallow a Town?" The *New York Times*, September 2.
28. The overall home ownership rate also declined, but by a smaller extent, from 69.2 percent to 68.2 percent. Although this seems modest, this drop meant that nationally the total number of home owner households dropped by nearly 500,000 between the third quarter of 2006 and the third quarter of 2007.
29. Temple University Center for Public Policy and Eastern Philadelphia Organizing Project. 2001. *Blight-Free Philadelphia: A Public-Private Strategy to Create and Enhance Neighborhood Value*. Philadelphia: Temple University Center for Public Policy.
30. Rokakis, Jim. 2007. "The Shadow of Debt: Slavic Village is Fast Becoming a Ghost Town. It's Not Alone." *Washington Post*, September 30.
31. Whitehouse, Mark. 2007. "Subprime Aftermath: Losing the Family Home." *Wall Street Journal*, May 30.
32. Zigas, Barry. 2007. "Where the Ball is Going to Be." Blog post, December 8. Zigas has been both a senior vice president at Fannie Mae and the executive director of the National Low Income Housing Coalition. Available at http://www.zigasassocates.com/blog/be_where_the_ball_is_going_to_be.

CHAPTER

10

Preserving Affordable Housing

PRESERVATION: A CRITICAL ISSUE

The focus of most of this book is on creating affordable housing, but making sure that affordable housing, once built, remains affordable and continues to serve the people for whom it was initially intended is as important and as complicated an issue as building it. Preservation has two distinct dimensions: how to keep from losing the affordable housing that has already been built, and how to make sure, going forward, that future affordable housing remains affordable.

The issue is far less a question of physical preservation than an organizational or financial one. Housing is an exceptionally durable product. Houses built hundreds of years ago are still in use throughout the world. Seventy percent of all of the American homes and apartments built before 1960 were still in use in 2006. Properly maintained, most of those housing units could still be accommodating families and individuals 50 years from now. While it is important that affordable housing—including public housing projects built from the 1930s on—be preserved physically through proper maintenance and repair, a far more complicated issue is preserving affordable housing *as affordable housing*, keeping units affordable to the households for whom few alternatives exist in the private market.

That this is a problem is a reflection of the way in which subsidized housing has been developed in the United States since the 1960s. Public housing was developed and owned by public entities whose mission was the ownership and operation of housing for low-income families and individuals; as such, it was assumed that the properties they owned would stay low-income housing indefinitely. The units that are still standing are still affordable housing today. From the 1960s on, subsidized housing has been built and owned by private entities, in most cases for-profit developers. Instead of the government paying the cost of the projects through grants, as had been the case with the public housing program, nearly 1.5 million units in new projects under both Section 236 and Section 8 were financed with a combination of subsidy contracts and mortgages, written for terms varying from 20 to 40 years. Once the mortgage was paid off or prepaid, the use restrictions on the property expired, and the owner's obligation to maintain the development as affordable housing was at an end. The owner was free to reset rents to market rates or convert the development to condominiums.

Since the late 1980s, the potential loss of well over a million existing affordable rental housing units created under the Section 236 and Section 8 programs has been a major issue across the United States. As will be discussed further below, efforts to hold onto this housing have led to a variety of actions by Congress, by the Department of Housing and Urban Development, and by a wide range of state and local actors. Even after 20 years of effort, however, the issue is far from being resolved. In the meantime, the same issue has arisen for state-funded affordable housing developments, units created through inclusionary housing, and the first generation of developments built under the Low Income Housing Tax Credit, which required that units remain affordable for no more than 15 years.

The importance of preservation is brought home by two considerations. First, relatively little new housing for lower income families is being created; second, much of the existing affordable housing is being removed. As Michael Stegman writes, "Between 1976 and 1980, the nation's supply of low-income units with rent restrictions running 20 years or more increased by more than 18 percent (390,000 units). Just between 1995 and 1999, however, the inventory declined 15 percent (almost 500,000 units), leaving the HUD-assisted housing inventory about the same as it was in 1982."[1] Production of affordable housing with the Low Income Housing Tax Credit, inclusionary housing programs, and state and local trust funds has not kept pace with the erosion of the federally funded housing stock, including the continuing demolition of much of the nation's public housing stock.

That situation demands that attention be focused on the new units being created today and in the future. It is now widely recognized that the policies of the past, in which billions of public dollars were used to create time-limited affordable rental housing with no thought for the long-term future of either the buildings or the millions of tenants that might be cast adrift into the marketplace, were at best shortsighted. The question remains, however, whether policy makers have learned enough to recognize that when one sets an end point on affordability—whether it is 20 or 40 years—that point will eventually be reached.

The issue has been rendered more complex, philosophically and practically, by the growing role of home ownership in the subsidized housing inventory. Few argue against the long-term preservation of rental housing, whether it be for 45 years, 50 years, or in perpetuity. Moreover, preserving affordability in rental housing is a straightforward matter of controlling rents and certifying the incomes of prospective tenants, procedures that have been thoroughly established over many decades.[2] When it comes to a buyer purchasing a home, preserving affordability means either that the resale price of the home must be controlled in order to keep it at an affordable level, or that the greater part of the gain realized by the home owner must be recaptured in order to subsidize another home to replace the one that is now no longer affordable. Either way, the home owner's opportunity to generate wealth from the sale of the home is being limited, perhaps significantly so.

To the extent that people see home ownership as an opportunity to build wealth through property appreciation, resale controls designed to preserve affordability in subsidized owner-occupied housing raise difficult issues of balancing individual gains against community benefits, and the importance of getting the most out of the public subsidies used to create the unit. In looking at this issue, however, it is important to remember that property appreciation is far from a constant in the marketplace. As of 2008, house values were plummeting in most parts of the United States, and far more home owners were losing wealth than gaining it. Public subsidies, by setting the initial price of the home well below its market value, protect their lower income buyer against similar losses. This issue will be addressed in further detail later in this chapter.

Finally, the great majority of lower income households in the United States do not live in housing that is formally "affordable housing" and subject to legal controls on its price or occupancy. Lower income home owners and tenants alike live in private market housing, which is often priced—particularly in older industrial cities and regions in the Midwest and Northeast—at levels not markedly higher, and sometimes even lower, than subsidized housing in the same communities. This housing, made up largely of modest single-family homes and "mom-and-pop" rental units in one- to four-unit properties, is also often at risk, either from deterioration through inadequate maintenance and repair, or through appreciation in gentrifying urban neighborhoods. While the ability of the public sector to preserve this stock may be more limited than when addressing housing that has benefited from public subsidies, there are ways in which it can intervene effectively in this arena as well.

The next section of this chapter will address the issue of expiring use restrictions on existing subsidized housing, followed by a discussion of the question of preserving housing built for affordable home ownership. The closing section will look briefly at affordability in the private market stock and some of the tools available to the public sector to address that issue.

THE PROBLEM OF EXPIRING USE RESTRICTIONS

The issue of expiring use restrictions on subsidized rental housing first arose in the 1980s, when emerging market opportunities, combined with increased financial stresses on owners, prompted a wave of owners of Section 236 housing projects to prepay their mortgages in order to relieve themselves of their subsidy contracts and use restrictions.[3] At that point, the Section 236 inventory contained some 540,000 units.[4] In response to the outcry from housing advocates and residents of affected developments, Congress enacted the Emergency Low Income Housing Preservation Act of 1987, imposing a moratorium on prepayments, and the Low Income Housing Preservation and Resident Home Ownership Act of 1990, providing incentives for owners to extend the use restrictions or sell projects to "priority purchasers"—tenants, nonprofit organizations, or public agencies. In 1996, however, Congress restored prepayment rights and effectively terminated these programs; by that point, approximately 100,000 units had been preserved. In the five years following the lifting of the moratorium, roughly 60,000 units were lost through prepayment.

Meanwhile, a further problem emerged with respect to units constructed under the Section 8 new construction/substantial rehabilitation program between the mid-1970s and mid-1980s. In order to fully cover the cost of development of these projects, HUD gave developers approval to charge rents that were high enough to ensure repayment of the government-insured mortgage. The rents were then made affordable to low-income tenants through project-based Section 8 vouchers. These projects, often built to high standards, were generally very expensive. As a result, in many cases, especially when Section 8 projects were built in distressed or high-poverty areas, the government-approved rents were far higher than those charged for private market housing in the same areas. This did not concern either the developers or HUD at first, since all of the tenants were receiving vouchers covering the difference between 30 percent of their income and the rent. As the Section 8 contracts began to expire in the 1990s, however, HUD found itself in severe difficulty. As Emily Achtenberg describes the situation, "The cost of renewing all the Section 8 contracts at current—often above-market—rents threatened to consume the entire HUD budget. On the other hand, if HUD declined to renew Section 8 contracts on HUD-insured properties, it could trigger a wave of mortgage defaults and foreclosures, resulting in staggering claims against the HUD mortgage insurance fund."[5]

Congress responded to this situation with the Multifamily Assisted Housing Reform and Accountability Act, enacted in 1997. This legislation authorized HUD to restructure the mortgages on Section 8 projects. Under a system known as "Mark to Market," HUD broke the initial mortgage into two parts; one, that could be supported by realistic market rents, which required regular monthly payments, and the other, an unsupportable balance, which became a deferred second mortgage. A parallel program, known as "Mark-Up to Market" permitted owners of Section 8 projects with below-market rents—who were beginning to opt out of the program in large numbers—to restructure their loans to permit them to charge market rents, thus increasing the financial desirability of remaining in the Section 8 program.

The Mark to Market program restructured and preserved roughly 200,000 units of subsidized housing before its sunset at the end of the 2006 fiscal year. Between 1995 and 2003, however, more than 300,000 HUD-subsidized units were lost, including roughly 220,000 units with project-based Section 8 assistance, as owners prepaid their mortgages and opted out of their Section 8 contracts.[6] The majority of HUD-financed or HUD-subsidized projects are still in the affordable housing inventory, but they remain at risk. Between now and 2013, HUD-subsidized mortgages on roughly 200,000 lower income rental units will mature.[7] By 2012, subsidy contracts on another nearly 50,000 subsidized units financed through state housing finance agencies will also expire.[8] In addition to properties whose mortgages will mature or contracts will expire, prepayment continues to be an option for additional thousands of projects. For public officials, housing advocates, and above all, lower income residents of these projects, what might be called a "rolling crisis" continues largely unabated. Large numbers of subsidized properties are still at risk, particularly well-designed projects in areas where market strength would enable them to maintain profitable rent levels without subsidies.

With the federal government less concerned with preservation in recent years, the focus, as in so many other areas of housing policy, has shifted to state and local government. States, and to a lesser extent, municipalities, have strong powers as well as some limited financial resources they can use to preserve expiring use properties. While in the end some financial involvement is often required, state regulatory powers are often enough "to bring owners to the negotiating table or otherwise facilitate preservation outcomes."[9] The power to regulate matters involving real property, including the rights of tenants and the responsibilities of property owners, is a state matter. States can exercise their power to promote preservation within the bounds of owners' constitutional property rights. Moreover, many subsidized housing developments are also subject to state-level use restrictions, imposed in return for any of many different forms of state or local assistance, such as below-market land sales, zoning variances, or tax abatements. In some cases, state use restrictions may extend for longer periods than the federal ones, and may survive a mortgage prepayment. An owner may be relieved of federal obligations by prepayment, but a state obligation incurred in return for tax abatement may still have many years to run before it is extinguished.

In addition to legal powers, state governments have used public resources to support preservation activities, including a growing share of their available allocations of Low Income Housing Tax Credits. Under this program, tax credit equity is used to cover not only the cost of acquiring the project from its former owner, but the cost—often considerable in buildings that are 20 or more years old—to perform necessary repairs, replace worn-out systems, and upgrade the building's energy efficiency. Since 2005, more than 60,000 units per year have been preserved through use of the LIHTC.[10] The downside of this use of the tax credit is that, in the absence of dedicated funding for preservation, preservation and creation of new affordable housing become a zero-sum proposition. Table 10-1 illustrates the range of potential state and local actions to preserve

TABLE 10-1 STATE AND LOCAL ACTIONS FOR PRESERVATION OF SUBSIDIZED HOUSING*

ACTIVITY	DESCRIPTION	EXAMPLES
State or local existing use restrictions	Projects receiving state or local assistance such as land, zoning variances, tax abatement, or public funds are often subject to state restrictions independent of federal use restrictions	Cambridge, Massachusetts, used its power under a tax relief agreement with a developer seeking to opt out to extend affordability for an additional 20 years
Notice requirements	State laws that require longer and more extensive notice of potential prepayment or opt-out than federal requirements	California requires 12 months' notice, while Rhode Island requires two years'. Minnesota and Maryland require owners to file a tenant impact statement
Fees	State laws that require owners to pay compensatory or mitigation fees in conjunction with prepayments or opt-outs	San Francisco and Seattle require owners to pay relocation costs for displaced tenants
Rent controls	Local rent control ordinances. Although rent control is preempted during the period that a project is subject to federal use restrictions, an existing rent control ordinance may become applicable to a property when the federal restrictions lapse	San Francisco has a strong rent control ordinance. Local officials attribute the near-absence of prepayments and opt-outs to the effect of that system
Right of first refusal or preemptive purchase right	State laws that require the owner to give a right of first refusal to buy the property to local government, a tenants organization, or a nonprofit housing corporation, or give preservation purchasers an exclusive period to make an offer	California law provides preservation purchasers with an exclusive right to make an offer during a six-month window after the owner has provided notice of conversion to market
Eminent domain	State or local laws that permit localities to use eminent domain to preserve affordable housing	Denver and Portland, Oregon, local laws authorize use of eminent domain for this purpose. New Jersey state law authorizes use of eminent domain for affordable housing generally
Low Income Housing Tax Credit (LIHTC) financing	State use of LIHTC allocations to support preservation, including providing set-asides of state allocations for preservation or points for preservation projects in the competitive process under the state's Qualified Allocation Plan (QAP)	The Massachusetts QAP sets aside 35 percent of the allocation for preservation; the Iowa QAP sets aside 20 percent. The California QAP sets aside five percent specifically for projects at risk of loss within the following two years
Direct state financing	Allocation of state funds for preservation of subsidized housing	Minnesota has appropriated $30 million to fund preservation efforts, while Massachusetts has created a preservation bond program financed by state revenues
Other state assistance	Tax relief for subsidized projects or their owners	Missouri has enacted a state tax credit for sellers that donate affordable housing properties to nonprofit purchasers

* Based largely on information in Achtenberg, *Stemming the Tide: A Handbook on Preserving Multifamily Subsidized Housing*

subsidized housing. It makes clear that there is indeed broad scope for states, and in some cases local governments, to play an important role in preserving subsidized housing, even where the projects were financed through federal programs.

PRESERVING AFFORDABLE HOME OWNERSHIP

After the demise of the ill-fated, short-lived Section 235 program, development of subsidized housing for home ownership revived in the 1980s and 1990s. Beginning with the first inclusionary programs and a handful of initial efforts using state and local trust funds, a growing number of communities began to offer houses and condominiums to lower income home buyers at prices that were often well below the market price for a comparable unit in the same area.[11] By the end of the 1990s, such programs were common in both urban and suburban areas. As subsidized owner-occupied housing programs proliferated, they raised a series of practical and philosophical issues. While these issues have been widely debated, and for the most part resolved in those communities that have already initiated such programs, as other communities embark on subsidized home ownership development, they need to explore and resolve these issues for themselves.[12]

Windfalls or community benefits

Few people question the premise that when a unit has been subsidized to sell at a below market price, the buyer's income should be too low to permit her to buy a house on the market. The real question is what should happen to that house when, as inevitably takes place, the initial buyer moves on and the house is sold to a new buyer. The resolution of that question hinges on the manner in which one balances community and private benefits.

From a communitarian standpoint, there is a compelling argument that the house should remain affordable to—and occupied by—lower income households for the longest possible period. First, the need for affordable housing is growing, rather than declining. The need for affordable housing is not a temporary condition resulting from a short-term emergency, but a continuing need driven by the realities of the housing market and the structural shortage of housing affordable to lower income families. Thus, the loss of any affordable housing unit negatively affects the housing choices of those families and the vitality of the community as a whole. Second, from a standpoint of fiscal efficiency, the longer the initial public investment in a subsidized home continues to benefit lower income owners, and the more owners it benefits, the greater the return on that investment to the community and to society.

This societal benefit, of course, is achieved by limiting the return to the home owner. This has led to objections, some ideological and some rooted in what people perceive to be the value of home ownership. From an ideological standpoint, many people are uncomfortable with the idea of limiting to any extent what is known as the "bundle of rights" associated with home ownership. Others argue that by limiting the owner's opportunity to benefit from the appreciation of his property, one is preventing a lower income family from building wealth and moving into the middle class. Each of these arguments needs to be addressed.

The core ideological argument should not be given undue weight. Limitations on that "bundle of rights" have been routinely imposed since the early years of the 20th century. Innumerable laws, including building codes, zoning ordinances, subdivision standards, environmental regulations, and fair housing laws limit the untrammeled use by a home owner of her property. While regulating the price of a transaction between the owner and a buyer of the property might be seen by some as a more intrusive regulation than any of these, the fact is that it is not an imposition so much as a *quid pro quo*, a trade-off for concrete benefits conferred the buyer as a result of public action.[13]

The second issue is more complex and goes to the nature of how housing is perceived in much of American society. To the extent that housing is perceived as shelter, a place where individuals can live and raise families in sound, affordable, and healthy conditions, appreciation is at most a matter of secondary importance. It is only when housing is seen as an investment rather than shelter that the issue of appreciation becomes significant. Even from that perspective, however, the argument that real estate appreciation is a predictable vehicle for upward mobility is not only flawed, but arguably dangerous in its implications if used as a basis for public policy.

First, as was noted earlier, appreciation is far from a sure thing. While it is true that real estate prices show an upward trend over the long term, it is a gradual one in which booms are followed by busts, often wiping out or significantly cutting into the short-term gains. While people who bought houses in the 1990s and sold them between 2001 and 2006 typically made impressive gains, people who bought houses in the 1980s and sold them during the 1990s often lost large amounts. As of 2008, house prices in most of the United States are dropping steadily, wiping out many of the earlier gains.

Second, the argument that real estate appreciation—which is, after all, not that far removed from speculation—is the only vehicle into the middle class is not only based on highly questionable assumptions, but does a disservice to the efforts of millions of lower income families who build income and wealth through education, entrepreneurship, and simple hard work. Indeed, the evidence shows that many residents of resale-controlled housing do indeed move out of subsidized housing into private market home ownership, not through appreciation but through growth in their household income.[14] Moreover, subsidized home ownership confers benefits to lower income households—unrelated to appreciation—that may work to increase their upward mobility.

These benefits include the lower monthly cost of housing, which means that the family will have more disposable income that can be used for savings or for expenditures such as education or improved health care, and the greater stability of tenure associated with affordable home ownership. To the extent that the homes are located in locations that are better—in the sense of better schools, greater safety, and similar features—than those the family could have afforded otherwise, that too confers benefits associated with upward mobility. This is particularly true of many of the home ownership units that have been created through inclusionary housing programs.

A further benefit of subsidized home ownership is the substantial, if not quite absolute, protection from loss in property value. Since the property is initially priced well below market value—typically 25 to 50 percent below—even if the market value of the property falls, it is unlikely to fall so much that the market value will drop below the subsidized price except under the most extreme conditions. The fact that the property is priced below market value means, moreover, that if the owner can sell it without controls, she is not merely gaining the appreciation that is associated with a rising market, but is reaping a windfall from the difference between the subsidized purchase price and the market price. An early example was a subsidized home ownership project built in Irvine, California, in 1976 without controls. After only three years, nearly a quarter of the owners had sold their houses at prices that averaged more than double what they paid.

As a general proposition, therefore, the case for controlling resale prices on a long-term basis, particularly where the homes have been subsidized to a below-market price, is a compelling one. It might be worth making an exception for subsidized home ownership projects developed in distressed inner city neighborhoods as a way of stabilizing and revitalizing them. In such areas, the home buyers are likely to receive fewer of the locational benefits that accrue to families of similar income buying houses in a suburban inclusionary development; they are, in a sense, pioneers who are making a commitment more to the neighborhood's future potential than its present reality. Given the low market values in these areas, the subsidized purchase prices are less likely to be below the market than those of their suburban counterparts.

Many community activists and CDC leaders in these neighborhoods argue that if prices begin to appreciate as a result of neighborhood revitalization, buyers should gain the full benefit of that appreciation, if only as a reward for their pioneering efforts. They also argue that, given the weak market conditions of the area, imposing resale price restrictions would deter some buyers who would otherwise make a valuable contribution to the neighborhood's vitality. Where the goal is neighborhood revitalization more than affordable housing per se, these arguments have merit. At the same time, it is important to recognize that if the neighborhood indeed does begin to appreciate at a significant rate, the need for affordable housing will also increase. Thus, even this issue may require some balancing of community and individual benefit.

The mechanics of resale controls

The purpose of controlling the resale of subsidized owner-occupied housing is twofold: to ensure that the price remains within the reach of households within the income range targeted by the locality, and to ensure that the household occupying the home falls within that range. A variation on resale controls, known as "recapture" of appreciation, permits the price of the unit to rise with the market, but captures the appreciation to be used to subsidize another housing unit elsewhere. As will be discussed below, recapture is usually a less desirable approach than direct resale controls.

Once the city or county has made the policy decision to impose resale controls on housing being built for affordable home ownership, and has decided how long it wants the controls to remain in place, it must address three technical issues:

1. Setting a formula to control resale prices
2. Adopting a legal mechanism through which the controls take place
3. Establishing a procedure for setting prices and qualifying buyers as resale transactions take place

Each of these has its distinctive features. The question of the duration of controls, however, must be resolved before anything else.

Duration

Any duration is theoretically possible, from not at all to forever, or in perpetuity.[15] Towns and cities that in the past have imposed no controls or controls of short duration have generally shifted to longer control periods: They recognized not only that many of their affordable units were being lost, but that it was becoming increasingly difficult to replace them with new units. Montgomery County, Maryland, which produced more than 10,000 units of owner-occupied affordable housing through inclusionary housing between 1977 and 1999, initially required only five years of affordability, increased to 10 years in 1981. By 1999, nearly two-thirds of the units created under their program were no longer subject to controls on resale or occupancy. In 2005, long after most of their units had been lost from the affordable housing stock, the county extended controls on future units to 30 years.

A California study that looked at the 10 "top-producing" cities in the state in terms of their inclusionary housing programs found that

- four cities required owner-occupied units to remain affordable for 30 years;
- one required units to remain affordable for 45 years;
- three required units to remain affordable for 55 years; and
- two required units to remain affordable in perpetuity.[16]

California law encourages cities and counties to preserve their affordable owner-occupied housing for at least 30 years.

The downside of any control short of a perpetual one is that it may expire even though the housing unit is capable of many more years of use. The New Jersey Council on Affordable Housing's rules governing affordable owner-occupied units require only a 30-year control period. When the house is sold for the first time after the end of the control period, however, the municipality must either purchase the unit at the restricted price or recapture the difference between the restricted price and the market price.[17] The funds collected as a result of the recapture are returned to the agency subsidizing the housing, or in the case of a home in an inclusionary development, are deposited in the municipal housing trust fund.

Appreciation formula
Having established the duration of the controls, the local agency responsible must adopt a formula for setting prices on resale. The purpose of a formula is to balance the goals of preserving the affordability of the home and permitting the owner to receive a reasonable amount of appreciation on resale. Davis notes, "What constitutes a return that is 'reasonable' or 'fair' is a subject of considerable debate among the organizers and supporters of shared equity housing."[18] As a result, formulas vary. Some are designed to ensure that the owner gains a minimum level of appreciation under all circumstances, even at the price of reduced affordability, while some are designed to ensure continued affordability at a particular income range, even if the owner gains little or no appreciation as a result.

The most widely used formulas are "index-based" and set the resale price on the basis of a readily available index. By tying the resale price to the change in the median household income in the area, the unit will be affordable on resale—subject to changes in mortgage interest rates—to a household of the same income level as the initial owner. The formula could in theory be refined to adjust the price to reflect changes in mortgage rates, but this could make the formula much more complicated and potentially force the seller to sell at a loss, even in a market where prices are rising. More commonly, formulas provide adjustments to reflect capital improvements made by the owner, and in some cases make downward adjustments if the seller has damaged the property over and above customary wear and tear.

Legal mechanism
To be of value, the resale controls must be legally enforceable. That means that they must be embedded in a legal mechanism that is not specific to the owner, but runs with the property. In practice, there are two fundamentally different ways in which this is handled—through a deed restriction or restrictive covenant, or through a land lease under the control of a community land trust (CLT) or similar entity.

Deed restrictions are a common way in which limitations are imposed on an owner's use of her property and incorporate the restriction into the deed in such a fashion that it cannot be removed by the owner. They are particularly common in condominium developments, where they are used to control things such as the color of the building or trim, the landscaping, or even the extent to which the owner can fly flags, hang laundry, or put a fence around her property.

When applied to resale controls governing affordable housing, the deed restriction will specify the duration of the restriction and the formula setting the maximum resale price, as well as the powers given the entity charged with enforcing the restrictions. The entity is usually either a governmental entity, such as a municipal or county housing office, or a private nonprofit entity, such as a CLT. In addition to setting the resale price, the entity's powers may include the right to intervene if the owner goes into default on the mortgage, or an exclusive right to refer prospective buyers to the property when the owner wishes to sell.

Community land trusts, of which there are now more than 150 around the United States, are nonprofit entities that create affordable home ownership, using a ground lease as the vehicle to ensure that the homes remain affordable on a long-term, often permanent basis. Under a ground lease structure, the ownership of the land is separated from the ownership of the building on it.[19] The buyer of a home developed by a CLT buys the home, not the land underneath and around it. The buyer instead leases the land, typically for a term of 99 years. The lease is renewable and inheritable, and gives the owner and her heirs the exclusive right to occupy the land on which the home is situated. The restrictions on resale, as well as other provisions to ensure that the unit remains owner-occupied and properly maintained, are embodied in the ground lease, which is enforced by the land trust. Typically, when a home owner subject to a CLT ground lease decides to sell, the land trust can either purchase the home itself and resell it to an income-qualified buyer, or monitor the conveyance of the property directly from seller to buyer at the formula resale price, making sure that the buyer meets the income qualifications set by the land trust.[20]

Both deed restrictions and CLT ground leases provide a solid legal basis for the imposition of resale controls. Historically they have represented distinct and separate models, with community land trusts typically being neighborhood-based, highly participatory entities engaged in community-building as well as real estate development. In recent years, however, the cities of Chicago and Irvine, California, have created land trusts as administrative vehicles that use both ground leases and deed restrictions to ensure the long-term affordability of the city's affordable housing stock.

Process
The most important thing is that there is a process. Maintaining affordability, whether for rental or owner-occupancy, does not take care of itself. Although some people have argued that one can rely on the title insurance company to enforce deed restrictions, that is not only wildly unrealistic but conjures up the specter of a closing being cancelled—after months of contracts, deposits, and other actions in good faith by both buyer and seller—when the title company representative discovers at the last minute that the buyer is not qualified or the resale price is not consistent with the formula in the deed restrictions. Some entity *must* be in place with the responsibility to manage the process and the legal authority to impose its will on the other parties in the transaction.

This entity can be a governmental agency or a nonprofit entity, such as a housing corporation or land trust. What form it takes is relatively unimportant, as long as it shares two salient features. It must be driven by the mission of preserving affordable housing, and it must have enough organizational substance to give it stability and the likelihood that it will be around for the long haul. In New Jersey, many towns where housing is being created through inclusionary developments have created affordable housing boards, which have the responsibility of enforcing resale controls, calculating resale prices, and screening prospective buyers for available properties. Those that do not may contract with a nonprofit entity or with the Housing Affordability Service in the state Housing and Mortgage Finance Agency to provide those services.

As mentioned earlier, some communities have used recapture of appreciation as an alternative to resale controls. While in theory the recapture of the subsidy amount should be fungible with resale controls, in the sense that it should permit the municipality to create a unit to replace the one lost, the reality is often otherwise. Depending on changes in market conditions, development activity, and land availability, by the time the recapture money is made available it may be substantially more expensive and more difficult to create an affordable housing unit than it was at the time the lost unit was constructed. As a result, the amount collected through recapture may not be enough to cover the cost of creating a replacement unit; in the worst case, it may not even be possible to create a replacement unit, and the money will end up sitting in the local housing trust fund.

Creating a new unit invariably requires more energy than preserving an existing unit. This is not only a matter of the time and creative energy involved in planning, finding sites, obtaining approvals, and so forth, but also a matter of environmental responsibility. As people are increasingly coming to appreciate, the preservation of existing housing is usually more environmentally responsible in light of the consumption of energy and natural resources associated with construction of new housing. Even when the new unit may be more energy-efficient or "green" in other ways, the expenditure of resources associated with its construction means that the crossover in terms of total energy expenditure may not come for decades, if ever.

PRESERVING AFFORDABILITY IN THE PRIVATE MARKET

Twenty-eight million U.S. households earn less than 50 percent of the median income in their areas, and 17 million earn between 50 and 80 percent.[21] Of these 45 million households, 15 to 20 percent live in housing that receives some form of public subsidy or assistance or receive housing vouchers to enable them to afford private-market housing. The other 80 to 85 percent rely entirely on the private market.

Lower income renters

Lower income households are more likely to be renters than the American population as a whole (Table 10-2). Fifty-five percent of all households earning less than $20,000 in 1999, roughly equivalent to those earning under 50 percent of AMI, were renters. In contrast to the widely held impression that most renters live in apartment buildings, more than half of the private market rental units in the United States are in one- to four-family properties, and more than half of those are in single-family houses.

These are the classic "mom-and-pop" properties. The overwhelming majority of them are owned by individuals or couples who typically own

TABLE 10-2 TENURE BY INCOME RANGE

INCOME RANGE	RENTERS (IN MILLIONS)	OWNERS (IN MILLIONS)	% RENTERS
0–$9,999	6.3	3.8	62%
$10,000–$19,999	6.8	6.6	51%
$20,000–$34,999	8.7	11.8	42%
$35,000–$49,999	5.8	11.6	33%

Source: 2000 Census

just one property, or at most a handful of similar properties, often in the same town or neighborhood where the owner lives. Many of the two- to four-family properties are owner-occupied, with the owner living in one unit and renting out the others. In many urban areas, particularly in the northeast, purchase and ownership of small rental properties is often an economic stepping stone for immigrant families, who often earn little more than their tenants.[22]

Low-income renters depend heavily on these properties. Seventy percent of all renters—close to 10 million households—with incomes below 50 percent of AMI living in private market housing live in properties with one to four units. Since these dwelling units, particularly those in single-family homes, tend to be larger than rental units in multifamily properties, they are more likely to be the homes of large families and families with children. Although only 21 percent of all renters are large families (with four or more members), 33 percent of all renters of single-family homes are large families; 57 percent of all Latino renters of single-family homes are large families. While the data do not make it possible to break down the extent to which lower income families with children are dependent on this segment of the housing stock, it is clearly the source of shelter for the overwhelming majority of those families.

In most urban areas, this rental sector provides housing at relatively affordable prices and of adequate quality, entirely financed through private, often informal, capital without any public sector assistance. The informal nature of the management and operation of this sector, as well as the extent to which many costs are either absorbed by the property owners or not accounted for, means that the operating costs reflected in the tenants' rents are far lower than in multifamily properties owned by either commercial entities or nonprofit organizations. To replace even a part of this sector with publicly subsidized housing would cost not only hundreds of billions in capital investment, but further billions in operating subsidies.

The continued health of this segment of the nation's rental housing inventory is critically important to the housing of America's lower income households. While its overall survival is not at risk, there are many issues that raise questions about the quality and stability of the accommodations it offers. Many small rental properties are of poor quality with significant defects in maintenance or repair, problems that can arise from a shortage of cash flow, excessive debt, or the owner's lack of skills or commitment. While many owners have a long-term commitment to their properties, others are speculators trying to make a short-term gain by flipping their properties. This has become a serious problem in many distressed older Rustbelt cities like Buffalo or Cleveland, where large numbers of investors have bought properties, sometimes on eBay, as short-term speculative investments with little concern for their long-term stability.

In cities like Cleveland or Buffalo, the problems for the tenants of one- to four-unit rental properties are associated with poor quality, deterioration, and in extreme cases, landlord abandonment; in cities experiencing strong market appreciation, however, the problem is the opposite. As home ownership in urban neighborhoods becomes more desirable and house prices increase faster than rents, prospective buyers are willing to pay more for single-family properties, leading to conversion of those properties from absentee to owner occupancy. While that may be a healthy change from the neighborhood standpoint, it can have damaging consequences for the lower income families living in those houses, who are being supplanted by more affluent home buyers.

A parallel trend is taking place in some urban areas where low-end multifamily rental properties are being upgraded, either as upscale rental housing or condominium conversion, or torn down in order to create sites for more valuable, higher density development. A case in point is the small city of Hoboken, New Jersey, across the Hudson River from New York City. A poor city in 1970, it had become an affluent outpost of midtown Manhattan by 2000.[23] Two thousand of the city's pre-1970 rental units, or roughly a quarter of the nonsubsidized rental stock, had been removed. Half of those had been converted into condominiums, and half demolished for construction of higher-density development in their place. The median rent had gone from $76 per month to $953 per month, or from 68 percent to 142 percent of the statewide median, despite the fact that one-third of the remaining rental units were subsidized for low- and moderate-income tenants. If it were not for the fact that more than one-quarter of all of the housing in Hoboken is subsidized housing—almost entirely constructed before 1980—few lower income families would live in the city today. Many of those units will see their use restrictions expire in the next few years, and may well cease being affordable to the city's lower income families.

Many tenants in small rental properties are facing a new crisis, arising from the wave of mortgage foreclosures that has swept many parts of the United States since 2006. As a rule, once a foreclosing creditor has taken possession of a property at sheriff's sale, it immediately moves to vacate the building. Many of the people living in the properties being foreclosed are tenants who then lose their homes, innocent victims of the landlord who defaulted on the mortgage or of the lender who made an irresponsible loan. Few states provide tenants with any protection against eviction in the case of foreclosure. While there is no way of estimating the magnitude of this problem nationally, a few snippets of local data provide some sense of the magnitude of this problem. In August 2007, of 9,500 properties sold in foreclosure auctions in California, 44 percent, or nearly 4,200, were not owner-occupied.[24] Similarly, 29 percent of the nearly 4,800 foreclosures in Massachusetts through mid-August of 2007 were multifamily—typically two- and three-family—properties.[25]

The problems associated with this segment of the rental housing market are often made worse by the lack of thoughtful public policies. Municipal regulations such as code requirements are often administered insensitively and punitively, with little attempt to distinguish between responsible but struggling landlords and outright speculators. While many cities provide loans or grants to struggling lower income home owners, few offer either financial or technical help to small landlords to help them upgrade their properties or improve their practices.[26] While helping hardworking or elderly home owners is politically popular, proposals to offer assistance to small landlords have been attacked as "rewarding slumlords."

Ultimately, there are two central public policy goals with respect to this stock. "First, to preserve—and perhaps even expand—the stock of one- to four-unit rental housing, while maintaining reasonable levels of quality and affordability; and second, to provide incentives for 'good' landlord behavior while continuing to punish 'bad' behavior."[27] This should not only involve incentives for responsible operation of rental property, and effective code enforcement and imposition of sanctions against irresponsible owners, but should include steps to discourage entry into absentee ownership by "bad actors"—the eBay speculators and their kin.

Lower income home owners

Lower income home ownership in the private market is an uncertain proposition. These homebuyers are at greater risk of losing their homes, while the homes they buy tend to be of poorer quality and lower value than those of more affluent home owners. Over the years, efforts have been made to ameliorate this situation by offering prospective buyers home ownership education and counseling or by providing home owners with access to low-interest loans and grants to make necessary repairs to their homes. These efforts, however, reach only a fraction of the buyers and owners who could potentially benefit from them. Indeed, as one research study has found, the disparity in home ownership rates between White and African American households has more to do with the latter's shorter spells of home ownership than with their relative likelihood of becoming home owners in the first place.[28]

While it is essential to protect prospective home buyers from buying properties that are in poor repair or overpriced by unscrupulous "flippers" or from being trapped in unsustainable mortgages, helping home-owning families keep them is equally important. Lower income home owners, in addition to being more susceptible to losing their homes as a result of personal situations, such as divorce, unemployment, or health crises, are the target of choice for predatory lenders and contractors. As was noted earlier, the greater part of the subprime foreclosure crisis has not come from mortgages that enabled families to buy a home, but from mortgages that families who were already home owners were induced to take out to refinance existing mortgages. If those families had sought responsible counsel before refinancing, many—arguably most—of those loans would never have been made, and the number of homes potentially lost to foreclosure in the United States reduced by more than a million.

In many cases, predatory lenders team up with shady contractors and together induce home owners to borrow money beyond their means for repairs for which they are charged unconscionable amounts, and in many cases may not even need. Less educated home owners in urban areas, particularly senior citizens, tend to be disproportionately targeted for these activities, which often feature aggressive door-to-door salesmanship.[29] Even in communities where local governments or nonprofit agencies offer low-interest loans or grants for home improvements for which these home owners are eligible, many are still victimized by home improvement scams. While this may reflect in part the red tape and other limitations associated with many government programs, it reflects even more the assertive promotional activities of the predators, and the passive "offer it and they will come" attitude of many government and nonprofit agencies offering programs for lower income families.

Pressures on low-income home owners in appreciating neighborhoods parallel those experienced by many rental units in such areas. Rising values can benefit those owners, but also carry risks for them. Although rising property values cannot directly force them out of their homes, increases in property tax burdens resulting from higher values can have that effect. This issue is particularly serious for elderly home owners, who may already be struggling with the cost of maintaining a home on an income that may be considerably less than it was when they bought the home.

Eighteen states have passed various forms of property tax "circuit-breaker" relief for lower income home owners, designed to limit the share of their income that a family is required to pay in property taxes. While formulas and eligibility ceilings vary widely from state to state, the basic principle is that if property taxes exceed some percentage of the household's income, the household can receive all or part of the excess back from the state, thereby keeping property taxes from becoming an excessive burden and helping them keep their home.[30] Not all programs are equally valuable. Some are available only to senior citizens and disabled home owners, while others cap the maximum benefit so low that they make little real difference. New York State offers a maximum benefit to nonsenior-citizen households of only $75 per year. Elsewhere, some local officials have designed targeted programs to address this issue, such as in Cook County, Illinois (which includes Chicago), where the county has created an expanded home owner exemption program to mitigate the impact of increases in property values.

Over the past few decades, the United States has spent far more, in both money and human energy, on trying to create more lower income home owners than on trying to help those owners keep their homes. As a result, lower income home ownership has become a revolving door for many families. They lose their homes within a short period after first becoming home owners, with little or no financial or social benefit to show for the experience. If there is a central lesson that can be derived from the home ownership issues of the past decade, including the foreclosure crisis that erupted in 2006 and 2007, it is the need for policies that focus on *preserving* home ownership, not mindlessly promoting it. Developing a home ownership preservation support system should be a priority for the public and nonprofit sectors in any community with a significant pool of lower income home owners.

NOTES

1. Stegman, Michael A. 2002. "The Fall and Rise of Public Housing." *Regulation* 25(Summer): 64.
2. There are other issues that arise with respect to the question of whether tenants should be allowed to remain in subsidized apartments when their incomes rise to exceed the ceiling income for the unit they occupy, but these issues do not bear on the affordability of the unit over time.
3. The expiration of the tax benefits allowed for depreciation and the loss of tax deductions for mortgage interest as principal repayments began to represent the lion's share of mortgage payments, coupled with the limitations on rent levels and cash return, meant that after 15 years many Section 236 project owners found themselves in a negative cash flow position, thus creating a powerful incentive to prepay, refinance, and convert the properties to market-rate housing. See Achtenberg, Emily P. 2002. *Stemming the Tide: A Handbook on Preserving Multifamily Subsidized Housing*. New York: Local Initiatives Support Corporation.
4. A much smaller number of units built under the earlier Sec. 221(d)3 program were also subject to the same provisions.
5. Achtenberg, *op. cit.*, 4.
6. National Housing Trust. 2004. *Changes to Project-Based Multifamily Units in HUD's Inventory Between 1995 and 2003*. Washington, D.C. The NHT website contains useful information on specific projects that have been lost as well as those that are at risk.
7. Government Accounting Office. 2004. *More Accessible HUD Data Could Help Efforts to Preserve Housing for Low-Income Tenants*. Washington, D.C.
8. National Housing Trust. "Potential Loss of State Agency Properties with expiring Section 8 Contracts, Developed without HUD/FHA Financing." This represents roughly one-third of all the units in this category. Available at http://www.nhtinc.org/documents/NHT_Expiring_S8_HFA_Brief.pdf.
9. Achtenberg, *op. cit.*, 22.
10. Since state definitions of "preservation" vary widely, these totals include some number of units from state-financed programs and inclusionary housing programs, as well as possibly privately owned formerly unsubsidized housing. The majority of the units, however, are likely to be HUD-subsidized projects.
11. This is very different from the approach used in the Section 235 program, where rather than subsidize the price of the dwelling unit, the federal government subsidized the interest rate on the buyer's mortgage, so that a lower income buyer could afford to buy a dwelling at market price.
12. An excellent description and assessment of these issues can be found in Davis, John E. 2006. *Shared Equity Homeownership: The Changing Landscape of Resale-Restricted, Owner-Occupied Housing*. Montclair, N.J.: National Housing Institute. This publication, which should be read by anyone eager to understand this subject in greater depth, can be downloaded from http://www.nhi.org/pdf/SharedEquityHome.pdf.
13. Other areas of public policy offer many analogies. No one questions, for example, the rule that a low-income family given food stamps is not permitted to sell them for a profit, but must use them to buy food. It is also important to note that many of the regulations that affect the bundle of rights also directly affect the price at which the unit can be sold, but work to create *minimum* prices (such as zoning regulations) rather than *maximum* prices. This issue is discussed in further detail in the author's book *Inclusionary Housing Programs: Policies and Practices*. 1984. New Brunswick, N.J.: Rutgers University Center for Urban Policy Research, 145–150.

14. In the course of the author's research in the 1980s, this point was made anecdotally by a number of officials responsible for administering resale controls in inclusionary developments. It was confirmed by a more recent study of families leaving subsidized homes created by the Burlington Community Land Trust. Davis, John E., and Amy Demetrowitz. 2003. *Permanently Affordable Homeownership: Does the Community Land Trust Deliver on its Promises?* Burlington Vt.: Burlington Community Land Trust.
15. A common law tradition known as the "law against perpetuities" is sometimes cited as a reason why perpetual controls may not be legally permissible. In reality, most states in the United States have enacted legislation either limiting its scope or eliminating it entirely, while even in those few jurisdictions where it may be applicable, there are a variety of legal means by which it can be neutralized.
16. Non-Profit Housing Association of Northern California. 2007. *Affordable by Choice: Trends in California Inclusionary Housing Programs*, 27.
17. N.J. Administrative Code, Sec. 5:80-26.5
18. Davis, *op. cit.*, 65.
19. The two-part ownership system, in which individual property owners own their unit or building, with the land owned by another and leased to the building owner through a ground lease, is rare in the United States but quite common in many other parts of the world. It is widely used in the United Kingdom, where even today a handful of ancient aristocratic families own large parts of the land on which central London's apartment buildings and offices sit; and in Israel, where the Israel Land Administration, a governmental agency, controls 93 percent of the land area of the nation on behalf of a number of governmental or quasi-governmental entities, leasing land to private entities for development or occupancy for either 49- or 98-year terms.
20. For a detailed discussion of CLTs and land leases, see Davis, *op. cit.*, 18–23.
21. Since income ranges are defined as a percentage of median, and incomes tend to be distributed along a curve approximating what statisticians refer to as a normal distribution, it is consistently the case that 25 percent of all American households (with modest variation by region) have incomes between 0 percent and 50 percent of their area's median, and 15 percent have incomes between 50 percent and 80 percent of AMI. In 2006, according to the American Community Survey, there were roughly 111,600,000 households in the United States.
22. For a detailed discussion of this section of the rental housing industry, the reader is referred to Mallach, *Landlords at the Margins: Exploring the Dynamics of the One to Four Unit Rental Housing Industry*, a working paper of the Harvard University Joint Center for Housing Studies, available online at http://www.jchs.harvard.edu/publications/rental/revisiting_rental_symposium/papers/rr07-15_mallach.pdf.
23. Between 1970 and 2000, the median family income in Hoboken went from 68 percent of the statewide median to 113 percent.
24. McAllister, Sue. 2007. "Renters Find They're not Immune to Effects of Foreclosure Crisis." *Oakland Tribune*, October 28.
25. Appelbaum, Binyamin. 2007. "Default Crisis is Evicting Renters." *Boston Globe*, October 21.
26. There are notable exceptions, most notably New York City, which offers a wide range of services and assistance through its Housing Education Program. For other programs to help preserve rental properties at risk, see Mallach. 2006. *Bringing Buildings Back: From Abandoned Properties to Community Assets*. National Housing Institute and Rutgers University Press, 24–30.

27. Mallach, *Landlords at the Margins*, 53. Different specific strategies that might be pursued to further these two objectives are discussed at 51–57.
28. Haurin, Donald R., and Stuart S. Rosenthal. 2004. *The Sustainability of Homeownership: Factors Affecting the Duration of Homeownership and Rental Spells*. Washington, D.C.: U.S. Department of Housing and Urban Development.
29. A more detailed discussion of home improvement scams targeting lower income, particularly senior citizen, home owners can be found on the National Consumer Law Center website at http://www.consumerlaw.org/issues/seniors_initiative/home_improv.shtml.
30. An excellent overview of state circuit-breaker programs is Lyons, Karen, Sarah Farkas, and Nicolas Johnson. 2007. *The Property Tax Circuit Breaker: An Introduction and Survey of Current Programs*. Washington, D.C.: Center for Budget and Policy Priorities. Available online at http://www.cbpp.org/3-21-07sfp.pdf.

CHAPTER

11

Homelessness and Affordable Housing

Although housing needs take many different forms, arguably the most urgent and problematic are the needs of the homeless, the people without a stable or predictable roof over their heads. While there have always been homeless people in the United States, homelessness as an urgent social issue emerged at the end of the 1970s and during the 1980s, as the sight of homeless people sleeping on streets and park benches and in abandoned buildings triggered first outrage and then widespread action. Since then, not only have vast amounts of public and private money been devoted to addressing the problems of the homeless, but ongoing debate has raged about almost every aspect of the problem: how many homeless people are there, why they are homeless, and what policies or strategies best address their undeniable needs.

Homelessness is a housing problem, but it is not only a housing problem. It is the compound nature of issues associated with homelessness that have fueled the intensity of the debate about how it should be addressed and that have often made it difficult for people dealing with affordable housing issues to understand how to think about homelessness and the homeless in the context of their efforts. During the course of the past nearly three decades, since homelessness first became part of the national policy agenda, the relationship between homelessness policies and those dealing with affordable housing has shifted back and forth. As will be discussed later in this chapter, current thinking, and the growth of what is known as the Housing First model for addressing homelessness, have begun to bring about a closer relationship between the two than has heretofore existed in many communities around the United States.

The first parts of this chapter provide a brief overview of the issue—what we mean by homelessness, who the homeless are, and what the reasons are for the increase in the number and the greater visibility of the homeless since the beginning of the 1980s. The latter parts will attempt to survey some of the strategies that have been pursued to address the problem, and discuss the ways in which efforts to end homelessness relate to the larger issue of the availability of affordable housing.

WHO ARE THE HOMELESS?

Simply stated, to be homeless is to lack a home, in the sense of a sheltered environment to which one has a legitimate, stable claim. As Christopher Jencks writes, "Any private space intended for sleeping can qualify as a home, as long as those who sleep there have a legal right to be there and can exclude strangers. The homeless have become those who have no private space of their own . . . "[1] As such, the homeless include all those who sleep in public places or in shelters, where they typically have no private space or assurance that they can regularly return.

Although not included in most estimates, the homeless could also be considered to include those sometimes called the "hidden homeless," the individuals and families who stay with friends or relatives and whose shelter is vulnerable from day to day at the whim of the legal tenants of the property or their landlord. There are many such households, not least in public housing and other subsidized housing projects. A recent analysis suggests that there may be as many as 3.9 million Americans living with family, friends, or nonrelatives (not including roommates, unmarried partners, lodgers, or people living in group quarters).[2]

Any attempt to define the precise number of homeless individuals and families is bound to be an estimate of uncertain reliability. In the 1980s, different experts made efforts to develop what are known as "point-in-time" estimates of the homeless; that is, the number of people who are homeless on a particular day or night, and came up with numbers that ranged from 250,000 to 700,000.[3] The 1996 National Survey of Homeless Assistance Providers and Clients came up with a range of 444,000 to 842,000. Based on her analysis of the data and her assessment of what it left out, Martha Burt, the survey director, concluded that a credible estimate was likely to be in the vicinity of

800,000. A more recent point-in-time estimate by the National Alliance to End Homelessness, in January 2005, was based not on a national survey, but on a projection from a large pool of local surveys; it elicited a figure of 744,313.[4] Even granting the uncertainties associated with the data, it would appear that the numbers of homeless people, after rising during the 1980s, have largely leveled off over the past decade.[5] In light of the amount of effort and money that has gone into addressing this problem, this is hardly good news.

Homelessness is a highly fluid condition, with the actual number of homeless people nationally or in any one community likely to fluctuate widely from day to day or from season to season.[6] For many of them—sometimes called the chronic homeless—homelessness is a long-term condition, but for most it is a short-term one, lasting sometimes only a few days or weeks. As a result, a second measure is often used, which is that of the number of different people who experience homelessness during the course of a year. This statistic is even more uncertain, because it is generated by extrapolating from a figure that is already an estimate. Using data in the 1996 survey, Burt and her colleagues concluded that between 2.3 and 3.5 million people, or roughly one percent of the nation's population, experience homelessness at some point during the course of a year.

Roughly one-quarter of all homeless people, or about 40 percent of homeless single individuals, fit the federal government's definition of being chronically homeless, a narrow definition that includes only those single individuals who have a disabling condition such as substance abuse or mental illness and have either been continuously homeless for a year or more or had at least four episodes of homelessness in the past three years. These individuals are estimated to make up 150,000 to 200,000 of the current point-in-time homeless numbers.

While most homeless people are single individuals, a significant percentage of them are families, and the majority of the members of those families are minor children. The 1996 survey found that 34 percent of all homeless people were family members, and 23 percent, or nearly one-quarter, were children, reflecting the fact that the overwhelming majority of homeless families are headed by a single, usually female parent. Among the single individuals who were homeless, 77 percent were male and only 23 percent female. Most of them were in their middle years (25 through 54); indeed, contrary to what may have been true many decades earlier, the elderly are significantly underrepresented in the homeless population, reflecting the dramatic increase in both income support and housing for senior citizens over the past 50 years. The 2007 estimate found that the percentage of homeless people who were members of families rather than single individuals had risen to 41 percent. Given the uncertainties of the measurement process, the authors concluded that it was uncertain whether this reflected a genuine trend, or was a product of the difference in methodology between the two studies.[7]

The homeless population is disproportionately African American, as shown in Table 11-1, and disproportionately urban. The 1996 survey found that 71 percent of the homeless are in central cities, far more than the urban share of the total poor population. Whether this reflects their origins, or whether homeless people tend to gravitate toward central cities because of access to services or for other reasons, is uncertain. With respect to other issues, such as the prevalence of addiction disorders or mental illness among the homeless, although there is no question that it is far higher than in the general population, different data sources disagree sharply on the extent to which these conditions are or are not pervasive among the nation's homeless population. This reflects not only the difficulty of measuring this population and the differences in scope and methodology from one study to the next, but also the use of statistics for polemical purposes, a practice that seems particularly common when dealing with this subject.

While one percent of the nation's population may not seem like a lot, the idea that in a country as rich as the United States as many as three million people could experience homelessness during the course of each year, including perhaps over a million children, is a legitimate cause for outrage. Understanding why this is so, however, is critically important if outrage is to be turned into constructive action.

TABLE 11-1 RACIAL AND ETHNIC DISTRIBUTION OF HOMELESS POPULATION

	FAMILIES	INDIVIDUALS
Non-Latino White	38%	41%
Non-Latino African American	43%	40%
Latino	15%	10%
Native American	3%	8%
Other	1%	1%

Source: 1996 National Survey of Homeless Assistance Providers and Clients

WHY ARE SO MANY PEOPLE HOMELESS?

Homelessness has existed in the United States since colonial times. Throughout most of American history, however, it was a very different phenomenon than it is today, largely made up of transient single men whose level of homelessness tended to rise and fall in ways paralleling changes in economic conditions. Homelessness grew during the depressions of the late 19th century and the Great Depression, and subsided as these episodes were replaced by periods of economic and job growth. Many of those who were considered homeless at the time actually lived in modest hotels and boarding houses, and would not be counted among the homeless by today's definitions. Every major city in the United States contained a skid row, which provided rudimentary but inexpensive accommodation to the city's down-and-out population. The number who actually slept in streets or on park benches was small, both because of the availability of cheap shelter in skid rows and the fact that such behavior was widely treated as criminal until the 1960s and 1970s.[8]

The emergence of homelessness as a seemingly new concern in the late 1970s and 1980s appears to have reflected two related, but separate, phenomena appearing over a short period: a growth in the number of homeless people, and their increased visibility to the rest of the nation. In seeking explanations for this relatively sudden transformation, analysts have come up with a variety of explanations, including changes in the housing market, in economic conditions and policies, and in social conditions and policies.

Housing market conditions

The erosion of the housing supply available to and affordable by the poor is a central element in the emergence of widespread homelessness. This is not the same as the loss of subsidized housing, or the curtailment of housing subsidy programs by the Reagan administration, which has at times been put forth as a primary cause of homelessness. Indeed, the initial growth in the number of homeless people took place before the most significant changes in housing programs. Even after those changes—which reflected in large part a shift from housing production programs to Section 8 vouchers—the number of poor receiving public subsidies did not change significantly. While the shortage of subsidized housing and the limited number of vouchers available in recent years has certainly had an effect on the nation's inability to make a significant dent in homelessness since the 1980s, it is unlikely that it was a major precipitating factor in the initial rise of homelessness.

As has been discussed earlier, only a small percentage of American low-income individuals and families benefit from housing subsidy programs. For those dependent on the private market, two powerful trends pushing people toward homelessness emerged during the 1960s and accelerated in the 1970s. The first was the broad national trend toward higher housing cost burdens for lower income families. In 1970, looking at the United States as a whole, there was a surplus of housing affordable to households in the lower quartile of the population—roughly speaking, those with incomes of 50 percent or less of the area median income. By 1980, that surplus had changed to a deficit of nearly two million housing units.[9]

The second trend was the loss of the single room and transient occupancy buildings of America's skid rows. While these buildings were often far from desirable and often well deserving of the widely used term "flophouse," they represented a crucial form of shelter of last resort, primarily for single men. Beginning in the 1960s, these properties became far scarcer, and where still available, often far more expensive. According to the census, 640,000 people with no other permanent address lived in hotels and rooming houses in 1960. By 1970, that number had declined to 320,000, and by 1980 to 204,000.[10] One estimate is that from 1970 through the mid-1980s roughly one million SRO units were lost through a variety of factors, including abandonment, redevelopment, gentrification, demolition, or conversion, reflecting economic changes as well as the pressures from rising housing code standards.[11] By the 1980s, hundreds of thousands of one-time skid row denizens were forced to find alternative places to live. Large numbers of them ended up homeless.

Economic conditions

As housing became increasingly expensive and out of reach of the poor during the 1970s and 1980s, changes in the economy and in American policies governing economic support to the poor had the effect of increasing the number of households in extreme poverty, further exacerbating the effects of the growing housing cost gap. During this period, *all* federal income support programs, with the notable exception of Social Security, lost value in constant dollars. AFDC (Assistance to Families with Dependent Children) and General Assistance programs were particularly hard-hit; in Illinois, the value of AFDC payments in 1985 was only 53 percent of the 1968 value, while the value of General Assistance payments was only 48 percent of what they had been worth in 1968.[12] These two programs were the principal income support for single women with children and for unemployable single individuals, two population groups that began to represent a growing share of the homeless.

It is harder to pin down how changes in the economy and the workforce affected homelessness. While homelessness grew with the sharp rise in unemployment at the end of the 1970s, it did not go down as unemployment declined during the course of the 1980s and 1990s. The effect on homelessness of changes in the labor market—such as the demand for unskilled labor—is hard to determine. What did change, however, was the value of a minimum wage job, which lost 23 percent of its purchasing power between 1981 and 1989. A single full-time worker at minimum wage would have earned enough to raise a family of three out of poverty in the 1960s, but that was no longer true by the mid-1980s.[13]

Social and behavioral conditions

Finally, there is little doubt that the extent of homelessness is significantly exacerbated by a variety of social conditions or changes in social policy that, in conjunction with poverty, have increased the number of individuals who are at risk. Among factors that have been identified as playing a significant role are such disparate ones as the deinstitutionalization of people with mental illness, the crack epidemic of the 1980s, and the overall weakening of kinship ties in modern American society.

The deinstitutionalization of people with mental illness began in the 1950s and was complemented by the creation of a network of community mental health centers beginning in the late 1960s. By the 1980s, however, more patients with severe disabilities were being discharged, while funding for community-based support for them was dwindling. Roughly 142,000 people who would have been sleeping in state hospitals under rules in effect in 1975 were sleeping elsewhere—many in shelters or on the streets—by 1990.[14]

Drug and alcohol use is high among homeless individuals, with estimated rates of substance dependence as high as 50 to 60 percent.[15] Alcoholism has historically been associated with homelessness in the United States, and a high, although undeterminable, percentage of the historical skid row population suffered from it. Drug use is a more recent addition;

the crack epidemic of the late 1980s is widely seen as a factor that not only increased the number of people at risk of homelessness because of their addiction, but weakened the community support systems that might have otherwise kept many of them from the streets and shelters.

Finally, although it is open to debate, some people see the weakening of family and kinship ties as a further exacerbating factor, whether in the sense of the growing number of single-parent families, the increasing number of single individuals without meaningful family relationships, or the growing reluctance of families to provide shelter to the "black sheep" of the family as they might have done in years past; as Wright and Rubin comment, many of the homeless are "family rejects who have exhausted the patience or resources of their kin networks, or family leavers who have fled a domestic situation so troubling or so abusive that life on the streets is the preferred alternative."[16] While the actual numbers vary widely from community to community, or from year to year, there is no question that flight from domestic violence or abuse is a major cause of homelessness among women, both as single individuals and as heads of families with children.

The foregoing survey suggests a number of points. Homelessness is the product of the interaction of many different factors, yet it seems clear that both systemic and individual factors are at work. Despite the limited availability of affordable housing and the increase in the extent of extreme poverty, which are the central systemic factors, most extremely poor households are not homeless. That suggests the importance of individual factors in determining whether a particular household will or will not experience homelessness. At the same time, if those households had more money, or if there were more affordable housing available, most of them would not be homeless.

Poverty, the shortage of affordable housing, and the fraying of the societal safety net place millions of American families and individuals at least potentially at risk of homelessness. It is easy enough to see that alcohol or drug dependency or mental illness, coupled with the inability to find even a modest room or apartment that the individual can afford on his SSI or General Assistance payment, could lead to homelessness. For others, the trigger can be any of many different things. To be poor in America is to lack a cushion against the many shocks that life can bring. A family spending 40 or 50 percent of its gross income in rent is in a poor position to withstand the economic shock of a divorce, loss of a job, a medical emergency, or the emergence of an addiction or mental health problem. Any of these shocks can readily plunge an individual or a family into homelessness. While for many homelessness is likely to be a short-term or one-time experience, others may turn to drugs or alcohol as a desperate coping mechanism, and become trapped in a cycle of long-term or repeated episodic homelessness. By its nature homelessness is a demoralizing experience.

Ultimately, though, the question keeps coming back to housing. As Wright and Rubin point out, where there are more extremely poor people than there is housing that they can afford, the situation becomes "an urban housing 'game' that some are destined to lose." Their conclusion seems incontrovertible: "There are . . . many routes by which people become homeless, but every route out of homelessness must sooner or later pass through stable, secure, affordable housing."[17] The questions that remain are how that is to be accomplished, and how efforts to house the homeless intersect with other actions, public and private, with respect to affordable housing.

CHANGING APPROACHES TO HOUSING THE HOMELESS

It has been nearly 30 years since homelessness first became a major public issue. In the course of those years, many different strategies have been used to address the problem and respond to the needs of the nation's homeless individuals and families, while an elaborate and extensive infrastructure of services and facilities for the homeless has emerged. That infrastructure, as described by the National Alliance to End Homelessness, "is made up of emergency shelters (short term, sometimes congregate living arrangements; sometimes only open in the evening and usually providing minimal services); transitional housing (longer term, often with single family units or smaller shared units, usually offering more intensive services, but often with time limits on how long a family can stay, ranging from six months to two years); and some permanent supportive housing (permanent housing linked with services, available to families with multiple barriers to housing or disabled household members). For the most part, nonprofit and faith-based organizations operate these programs, which are funded by the federal, state and local governments, and private donations. Most of the organizations that provide housing and services to homeless populations participate in Continuums of Care, local or regional bodies that coordinate services and funding for homeless people and families; there are approximately 500 Continuum of Care [organizations] across the country."[18]

Throughout most of the past decades, the response to the issue of homelessness has been most widely seen as a matter of providing services to the homeless individuals and families that appeared across the United States. The initial response addressed what was not unreasonably perceived as their immediate needs for food and shelter. Gradually, first with local resources and then with growing assistance from state and federal funds, a network of shelters, soup kitchens, food banks, and other facilities emerged, which today feed hundreds of thousands of people during the day and give them a bed at night. As of 2005, the Department of Housing and Development estimated that there were 217,900 emergency shelter beds in the United States.[19] As emphasis has shifted toward transitional and permanent supportive housing, the number of emergency shelter beds, after rising dramatically between 1984 and 1996, has gradually declined since the mid-1990s.

While part of the purpose of providing shelters for the homeless was to address their immediate needs, creating them was based at least in part on the premise that for most of their occupants, the shelter stay would be a short-term, one-time experience until the individuals were able to get back on their feet. While this was true for many homeless people, it soon became apparent that for many others that was not the case. By the mid-1980s, the concept of transitional housing for the homeless, along with the development of permanent supportive housing, had begun to take root. These two strategies were institutionalized in the form of the Supportive Housing Program in the McKinney-Vento Act, the principal federal law addressing the needs of the homeless, which was enacted in 1987.[20]

Transitional housing was initially seen as a way of dealing with the needs of people with significant problems of mental illness and substance abuse but gradually grew to be used for a wide spectrum of homeless families and individuals. It was grounded in the idea of "housing readiness"—that "a period of stabilization, learning and planning [is] needed if they are ultimately to leave homelessness and stay housed."[21] Initially funded by Congress as a demonstration program, transitional housing became a permanent part of the federal funding stream in 1992, and has remained there since. By 2005, there was a total of 220,400 transitional housing beds available across the United States. These represented roughly 100,000 beds for single individuals and 40,000 family units, with the average family containing three members. As Fig. 11-1 shows, both transitional housing and permanent supportive housing, driven by both federal and local priorities, grew dramatically between 1995 and 2005. At that point, there were an additional nearly 32,000 beds for the homeless in the development pipeline, of which over half were permanent supportive housing and only 4,600 emergency shelter beds.

Transitional housing takes many different physical forms, from buildings that are specifically built or rehabilitated for the purpose to scattered-site housing, where participants are housed in homes or apartments scattered within a neighborhood or city. Single individuals are most likely to be housed in rooms in purpose-built multiunit buildings with common lounging and dining areas, while families are more likely to be housed in individual apartments, often in scattered buildings rather than a single facility. A transitional housing program for families built in Trenton, New Jersey, during the 1990s provided separate row houses for each family in the program, with no more than two on any city block.

Transitional housing is fundamentally a social service delivery program operating within a housing framework, based on the requirement that residents participate fully in the social service program. Residents are provided with a wide range of services and must participate in a variety of activities, usually organized around a "program plan" that sets behavioral goals developed by a social caseworker with the family or individual. The typical program provides the participants with both on-site services—at the building or apartment—and more specialized services provided elsewhere. More or less standard services provided on-site include case management, tenant stabilization, meeting basic needs for food and clothing, daily living skills, conflict resolution training, budgeting and money management training, and assistance in accessing entitlements, job opportunities, and ultimately, permanent housing. In family transitional housing, services also usually include school support and after-school programs, as well as programs to help families deal with domestic violence.

Under federal regulations, residents may stay in transitional housing no more than 24 months. Most service providers permit 24-month stays, although some require their residents to be "up and out" within a shorter time. In most cases, residents completing their transition must move, but a number of programs permit residents to convert their housing to permanent housing. Some nonprofit organizations have created developments that combine transitional and permanent units in a single complex, thus enabling families to remain in the development, if not always the same dwelling.

YMCA Family Village, a transitional housing development for homeless women with children in Redmond, Washington. The architect of record was Stickney Murphy Romine, and the design architect was Pyatok Architects, Inc.

Pyatok Architects, Inc.

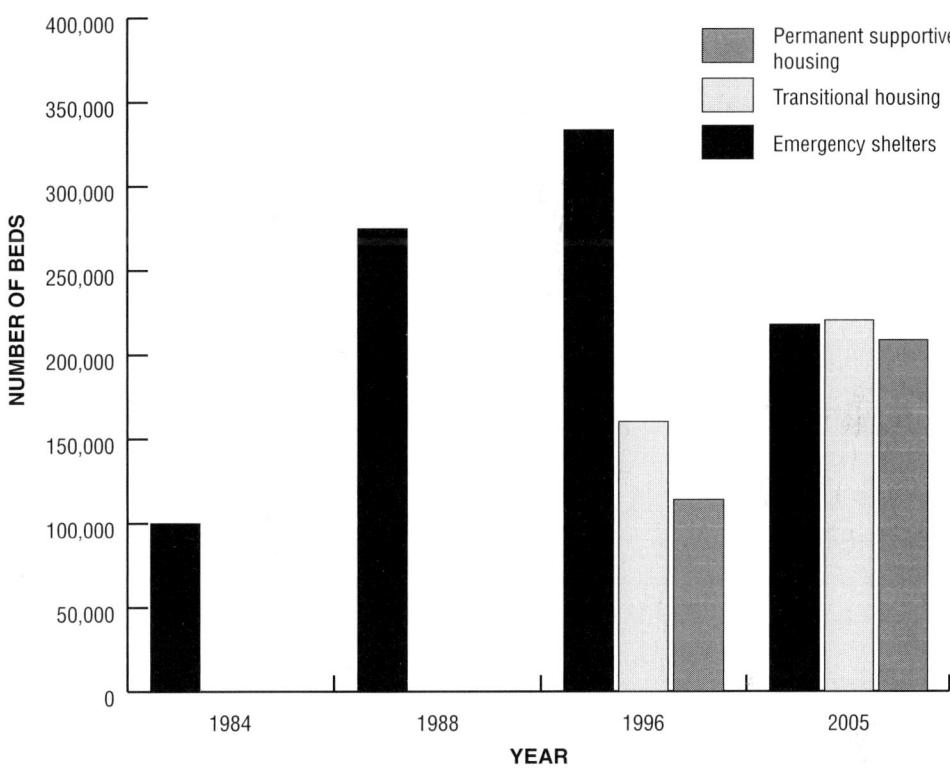

Source: U.S. Department of Housing and Urban Development

Figure 11-1 National Inventory of Facilities for the Homeless, 1984–2005

The questions of whether transitional housing works as a means of reducing homelessness, and what aspects of the combination of housing and services that it offers have an effect on the participant's ultimate success or failure, are complicated and not easily answered. There appears to be some evidence that the immediate outcome for many of those "graduating" from transitional housing is positive. The majority move into permanent housing, with about half of those moving into subsidized housing and the other half into private market housing. There is only limited data, however, on whether they retain their housing, and for how long. In the Sound Families initiative, a large-scale transitional housing program in the state of Washington underwritten by the Bill & Melinda Gates Foundation, 88 percent of the families moved into permanent housing. Although 40 percent of the families had moved within a year, nearly all were still in permanent housing at the end of the year, and only six percent were homeless.[22]

According to various research studies, 88 percent is an unusually high rate of successful placement in permanent housing from transitional housing, reflecting the fact that the Sound Families initiative was able to provide its graduates with portable Section 8 vouchers. Over three-quarters of those placed from the initiative used the vouchers to find permanent affordable housing. Other programs typically report much lower successful housing outcome rates, usually in the vicinity of 50 to 70 percent. A study of transitional housing participants from the Madison, Wisconsin, area found that less than half left the program for "positive housing outcomes." Of those, one-quarter moved in with family or friends, under conditions the researchers considered positive.[23]

The picture is further muddied by the wide variation between programs in the number of residents who complete the program compared to those who voluntarily leave or are asked to leave by the staff prematurely. These latter categories may represent anything from 20 to 50 percent of those entering many programs. Moreover, to the extent that transitional housing leads to successful outcomes, there appears to be little evidence to identify what features of the program contribute to success. The importance of affordable housing availability—whether in the form of bricks and mortar or through housing vouchers—in determining the probability of successful outcomes is a recurrent theme in the literature.

The extent to which positive transitional housing outcomes depend on the availability of affordable housing, coupled with the difficulty of showing specific connections between positive outcomes and any particular features of these programs, led many practitioners and researchers in the 1990s to wonder whether it was the availability of housing in the first place, rather than the programs, that brought about those outcomes. These questions led in turn to the growth of the Housing First model, described by the National Alliance to End Homelessness as "an approach to ending homelessness that centers on providing homeless people with housing quickly and then providing services as needed."[24]

Housing First models vary widely, but share a body of common features, as described by the Alliance:

- They focus on helping individuals and families access and sustain permanent rental housing as quickly as possible.
- The housing is not time-limited.
- A variety of services are delivered primarily following a housing placement to promote housing stability and individual well-being.

- Services are time-limited or long-term depending upon individual need.
- Housing is not contingent on compliance with services; instead, participants must comply with a standard lease agreement and are provided with the services and supports that are necessary to help them do so successfully.

The Housing First model was pioneered in the 1990s by Pathways for Housing, an organization founded by Sam Tsemberis, a New York City psychologist. Pathways concentrated on housing mentally ill homeless adults, the great majority of whom are also either alcohol or drug dependent. "Unlike traditional housing programs," as the Pathways website describes the program, "admission requirements are minimal: to be eligible, clients must be homeless, have a psychiatric disability, and elect to participate in the program. After settling into new apartments, clients are offered a wide range of support and clinical services."[25] Pathways serves more than 500 individuals in New York City and vicinity, and its placements have an exceptional retention rate; a 2007 sample study found that 88 percent of the individuals placed by Pathways were still in permanent housing after two years.[26]

The Pathways program is service-intensive, providing services to its clients through seven Assertive Community Treatment (ACT) teams, each one containing a social worker, substance abuse counselor, nurse, psychiatrist, peer counselor, family specialist, and employment specialist. Each ACT team provides services 24 hours per day, seven days per week to approximately 70 clients. Even with this intensive level of services, Pathways finds that their total cost to house and provide services to their clients is approximately $22,500 per year, or less than half of the cost of serving a chronically homeless individual through the emergency shelter system, and considerably less than serving that individual in transitional housing.

Given the success that organizations such as Pathways have had in using the Housing First model with chronically homeless people generally considered to be the most difficult to house, it was a logical step to extend the model to homeless families. In contrast to homeless individuals, homelessness among families is less often triggered by distinct behavioral problems. As Dennis Culhane, a prominent scholar and advocate of Housing First strategies puts it, "Homeless families ARE poorer, more likely to be pregnant, from an ethnic minority, and less likely to have a housing subsidy. Homeless families ARE NOT more likely to be mentally ill, depressed or less educated. As a group, homeless families are poorer, not more 'troubled'."[27] Homeless families are extremely poor, typically headed by single women with small children, limited education and employment levels, and with weak family and friendship support networks. In these respects, they are not markedly different from other very poor families who are housed.[28] While not all of those involved with addressing family homelessness agree with Culhane, his position has become widely accepted and has formed an important part of the basis for moving from a focus on the service-driven model of transitional housing to a housing-driven model represented by the Housing First approach.

Beyond Shelter, a pioneering effort in Los Angeles to apply that approach to homeless families, was founded by Tanya Tull in 1988. The Beyond Shelter model requires that the family agree to an initial Family Action Plan, developed together with a caseworker on intake, but makes continued participation in case management voluntary after the family is placed in a housing unit. Between 1989 and 2003, Beyond Shelter had placed in permanent housing, with substantial success rates, some 2,800 multiproblem homeless families, most of whom had substance abuse problems.[29] Since then, a growing number of communities around the country have adopted the Housing First approach for homeless families, either across the board or for those families that do not display significant behavioral barriers to housing stability on the basis of initial screening. In Columbus, Ohio, a Community Shelter Board screens homeless families, referring most to Housing First strategies but targeting higher cost and more intensive interventions to a smaller group of families with multiple problems. In Columbus, as elsewhere, rapid placement of families in permanent housing appears to lead to both substantial residential stability for the families and lower costs for the social service system.

AFFORDABLE HOUSING AND HOUSING FIRST

The availability of affordable housing remains a central issue with Housing First, as it ultimately does with any strategy to reduce homelessness. Homeless individuals and families are very poor. Since homeless families are largely headed by single women with low levels of education, the likelihood that their incomes will rise significantly above the poverty level is not great, even under the most positive conditions. Except to the extent that they can find housing in subsidized affordable developments or are able to obtain vouchers to reduce the cost of housing in the private market, they will continue to have difficulty achieving stable housing conditions, particularly in high-cost urban areas. Not surprisingly, studies have found that whether a poor family has a housing voucher or other subsidy has a significant impact on the likelihood that they will become homeless; one study concluded that "subsidized housing was virtually the only predictor of residential stability after shelter."[30]

In light of this, it is not surprising that many Housing First programs and programs to place graduates of transitional housing in permanent housing are engaged in a never-ending struggle to gain access to enough housing subsidies for their clients. Some programs, such as the Sound Families initiative in Washington, have been able to obtain access to a pool of housing vouchers. In other cases, homeless families are given priority for available subsidized housing units within the community. In Westchester County, New York, a high-cost area with a limited supply of subsidized housing, the county's department of social services was able to obtain the state's approval to add a "housing allowance" to each family's welfare (Temporary Assistance to Needy Families or TANF) benefit so that it would be able to afford housing on the private market. The state also authorized the county to provide a rental assistance program to working families moving out of the TANF program, in order to provide them with a one-year bridge subsidy in the expectation that the family would be able to obtain a voucher within a year.[31]

Many programs work hard to mobilize local resources to supplement the limited pool of state and federal resources for affordable housing. In addition to tapping multipurpose local housing trust funds, a large number of communities have dedicated public funds specifically to housing for the homeless. In 2006, the city of Portland, Oregon, provided $2.1 million in general fund revenues for a variety of both capital and operating needs and approved a $9 million bond issue for permanent supportive housing. Denver's ambitious Road Home program has established a goal of raising nearly $6.4 million per year from foundation, corporate, and individual sources to supplement public funds. The program has carried out a number of unconventional fund-raising efforts, including placing "donation meters" in key downtown locations and hosting an annual pajama party to raise money. The 2008 party raised $185,000 for the program.

Because of the connection between homelessness and the availability of affordable housing, increasing the affordable housing inventory has become an important element in many current local strategies to reduce or end homelessness. The Denver Road Home program has set a 10-year goal to create an additional nearly 3,200 permanent and transitional housing units, and by the end of the second year had created 789 new units. By 2007, Beyond Shelter's housing development arm had created 620 affordable rental units in Los Angeles, with another 242 in their development pipeline. Another L.A.-based organization, the SRO Housing Corporation, has as its mission the rehabilitation of the old residential hotels and boarding houses of the city's East Central district, its former skid row, turning them into high-quality affordable housing for single individuals. Initiated in 1984 under the leadership of long-time housing advocate Andy Raubeson, SRO Housing has created nearly 1,200 permanent units of housing along with 134 units of transitional housing and over 400 emergency shelter beds. In addition, it maintains two community parks and the James M. Wood Community Center, a visual landmark as well as a center of activity in the East Central area.

In the final analysis, given the paucity of the existing affordable housing inventory, the scarcity of vouchers, and the limited resources available to create new affordable housing, there is not and will not be in the foreseeable future enough subsidized housing to accommodate all those in need, whether they are currently homeless, ill-housed, or cost-burdened. While there is a credible argument that the needs of the homeless should take precedence for the scarce resources available over those who have a roof over their heads, that cannot but raise other questions, and potentially create perverse incentives for people to become homeless. Millions of poor families live in difficult housing situations, including those doubled up, those paying 50 percent or more of their income for shelter, or those living in overcrowded or substandard housing. For many of those households, staying out of homelessness is itself a struggle. On any given day, the number of families who are potentially at risk but are managing, often at considerable effort, to avoid homelessness is far greater than those who are homeless.

While few people consider homelessness in itself to be an attractive prospect, the more programs reduce the burdens of homelessness and offer what can be considered rewards—in the form of preferential access to the scarce and highly desirable commodity represented by a voucher or a subsidized apartment, more people may find it preferable to give up the struggle to avoid homelessness and enter the shelter system. There is some evidence that this indeed happened in the late 1980s and

Denver's Road Home uses "donation meters" on downtown streets both to raise money and raise peoples' awareness of homelessness.

Photo © Rich Miller, courtesy of Jamie Van Leeuwen, Denver's Road Home

early 1990s in New York City. When the city, under court order, sharply reduced the wait time for homeless families to qualify for permanent subsidized housing, the number of families entering the system grew; as Jencks points out: "The homeless are not just passive victims. They make choices like everyone else."[32]

This is not an argument to refrain from providing permanent housing to the homeless, or to return to the regime of dangerous shelters or welfare motels. It is a commentary, however, on the dangers that arise whenever a fundamental condition of a decent existence such as safe affordable housing is offered as a lottery only to a select few from among the population in need, rather than as an entitlement. As long as that is the case, there will be winners and losers, and people will continue to try to game the system to their advantage.

NOTES

1. Jencks, Christopher. 1994. *The Homeless*. Cambridge, Mass.: Harvard University Press, 3–4.
2. National Alliance to End Homelessness. 2007. *Data Snapshot: Doubled Up in the United States*. Available at http://www.endhomelessness.org/content/article/detail/1779. The report was based on an analysis of data in the 2005 American Community Survey.
3. See Cordray, David S., and Georgine M. Pion. 1991. "What's Behind the Numbers? Definitional Issues in Counting the Homeless." *Housing Policy Debate* 2:3.
4. National Alliance to End Homelessness. 2007. *Homelessness Counts*. Available at http://www.endhomelessness.org/content/article/detail/1440.
5. One publication of the National Coalition for the Homeless, *Fact Sheet #2 How Many People Experience Homelessness?* argues that homelessness is increasing, citing the increase in the number of shelter beds provided by social service agencies. This would appear to be highly circular reasoning. An increase in shelter beds is more likely to be a response to a given amount of homelessness, starting with a base condition in which the number of beds is likely to be significantly below the potential demand; it may also be a response to the increased availability of funding for shelter beds. Jencks raises the question of whether the increased availability of shelter beds under some circumstances may even act as a trigger to increase the size of the homeless population; see *op. cit.*, 103–106.
6. Since people in shelters are easily counted, but people living in the woods or abandoned buildings are not, it is reasonable that winter counts tend to be higher than those conducted in warmer weather.
7. National Alliance to End Homelessness, *op. cit.*, 12.
8. The issue of "recriminalization" of the homeless is a complex one, beyond the scope of this chapter. For an admittedly partisan perspective, see National Law Center on Homelessness & Poverty. 2002. *Illegal to be Homeless: The Criminalization of Homelessness in the United States*. Available at http://wiki.nlchp.org/pages/viewpage.action?pageID=65600.
9. Burt, Martha R. 1992. *Over the Edge: The Growth of Homelessness in the 1980s*. Washington, D.C.: The Urban Institute Press, 46.
10. Jencks, *op. cit.*, 64.
11. Hartman, Chester, and Barry Zigas. 1991. "What's Wrong with the Housing Market?" cited in Wright, James D., and Beth A. Rubin. "Is Homelessness a Housing Problem?" *Housing Policy Debate* 2(3): 937.
12. Rossi, Peter H. 1989. *Down and Out in America: The Origins of Homelessness*. Chicago: University of Chicago Press, 190–191.
13. Burt, *op. cit.*, 73.
14. Jencks, *op. cit.*, 39
15. Wright and Rubin, *op. cit.*, 942.
16. Ibid., 946.
17. Ibid., 952–953.
18. National Alliance to End Homelessness. 2006. *Promising Strategies to End Family Homelessness*. Available at http://www.endhomelessness.org/content/article/detail/999.

Under the HUD funding structure for transitional and permanent supportive housing, a community must have a continuum of care structure in place to be eligible.

19. U.S. Department of Housing and Urban Development. 2007. *The Annual Homelessness Assessment Report to Congress*. Available at http://www.huduser.org/publications/povsoc/annual_asssess.html.
20. The legislation (PL100-77) was initially known as the McKinney Act, after its principal sponsor, Rep. Stewart B. McKinney (R–Conn.). It was renamed the McKinney-Vento Act in 2000 to honor the late Rep. Bruce Vento of Minnesota, a longtime advocate for the homeless.
21. Burt, Martha R. 2006. *Characteristics of Transitional Housing for Homeless Families*. Washington, D.C.: The Urban Institute.
22. Northwest Institute for Children and Families, University of Washington School of Social Work. 2007. *How Are They Faring? Findings on 51 Families One Year After Exiting Transitional Housing*. Seattle: Bill & Melinda Gates Foundation.
23. Silva, Kristin, and James P. Winship. 2005. *Measuring the Success Rate of Clients in Transitional Housing*. Madison: Wisconsin Partnership for Housing Development, Inc.
24. Available at http://www.endhomelessness.org/section/tools/housingfirst.
25. Available at http://www.pathwaystohousing.org/TopMenu/AboutUs-2.html.
26. Stefancic, Ana, and Sam Tsemberis. 2007. "Housing First for Long-Term Shelter Dwellers with Psychiatric Disabilities in a Suburban County: A Four-Year Study of Housing Access and Retention." *Journal of Primary Prevention* 28, nos. 3–4 (July): 265–279.
27. Culhane, Dennis. 2004. "Family Homelessness: Where to From Here?" Presentation delivered at the National Alliance to End Homelessness National Conference on Ending Family Homelessness in October. A detailed paper in which Culhane and his colleagues study these questions in more detail is Culhane, Dennis, Stephen Metraux, Jung Min Park, Maryanne Schretzman, and Jesse Valente. 2007. "Testing a Typology of Family Homelessness Based on Patterns of Public Shelter Utilization in Four U.S. Jurisdictions: Implications for Policy and Program Planning." *Housing Policy Debate* 18(1) (May). A dissenting view, which argues for a greater emphasis on mental health issues of homeless families, is expressed in the comment to this paper by Ellen L. Bassuk in the same issue of *Housing Policy Debate*.
28. For a detailed survey of the research literature on these issues, see National Alliance to End Homelessness. 2005. *Family Homelessness in our Nation and Community: A Problem with a Solution*. Available at http://www.endhomelessness.org/content/article/detail/1224.
29. Tull, Tanya. 2004. "The Housing First Approach for Families Affected by Substance Abuse." *The Source* 13(1) (Spring).
30. The research is described in Khadduri, Jill. 2008. *Housing Vouchers are Critical for Ending Family Homelessness*. Washington, D.C.: National Alliance to End Homelessness.
31. National Alliance to End Homelessness. 2007. *Community Snapshot: Westchester County, N.Y.* Available at http://endhomelessness.org/content/article/detail/1524.
32. Jencks, *op. cit.*, 104. The New York City experience has been described by Gordon Berlin and William McAllister. 1992. "Homelessness." In *Setting Domestic Priorities: What Can Government Do?* ed. Henry Aaron and Charles Schultze. Washington, D.C.: The Brookings Institution, and J. Phillip Thompson. 1996–1997. "The Failure of Liberal Homeless Policy in the Koch and Dinkins Administration." *Political Science Quarterly* 111(Winter): 4.

CHAPTER

12

Inclusionary Housing: Using the Market to Create Affordable Housing

From the earliest days of affordable housing development, projects for lower income households were seen as a thing apart from the housing market. First developed by philanthropists, and then by government agencies, they occupied a separate physically distinct space, driven by different impulses than those driving developers of private-market housing. Even when government began to provide funds for private for-profit developers to build low-income housing in the 1960s, the projects they built were no different in concept from those government had built a generation earlier: separate containers for low-income families. Indeed, at the time it would have been hard for most developers, not to mention housing officials and city planners, to think that it could, or should, be otherwise.

This began to change in the 1970s, as two ideas about affordable housing began to capture the attention of planners, housing developers, and local officials. The first was that, contrary to the conventional wisdom, there was not only no good reason why lower income families could not live in the same development as more affluent ones, but that there were good reasons why they *should*. The second was that more affordable housing could be created if it was made part of the process of building housing for the market, taking advantage of the considerable energy and resources possessed by builders and developers in the private market as well as the power of the market itself. The terms that came into use to describe such efforts were *inclusionary zoning* or *inclusionary housing*,[1] phrases that deliberately played on the contrast with the exclusionary zoning practices of suburbia, to which they were seen as at least a partial antidote. Today, inclusionary land-use regulations are a widely recognized—although still intermittently controversial—strategy for creating affordable housing, used by a large and growing number of both affluent suburbs and older cities.

This chapter will provide an introduction to the varieties of inclusionary housing strategies, and describe how different municipalities use these strategies as a means of creating affordable housing and integrating it with their larger land-use planning activities. The first section will describe what inclusionary housing is, how it emerged, and how it has spread outward from its roots in a handful of affluent suburban communities. Two sections then focus on the legal and the economic issues associated with inclusionary housing; the final section looks at the policy and operational choices that determine its success, including the role the public sector must play in making inclusionary housing work.

WHAT IS INCLUSIONARY HOUSING?

Inclusionary housing uses the market to create affordable housing. It refers to programs or regulations that require or provide incentives to private developers to create affordable housing as part of their market-driven development activity, either by including the affordable housing in their developments, building it off-site, or contributing cash or land in lieu of construction so others can provide it. In most cases, a developer, either as a condition of approval or in return for incentives such as density bonuses, sets aside a percentage of the housing units in a development for affordable housing, selling or renting them to households whose incomes fall below specified income ceilings at affordable prices or rents. In other cases, a developer may contribute a cash in-lieu payment to a local housing trust fund, or donate a parcel of land to a municipal land bank or a community development corporation.

Inclusionary housing can be voluntary or mandatory. Under a voluntary program or ordinance, developers are offered incentives, such as increased density, in order to provide affordable housing, but are not required to do so. Under a mandatory program, they must provide the affordable housing—or an alternative such as an in lieu fee—and are often provided with incentives to offset the cost of doing so. In practice, voluntary programs are generally ineffectual. While developers who are required to provide affordable housing under reasonable ground rules figure out how to make it work, few voluntarily take on the obligation given the choice. As a result, except in those settings where a voluntary program is dictated by legal or political considerations, the thrust of inclusionary housing in recent years has been toward mandatory programs.

Inclusionary housing can apply to nonresidential projects, as well. Developers of office buildings or shopping centers are rarely expected actually to build affordable housing, but they may be required to contribute to a housing trust fund. Such programs or policies are generally known as "linkage." Boston and San Francisco have had linkage programs in place for decades, generating hundreds of millions of dollars to support a wide range of affordable housing activities.

Inclusionary programs serve a number of purposes. Most fundamentally, they are a way of producing affordable housing units, an important goal in itself in an era of limited public resources for affordable housing. They enable a city or county to leverage limited public resources by enlisting the development capacity, and in some cases the financial resources, of private developers to help further affordable housing programs. In addition, they can make it possible to integrate affordable housing into mixed income, socially inclusive developments, avoiding the concentration of poverty that has bedeviled so many affordable housing programs. They enable lower income families to share in the opportunities and quality of life available in more affluent communities, often with far less conflict and controversy than often accompany efforts to develop more conventional affordable housing projects in those same communities.

Inclusionary programs came into being more or less simultaneously in the early 1970s in a handful of affluent suburban communities and counties in the San Francisco Bay and Washington, D.C., metropolitan areas. No one community or individual can be cited as the "inventor" of inclusionary housing. It grew out of many different strands, including the struggle against suburban exclusionary zoning, which had its roots in the civil rights movement, and the growing awareness among liberally inclined officials and civic leaders in affluent suburban communities such as Fairfax County, Virginia, or Palo Alto, California, of the extent to which the cost of housing in their communities was rising beyond the reach not only of the poor, but of the young couples and families of the struggling middle class.

The first zoning ordinance that incorporated inclusionary requirements was most probably that of Fairfax County, which was adopted in 1971 and required that developers set aside 15 percent of their new homes or apartments for affordable housing. Although that ordinance was struck down by the Virginia Supreme Court two years later, other ordinances enacted during the next couple of years, including those adopted in Palo Alto and in Montgomery County, Maryland, a large, affluent suburban county north of Washington, D.C., have remained. Montgomery County's Moderately Priced Dwelling Unit or MPDU ordinance, enacted in 1973, has been exceptionally productive, leading to the construction of some 15,000 affordable housing units over 35 years.

The 1980s saw the first linkage ordinances; San Francisco broke ground with its ordinance in 1981, followed by Boston in 1986. The San Francisco ordinance initially required developers of office buildings to contribute $7.05 per square foot to the city's housing trust fund. Today, after many adjustments and the extension of the program to retail, hotel, and research and development projects, the linkage fee ranges from $13.25 to $19.89 per square foot depending on the type of development.

While local inclusionary housing activities in California, Virginia, and Maryland preceded state laws, state laws or court decisions elsewhere drove the spread of inclusionary housing. The Massachusetts Comprehensive Permit Law[2] gave developers of affordable housing—including developers who set aside at least 20 percent of their units as affordable housing—the right to go to the state Housing Appeals Committee to overturn municipal rejections of their projects. Although enacted in 1969, it became highly popular with developers in the 1980s, who used its provisions repeatedly since then to gain approval for inclusionary developments in recalcitrant towns. As a result, although relatively few Massachusetts towns have incorporated inclusionary requirements into their zoning ordinances, the state is a leader, along with California and New Jersey, in the production of affordable housing through inclusionary development.

Although a handful of New Jersey towns also enacted inclusionary ordinances in the 1970s, they were little more than symbolic gestures until the situation changed dramatically with the New Jersey Supreme Court's seminal 1983 decision in *Southern Burlington County v. Township of Mt. Laurel*[3] (known as the *Mt. Laurel II* decision). Affirming the court's earlier opposition to exclusionary zoning, the court not only held that inclusionary development was a desirable way for municipalities to meet their obligations to provide for their fair share of the region's affordable housing need, but that if a municipality failed to act, the courts would grant approvals—the so-called "builder's remedy"—to developers offering to build developments with a reasonable percentage of low- and moderate-income housing units.

Within little more than a year from the decision, the three special judges the court appointed to hear *Mt. Laurel* cases were deluged with over 140 separate cases from developers looking for a builder's remedy for their projects. Although few builder's remedies were actually granted by the courts, the threat spurred previously recalcitrant towns to negotiate settlements with developers. The first inclusionary development in New Jersey, in the hitherto exclusive and exclusionary central suburb of Bedminster, opened its doors in the summer of 1985. Two hundred and sixty affordable condominium units selling for as little as $30,000 were part of a larger 1,287 unit planned development, which was approved as part of a settlement of protracted litigation.

The enactment of the New Jersey Fair Housing Act in 1985 and the creation of the state Council on Affordable Housing led municipalities across the state to develop affordable housing plans to meet their fair share obligations as determined by the council. By this point, with most federal housing programs a thing of the past, inclusionary zoning was seen as the way communities could fill the gap left by the demise of those programs. Since then, it has been the largest single means by which affordable housing has been provided in New Jersey. By the early 2000s, more than 150 different towns, villages, and townships had enacted zoning ordinances or adopted zoning changes incorporating set-asides of affordable housing, and nearly 20,000 affordable housing units had been created as a result.

While inclusionary housing in California began with Palo Alto in 1973, it too was limited to a handful of cities and counties until the 1980s, when the state enacted laws requiring local governments to prepare housing elements and accommodate their fair share of regional housing needs. From that point on, the number of cities and counties with inclusionary housing ordinances has grown steadily. The number has exploded since the 1990s, going from 60 in 1994 to over 100 by 2002, and 170 by 2006—nearly one out of every three California local governments. Between 1999 and 2006, affordable housing created through inclusionary programs represented more than 10 percent of total housing production in 24 of California's cities and counties.

Inclusionary housing grew steadily in New Jersey, Massachusetts, and California during the 1980s, and appeared during that period in a handful of other towns and cities, such as Boulder, Colorado, and Lewisboro, New York. Its emergence as a national—and an urban as well as suburban—phenomenon, however, began during the 1990s and grew most notably in the years following the millennium. This reflected not only the dramatic revival of housing market demand in a host of cities that had seen little private housing development for decades, but also the growing popular acceptance of the ideas that housing should be economically integrated and that developers should be engaged in providing that housing.

To urban planners and housing advocates in these cities, the revival of market demand was seen as both a threat and an opportunity. While many saw gentrification as a threat to housing and neighborhoods that had been affordable to lower income families, others saw the rise of market-driven development as an opportunity and inclusionary housing strategies as a vehicle for realizing that opportunity. The first of the wave of urban inclusionary programs were enacted in 2002 in Stamford, Connecticut, and Denver. They were followed over the next few years by Chicago, San Diego, Washington, D.C., Baltimore, and most recently, Philadelphia.

In contrast to most of the earlier suburban programs, which were driven by liberal political leadership or state mandates, most of the urban programs emerged out of community-based advocacy, which ultimately compelled hesitant mayors and city councils first to take notice, and then to act. While Stamford's Mayor Dannel Malloy did not initiate that city's effort, he quickly recognized the breadth of the community's support for inclusionary housing and embraced it energetically. In other cities, including Chicago, Washington, D.C., and Baltimore, the enactment of inclusionary zoning ordinances took place only after sustained coalition building and advocacy efforts. In Chicago, the city's community development corporations played a central role in those efforts, while in Baltimore, the national organizing group Acorn pulled together a broadly based coalition, including nonprofit organizations, religious institutions, and trade unions.

At the same time, inclusionary housing was spreading more widely around the United States, prompted by the increased pressure coming from the steady rise in house prices that began toward the end of the 1990s. The past decade has seen it emerge as an important part of local housing strategies in towns and cities in many different states, including Florida, North Carolina, New York, Illinois, and Washington, among others.[4] Today, as towns and cities develop their affordable housing strategies, inclusionary housing routinely figures in their discussions. They may or may not in the end choose to enact an inclusionary housing program, but the idea has become an integral part of the planner's toolkit. At the same time, opposition to inclusionary housing programs from the home building industry remains strong, with the National Association of Home Builders and its state affiliates continuing to devote considerable time and money to fighting it at the state and local levels.

Any attempt to estimate how many affordable housing units have been created in the United States through inclusionary housing is likely to be little more than a barely educated guess. There is no central clearinghouse for such information, and many cities and counties do not even have accurate tabulations of their own efforts. While there are figures for affordable housing created through Massachusetts's 40B program, the published statistics do not distinguish between units in inclusionary developments and those in conventional affordable housing projects.

The matter is compounded by the fact that many programs permit developers to contribute to a housing trust fund either as their sole option, in the case of linkage, or as an alternative to building affordable housing. Tracking how that money is spent, and how many affordable housing units are created as a result, is even more difficult. Trust fund money may be spent on a variety of housing-related activities that do not result in new units, including assistance to struggling lower income home buyers or home owners.[5]

Still, a rough estimate suggests that the total might be in the vicinity of 120,000 to 150,000 affordable housing units, taking into account units financed in whole or part with linkage fees. California most probably accounts for nearly half of that total.[6] This figure is modest compared to federal housing programs such as the low income housing tax credit, because until recently few jurisdictions outside California, Massachusetts, and New Jersey had inclusionary programs. Even in California, such programs were relatively sparse until the 1990s. Since 1999, California cities and counties have produced more than 29,000 units through inclusionary housing programs, nearly 4,000 units per year. The cities of Sacramento, San Diego, Carlsbad, Roseville, and Irvine are each currently producing more than 150 units per year through their inclusionary programs.[7]

THE LEGAL STATUS OF INCLUSIONARY HOUSING

The legal issues surrounding inclusionary housing programs are more complicated than those for other affordable housing programs. Questions of land-use law, exactions, and price controls can arise when local governments obligate private developers to produce affordable housing or contribute to a housing trust fund.

While the purpose and outcomes of inclusionary housing are clear, it has not always been clear how inclusionary housing fits legally into the regulatory framework of state and local government. Inclusionary housing has been variously characterized as a land-use regulation, such as a part of a zoning ordinance; as an exaction, similar to impact fees that many cities and counties charge for road or park improvements; and in a few cases, as a form of price regulation similar to rent control.[8] One inclusionary ordinance has been invalidated as a taking.[9] This is not mere hairsplitting, since depending on how it is defined, the legal or even constitutional standards that determine whether a program passes muster may be very different ones.

An exaction takes place where a municipality or county requires, or "exacts," as a condition of approval, a financial contribution from a developer for improvements to the public infrastructure or other facilities or activities benefiting the public, ranging from improving roads or sewer systems needed to serve the development to contributing to the cost of building or maintaining parks, schools, or firehouses. Under the laws of most states, as well as basic constitutional principles embodied in the U.S. Supreme Court's *Nollan* and *Dolan* decisions,[10] there must be a clear relationship of proportionality or a "nexus" between the nature and amount of the exaction and the impact of the development on the community. Thus, the amount of an impact fee (as these exactions are sometimes called) for school construction needs to be closely related (or proportional) to the cost of accommodating the additional pupils likely to be generated by the development, and cannot be used to alleviate overcrowding unrelated to the development's impact. How precise that relationship needs to be, and whether a municipality can in fact exact money for a school building project at all, will depend on the law of the particular state.

By contrast, a land-use regulation requires no such test; it is determined by the suitability of the land for a particular use or activity and the reasonableness of the local authority's regulations. It has long been recognized that land-use regulations have major financial implications. They largely determine the opportunity for profit from developing the land, and by extension, the value of the land itself. American law, however, has consistently held that towns and cities have broad discretion to change the regulations governing a particular piece of land, even if the change significantly diminishes the value of the land, without being required to compensate the owner—as long as the change furthers the public purposes of land-use regulation and the owner is not deprived of all potential use of the land. On that basis, courts have consistently upheld zoning ordinance changes that have reduced the density permitted in an area, or restricted what the owner can use the land for, as long as some beneficial use remained and the local government had sound reasons for its actions.

These differences have significant implications for inclusionary housing. If the obligation placed on a developer to incorporate affordable housing in a project or make a payment into a housing trust fund is categorized as an exaction, it will have to meet the so-called nexus test, meaning that the municipality must establish a strong relationship between the impact of the development and the affordable housing obligation. If that obligation is treated as a land-use regulation, no such relationship needs to be established, but the regulation must be shown to be within the municipality's power to regulate land use, be grounded in a sound public purpose, and not so limiting on the owner's ability to use the property that it can be considered a taking of the property. Moreover, the regulations must be broadly applicable to similarly situated properties, rather than reflecting individual treatment of specific properties.

As a rule, ordinances or regulations that require inclusion of affordable housing within a development—as distinct from linkage programs—have been construed as land-use regulations rather than exactions. This was part of the rationale used by the Virginia Supreme Court in striking down the Fairfax County ordinance in *DeGroff v. Fairfax County*.[11] The court held, in a ruling weak in both analysis and historical understanding, that because inclusionary zoning was "socioeconomic" in nature, it had no place in a land-use regulatory scheme.[12] Both the reasoning and conclusion of the Virginia court were dismissed, however, in the New Jersey Supreme Court's *Mt. Laurel II*.[13] The court pointed out that zoning regulations are inherently socioeconomic in nature, adding, in a pointed rejoinder to the Virginia decision, "It is nonsense to single out inclusionary zoning and label it 'socio-economic' if that is meant to imply that other aspects of zoning are not." The New Jersey court found that inclusionary ordinances were a permissible form of land-use regulation. The California courts reached a similar conclusion in that state's key case, *Home Builders Association of Northern California v. City of Napa*,[14] holding that Napa's inclusionary zoning ordinance was "a generally applicable legislative enactment rather than an individualized assessment imposed as a condition of development."[15]

While most state laws are silent on inclusionary housing, those that do address it consistently do so within the framework of land-use regulation, as is the case in Connecticut and Washington. It seems likely that, in those states that currently lack either statutes or case law establishing its legal status, future court cases will be heard in the framework of the state's body of laws dealing with land-use regulation.[16]

The principal reason why inclusionary zoning ordinances are treated as land-use regulations is that they control an aspect of the development itself; that is, they specify standards for the affordable housing units that are part of the development, and thus are inextricable from the manner in which the development must use the land on which it is to be constructed. Although some such ordinances permit developers to make a payment to a local housing trust fund in lieu of constructing the units, such options are considered secondary to the principal purpose of the ordinance, which is the construction of housing. Linkage programs are fundamentally different, since the developer's payment of a fee is the purpose of the ordinance or policy, rather than a secondary feature.

As a result, linkage ordinances are widely considered to be exactions falling under the nexus standard, meaning that the municipality must demonstrate that a clear relationship exists between the impact of the development and the fee being charged. In practice, however, this raises little difficulty. New shopping centers and office buildings bring large numbers of workers into a community, many of whom are low-wage workers and members of lower income households. Planners and economists, given information about the size of a particular nonresidential development and the nature of the planned use—office, retail, warehouse, etc.—can predict with reasonable accuracy the number of lower income households that will need housing in or near the municipality as a result of the construction. Such a study, called a nexus study, is required in California as a condition preceding enactment of a linkage ordinance.

As more states enact statutes authorizing local governments to enact inclusionary ordinances, questions about their legality are likely to become rarer. At this point, however, in those states that have not enacted such ordinances, they still remain. To determine whether a municipality can indeed enact an inclusionary ordinance in a state in which explicit authority is lacking, two questions are likely to be paramount. First is the nature and scope of the state's statutes authorizing land-use regulation generally, and the extent to which they provide flexibility to local governments and recognize the socioeconomic dimension of land-use regulation. Second is the breadth of discretion permitted to local government generally to exercise its police power within the overall framework of state law, rather than being limited to those powers explicitly authorized by the state.

ECONOMICS OF INCLUSIONARY HOUSING

The way that inclusionary housing interweaves the creation of affordable housing with the development of housing for the private market triggers a series of economic questions that do not arise when a developer builds an affordable housing development through a public subsidy program. The most important distinction between inclusionary housing and other ways of producing affordable housing is that it depends on the marketplace and on the readiness of developers to build for the market. This means not only that enough market demand, and development activity responding to that demand, must exist in the locality to justify establishing a program, but that the program itself must be designed so that developers can comply with it without impairing the economic viability of their projects. If the inclusionary requirements—in terms of the percentage or price range of affordable housing—or the linkage fee are too demanding, they could potentially discourage development, thereby defeating the purpose of the program.

The central features that determine the economic feasibility of an inclusionary program, over and above the critical threshold conditions of market demand and development profitability, are the percentage and affordability level of the affordable housing units required, and the extent to which any costs imposed on developers as a result of those requirements are offset by public sector incentives or assistance.

A typical inclusionary ordinance will specify both the percentage of affordable units required of developers, often referred to as the "set-aside," and the income range or ranges of the tenants or buyers to whom the units must be affordable. Percentages vary widely, from as little as five percent to more than 25 percent, but most suburban ordinances require that 15 to 20 percent of the units in developments subject to an inclusionary program be affordable housing, while urban programs usually require less. This reflects both the remaining uncertainties associated with urban housing markets and the higher cost of construction typical of urban centers.[17] Chicago's inclusionary ordinance requires that 10 percent of the units in new developments be affordable housing, as do those of Boston and Denver. Under the Baltimore ordinance, that percentage is exceeded only where the project is benefiting from "major public subsidy."

The affordability targets of inclusionary housing programs vary even more widely. In California, which gives its cities and counties broad discretion to design their own inclusionary programs, some programs require that units be priced to be affordable to households earning 100 to 120 percent of the area median income, while others require that at least some of the units be affordable to households at 50 percent or even 30 percent of AMI. Many California ordinances provide for a mix of different affordability ranges, such as the city of Irvine's ordinance, which requires a 15 percent set-aside, equally divided between households with incomes below 50 percent, between 51 to 80 percent, and between 81 to 120 percent of AMI.

In New Jersey, the Council on Affordable Housing has adopted regulations that specify in detail the affordability range that must be built into all local inclusionary ordinances. At least half of the units must be affordable to households earning below 50 percent of AMI, with the balance affordable to households earning between 50 and 80 percent of AMI. Within each of these two ranges, the state further specifies a series of pricing subranges to ensure that towns do not price their units to households at the very top of each income range. While understandable in principle, the proliferation of different prices for the same or similar housing units, particularly in a small development, can be quite burdensome to the developer.

The cost of meeting a community's inclusionary requirements are a function of the percentage of affordable housing required and the income range or ranges to which it must be affordable. In most cases, the price of an affordable unit will be less than the cost to produce it. The lower the income of the target household for that unit, the greater the gap is likely to be. If it costs $250,000 to produce a hypothetical unit, and a would-be

TABLE 12-1 COMBINED EFFECT OF PERCENTAGE AND AFFORDABILITY RANGE ON COST OF SATISFYING INCLUSIONARY REQUIREMENTS

TARGET HOUSEHOLD INCOME	SUBSIDY COST PER AFFORDABLE UNIT	TOTAL SUBSIDY COST FOR 100-UNIT PROJECT		
		10%	15%	20%
$20,000	$190,000	$1,900,000	$2,850,000	$3,800,000
$40,000	$130,000	$1,300,000	$1,950,000	$2,600,000
$50,000	$100,000	$1,000,000	$1,500,000	$2,000,000
$75,000	$25,000	$250,000	$375,000	$500,000

Assumptions: Cost per unit is $250,000 and household can afford to pay 3 times household income

targeted household can afford to pay three times its income of $75,000 for the unit, the household will be able to pay $225,000 and the gap will be $25,000. If the unit is to be targeted to a household with an income of $50,000, the gap will grow to $100,000. This figure is generally known as the "affordability gap."

The effect of the affordability range and the percentage of affordable units are illustrated in Table 12-1 for a hypothetical development of 100 units, where the cost of producing each affordable unit is $250,000. Depending on the combination of options chosen, the total subsidy cost associated with the development could range from a modest $250,000 to the considerable sum of $3.9 million. The former, which is likely to be less than one percent of the developer's total project cost, can be accommodated by most developers under most circumstances without difficulty, while the later is likely to require help in the form of cost offsets or incentives from the public sector. An analysis of this sort can help local governments assess the extent to which they may have to provide offsets or incentives as part of their inclusionary programs.

Offsets and incentives

Public sector cost offsets play an important role in inclusionary housing programs. Offsets are public sector actions or incentives that reduce the affordability gap, either by reducing the developer's costs or by increasing the return. Waivers of application or sewer hookup fees are offsets that reduce developer costs. A tax abatement that reduces the carrying cost to the future lower income home owner, allowing the developer can charge more for the unit, increases revenues. In both cases, the effect is to reduce the gap and mitigate the economic effect of the ordinance on the developer.

Nothing in law or economics dictates that cost offsets must necessarily eliminate *all* economic effects of the ordinance. To some extent, meeting the requirements of an inclusionary zoning ordinance can be seen as part of the developer's cost of business, similar to a host of other requirements that may be imposed, from planting shade trees along sidewalks to contributing to the cost of the local public schools. Many developers see inclusionary requirements in that light, and will go forward without cost offsets if the project "pencils out"; that is, can be counted on to generate an adequate rate of return.[18] This is particularly true in prime up-market locations, where the sheer opportunity to build is worth almost any concession that the municipality might demand.

There is a difference, however, between the cost of inclusionary housing and other costs typically imposed by local land-use regulations or impact fees. In the case of the latter, the costs either translate into benefits for the development—such as shade trees—or mitigate public sector costs made necessary by the development—such as a public school. In the case of inclusionary housing, the municipality is requiring the developer to participate in addressing a social or economic condition that the developer did little or nothing to create.[19] Thus, there is a credible argument, which has been acknowledged in the laws of a number of states, that where a municipality wants to take advantage of a developer's energy and initiative to address this condition by imposing an inclusionary requirement, it must, in the words of a recent New Jersey court decision, offer the developer an "offsetting benefit."[20] Thus, under the Washington state law authorizing inclusionary zoning,[21] municipalities must offer one of a number of such benefits or incentives, including

- density bonuses;
- height and bulk bonuses;
- fee waivers or exemptions;
- parking reductions; and
- expedited permitting[22]

These are only a few of the potential offsetting benefits that a municipality or county can offer.

The most common offset links the inclusionary requirement either to a density bonus or a rezoning of property. Under a density bonus program, the municipality provides a "bonus" number of market units in return for the developer providing affordable housing, often at a rate of one additional market unit for every affordable unit. Thus, if the baseline density in a zone is 10 units to the acre, by imposing a 20 percent set-aside and a 20 percent density bonus, the developer can build 12 units to the acre. In principle, the additional profit from the incremental market units will offset the cost of the affordable units.[23]

Where a developer wants to rezone a property, either from a lower to a higher residential density or from nonresidential to residential use, or where the municipality is planning to rezone land in ways that will significantly increase its value, a compelling argument can be made that the inclusion of an affordable housing set-aside should be part and parcel of that rezoning. The cost of the set-aside in such cases is being offset by the windfall benefit being given by the public to the property owner and developer as a result of the rezoning. In cases where land was previously zoned for a low-demand use, such as industrial use in many older cities, a rezoning allowing high-density residential development is likely to cause a considerable windfall. In a strong market environment, the increased value resulting from the rezoning can justify a substantial set-aside of affordable housing.[24]

The most common other offsets, as suggested by the Washington statute, are likely to be either in the form of land-use regulatory changes that reduce the cost of development or fiscal benefits, such as fee waivers or expedited processing. While none of these offsets involve the direct transfer of public funds, they nonetheless can have a significant effect on the public cost of the project. Changes in the density of development, for example, can have significant impacts on traffic, service delivery, and the quality of life, although the change—depending on the particular circumstances—can be either positive or negative. Waiving fees otherwise used to support municipal functions, such as development plan review or sewerage service, shifts the cost of providing those functions onto other developers or onto the taxpayers as a whole. Expedited processing for one class of project may result in additional delays for other projects awaiting action, which may also confer public benefits.

Finally, as noted earlier, a city or county can use its resources to increase the developer's revenues indirectly by providing a tax abatement on the affordable units, or directly, by providing capital subsidy funds from HOME or from a state or local housing trust fund.

A sophisticated application of offsets, involving cost reductions and revenue increases in a variety of different settings, appears in the inclusionary ordinance enacted by the Baltimore city council in 2007. The ordinance provides for different inclusionary requirements for three different project types:

- Projects receiving a "major public subsidy" such as discounted city land, tax abatement, tax increment financing or city grants, loans or infrastructure above a certain percentage of project cost
- Projects that are the subject of a planned unit development density increase or a rezoning from nonresidential use
- Projects receiving no subsidy or benefit from the city

The ordinance varies both the set-aside percentage and the affordability targets for each of the three categories, and provides for a variety of adjustments, including the possibility of increased subsidies or waivers of all or part of the inclusionary requirements as necessary to ensure that projects are economically feasible. These adjustments and the substantial public incentives reflect the still-uncertain real estate market conditions in a city where gentrifying neighborhoods and strong downtown housing demand coexist with other parts of the city where widespread abandonment and economic distress remain the norm.

MAKING INCLUSIONARY HOUSING WORK

Like any other affordable housing strategy, inclusionary zoning does not run itself. Since developers have a compelling interest in maximizing their returns and minimizing their costs, the public sector has to be particularly diligent in designing and managing an inclusionary program to make sure it accomplishes the greatest benefit to the public while being consistent with developer profitability. Clear, well-thought-out ground rules must be drafted and incorporated in an ordinance or policy in advance of any specific application, and development applications must be carefully reviewed and monitored to ensure that they indeed comply with the provisions of the ordinance. Procedures must ensure that buyers or tenants are properly qualified and selected without favoritism, as in an affordable housing development, and resales and rerentals must be monitored over time to ensure that the housing units remain part of the affordable housing stock. Finally, if developers are permitted to contribute land or money for development of affordable housing elsewhere in the community, procedures must be in place to determine when those alternatives are acceptable, and how—once the land or money has been received by the municipality—it will be used to create affordable housing rather than sit idle.

Addressing the issues

Table 12-2 offers a checklist of issues that need to be considered in designing and implementing an inclusionary housing ordinance. Some are straightforward, while others may require considerable discussion and evaluation before reaching consensus and resolution.

An inclusionary ordinance needs to go into considerable detail to make clear precisely what the city or county expects of the developer with respect to the affordable housing units. Once the number and affordability mix of the units has been established, the city must specify how they are to be provided within the development. Many of the issues that arise are not matters of right or wrong, but matters of judgment and policy. There is nothing inherently wrong about a developer clustering the affordable units in a particular part of the site—as long as it is not isolated or otherwise unsuitable—but there are legitimate policy reasons for a city to require a developer to disperse the affordable units within the development. Similarly, with respect to the distribution of the affordable units by size or number of bedrooms, the city can require that it be similar to that of the market units or may want to specify a particular mix based on its assessment of the community's housing need. It is important, however, that the ordinance specify the bedroom mix; otherwise the developer might be tempted to save money by making all the affordable units one-bedroom or studio apartments.

The importance of detailed standards and careful review and monitoring cannot be overstated. Developers, even responsible and ethical ones, are ultimately most concerned about the bottom line. Seemingly modest differences in how the sales prices of affordable units are calculated—such as permitting buyers to qualify on the basis of an adjustable-rate mortgage rather than a fixed-rate one, or setting unrealistically low condominium fees for the affordable units—can mean millions of dollars in additional revenues to the developer through higher prices for the required affordable units. Similarly, if the developer is given responsibility for screening and selecting the buyers and tenants of the affordable units, the temptation to cut corners in order to fill the units quickly and minimize the interest on the developer's construction loan may be hard to resist.[25]

TABLE 12-2 INCLUSIONARY ZONING ISSUES CHECKLIST*

ISSUE	COMMENT
Is the ordinance clearly or arguably legal under applicable state law?	In many states this will be clear, based on existing statutes or case law. In some states, however, existing law will not provide a clear direction, in which case the city attorney will have to make a judgment based on drawing inferences from general state law dealing with municipal powers, land-use regulation, and the like.
How broadly should the ordinance apply?	Ordinances can apply to a limited number of zoning districts, all residential development, or both residential and nonresidential development, by building in a linkage program. The ordinance may want to set separate standards to govern situations where rezoning results in significantly enhanced land values.
What inclusionary percentage should be required?	The percentage can range from as little as five percent to more than 30 percent and should reflect a balance of economic feasibility considerations and the city's housing goals. In addition to setting the percentage, the ordinance must address how fractional amounts should be calculated.
What is the minimum threshold size of projects to which the ordinance applies?	Ordinances typically set a minimum development size to trigger the ordinance, which can range from five to over 50. Ordinances may impose an in lieu fee on developments below the threshold.
What should be the income mix of the affordable housing units required?	Ordinances can set standards that range from below 30 percent of AMI to as high as 120 percent of AMI. Many ordinances require a mix of different affordability levels, particularly in large-scale developments.
To what extent should developers be permitted to pay fees in lieu of building housing, and how should the fee be set?	The fee should bear a reasonable relationship to the developer's cost of providing the unit or the cost of providing the unit elsewhere. The city must decide whether it wants more to obtain units from the developer or receive cash in order to permit construction of units elsewhere, and calibrate its policies to govern in-lieu fees accordingly.
To what extent should developers be permitted to build housing off-site or donate land for housing off-site in lieu of building?	These alternatives should also be determined in the context of the city's overall housing goals. Care should be taken to ensure that off-site options do not further concentrations of poverty and affordable housing and that they benefit the neighborhoods in which they are situated.
What are design and size standards for affordable housing?	The ordinance should make clear the extent to which the affordable units do or do not need to share the same design features, size, and bedroom mix of the market units. Many ordinances permit smaller units with more modest interior furnishings, as long as the exterior appearance is similar to the market units.

ISSUE	COMMENT
How should affordable units be situated on the development site?	Some ordinances require that affordable units be dispersed among the market units, while others permit them to be clustered. If the latter, standards may be appropriate to ensure that they are not isolated or sited in unsuitable parts of the site.
When will the units be built?	The ordinance should make sure that the affordable units are built in parallel with the market units and that no affordable units are "left over" to be built after the last of the market units has been completed.
What incentives or offsets, if any, will be offered to developers?	The city must determine what incentives it will offer from those available (density bonuses, fee waivers, etc.), based on its understanding of what is necessary to ensure the economic feasibility of the ordinance as well as its assessment of any public costs involved. The laws of some states require cities to offer some incentives as part of an inclusionary ordinance.
How will households qualify for the units and who will be responsible for qualifying them?	Specific criteria—which can be taken from existing housing subsidy programs—can be used to determine qualifications for the buyers and tenants of the affordable units. A public or nonprofit entity independent of the developer should be identified and charged with the responsibility of recruiting, screening, and selecting buyers and tenants.
How will initial rent and sales prices be calculated?	The ordinance or accompanying regulations should specify precisely how a unit is considered "affordable" based on the appropriate percentage of income spent on monthly housing costs. Particularly with respect to units for sale, the ordinance must specify the way cost is calculated, to ensure that the costs are not low-balled by the developer in order to inflate the price.
How long should the units remain affordable?	Affordability controls can vary from not at all to permanent. Most cities are finding that longer terms of affordability, with reasonable but modest appreciation permitted for owner-occupied units, best serve the public interest.
How will the resale of affordable units be handled?	The ordinance or accompanying regulations need to provide a formula to govern the appreciation permitted on resale of an affordable unit. A public or nonprofit entity such as a community land trust must be put in place to calculate resale prices, ensure that new buyers are income-qualified, and generally monitor the affordable inventory being created through the inclusionary program.
How will the program be monitored and adjusted over time?	The ordinance should provide for ongoing monitoring of the effects of the ordinance as well as changes in market conditions that may affect the ordinance, and may justify modifying the terms of the ordinance. Monitoring can ensure that the city gets the maximum benefit from the program and that developers are not unfairly burdened with unrealistic conditions.
Does the ordinance provide for modifications or waivers in the case of hardships or special conditions?	It may be appropriate to permit developers to seek adjustments or waiver of inclusionary requirements in the event of hardship or unusual conditions, in which case the ordinance should specify what a developer must provide in terms of evidence to justify an adjustment or waiver.

* This checklist has been adapted freely from one prepared by the California Institute of Local Government

Similar responsibilities arise with respect to resale or rerental of affordable units. While it is easy to understand that a management entity must be in place to handle rerentals, it is equally important that an entity be in place to handle resales. Typically, affordable units in inclusionary developments built for sale are subject to what are known as deed restrictions or covenants, which govern the price at which the unit can be resold and the income qualifications of future buyers. Although these conditions are attached to the deed, they still need effective management. Someone must calculate the resale price and explain it to the seller,[26] screen potential buyers, and make sure that when the closing takes place, all of the conditions are satisfied and the unit remains affordable.

Offering alternatives to on-site construction

The extent to which an inclusionary ordinance should offer alternatives to building affordable units within the development triggering the obligation is another issue that demands careful consideration. Five potential alternatives—including on-site development—are at least theoretically possible, as shown in Table 12-3. In practice, however, not all may be feasible or desirable in all communities. Since it is fundamentally the city's choice to decide which alternatives to offer developers, if any, it is the city's responsibility to determine which alternatives—and under what terms—best serve the public interest.

That determination will hinge on two factors, one a policy issue and the second a practical one. The policy issue is the extent to which units in the anticipated market-rate developments will better address community needs than alternative affordable housing types or locations, or

TABLE 12-3 INCLUSIONARY HOUSING ALTERNATIVES

	ON-SITE	OFF-SITE
Construction	Developer constructs affordable housing units as part of development project	Developer constructs affordable housing units on separate site elsewhere in community
Land	Developer dedicates portion of site to be developed by other entity	Developer dedicates site for affordable housing elsewhere in community
Money	N/A	Developer makes contribution to housing trust fund for development or improvement of affordable housing in the municipality or county

whether alternatives will better address community needs. The practical issue is the extent to which the capacity exists—or can be created—within the community to create those alternatives.

The policy issue is not a simple one. In many older cities, a large percentage of market-rate construction is in high-rise buildings in or near the city's downtown. Affordable units in those buildings are likely to be small units. Even if the units contain two or three bedrooms they may not be as appropriate for families with children as units without elevators and with private yards. Moreover, since high-rise buildings are very expensive to build, the cost to the developer to create each affordable unit may be greater than the cost to build an equally affordable unit on a vacant lot in a residential neighborhood in the same city. As a result, an in-lieu fee might potentially not only lead to the construction of units more suitable for families with children, it might even result in a greater number of affordable units.

Even if this is the case, there are countervailing factors to consider. Are adequate building sites available in suitable locations for the affordable housing to be built? In many cities, the alternative sites may be in both high-poverty and predominately minority areas. Thus, while a strategy of collecting in-lieu fees from downtown developers might result in more housing units, it also might result in the continuing concentration of affordable housing in lower income, heavily African American or Latino areas. In other cities, however, building sites might be available in areas that are beginning to show signs of gentrification. A strategy that targeted those sites for affordable housing, acquiring them with in-lieu fees, might be an effective way to preserve economic integration in areas that might otherwise gradually lose their existing lower income residents.

Capacity also varies from city to city. Most large cities in the United States have what might be called an affordable housing development "infrastructure." City governments employ individuals with housing expertise, one or more community development corporations or nonprofit developers have the ability to build or rehab affordable housing, lenders and intermediaries provide financial support, and, for the most part, it is possible to find suitable sites for development or redevelopment. This infrastructure is often weaker or nonexistent in small cities and suburban or rural areas. Small towns lack expertise, few of them have local CDCs or nonprofit developers, and sites may be scarce or available only at excessive cost.

The political climate, moreover, will also vary. While opposition to affordable housing is far from unknown in large cities, overall it is more generally accepted. With large lower income constituencies, urban politicians are more likely to be attuned to their needs, while groups like Acorn can mobilize large bodies of residents in support of affordable housing initiatives. In many growing suburban communities the climate is very different. While people may not be opposed to affordable housing in principle, they may object to it being located in their backyard, fearing that it will affect their property values and bring unsuitable people into their neighborhood. In the absence of a large low-income constituency, local officials are unlikely to promote affordable developments in the face of neighborhood opposition.

As a result, while housing trust funds—whether created through in-lieu fees, linkage fees, tax increment financing, or other means—may be a godsend in cities like Philadelphia or Boston, they may end up accumulating cash, rather than creating housing units, in communities that lack either the development infrastructure or the political climate to create affordable housing. Where they are used, the money may go to noncontroversial purposes such as down payment assistance or fix-up grants to lower income home owners rather than to create affordable housing units.

In New Jersey, municipalities have been legally permitted since 1990 to collect development fees, including in-lieu fees, for affordable housing. With few exceptions, the municipalities doing so are affluent, growing, suburban municipalities. Since 1990, they have collected a total of nearly $360 million. Only a little more than half of the funds, or $189 million, has been spent, leaving a balance at the end of 2006 of $171 million. Of the amount spent, a great deal—most probably more than half—has been spent on Regional Contribution Agreements, sending money to other municipalities—usually older cities and small towns—to build affordable housing in their stead. As a result, the New Jersey legislature has recently amended the state's Fair Housing Act to introduce a "use it or lose it" provision. Under the amendment, local trust fund monies that have not been committed within four years after their receipt will revert to the state's housing trust fund for use in cities or towns more favorably disposed to affordable housing.[27]

All of these considerations must be weighed by local officials in designing their inclusionary housing program. A rapidly growing suburban community would most probably be well advised to maximize developer production of affordable housing units, and set the bar extremely high for in-lieu fees or not permit them at all. A city such as Philadelphia, where nearly all market-rate development takes the form of expensive downtown and waterfront high-rise buildings, might want to maximize either in-lieu payments or off-site construction of affordable housing, with appropriate safeguards to ensure that the new housing was built in the city's appreciating neighborhoods rather than in its areas of greatest poverty concentration.

In closing, inclusionary housing has proven itself as a workable strategy to create affordable housing, often fostering social inclusion and economic integration in the bargain. At the same time, even more than with many other housing programs, the devil is in the details. Unless an inclusionary program is thoughtfully designed and, above all, carefully and rigorously managed, the results can fall far short not only of its intentions, but its potential community benefit.

NOTES

1. While the use of the term inclusionary *zoning* to describe the strategy in general is arguably inaccurate, in that inclusionary housing is often created through procedures unrelated to local zoning ordinances, it is nonetheless used all but interchangeably with inclusionary housing. Alternatively, inclusionary zoning is sometimes used to refer to the process by which inclusionary housing—that is, the mixture of affordable and market-rate housing in a development—comes into being.
2. See page 168 for a more detailed description of this law.
3. 92 NJ 158, 456 A.2d 390.
4. A typical example is Bozeman, Montana, where a newly elected city commission began to investigate inclusionary zoning as a response to the local housing crisis in Smith, Marjorie. 2006. "Affordable Housing: Taking Bites out of the Elephant." *New West*, February 20.
5. For example, under the New Jersey Fair Housing Act, municipalities were permitted until recently to send a percentage of their fair share obligation to another municipality by making a cash payment known as a Regional Contribution Agreement. While strictly speaking the money comes from the sending municipality's funds, it is general practice for sending municipalities to take money from their housing trust fund—mostly, but not entirely, generated through in-lieu payments or linkage fees—for this purpose. The question then arises: For purposes of this tabulation, are the housing units built by receiving municipalities with the assistance of Regional Contribution Agreements to be considered the product of inclusionary housing policies?
6. The author's state-by-state estimates are 65,000 to 70,000 for California, 25,000 to 30,000 for New Jersey, 14,000 to 20,000 for Massachusetts, 15,000 for Montgomery County, and between 10,000 and 15,000 elsewhere.
7. Non-Profit Housing Association of Northern California. 2007. *Affordable by Choice: Trends in California Inclusionary Housing Program*. This report offers a wealth of information about the status and trends of inclusionary housing in California, and is

available online at http://www.nonprofithousing.org. The data given in the report are for a 7.5-year period from January 1999 through June 2006.
8. Many states have laws banning or restricting the imposition of rent control by local governments. A Colorado court invalidated a ski resort's inclusionary ordinance on the grounds that it constituted rent control; see *Town of Telluride v. Lot Thirty-Four Venture, LLC*, 3 P.3d 30 (2000). This was an eccentric ordinance, however, that required developers to provide housing for 40 percent of the employees generated by the development, and established base rent levels for the units. The city of Boulder was able to design an inclusionary ordinance that was able successfully to navigate the constraints of state law. A more conventional inclusionary ordinance enacted by the city of Madison, Wisconsin, was invalidated in 2006 by the state Court of Appeals on the grounds that it violated the state's ban on rent control; *Apartment Association of South Central Wisconsin, Inc. v. City of Madison*, 2006 WI App 192, 717 N.W. 2d 614.
9. In *DeGroff v. Fairfax County* (see note 11 below). This eccentric 1973 ruling, which appears to have been supported by no factual findings whatsoever with respect to the impact of the ordinance on the developer's ability to use his property profitably, has not, to the author's knowledge, been followed by any court since.
10. *Nollan v. California Coastal Commission*, 483 US 825 (1987) and *Dolan v. City of Tigard*, 512 US 687 (1994) are the leading U.S. Supreme Court cases on exactions and regulatory takings.
11. 214 Va. 235, 198 S.E.2d 600 (1973). Virginia is perhaps the most extreme state in the United States with respect to its application of "Dillon's Rule," the doctrine that holds that local governments may not take any actions except those explicitly authorized by state statute.
12. The court also held that the ordinance was a taking of the developer's property, because the prices for the affordable units would not be "fixed by the free market."
13. See especially 456 A.2d at 448.
14. 108 Cal Rptr. 2d 60 (2001), *cert. denied*, 535 U.S. 954 (2002).
15. Ibid., at 64.
16. A potentially important pending case has been brought by the Florida Builders Association and others against the city of Tallahassee, which adopted an inclusionary ordinance requiring that 10 percent of the units in all developments of 50 units or more be affordable housing. The outcome of the case is being awaited by many other Florida cities and counties that are contemplating adopting inclusionary zoning ordinances.
17. Notably, in many urban centers, typically in downtown centers, the greater part of the market-driven development takes the form of high-rise construction, a substantially more expensive form of construction than typical suburban two or three-story wood frame housing. Moreover, urban development often requires the construction of parking structures, which can increase the per-unit cost (depending on the nature of the structure, and the number of spaces per dwelling unit) between $10,000 and $40,000 over the cost of accommodating cars in surface parking areas.
18. In practice, the developer is unlikely to bear the cost, instead passing it backward to the landowner in the form of a lower purchase price for the undeveloped land.
19. Some have argued that in the "nexus" framework discussed earlier there is a causal relationship between the construction of expensive houses and the need for lower income housing; the residents of those houses create economic activity, and there is an attendant growth of low-wage jobs in the community in services such as landscaping or retail trade. This is plausible enough in principle; when one does the arithmetic, however, the number of lower income units as a percentage of market units that can

be justified on this basis is often far smaller than the typical inclusionary set-aside percentage. This is not the case with respect to linkage, where the arithmetic usually finds that under the nexus test the municipality could legally impose a substantially larger fee than is likely to be economically sustainable.

20. *In the Matter of the Adoption of N.J.A.C. 5:94 and 5:95*, 390 N.J. Super 1 (App. Div., 2007), *cert. denied*, 192 N.J. 72 (2007).
21. The law refers to the program, however, as an "affordable housing incentive program."
22. Revised Code of Washington, 36.70A.540, enacted 2006.
23. If the 20 percent set-aside is recalculated based on the higher density, the actual bonus is less than 1:1, because at 12 units per acre, the set-aside is 2.4/acre, and the value of the bonus, therefore, is reduced to 0.8:1. Thus, in order to ensure that the bonus is 1:1, the ordinance must specify that the set-aside is calculated on the base density. The regulations proposed by the New Jersey Council on Affordable Housing in January 2008 contain such a provision, at N.J.A.C.5:94-6.4(b)(2)i.
24. This is, in fact, the law in England, where the local authority granting planning permission, as it is called in the United Kingdom, has the authority to recapture a significant part of this increased value (known as "planning gain") in the form of affordable housing or other community benefits. In 2008, New Jersey amended the state Fair Housing Act to require an affordable housing set-aside in all residential development where the property had been rezoned from nonresidential use within the preceding two years.
25. Typically, developers borrow money from lenders to cover the construction period, paying interest up to the point they sell each unit; from that point on, the new buyer is responsible for paying the mortgage. The more quickly the unit is sold after completion (or in some cases, even before), the less interest the developer must pay, and therefore the profit is higher. In the case of modestly priced units, this cost can amount to $1,000 to $1,500 per month per unit.
26. A corollary to this is that the controls must be carefully explained to the initial buyer so that she clearly understands what will take place at such point that she decides to sell the unit. In order to minimize subsequent misunderstanding and what one California housing officer has called "situational amnesia," some housing agencies have started to videotape the sessions in which these provisions are explained to prospective buyers.
27. Public Law 46 of 2008. The same law abolished Regional Contribution Agreements.

CHAPTER

13

Policies, Politics, and the Future of Affordable Housing in the United States

Today's affordable housing scene in the United States is the product of the policy and program choices of the past. Those policies have constantly changed over the last 70 or more years, and they are likely to change in the future. As this book was being written, the collapse of the housing bubble and the spreading subprime foreclosure crisis, two phenomena that were only tangentially related to affordable housing as such, have profoundly changed the context in which affordable housing strategies operate. Changes in public policy that reflect the growing concern over energy sustainability and global warming, and their implications for the course of future development, are likely to have an even greater impact over the long term.

The United States is a changing nation. We are changing as the global forces affecting us and our understanding of them also change. Changes in the nation's housing markets, its social and demographic makeup, and its patterns of settlement and growth will all affect the demand for and supply of affordable housing. Furthermore, the way in which affordable housing is developed in the future, as is true of every area where our actions influence our physical surroundings, will change as we better recognize how those actions affect the environment and what we must do in the future to be able to continue to live on this planet. The effect of these trends and forces may well constrain the scope of future affordable housing policies. They may also offer opportunities for future creativity and change. Indeed, change and creativity in this field, particularly at the national level, is long overdue. While some innovations have emerged at state and local levels over the past decade, recent years have not been fertile ones for housing policy at the national level.

This chapter will explore some of those changes and their implications for future affordable housing policies, beginning with a discussion of some of the key trends, policies, and political issues that are likely to influence the direction of those policies. To predict specific policies, of course, would be no more than an exercise in guesswork. The chapter will conclude, therefore, not with predictions, but with an overview of the key themes that future policies should address, at such time that American policy makers are once again ready to explore these issues and think more seriously about how the United States will afford its less affluent citizens the quality of life appropriate for a resident of a land so well endowed with resources and opportunities.

DRIVERS OF HOUSING POLICY CHANGE

Demographic change

Future demand for affordable housing will be deeply affected by changes in the demographic makeup of the nation's households. As the United States becomes an increasingly diverse, multicultural nation, different language and cultural patterns will become increasingly important in our towns and cities. The nation's Hispanic population, which was 42 million in 2005, may triple to 128 million by 2050 according to a study by the Pew Research Center, at which point 29 percent of the population will be Hispanic and another nine percent of Asian origin.[1] The type of housing that we build will increasingly have to reflect the distinct cultural patterns of these emerging ethnic communities, a trend already reflected in many of the affordable developments going up in multiethnic cities such as Los Angeles, San Francisco, or Oakland.

During the same period, the elderly population will grow almost as quickly as the immigrant population, reflecting the aging of long-term residents. Thirty-seven million Americans were older than 65 in 2005. That number is expected to more than double, reaching between 81 and 87 million by 2050.[2] By that point as many as a quarter of the nation's households will be headed by an elderly person or couple.

The conventional nuclear family with a husband and wife raising their children still exists, but it no longer dominates. Half of all low-income families with children are single-parent families, while in 2006, 4.7 million children, including 2.2 million under the age of six, were living with a grandparent. Households are continuing to grow smaller; in 2006, 60 percent of the nation's households contained one or two members, and only 24 percent had four or more members. Overall, the typical lower income household is no larger than the typical household in the rest of the population, except among households of Hispanic origin, whose households are significantly larger than non-Hispanic households.

As Figure 13-1 shows, household growth over the coming decade will largely take place among couples without children—young couples and empty-nesters—and single persons. While the number of married couples without children will grow by nearly seven million, and the number of single-person households by more than four million, the number of households with children will grow by barely more than two million, of whom a significant percentage will be nonfamily households. More than half of the growth in the number of minority—largely Hispanic—families with children will be offset by the decline in the number of non-Hispanic

Figure 13-1 Projected Change in Households, 2005–2015 (Millions)

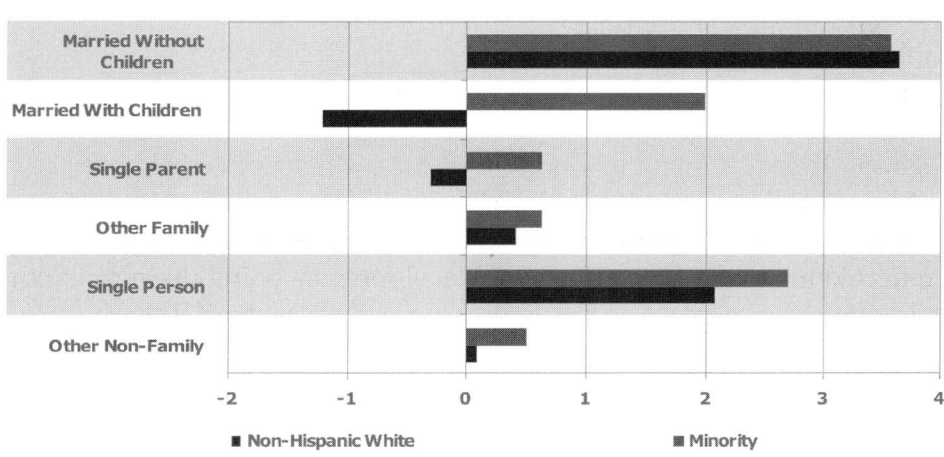

Note: JCHS projections assume 1.2 million annual average net immigration.

Source: Reprinted with permission from the Joint Center for Housing Studies of Harvard University

White families with children, as the latter population ages. Increasingly fluid family dynamics will call for more fluid forms of housing that can more easily be adapted to changes in occupancy over time.

The changing geography of housing market demand

Housing market demand has shifted significantly during the past decade, setting trends in motion that are likely to continue into the future. After a long period that began soon after the end of World War II, during which time mainstream America turned its back on its older cities and marched off to the suburbs, recent years have seen a dramatic reversal. Global cities like New York, Chicago, and San Francisco, as well as smaller cities like Providence and Chattanooga, have seen a revival of market demand and a steady increase in the pace of new construction. Figure 13-2, which compares the median house price in four historically distressed New Jersey cities to the statewide median, shows how, after reaching rock-bottom in the 1980s, urban house prices have revived to the point where today they approach, and, in the case of the city of Elizabeth, exceed the statewide median price. As demand for housing in urban areas grows,

Figure 13-2 Change in House Prices in Selected New Jersey Cities, 1960–2006

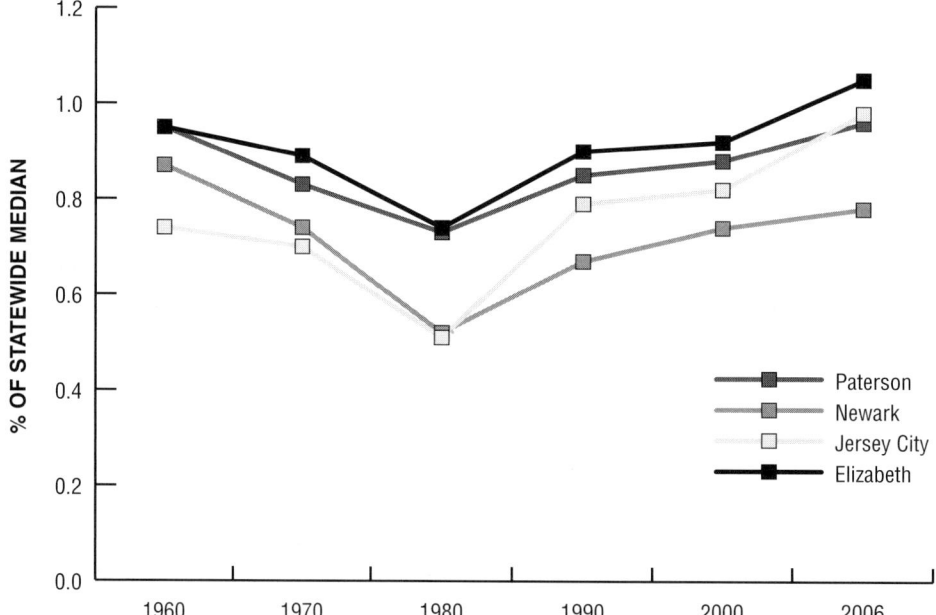

and the price of housing in historically inexpensive, lower income neighborhoods rises, the affordable housing supply is reduced and increasing pressure is exerted on the city's less affluent residents.

While the national housing market decline that began late in 2006 or 2007 has temporarily slowed the growth of the urban market, the trend of rising urban property values is likely to be a long-term one. This is fueled both by changing demographics, such as the bulge of baby boom empty-nesters, and by growing appreciation for the virtues of density, pedestrian-oriented living, and the creative, varied combinations of uses and activities that characterize urban environments, which are in sharp contrast to the automobile-oriented suburban monoculture. Equally striking is the extent to which sprawling western cities like Tucson or San Jose are investing billions of dollars to reinvent themselves as denser, more classically urban, places—while new developments such as Westgate Center in Glendale, Arizona, or The Woodlands outside Houston, have taken on quasi-urban (or perhaps "faux-urban") forms. Abandoning the suburban housing models of years past, they now advertise their "bold, new urban destination," adding that "Westgate living means a life that's nonstop excitement . . . entertainment . . . action."[3]

As demand grows in urban areas, or in those suburban areas that can offer similar lifestyle choices as well as transportation efficiencies, demand could decline elsewhere. It is not unreasonable to speculate about a future America in which the spatial distribution of rich and poor is much more like that in many European cities, where city centers and nearby residential areas are populated by the prosperous, and the poor are largely relegated to outlying districts of the cities or to the suburbs. The French word *banlieue*, which was once a neutral word used to describe areas outside central cities, is associated today in the French mind with poverty and violence, and used as a generic term to describe the ring of massive high-rise suburban public housing projects surrounding Paris and other major French cities largely inhabited by the impoverished descendants of immigrants.

The French experience, which exists to varying degrees in many other European countries, is unlikely to be repeated in that form in the United States, but similar patterns are beginning to emerge in many of the older inner-ring or first-tier suburbs surrounding central cities in American metropolitan areas. These suburbs, which were largely developed either before or immediately after World War II and often contain the modest homes and garden apartments that accommodated the first generation of the suburbanized working class, are widely succumbing to increasing social and economic pressure. As urban analyst William Hudnut has recently written, "Problems of decline, traditionally associated with inner cities, have appeared, and most first-tier suburbs are struggling to hold their own against these adverse trends."[4] A recent study of the inner-ring suburbs in the Philadelphia metropolitan area found that they "exhibit symptoms of decline typically associated with inner cities such as White flight, decrease in population, increase in minority and low-income households, and rising poverty levels."[5]

While the extent to which inner-ring suburbs are at risk has been the subject of attention for a number of years, questions have more recently begun to be raised about the future of suburbia in general, prompted in part by the foreclosure crisis but in part by a growing awareness of the vulnerability of suburban communities to changes in market demand and transportation and energy costs. In a recent article, developer and commentator Chris Leinberger wrote provocatively that, as the swing back to urban living continues, "Many low-density suburbs and McMansion subdivisions, including some that are lovely and affluent today, may become what inner cities became in the 1960s and '70s—slums characterized by poverty, crime and decay."[6]

Environmental and energy issues

Transportation and energy costs are likely to play a significant role in driving future directions of development activity and real estate value and determining whether in fact today's McMansions will be the slums of tomorrow. There is little doubt that these costs are going to continue to rise, although to what extent and how American society will adapt to higher costs is uncertain. How fast and to what levels they rise will be powerfully affected by public actions and policy decisions—such as how future administrations decide to move toward energy independence or the extent of future instability in the Middle East—in the United States and throughout the world. How people's behavior will be changed by higher costs is hard to predict. Although public transit use has already begun to increase, higher gasoline prices are more likely to translate into purchase of more energy-efficient cars than dramatic changes to modes of transportation. Higher energy prices may also translate into higher prices for properties located close to existing rail and light rail lines, with corresponding declines for properties that require extended automobile trips for work, shopping, and recreation.

Higher energy costs may also change the way affordable housing is developed. Today, public funders try hard to minimize the amount of subsidy going into a new development and to spread scarce funds more widely. As a result, developers are pressed to save money on initial costs at the expense of higher maintenance and higher energy costs over time. This is already beginning to change, however, as developers—particularly nonprofits planning to retain long-term ownership of their projects—and government agencies focus increasingly on life cycle as well as initial costs and on the long-term savings potentially available from green, energy-efficient buildings. In the future, moreover, housing capital funds may well be redirected from new construction and spent on retrofitting older buildings. Depending on the nature of the retrofit, energy-efficiency improvements tend to pay quickly for themselves in operating savings, often in as little as two years, and rarely in more than 10.

It may not be too far-fetched to imagine a not-too-distant future in which home prices actually decline as the size of a house exceeds what will be seen as a "reasonable" amount of space for a family, rather than the current norm of paying a premium for additional interior floor space. Will the increasing number of single individuals and childless couples, who make up the greater part of housing demand, want to pay a steadily rising energy premium in order to live in a house that may be far larger than what they need, or choose to live in a smaller home—likely an apartment—in a more central area with greater amenities? Centrally located housing in many urban downtown areas is already commanding a significant premium, as measured in sales price per square foot of floor area, over upscale suburban locations. Perhaps at that point, McMansions may start to be subdivided into apartments, although such steps are likely to be greeted with considerable hostility by neighbors and local officials.

Land-use and environmental policies will continue to have significant impacts on affordable housing. Smart growth, in the form of growth restrictions and measures to curb sprawl, may have an impact on housing costs and the ability to address affordable housing needs, although not necessarily more so than exclusionary zoning practices that serve few or no sound policy ends.[7] While many smart growth programs have tended to focus on discouraging inappropriate development—or development in inappropriate locations—at least some have balanced those efforts with parallel ones to encourage higher density development in areas more suited for growth, such as infill sites and areas served by public transportation. This is the case in Portland, Oregon, where the growth management scheme of Portland Metro, the regional planning agency, limits growth outside the urban growth boundary and mandates higher densities in appropriate areas within the boundary, while also requiring local governments to consider strategies to foster more affordable housing development.[8]

These trends are likely to have significant impacts on housing development generally, and by extension on affordable housing. The limited availability of vacant and buildable land, particularly in the more developed coastal areas, water use restrictions in many parts of the South and Southwest, hurricane standards in Florida and earthquake standards in California, and many other regulatory constraints all affect both the amount of housing produced and its cost. To the extent that regulatory constraints on housing development do push prices up, the demand for affordable housing is likely to increase, particularly from moderate-income households. Regulatory constraints, however, in the absence of strong countervailing provisions such as fair share or inclusionary housing standards, tend to make it even more difficult to develop affordable housing because of the financial constraints on such housing and the political opposition with which it must contend.

As more people become aware of the relationship between the availability of affordable housing and a community's economic vitality, there appears to be a growing recognition of the need to accommodate affordable housing within local or regional land-use regulations. HOME Connecticut, a broad coalition that includes business, civic, and neighborhood leaders, has campaigned for increasing the stock of affordable housing, arguing that "High housing costs are driving workers out of Connecticut, threatening our labor pool and causing concern among businesses throughout the state."[9] Their argument has resonated widely; in 2007, the group successfully gained legislative approval of a law that will provide incentives to communities that create zones to permit high-density, mixed income housing developments.

These trends and policy shifts will not affect all parts of the country equally. The United States is a big country, with great geographic variation in economic conditions, housing demand, social patterns, and climate. Increasingly stringent land-use regulations are likely to have the most dramatic impact in the areas where strong housing demand meets equally strong constraints, such as in the major metropolitan areas of the two coasts and certain inland locations like the Chicago area. At the same time, environmental pressures could see increasing constraints being imposed on housing in areas of traditionally modest regulation, such as the Las Vegas area.

Areas with more compact suburban development patterns, such as much of the Pacific Coast and the Southwest, and areas with climates requiring less heating or air conditioning[10] may see less wrenching change as a result of rising energy and transportation costs. Many of the nation's older industrial cities are still struggling, and are seeing little of the revival of market demand that is so potent in cities like Chicago or Denver. Cleveland, Detroit, and many other Rustbelt cities are not only still in dire economic straits, but have been far more severely affected by the foreclosure crisis than their more prosperous counterparts. In these areas, which are losing population and have a substantial surplus of housing, price pressures are modest at best, and production of affordable housing is a less compelling need than in other parts of the country. Cities with severe winter climates are likely to be most affected, at least in the short run, by higher energy costs, although perhaps they can console themselves with the thought that in the long run they may be beneficiaries of global warming.

SHAPING FUTURE AFFORDABLE HOUSING POLICY

Policies and politics today

The recent past offers little to suggest the direction of future federal housing policy. Federal housing activities today, without significant exception, reflect the survival of programs—often considerably scaled down—established during the 1970s (CDBG and Section 8), the 1980s (Low Income Housing Tax Credit and McKinney Act) and the 1990s (HOME and HOPE VI). In constant dollars, the HOME appropriation for the 2008 fiscal year was just over three-quarters of the program's first appropriation in 1992. The CDBG appropriation has declined from $4.3 billion in 2004 to $3.6 billion in 2008, and would be further reduced to $2.9 billion under the administration's pending FY 2009 budget proposal.

The one new affordable housing policy initiative that has generated significant traction during the past decade has been the idea of a national affordable housing trust fund supported through a charge on the revenues of Fannie Mae and Freddie Mac, the two gargantuan, government-supported secondary mortgage market entities. The trust fund would be designed to foster the production, preservation, or rehabilitation of

1.5 million affordable housing units over the next 10 years, or 150,000 units per year. Under the provisions of H.R. 2895, the National Affordable Housing Trust Fund Act of 2007, which passed the House of Representatives in October 2007, the funds would be allocated on a formula basis to states and localities to be used to produce new housing, preserve existing federally assisted housing, and rehabilitate existing private-market housing, including manufactured housing and community land trusts. All funds would have to be used for households earning less than 80 percent of the area median income, and three quarters of the funds would be used to assist extremely low-income families; that is, families earning 30 percent or less of area median income.

The campaign to enact the national affordable housing trust fund began in the 1990s under the leadership of the National Low Income Housing Coalition, which led to the introduction of the first trust fund legislation in Congress, sponsored by Sen. John Kerry of Massachusetts in 2000. Support has gradually built for the proposal, which passed the House in 2007 despite opposition from the Bush administration. The significance of the trust fund, however, is less in the number of units that it would create as in its focus on the extremely low-income households who are too poor to benefit from most of the housing created through the Low Income Housing Tax Credit, most HOME activity, and most state housing programs.[11]

The Trust Fund's focus on extremely low-income households, although important, raises the question of the extent to which such a program can fully respond to the needs of families who may not be able even to carry the operating costs of the housing being created for their use. The campaign's materials state that "projects funded through the Trust Fund should assure that any operating subsidy needed to make the housing affordable for a range of extremely low income people is provided. That could be by using Trust Fund assistance to underwrite the operating subsidy for new or rehabilitated units for one year, *after which the operating subsidy funding should come from other sources*" (emphasis added).[12] In the absence of a significant increase in housing vouchers or some other form of ongoing support, this may not be a realistic prospect. Given the potential costs involved, converting the housing voucher program to one that is available as an entitlement to all eligible households, as is the case in a number of European countries, does not appear likely in the foreseeable future, although it is worth exploring as a long-term policy.[13]

The political prospects of the Housing Trust Fund are enhanced by its ability to draw upon an off-budget revenue source in the form of the activities of the government-supported secondary mortgage market entities. Given the current federal budget climate, it is hardly realistic to expect any significant increase in federal funding for affordable housing in the foreseeable future. Even if a future Democratic president and Congress were to restore some of the Bush administration's tax cuts, major increases in housing support are highly unlikely due to economic uncertainties, budget deficits, and the demands of competing and arguably higher priorities such as environmental issues and health care.

Housing advocates have reluctantly come to realize that although housing is a fundamental human need, increasing spending for that purpose beyond today's modest levels—representing in recent years slightly more than one percent of federal spending—is not seen as an overriding priority on either side of the political aisle. As shown in Figure 13-3, after peaking during the 1990s at roughly 10 percent of nondefense discretionary spending, federal spending on housing has steadily declined.

Except for the foreclosure crisis, housing was not a major issue in the 2008 presidential primaries or in the general election campaign. This is

Figure 13-3 Housing Assistance as a Share of Nondefense Discretionary Spending (Percent)

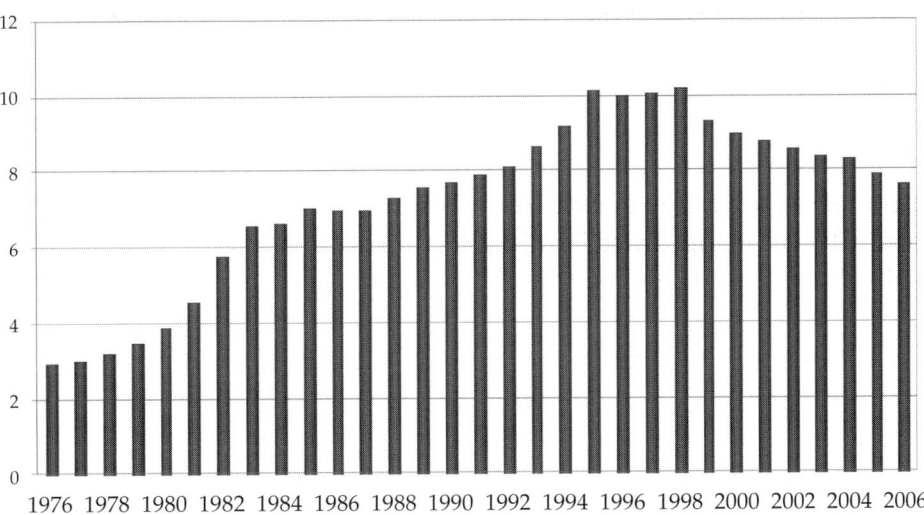

Source: Reprinted with permission from the Joint Center for Housing Studies of Harvard University

nothing new; as Jason DeParle wrote in 1996, "Housing has simply evaporated as a political issue."[14] Most American households are well housed. While many middle-class families have high housing cost burdens, they are unlikely to see this as a systemic problem in the same sense that they see their issues with the health care system. Moreover, while a struggling middle-class family may hope to gain a direct benefit from a restructured and more affordable health care system, they have no similar stake in affordable housing initiatives. They are unlikely to get any relief from their housing costs through programs that finance future affordable housing construction or provide poor families with housing vouchers.

In the near future, as will be discussed in the next section, advocates' attention is more likely to be directed instead toward changes in existing programs to make them more effective both as ways to house lower income people and to simultaneously further sound planning and environmental policies. National policies that promote lower income home ownership are likely to come under particularly close scrutiny in the next few years. The foreclosure crisis that is currently ruining millions of home owners and placing hundreds of urban neighborhoods and small towns at risk has demonstrated that the combination of laissez-faire and mindless boosterism that has characterized recent home ownership policies has done the nation great damage. The current crisis is not likely to fundamentally change the desire of most Americans to be home owners. Promoting home ownership opportunities for lower income families is likely to continue to be, in some fashion, an important part of national housing policy. In the future, however, that policy may become a more thoughtful one, better attuned to the risks as well as rewards of home ownership and one which recognizes that the nation's households will also need decent affordable rental housing.

Housing policy, resources, and the right to housing

Affordable housing policy, by its nature, is multidimensional. No single size fits all. It must address the needs for affordable home ownership as well as rental housing, and the needs of the very poor as well as those of middle-class households struggling to find housing they can afford in high-cost areas such as New York or San Francisco. It means different things in different parts of the country. Affordable housing policy, moreover, is inextricably interwoven with the nation's policies toward housing development and real estate investment generally, which in turn are intertwined with broader environmental and fiscal policies.

Perhaps reflecting the nation's bias toward ad hoc rather than systematic policy making, politicians and policy makers rarely address the global question of defining national policy for housing those who cannot complete effectively in the marketplace. Since the Reagan administration's Presidential Commission on Housing in 1982, which led to the last major policy shift from an emphasis on housing production to a greater focus on housing vouchers, housing policy efforts have involved programmatic tinkering rather than strategic thinking, a bias reflected in the report of the Millennial Commission on Housing as well as in the actions of the last few presidential administrations.

Despite this bias, it is important to at least briefly address the fundamental question of the scope of affordable housing policy before exploring some of the specific issues that should be considered in framing more effective housing policies for the future. This reflects not only the realities of the American policy environment today, but the importance of seeing affordable housing policy not just as a matter of individual dwelling units, but as a critical building block in creating healthy neighborhoods and cities.

Since the Housing Act of 1949 famously called for a "decent home in a suitable living environment" for every American household, housing conditions have changed dramatically for the nation as a whole, including for its lower income families and individuals. Home ownership has increased, houses are larger, better equipped, and inevitably, more expensive. Housing conditions have changed dramatically for lower income households as well. The percentage of those households living in substandard housing has dropped sharply, as has the percentage of people living in overcrowded conditions, although not to the same degree. Both, however, continue to be problems for millions of households. At the same time, housing costs have increased dramatically, to the point where today the majority of lower income households are significantly burdened by excessive housing costs. As Michael Stone has written, "The now-platudinous National Housing Goal of 'the realization as soon as feasible of a decent home and a suitable living environment for every American family' makes no mention of affordability."[15] The greatest improvement in the physical conditions of lower income housing, however, took place between 1950 and 1980. Since then, there has been little change in those conditions, while more and more households find themselves increasingly cost-burdened.

This shift in the nature of the nation's housing problems leads one to focus on the recurrent question: whether affordable housing problems should be seen as problems of inadequate supply or of inadequate demand. Is housing in short supply, or do large numbers of households simply lack the financial resources to access an ample, but overly expensive, supply of housing? A corollary to that question, in areas of the United States where the supply of housing is clearly inadequate, is how best to add to the supply of housing and how future affordable housing production should relate to the larger housing market and housing stock. The experience with inclusionary housing strategies here and in Europe has demonstrated that increases to the affordable housing supply can be created successfully not only by building affordable housing projects, but by pursuing approaches that physically integrate affordable housing into larger mixed income and mixed use developments.

Regardless of whether supply or demand strategies are to be pursued, or in what combination, the starting point needs to be the question of whether society should offer a right to housing, and if so, what that right entails. While the 1949 Housing Act implied that right, it is—as Stone and others have recognized—at best the expression of a pious hope, and at worst an empty platitude. The concept of a right to housing is disconnected from the reality of affordable housing policy as it has evolved and devolved in the nearly six decades since then. Instead, the present system takes the form of a competition, with a small body of winners and a larger body of losers; as a recent article described getting an affordable apartment in New York, "most of the homes can be had only by entering lotteries, which carry odds that are barely better than those for most casino jackpots."[16] In expensive cities like New York, Boston, or San Francisco, hundreds of families may apply for each new unit or housing voucher that becomes available.

The concept of a right to housing at some level has become a central part of the social safety net as it is understood in many European nations. A financial stipend that permits low-income families to afford housing in the private market, known as housing benefit or housing allowance, has become an entitlement in the United Kingdom and in Germany. In both countries, families meeting the statutory conditions have a legal right to the benefit; as the website of the United Kingdom Department of Work and Pensions puts it, "Are you on a low income?

Paying rent? If yes to both, claim housing benefit."[17] While the share of dedicated affordable housing in Germany's housing stock is not much larger than in the United States, most lower income German families are better housed and pay a smaller share of their income for rent as a result of the housing benefit.

The question of housing benefit, however, cannot be separated from larger economic issues. The extent to which lower income households are cost burdened in the United States is a function not only of the cost of housing itself, but the widening income inequality of American society and the growing impoverishment in relative terms of the less affluent sectors of the population. This can be counteracted to some degree by the creation of an adequate economic safety net for those whose incomes do not enable them to afford the necessities of existence; the United States provides many of those in need with Medicaid, Food Stamps, and the Earned Income Tax Credit.[18] All of these have some effect on families' housing cost burden, in that they supplement their income or free up funds that would otherwise be needed for groceries or health care. While American society has accepted that government should ensure access to food or health care, at least for the poorest households, no such notion has been adopted with respect to housing.

The concept of a right to housing raises some difficulties in practice, although not insurmountable ones. Two basic questions arise: Who should be entitled to assistance to exercise that right, and what, exactly, should the exercise of that right entitle one to? The suggestion that the voucher program should be expanded to encompass the six million households that have what HUD has defined as "worst-case housing needs"—households with incomes below 50 percent of the area's median income and that either pay 50 percent or more of their monthly income for rent or live in substandard housing—while appealing in concept, is questionable in practice in that, as HUD's research has shown, large numbers of households regularly move in and out of "worst-case" status as their incomes and housing circumstances fluctuate.[19] Establishing appropriate standards for eligibility and level of assistance is not impossible, but it is difficult. The task is further complicated by the politically charged tension between addressing the needs of the poor and those of the struggling middle class, who find it increasingly difficult to afford homes of decent quality in their communities, particularly in the expensive coastal states. The problem is rendered doubly difficult in that how eligibility and the standard of assistance are defined defines, in turn, the magnitude of public expenditure needed to make the right a reality.

Determining the quality or affordability of housing that should be guaranteed by right is the second question. The definition of "reasonable" housing conditions changes regularly over time to reflect shifts in societal standards and reality. Overcrowded conditions that officials considered unhealthy and dangerous in 2000 would not have been considered even moderately bothersome in the 1930s, while the idea that poor families should spend 30 percent of their gross income for shelter—all but universally accepted today—would then have been considered highly unreasonable. Similarly, the standards for acceptable equipment and facilities in housing units are constantly being upgraded; recently, the New Jersey Department of Community Affairs has proposed that all new affordable housing units be provided (at considerable cost) with fully activated sprinkler systems.[20] While no one argues that the government should guarantee everyone a McMansion, the question of what is "good enough" housing remains an open and highly controversial one.

Ultimately, many of these issues come down to resources. Proposals such as those to extend vouchers only to worst-case households, although raising problems of their own, are driven by the desire to find a way of extending housing opportunities at a cost that will be generally perceived as reasonable in light of fiscal constraints and priorities.[21] What is ironic, in the context of the difficulty of increasing federal expenditures for affordable housing, is the continued and well-known profligacy of the federal government in subsidizing the housing of the well-to-do through tax expenditures. Tax expenditures related to housing grew from less than $30 billion in 1977 to more than $120 billion by 2000. The Joint Committee on Taxation estimated that in the 2007 fiscal year, the mortgage interest deduction alone will reach $74 billion, with other home owner deductions on property taxes and the capital gains exclusion adding another $45 billion. The committee projected the cumulative total projected tax expenditure for 2007 through 2011 to be $671 billion. By comparison, the cumulative total tax expenditure for all programs that benefit lower income households, the low-income tax credit and the exemption from taxation on tax-exempt bonds, will barely total $40 billion.[22] As has been extensively documented, the majority of expenditures flow to upper-income households, with nearly half of the benefit going to households in the top quintile of the income range.[23]

Contrary to the real estate industry's rhetoric, there is no evidence that these deductions have any effect on the home ownership rate. Australia, Canada, and Great Britain, none of which offer similar tax deductions, all have comparable or greater home ownership rates.[24] What the deductions actually do is push the cost of housing upward, by increasing the amount that a person who itemizes tax deductions can afford to spend on housing. This is the secret of its political untouchability. Major sectors of the American economy, including the home building, real estate, and mortgage credit industries, have a powerful vested interest in house prices being high, since ultimately their revenues are driven by the cost of the housing they sell, build, or finance. Unfortunately, the effect of the deduction is to make housing that much less affordable to those who do not itemize deductions. In the final analysis, the mortgage interest and property tax deductions represent a vast regressive income transfer from the less affluent—who pay the price for more expensive housing without being able to benefit from the deductions—to the more affluent, and through them to the various sectors of the housing industry. These tax deductions, however, have withstood repeated attack and appear to be politically all but indestructible. Moreover, in the event that they should be curtailed in some fashion, under current conditions it is highly unlikely that the savings will be made available for affordable housing programs, rather than for deficit reduction or some other higher policy priority.

Although in the short run it may appear unrealistic, in the long run a basic housing allowance for all families who need it is neither unworkable nor fiscally out of reach. In the more near-term future, however, if affordable housing policy in the United States is fated to continue to function as a lottery, housing policy goals should focus on improving the efficiency of that lottery, not only in the sense of improving the odds for the players, but in terms of making the outcomes more rational in terms both of who benefits and how the lottery affects others on whom it has an indirect effect. This means using available resources more efficiently so that the number of beneficiaries and the quality of their benefits can be increased without spending more money; targeting resources more effectively to ensure that the beneficiaries are those with the greatest need; and finally, using those resources so that they enhance the economic and social viability of the communities in which they are used, rather than undermining them. How these goals can be pursued, within the framework of economic and political plausibility, will be discussed in the following pages.

The foregoing discussion has concentrated on the national picture and the role of the federal government in affordable housing policy. This is not to minimize the role of state and local government, but simply recognizes that any fundamental change in the scope or direction of affordable housing policy or in the resources devoted to it will ultimately have to come from the federal government. Despite the heroic efforts by advocates and policy makers, no state or local government currently devotes resources to affordable housing that are remotely equivalent even to the current diminished level of federal spending in those states and cities. What state and local governments have done, however, is demonstrate creativity in the use of limited public resources; far more so, particularly in recent years, than the federal government. Should the federal government seek to reassert a meaningful role in housing policy in coming years, it is critical that it build on that creativity, and be sensitive to the many significant local variations in needs and market characteristics, rather than simply trying to reimpose federal standards and bureaucratic imperatives on a diverse nation.

Home ownership

The benefits of home ownership for family and neighborhood stability justify public policy efforts to foster home ownership. While the benefits of home ownership *may* include wealth building in the form of equity in an appreciating asset, that particular outcome is uncertain and speculative. Those who promote home ownership as an all-but-guaranteed path to wealth, encouraging poorly prepared home buyers to purchase houses beyond their means or take on unsupportable mortgage debt, do those home buyers and the public a grave disservice. There are significant risks associated with home ownership, particularly for low-income owners who are likely to purchase properties in need of repair in distressed neighborhoods and who may lack the financial cushions to deal with unanticipated repairs or economic shocks.

Sound public policy should maximize the positive and reduce the negative aspects of home ownership for lower income buyers. Buyers should be able to gain access to ownership at a cost that is not burdensome. Once they have become owners, they should have a reasonable opportunity to gain the potential economic and noneconomic benefits offered by home ownership. More than anything else, that opportunity will depend on whether their home ownership is stable and long lasting. The current system, as has been more than amply demonstrated in recent years, offers neither reasonable cost nor stability.

The starting point for a sound home ownership policy must be to make available mortgages that do not require home buyers to spend an excessive percentage of their income on housing costs. While many lower income households may be higher risks than the average home buyer, the subprime meltdown has demonstrated that it is dangerously counterproductive to make those buyers pay higher interest rates and incur higher monthly costs on the theory that that will mitigate those risks. For that reason, we need a new way of looking at mitigating risk, one not based on raising the cost of the loan to reflect the risk, but based on creating other mechanisms to mitigate lender risk without burdening the borrower.

One way to do that is to require prospective home buyers to participate in meaningful home ownership education and counseling, a step that has been shown to significantly reduce mortgage delinquencies. The word "meaningful" is important, since there is no evidence that the telephone conversations that much of the lending industry considers "counseling" has any effect on credit risk.[25] In the course of counseling, the prospective buyer should be given enough information to evaluate whether home ownership is indeed an appropriate step, and to change course without having incurred any liability. This preownership period should also be treated as an opportunity for credit repair so the prospective home owner can qualify for the lowest cost mortgage available. Communities contemplating initiating new programs or expanding existing ones for lower income home ownership should ensure that counseling available for new buyers and that it meets high standards of quality.

Another approach worth exploring is the shared-equity mortgage, under which the lender shares the future equity appreciation on the property with the borrower in return for lower current monthly payments. As a result, the buyer trades greater affordability for a reduced potential gain from future appreciation. Widely used as a means of fostering affordable home ownership in the United Kingdom, shared-equity mortgages can be structured in a variety of ways, including models under which the borrower can "buy back" the lender's equity share, either by direct cash payment or by continued timely mortgage payments over some number of years. Financial analyses suggest that shared-equity mortgages could be a potentially attractive option for the investment community.[26]

In addition to mortgage financing, creating housing for owner-occupancy that is affordable to lower income buyers often requires capital subsidy to reduce the price of the home below the cost of production. As discussed earlier, the cost of such subsidies can easily exceed $100,000 per house, making it difficult for many local governments and CDCs to produce more than a handful of affordable home ownership opportunities. Many communities end up producing rental housing when they would prefer to build for home ownership, simply because of the ready availability of equity investment for low-income rental housing under the Low Income Housing Tax Credit. To offset this imbalance, housing advocates have proposed the creation of a home ownership tax credit that would parallel the rental credit. The credit would go either to the home buyer, the developer of the housing, or to a lender to further reduce the cost of the mortgage loan.[27]

Having a support system for lower income owners is as important as the process by which they became home owners. By definition, to be a lower income home owner is to be at risk. Lower income home owners have a thinner financial cushion with which to withstand either the impacts of negative life experiences such as unemployment or serious illness or of unanticipated repair costs. By virtue of their limited housing choices, they are more likely to buy houses that will need repair either immediately or within a few years of occupancy.

Such a support system could take many different forms; indeed, to be effective, it is likely to have to be multifaceted. Postpurchase counseling, both on an ongoing basis and in the event of delinquency and foreclosure risk, is important.[28] Other valuable elements of a home ownership support system include locally based emergency assistance funds that can respond quickly to financial crises, and mortgages that respond to short-term risks such as income disruptions by providing flexibility and the ability for the borrower to make up missed mortgage payments. In many urban areas, where unscrupulous lenders and contractors prey on vulnerable lower income and elderly home owners, programs that provide those owners with access to affordable funds for urgently needed repairs are other important pieces in the system.

Finally, policy makers should seriously consider expanding the place of shared-equity models of home ownership as alternatives to conventional fee simple ownership as ways to increase the magnitude and the long-term sustainability of lower income home ownership. A particular advantage of community land trusts, limited-equity cooperatives, and deed-restricted condominiums is that in return for limiting the owner's equity return, they offer the potential of an institutionalized support system that can protect the owner from many of the downsides of home ownership, and may even enhance some of ownership's noneconomic benefits.[29]

Since, as noted earlier, large numbers of lower income owners do not actually benefit from significant appreciation of their housing values under conventional home ownership structures, limits on equity return, either in the form of a controlled resale price or the recapture of gain, may not be as great a loss in practice as some might imagine. This is particularly true if prospective buyers, rather than being subjected to one-sided propaganda, are made aware of the actual balance of risks and rewards involved in home ownership.

Creating a system that provides future lower income home owners with sound financing products along with a support system to sustain their ownership over time will require major changes in current practices. It will not be easy to create mortgage instruments that both meet the needs of lower income buyers and appeal to the investment community, a necessary condition if they are to be brought to the scale necessary to have a meaningful impact on the magnitude and stability of lower income home ownership. Moreover, simply making products available is not enough. As long as mortgage lenders and brokers are strongly motivated by financial gain to offer more expensive products to potential borrowers, they are likely to continue doing so. Unless these alternative products are aggressively marketed, they may be crowded out by the noise created by the promoters of expensive and dangerous mortgages. The Federal Housing Administration needs to reestablish its role as a leader in fostering affordable home ownership, as do Fannie Mae and Freddie Mac. The evidence from recent years suggests that both entities, rather than attempt to maintain responsible standards in the lending industry, joined in the feeding frenzy with what now appear to have been predictable results. Should they survive the current crisis, Fannie and Freddie have the obligation to set and enforce standards for acceptable practice in the lending industry. At the same time, mortgage features and underwriting practices that are clearly abusive, such as many of those that led to the current foreclosure crisis, need to be prohibited by law as a form of consumer fraud.

Beyond that, however, if the American political system places a value on expanding home ownership, the public and private sectors must provide the necessary financial resources to create a true support system for lower income home buyers and owners along the lines of the system outlined above in order to ensure that expanded ownership does indeed benefit both the families involved and the communities in which they live. This is not only a rational economic imperative, it is an ethical one.

Rental housing

However successful future policies to foster lower income ownership might become, home ownership can never be the beginning and end of a sound housing policy. At any given time, roughly one-third of the nation's population and half of its lower income households are likely to be renters.[30] Some of these households will be lifelong renters, while others will move back and forth between home ownership and rental, based on changes in economic circumstances and family composition. While some of these households live in subsidized housing, and some have housing vouchers, the great majority of these households are dependent on the private rental market, a sector of the housing market that is often treated with indifference or disdain by government at all levels.

Low-income renters are far more likely to suffer from severe housing problems than home owners of similar economic status.[31] They are more likely to live in poor quality housing, far more likely to experience overcrowding, and—at least until the last few years—much more likely to be cost-burdened. Whether they live in subsidized housing, have a housing voucher, or rent on the private market, they are more likely to live in areas of concentrated poverty and limited opportunity. Those who have not been lucky in the affordable housing lottery are dependent on the uncertainties of the private market. Without an adequate pool of good quality and affordable rental housing in our cities, towns, and rural areas, millions of families will continue to find themselves in unsound, overcrowded, or cost-burdened conditions, at constant risk of homelessness.

Rental housing has received little policy attention in recent years, particularly at the national level. While the Low Income Housing Tax Credit continues to produce a steady stream of affordable rental units of generally good quality, the way it is used and where those units tend to be located, as will be discussed below, raise serious public policy concerns. Efforts to preserve the existing affordable housing stock, including both public housing projects and privately owned projects with expiring use restrictions, have been erratic and inconsistent. While many projects have been saved through determined local efforts, many more have been lost. Meanwhile, as urban neighborhood housing markets revive, thousands of once-affordable private market rentals are lost as single-family rental properties and sold to affluent home buyers, while multifamily buildings may be upgraded in order to charge higher rents or converted to condominiums.

This housing is not being replaced. The MacArthur Foundation has found that "Over the past decade, for every unit of affordable rental housing built, two were lost to condo conversion, demolition or rising rents."[32] Restrictive land-use policies have made it increasingly difficult for developers to create new rental housing in many parts of growing metropolitan areas. Although upscale rental housing is being built in reviving urban downtowns, and some small percentage of that housing is affordable housing through inclusionary zoning programs, economic and regulatory constraints often make construction of new rental housing of a more modest character in urban neighborhoods all but impossible. As Table 13-1 shows, the share of rental housing produced in recent years, in all parts of the country, is substantially smaller than its share of the total housing stock. The nation's rental housing inventory, as a result, is growing substantially older than its owner-occupied housing, which is more readily replaced and replenished.

TABLE 13-1 RENTAL HOUSING SHARE OF TOAL HOUSING PRODUCTION, 1995–2000, AND RENTAL HOUSING AS SHARE OF TOTAL HOUSING STOCK BY GEOGRAPHIC DIVISION, 2000

GEOGRAPHIC DIVISION	% OF RENTAL HOUSING IN 1995–2000 PRODUCTION	% OF RENTAL HOUSING IN TOTAL HOUSING STOCK
New England	18.1%	35.1%
Middle Atlantic	25.6	38.5
East North Central	20.7	30.1
West North Central	21.4	28.9
South Atlantic	21.6	30.9
East South Central	19.8	28.8
West South Central	24.7	34.5
Mountain	23.0	32.0
Pacific	30.1	41.3

Source: 2000 Census

Most of this stock is located neither in subsidized housing projects nor private apartment buildings. Just over half of all rental dwellings in the United States are in one- to four-family buildings—of which over half are investor-owned, single-family houses. These properties include modest Philadelphia or Baltimore row houses, Boston "triple-deckers" where the owner occupies one unit and rents out the other two, small shotgun cottages in southern towns, and large Victorian houses in older industrial cities, often inelegantly carved up into two or three apartments. These small rental properties are the largest reservoir of housing for low-income families in the United States, housing 70 percent of all lower income renters.[33]

Rental housing conditions vary widely across the United States. In areas of high demand, such as the New York or San Francisco areas, rental housing—except for the affluent—is generally in short supply. Vacancy rates may be as low as two or three percent, and even modest apartments in modest neighborhoods will rent for well over $1,000 per month. In these areas, even households earning 80 or even 100 percent of the area median income may feel the pinch of high rents. As many as half of the families that receive housing vouchers in high-cost areas turn them back to the local housing agency because they cannot find a suitable house or apartment within the Fair Market Rent limits. In low-demand areas, rents are far lower and vacancy rates far higher. In Flint, Michigan, for example, the median rental dwelling is affordable to a family earning less than 40 percent of area median income, and in 2000 the rental vacancy rate was an astronomical 13 percent. While the very poor are still cost-burdened in those areas, most low- and moderate-income families have no trouble finding rentals they can comfortably afford.

What does this mean for a rental housing policy? Ideally, the government would provide a housing allowance to ensure that no low-income family would be unduly cost-burdened, while providing incentives to private developers to build modest apartment buildings that would rent at moderate rents. This would minimize the gap between the market and what low-income families can afford and reduce the cost of a housing allowance program, while providing subsidies to build affordable housing in high-demand, high-cost areas to ensure that the supply of rental housing is adequate to meet the need. While reality will inevitably fall short of this ideal, we can do better than we are doing now—even with the resources currently available or potentially available in the near future. This will require both a rethinking of resources devoted to production of new affordable housing and a far greater emphasis on preservation than has been the case up to now.

The housing choice voucher program needs to remain the cornerstone of the nation's affordable rental housing policy. To the extent that in much of the United States housing burdens are more a product of inadequate demand rather than supply, they can be addressed most effectively with programs that supplement the incomes of low-income households, so that even the poorest families can afford modest but sound housing on the private market. Given the high costs associated with building and operating most subsidized housing, creating a program under which government will provide developers with capital subsidies to build subsidized housing for families earning 30 percent or less of the area median income is likely to be a wasteful exercise. Even if government picked up the entire cost of development—which is currently as much as $250,000 per unit in some high-cost areas—public money would still have to subsidize the operating cost of the project might if it is to be affordable to the households in greatest need.

Where the existing stock is adequate, it is most appropriate to provide those families with vouchers to use in the private market. In high-demand areas where the existing affordable housing supply is limited, "project-based" vouchers that are tied to the unit (or an interchangeable unit within the project or building), rather than to the tenant, should be allocated to existing subsidized housing or modest private rental housing. Although project-based vouchers—which are currently permitted by HUD on a limited basis—remove some units from the supply that would otherwise be available to only slightly better-off households (typically earning 50 to 80 percent of area median income), those households are more likely to find acceptable accommodation in the private market than the families that benefit from the vouchers.

There are areas in the United States where housing problems are the result of an inadequate supply of affordable housing, and where the production of additional rental housing, whether subsidized or developed in the private market, is still needed. The principal, and almost the only, vehicle that currently exists to serve this goal is the Low Income Housing Tax Credit program. It is a highly productive program from a purely quantitative standpoint, but is flawed in other important respects, over and above the inherently fiscally inefficient nature of a tax credit compared to a direct governmental appropriation.

The manner in which tax credits are allocated, with each state receiving an amount directly proportional to population, while politically appealing, fails to reflect the unevenly distributed need for additional affordable rental units. In Stamford, where not even a household earning 80 percent of median income can afford the median rent, a new tax credit project fills a gap that is not being met by the private market. In Flint, a new tax credit project simply drains demand from the private market, exacerbating an already excessively high vacancy rate and increasing the risk that property owners will abandon their properties. While not *every* proposal to build tax credit housing in Flint is necessarily a mistake—there may be cases where the project adds value by reusing a valuable historic building or anchoring a neighborhood revitalization strategy—the last thing that city needs is more housing built simply for the sake of adding to an already excessive supply.

Even in areas where the need for additional supply exists, the structure of the program makes it difficult to meet those needs in the most rational or appropriate fashion. It is perverse that, at a point where policy makers and the public have largely recognized the value of economic integration and the ills of concentrated poverty, the tax credit program offers a generous bonus to developers who build projects in high-poverty areas, while making it difficult, although not impossible, for developers to use low-income tax credits in mixed income developments; as the National Association of Home Builders comments, "While this is technically allowable under the LIHTC, it is difficult in practical application and investors shy away from this approach."[34]

These problems should not be overstated. Many mixed income projects have been developed through the tax credit program. Despite the bonus for projects in high-poverty areas, state allocating agencies that have sought to direct tax credit projects into low-poverty areas have been able to do so by offering preference for such projects in their Qualified Allocation Plans. As a result, in a number of states, including Utah, Wisconsin, New Hampshire, Delaware, and Nebraska, more than 60 percent of tax credit housing units have been built in low-poverty (under 10 percent) census tracts.[35] It is notable that these are all states with few large, distressed older cities. By contrast, in many large states, including California, Illinois, Pennsylvania, and Texas, less than 30 percent of tax credit units are in low-poverty areas.

The tax credit program is past due for an extensive overhaul. The state-by-state allocation formula should be revised to reflect the varying needs for additional housing supply in each state, perhaps by using such measures as market rent levels or vacancy rates. Although such a change may face some resistance, it is worth noting that both CDBG and HOME funds are allocated on the basis of formulae that take need into account, rather than simple proportionality of population.[36] The incentive structure should be reversed, with developer bonuses for building in low-poverty areas and for integrating tax credit units into mixed income and mixed tenure developments. Finally, the program should move away from the time-honored but obsolete notion that tax credit projects should be "projects," in the sense of distinct, separate buildings constructed or rehabilitated for that purpose.

The United States can learn a valuable lesson from France, where a creative turnkey approach has enabled more of that nation's affordable rental housing to be integrated into mixed income developments in a highly cost-effective manner.[37] Under this approach, a developer building private market condominiums enters into a contract with a nonprofit housing corporation or public housing agency. The housing corporation agrees to buy a share of the units—usually 10 to 20 percent, and never more than 50 percent—upon completion of construction. The housing corporation receives a package of tax breaks, low-interest loans, and capital grants from the national government to cover the cost of purchasing the units from the developer. The housing corporation thus becomes the owner of its share of the condominiums, which become affordable rental units. While the corporation selects the tenants, the maintenance of the rental units is subsumed within the maintenance of the condominium development as a whole.

This approach, which is not strictly speaking prohibited under the Low Income Tax Credit program, but which has been applied only rarely and with considerable difficulty, offers many advantages over the way tax credit units are now created and should become the norm rather than the rare exception. Since the developer is building a conventional private development, without the extra costs dictated by the subsidized housing development process, per-unit costs are likely to be substantially lower than the cost of an equivalent unit in a purpose-built tax credit project. Moreover, the developer is likely to be willing to sell the units to the housing corporation at a substantial discount below the market price of the units—as is the case in France—because she knows that she will save money by selling a bloc of units immediately on completion without marketing and postconstruction holding costs. The developer is doing what she does best—building housing—while the housing corporation can concentrate on rental management and tenant selection.

A tax credit program restructured this way would significantly increase production of affordable housing units with no increase in the level of the federal government's tax expenditure. Of equal importance, a greater share of the units that it would create would be built in those parts of the country where the need for additional housing supply is greatest. Within those areas, new affordable housing would be more likely to be integrated into economically diverse housing developments and communities, enabling lower income families to live in areas with better public services, schools, and job opportunities.

The tax credit program, valuable as it is—and can become—cannot in itself address the steady erosion of the moderately priced rental housing that represents the principal housing resource for most lower income households. That will require far more sustained attention to preservation that has hitherto been the case, combined with incentives to build rental housing developments that will be affordable, modest homes in sound but unpretentious moderate and middle-income areas. This housing might be similar in character to the garden apartments that were constructed by the thousands during the 1950s and 1960s in growing suburbs and urban neighborhoods, and which 50 years later are still largely in good repair, representing a significant part of the unsubsidized housing affordable to moderate income households in these communities.

The impediments to construction of such housing are both regulatory and economic. While modest rental developments can still be built in outlying areas in the South and Midwest, which often have undemanding zoning codes or no zoning at all, they are rarely permitted in the suburbs of coastal states where the demand is greatest. Massachusetts and Connecticut have taken small steps forward by passing laws giving municipalities financial incentives to zone land for and to approve high-density or multifamily developments. The state regulations do not specify, however, that the developments must be rental housing, and many of them are likely to be expensive condominium projects with a required set-aside of affordable units. These are, at best, modest gestures.

Economic impediments also play a role. It is difficult, particularly in high-cost areas where the need is greatest, to build new rental housing of good quality with conventional financing, provide a good level of services and maintenance, pay full property taxes, and still rent the apartments at levels that moderate-income families can afford. Coupled with regulatory changes that will provide greater opportunities to build multifamily housing, such development could be rendered financially feasible with no more than modest financial incentives. Those incentives could include measures such as greater access to tax-exempt bond financing,[38] tax incentives such as waivers of sales tax on building materials and reduced property taxes, waivers of municipal fees (such as building permits, sewer hookups, or impact fees), and low-interest or deferred-payment second mortgage programs. Although each incentive is modest in itself, collectively they could reduce the rent needed to break even on a new rental housing project by as much as 30 percent.[39]

In the end, however, no production strategy can replace a sound preservation strategy. Public support for rental housing preservation has been sporadic, at best. Large numbers of public housing units are gone, replaced with housing vouchers—if anything. Efforts to save the privately owned affordable housing stock built under the Section 236 and Section 8 programs during the 1970s have had some impact. If appropriate steps are taken over the next few years, hundreds of thousands of units at risk can still be saved. Preservation, however, must be more than an intermittent response to predictably imminent crises. As long as subsidized housing is built with time-limited use restrictions, those restrictions will expire. Thousands of units in projects built under Section 236 and financed by state housing finance agencies will see 40-year restrictions expire during the decade beginning in 2010, while thousands more built with the Low Income Housing Tax Credit will see 30-year restrictions expire in the 2020s.

An ongoing commitment to the preservation of subsidized housing with expiring use restrictions must also address the condition of many of these projects. Many of them were constructed with inexpensive materials and systems and now, after 20, 30, or 40 years, the buildings are in urgent need of improvement and systems replacement, as well as energy efficiency retrofits to reduce the amount of money tenants need to pay for utilities. Despite the lack of recent action at the national level, a growing number of states and localities are addressing these issues, many of them with the support of the MacArthur Foundation, which has made a commitment to invest $150 million over 10 years to assist in the preservation of 300,000 affordable rental units, both in projects with expiring use restrictions and in the private market.

Merely preserving subsidized housing with expiring use restrictions is not enough. Preservation policies need to focus not only on subsidized housing, but on unsubsidized but affordable private-market housing as well, to keep valuable units from being lost through demolition, rent increases, or condominium conversion. Efforts need to focus on the quality of the housing as well as the quantity, to make sure that all affordable housing, whether subsidized or not, meets reasonable standards of condition and maintenance. It is reasonable to support nonprofit entities in their efforts to acquire properties from private owners in order to preserve them as affordable housing, particularly in areas showing significant market appreciation, but the great majority of rental units will remain in highly dispersed private hands. Ultimately, the availability of decent, affordable housing in the United States may depend more than anything else on the ability of the public sector to orchestrate the right conditions—both carrots and sticks—to motivate the millions of individuals, couples, and business entities that own rental properties to maintain them in good order and keep them affordable to the households that depend on them for shelter.

This is particularly true of the roughly 18 million one- to four-family properties in the rental stock. Nearly nine out of 10 owners of these properties are individuals or couples, and more than two-thirds own only one or two properties. Most of them are or want to be responsible owners, although many of them may lack the management and financial skills to be fully successful. More owners barely break even, or even lose money, than see a positive cash flow from their properties. While that may not be a critical concern for irresponsible speculators or flippers, who buy properties for short-term gain without concern for their long-term condition and viability, most owners plan to hold onto their properties for the long term. Good and bad owners alike tend to see their relationship with government as adversarial, with little interaction beyond irregular visits by often punitively minded housing inspectors.

Public policy, particularly at the local level, should focus on building cooperative relationships and strengthening the responsible owners of small rental properties while discouraging the presence of speculators and other bad actors. Specific efforts should include more regulatory flexibility, training, and support for owners to become more effective landlords, and financial assistance in the form of low-interest loans for property improvements. The Community Investment Corporation, a nonprofit entity that provides loans to rental property owners in Chicago, offers a property management training program to its borrowers and other landlords, covering subjects from marketing and fair housing to real estate tax issues, maintenance, and budgeting. CIC also provides a free downloadable online property management manual.[40] New York City, in addition to offering training through its Housing Education Program, offers small-group and one-on-one technical assistance and mentoring to landlords through its Owner Service Program.

While government has no direct control over who enters the rental housing industry as a property owner or how long they hold onto their property, it can craft policies to discourage unqualified or inappropriate owners and short-term speculative holding. Known bad actors should be prevented from bidding on properties at auctions or tax sales; other measures can also help. Higher real estate transfer taxes on properties held only for a short period, and measures to discourage property flipping, such as disclosure requirements, targeted code enforcement, and greater state oversight of appraisal practices, are effective ways to discourage speculative holdings.

Preservation is consistently less expensive than new construction. In most cases, it is also more environmentally responsible. Similarly, it is far less costly to create incentives to promote a stronger private rental sector than it is to replace those housing units with far more expensive units constructed under the Low Income Housing Tax Credit or other housing subsidy program. The more government uses its powers and resources to preserve existing affordable housing and foster a strong and responsible private sector rental industry, the further public dollars will go to meet the goal of providing decent, affordable housing for America's lower income households.

In closing, it is important to always bear one fundamental principle in mind. Housing policies, programs, and strategies are not, ultimately, about bricks and mortar, but about people and the communities they live in. This reality is often easily lost in discussions of financing alternatives and program regulations, in which the bloodless, distancing term "housing units" is routinely used to refer to people's homes. All of the complex procedures and regulations involved in the production, rehabilitation, or preservation of affordable housing are means to an end: to improve the lives of individuals and families who cannot afford decent housing on the private market, and to improve the communities in which they live.

In the United States, as in most developed nations, that process has become a complex and time-consuming one. It is further complicated in the U.S. by the degree to which only limited resources are devoted to affordable housing. Every decision about where money will go becomes a zero-sum decision, in which one project or one family gains and another loses. It is even further complicated by the extent to which the phrase "affordable housing" itself too easily becomes a code word reflecting the economic, social, and racial conflicts that still underlie so many decisions about how and where people live in our society.

Those realities cannot be wished away, but they should not allow us to lose track of the central issue. A wealthy nation such as the United States has a responsibility to ensure that its less affluent citizens have a decent roof over their heads, in a community where they can share a decent quality of life and the opportunities that the nation offers. Each effort to develop tax credit housing in a neighborhood where it is in short supply, to restore a dilapidated building to sound, livable condition, to help landlords better maintain their properties, or keep a low-income home owner from losing her house through foreclosure, is a small step in that direction.

NOTES

1. Passel, Jeffrey S., and D'Vera Cohn. 2008. *United States Population Projections 2005–2050*. Washington, D.C.: Pew Research Center. The projections published by the Census Bureau are somewhat more modest and project an increase in Latino population to 102 million, or 24 percent of a somewhat smaller total, by 2050.
2. The lower figure is from the Pew study, the higher from the Census Bureau.
3. Available at http://www.westgate-living.com.
4. Hudnut III, William H. 2003. *Halfway to Everywhere: A Portrait of America's First-Tier Suburbs*. Washington, D.C.: Urban Land Institute.
5. Green, Nancey Leigh, and Sugie Lee. 2005. "Philadelphia's Space In Between: Inner-Ring Suburb Evolution." *Opolis: An International Journal of Suburban and Metropolitan Studies* 1(1).
6. Leinberger, Christopher. 2008. "The Next Slum?" *The Atlantic Monthly*, March. The thesis of this article is explored further in Leinberger's book *The Option of Urbanism*. 2007. Washington, D.C.: Island Press.
7. A good analysis that compares the impacts of growth management with other land-use regimes is Nelson, Arthur C., Rolf Pendall, Casey J. Dawkins, and Gerrit J. Knapp. 2002. "The Link Between Growth Management and Housing Affordability: The Academic Evidence." Brookings Institution Working Paper.
8. In contrast to most other regional planning agencies, which have at most an advisory land-use role, Portland Metro, which was created by referendum and is governed by an elected council, has substantive land-use authority.
9. Available at http://www.homeconnecticut.org/index.php?option=com_content&task=view&id=3&Itemid=6.

10. It is important to distinguish between the two. Heating in a cold climate is a necessity. Air conditioning is not a necessity for healthy individuals in most hot climates. As a result, the latter areas offer more room for cost savings through adaptive behavior.
11. The National Housing Trust Fund became law as a part of the Housing and Economic Recovery Act of 2008, which was reluctantly signed by President Bush on July 30 of that year. Under the act, however, proceeds of the Trust Fund for the first three years will be earmarked for foreclosure prevention; moreover, the uncertain financial status of Fannie Mae and Freddie Mac as of this writing makes the actual financial prospects for the Trust Fund equally uncertain.
12. Available at http://www.nlihc.org/detail/article.cfm?article_id=3834.
13. In 2003, the United Kingdom spent £11 billion on housing benefit, the equivalent of the U.S. housing voucher program. Adjusting for the difference in the value between the pound and the dollar and the relative population of the two countries, this would be the rough equivalent of $110 billion in the United States. The U.S. government budget for fiscal year 2008 appropriated $23.5 billion for housing vouchers, less than a quarter of that amount.
14. DeParle, Jason. 1996. "Slamming the Door." *New York Times Magazine*, October.
15. Stone, Michael E. 2006. "Housing Affordability: One Third of a Nation Shelter-Poor." In *A Right to Housing: Foundation for a New Social Agenda*, ed. Rachel G. Bratt, Michael E. Stone, and Chester W. Hartmann. Philadelphia: Temple University Press.
16. Toy, Vivian S. 2008. "Winning that One in a Million." *New York Times*, March 2, Real estate section.
17. Available at http://www.dwp.gov.uk/lifeevent/benefits/housing_benefit.asp#caniget.
18. The food stamp program permits families to deduct a certain amount of their shelter costs from their income in computing their eligibility.
19. See U.S. Department of Housing and Urban Development. 2007. *Affordable Housing Needs 2005: A Report to Congress*. Available at http://www.huduser/org/Publications/pdf/AffHsgNeeds.pdf. HUD's choice to call their report "affordable housing needs" rather than "worst-case housing needs," which is what they are required to report to Congress, may be an attempt to conflate the two, thereby minimizing the large number of households that have significant affordable housing needs but do not fit into the narrow "worst-case" category.
20. Few people question that, all things being equal, sprinkler systems provide some benefit. The reality is that all things are not equal. Assuming that a sprinkler system adds five percent to the cost of a unit—a conservative figure—and that public resources are not increased to cover this added cost, as is likely, the imposition of this requirement will reduce the number of affordable housing units built by five percent. The question then is: do the benefits of the sprinklers to those incremental units provided with the systems exceed the costs to the households who will be denied affordable housing because of the reduction in the number of units produced?
21. This argument is made by Harvey, Bart. 2006. "A Decent Home and a Suitable Living Environment for All Americans: Rhetoric or Legitimate Goal?" John T. Dunlap Lecture, Joint Center for Housing Studies of Harvard University. Harvey writes that "currently, the cost of HUD's tenant-based housing voucher program is approximately $16 billion and it serves 2.1 million households—for an annual per-voucher cost of roughly $7,600. Providing a voucher for every household with worst-case housing needs would cost an additional $38 billion a year."
22. U.S. Congress Joint Committee on Taxation. 2007. *Estimates of Federal Tax Expenditures for Fiscal Years 2007–2011*. September 24.

23. Dolbeare, Cushing N., et al. 2004. *Changing Priorities: The Federal Budget and Housing Assistance 1976–2005*. Washington, D.C.: National Low Income Housing Coalition.
24. Home ownership rates in Italy, Spain, and most Eastern European countries are significantly higher than in the United States and other Anglophone countries.
25. See Hirad, Abdighani, and Peter M. Zorn. 2002. "Prepurchase Homeownership Counseling: A Little Knowledge is a Good Thing." In *Low-Income Homeownership: Examining the Unexamined Goal*, ed. Nicolas P. Retsinas and Eric S. Belsky. Washington, D.C.: The Brookings Institution.
26. See Caplin, Andrew, James H. Carr, Frederick Pollock, Zhong Yi Tong, Kheng Mei Tan, and Trivkraman Thampy. 2007. "Shared Equity Mortgages, Housing Affordability and Homeownership." *Housing Policy Debate* 18(1). As with any other financial instrument, great care must be taken to ensure that the benefits accruing to the borrower and those accruing to the lender are appropriately balanced, something that is not necessarily the case with some of the shared-equity mortgage models currently under discussion.
27. The establishment of a home ownership tax credit was a major recommendation of the Millennial Housing Commission. See *Meeting Our Nation's Housing Challenges: Report of the Bipartisan Millennial Housing Commission Appointed by the Congress of the United States* (2002).
28. A number of issues are raised by this recommendation. There has been little sustained experience with ongoing postpurchase counseling, as distinct from counseling triggered by a default crisis. As a result, even though intuitively it can be seen as beneficial, its value has not been clearly established. Moreover, the concept may be seen as an overly paternalistic form of hand-holding, raising the specter of the so-called "nanny state." At the same time, the experience of the recent home ownership meltdown would tend to validate its potential importance.
29. Nearly 200 Community Land Trusts have been created in all parts of the United States, while many thousands of affordable units have been created primarily in the New York and Washington, D.C., areas through limited-equity cooperatives, which allow buyers to own a share in the cooperative, rather than individually owning their dwelling.
30. One might argue that if shared-equity home ownership alternatives were to become widespread, they might significantly reduce the percentage of renters in the population. This is unlikely; shared-equity home ownership is more likely to be an alternative—and in many cases, an appropriate one—to conventional home ownership, rather than to rental tenure.
31. Low-income home owners are more likely to be elderly people who in many cases bought their homes when their incomes were higher. Many of these households have no mortgages and relatively low housing costs.
32. Presentation by Erika Poethig, associate director for housing, The MacArthur Foundation, at *Affordable Housing: What's Next Nationally and in Nashville* conference, Vanderbilt University, March 11, 2008.
33. Donovan, Shaun. 2002. *Background Paper on Private Multifamily Rental Housing*. Prepared for the Finance Task Force, Millennial Housing Commission. Available at http://govinfo.library.unt.edu/mhc/papers/mrmf.doc.
34. NAHB policy on Low Income Housing Tax Credit program. Available at http://www.nahb.org/generic.aspx?genericContentID=3552.
35. Khadduri, Jill, Larry Buron, and Carissa Climaco. 2006. *Are States Using the Low Income Housing Tax Credit to Enable Families with Children to Live in Low Poverty and Racially Integrated Neighborhoods?* Washington, D.C.: Poverty & Race Research Action

Council. The data are for tax credit units in major (more than 250,000 population) metropolitan areas in those states. Overall, 58 percent of America's metropolitan population lived in low-poverty tracts.

36. Perhaps some of the political resistance to such a change could be overcome by balancing the redirection of tax credit allocations to high-cost areas with a parallel redirection of a larger share of housing vouchers to lower-cost areas. Even in Flint and similar cities, families earning 30 percent or less of the area median income may have difficulty finding sound, decent housing without assistance.

37. Since the 1990s, French housing policy has emphasized social inclusion and the integration of affordable housing into the larger community. This policy reflects France's desire to avoid the mistakes of the 1960s and 1970s, when it built great numbers of massive and isolated suburban housing projects.

38. At present, federal law limits each state in the amount of tax exempt debt it can issue for private end users, a limitation known as the "volume cap." Many states further limit the amount of tax exempt debt that can be used for housing by targeting the greater part of the state's volume cap to economic development projects.

39. Fee waivers, waiver of sales tax on building materials, and the lower construction interest cost associated with tax-exempt financing should reduce development costs by roughly 10 percent. Tax-exempt bond financing will reduce the monthly debt carrying cost by 12 percent to 15 percent, while a 50 percent reduction in property taxes will reduce monthly operating costs by six to nine percent in a typical jurisdiction.

40. Available at http://www.cicchicago.com/htdocs/training/pmmanual.html.

APPENDIX

Resources for Further Information

A vast body of information is available on affordable housing, including detailed data on housing needs, case studies of successful, well-designed housing developments, guides to financing projects under programs such as the Low Income Housing Tax Credit, and much more. This appendix is designed to highlight particularly valuable or useful books, reports, articles, and websites in each of the areas covered by this book, along with comments on the most important of these documents and sources. At the same time, this is not an exhaustive bibliography, but at most a modest selection of the thousands of books, articles, reports, and other documents on this subject. The reader is urged to look beyond these citations and discover the wealth of information and knowledge available on this subject. Although some of the web addresses for specific documents may have changed by the time this book is in a reader's hands, the reader will almost always be able to find the document by going to the website indicated and searching there.

In addition to specific documents and sources, which are given in sections of the appendix corresponding to the relevant chapter of the book, the housing field is fortunate to have a number of online libraries, where a wide variety of valuable materials covering different aspects of affordable housing can be found in one place. These sites are highlighted and described in the first section of this appendix, listed in alphabetical order. Many of them are well organized for browsing, either by topic or directly by publication, an activity that is likely to lead to valuable serendipitous discoveries.

ONLINE HOUSING LIBRARIES

American Planning Association, http://www.planning.org. The Knowledge Exchange section of the APA website has a section called the Affordable Housing Reader, which contains over 100 documents, reports, and articles on affordable housing from the *Journal of the American Planning Association, Planning* magazine, and other APA publications.

The Brookings Institution Metropolitan Policy Program, http://www.brookings.edu/metro.Brookings publishes consistently solid and often provocative pieces ranging from in-depth research papers to op-ed pieces dealing with housing and many other issues facing today's American cities and metropolitan areas.

Center for Housing Policy, http://www.nhc.org/housing/chp-index. The research arm of the National Housing Conference publishes well-researched, solid pieces on many different housing issues of direct interest to planners and other practitioners, including workforce housing, shared equity development, and inclusionary zoning. Its other website, http://www.housingpolicy.org, offers excellent introductory materials on affordable housing issues.

Housing Policy Debate, http://www.mi.vt.edu/web/page/916/sectionid/580/pagelevel/2/parentid/580/interiorHPD.asp. *Housing Policy Debate* has been the nation's outstanding scholarly journal on matters of housing policy since 1990. It has published articles and forums on almost every issue and controversy of concern to practitioners as well as scholars. In contrast to most scholarly periodicals, its entire contents are available without charge online.

HUD User, http://www.huduser.org. This website is the gateway to the policy and research arm of the U.S. Department of Housing and Urban Development. In addition to hundreds of publications (largely, but not entirely, those sponsored by HUD over the past 40 years), the site includes a searchable bibliographic database containing more than 10,000 entries. Almost all materials can be downloaded without charge.

The Joint Center for Housing Studies at Harvard University, http://www.jchs.harvard.edu. The Joint Center conducts and sponsors some of the best research into housing issues in the United States, including an annual report, *The State of the Nation's Housing*. Online materials include formal research publications, working papers, conference proceedings, and research notes.

KnowledgePlex, http://www.knowledgeplex.org. The Fannie Mae Foundation, now sadly defunct, created this resource center for affordable housing and community development; the site continues to function, at least for the time being. It contains a wealth of information, ranging from downloadable articles, research papers, and reports to news articles and information about upcoming housing-related events. Readers can subscribe to a highly informative weekly digest of housing news and events.

National Association of Realtors, http://www.realtor.org/libweb.nsf/pages/fg327. The Field Guide to Affordable Housing at the web address above offers links to a wide variety of articles on different aspects of affordable housing. NAR offers other field guides on specific housing-related topics, many of which are cited in some of the sections below.

Shelterforce **magazine**, http://www.nhi.org/online/index.html. *Shelterforce* has published timely and incisive articles on affordable housing and community development issues for more than 30 years, and is essential reading for anyone engaged with the rebuilding of American cities. The entire archive of articles from more than 150 issues is available online, and is particularly rich in articles that describe important affordable housing issues and controversies at the state and local levels.

CHAPTER 1: THE CASE FOR AFFORDABLE HOUSING

Some of the best and most current information on housing needs in the United States is available from the Joint Center for Housing Studies at Harvard University, as noted above. The National Low Income Housing Coalition also provides data and research on housing needs, including the annual *Out of Reach* report, which compares incomes and housing costs by area around the United States. This report is available at http://www.nlihc.org. Reports on housing needs, with particular focus on working families, are also available from the Center for Housing Policy of the National Housing Conference.

A HUD report, *Affordable Housing Needs: A Report to Congress on the Significant Need for Housing*, addresses the nation's "worst-case" housing needs in detail as of 2005, and can be downloaded from http://www.huduser.org/publications/affhsg/affhsgneed.html. Detailed information on housing needs for states, larger municipalities, and counties is available in consolidated plans prepared by those jurisdictions as a condition for receiving federal Community Development Block Grant funds.

A good introduction to housing market analysis, and the relationship between the market and affordable housing is Green, Richard K., and Stephen Malpezzi. 2003. *A Primer on U.S. Housing Markets and Housing Policy*. Washington, D.C.: The Urban Institute Press. A dissenting view from the right is Husock, Howard. 2003. *America's Trillion-Dollar Housing Mistake: The Failure of American Housing Policy*. Chicago: Ivan R Dee.

For readers interested in tracking specific data sets, two sites are most useful. The Census Bureau site, http://www.factfinder.census.gov, contains data not only from the decennial census but also from the American Housing Survey and the American Community Survey. The AHS contains housing data that is far more detailed than that of the census, but for a relatively small sample of housing units. It is available for the United States as a whole and for major cities and metropolitan areas. The ACS is also based on a sample, but a larger one than the AHS. It contains limited housing data nationally and for states, metropolitan areas, and large cities. HUD's special census tabulations of housing needs by race and income range to assist local governments in preparing consolidated plans can be downloaded for states, counties, and places from http://socds.huduser.org/scripts/odbic.exe/chas/index.htm.

DataPlace, http://www.dataplace.org, created as an adjunct to KnowledgePlex, is a valuable data resource for housing and community development, and contains a wide variety of useful data at the state, metropolitan area, city, and census tract level. Its annual compilations of housing market activity data from the Home Mortgage Disclosure Act (HMDA), beginning in 1997, are particularly useful for tracking local housing trends.

The literature on deregulation and its effects on affordability is considerable, but often highly tendentious and partisan. Two HUD publications frame the topic: *"Not in My Backyard" Removing Barriers to Affordable Housing* (1991), and its sequel, *"Why Not in Our Community?" Removing Barriers to Affordable Housing* (2005). Both are available at http://www.huduser.org. HUD has also established a Regulatory Barriers Clearinghouse at http://www.huduser.org/rbc, which offers a number of reports and analyses, and above all, a large number of examples from the field. The information from the Clearinghouse must be used with care, however, since it presents its materials totally without any filter or critical assessment, making no distinction between highly valuable initiatives and those that are trivial or even misleading. The author has published an article, "The Fallacy of Laissez-Faire: Deregulation, Housing Affordability and the Poor." 1986. *Journal of Urban and Contemporary Law*, (30), designed to offer some perspective on the conflicting claims for the effects of deregulation.

Two strong case studies of the impacts of regulation are Luger, Michael I., and Kenneth Temkin. 2000. *Red Tape and the Cost of New Residential Development*. New Brunswick, N.J.: CUPR Press (Rutgers University), which compares the regulatory regimes of New Jersey and North Carolina and their effects on housing costs; and *Regulatory Barriers to Publicly Subsidized Housing and Recommendations* from the Drachman Institute of the College of Architecture and Landscape Architecture at the University of Arizona. The latter is a detailed analysis of a development case study in Tucson, and can be downloaded from http://www.drachmaninstitute.org/SpecialEvents/AffordabiltySymposium/Regulatory_Barriers_to_Publicly_Subsidized_Housing.pdf.

CHAPTER 2: A SHORT HISTORY OF AFFORDABLE HOUSING

Perhaps the best single overview of American housing policy over the past 100 years is Wright, Gwendolyn. 1981. *Building the Dream: A Social History of Housing in America*. Cambridge, Mass.: The MIT Press. Housing issues under the New Deal are discussed in Radford, Gail. 1996. *Modern Housing for America: Policy Struggles in the New Deal Era*. Chicago: University of Chicago Press. Two good books that offer a perspective on housing issues from the 1960s are Abrams, Charles. 1965. *The City is the Frontier*. New York: Harper & Row, and Fried, Joseph P., *Housing Crisis U.S.A.* 1971. New York: Praeger Publishers. The *Report of the President's Commission on Housing*. 1982. Washington, D.C., offers a similar perspective from the beginning of the 1980s. An excellent and highly readable overview, with good sections on public housing, urban renewal, and housing policy of the time is Mayer, Martin. 1978. *The Builders*. New York: W.W. Norton & Co.

Two excellent overview articles are Orlebeke, Charles J. 2003. "The Evolution of Low-Income Housing Policy, 1949 to 1999." *Housing Policy Debate*, (11)2, and von Hoffman, Alexander. 1996. "High Ambitions: The Past and Future of American Low-Income Housing Policy." *Housing Policy Debate*, 7(3). A more detailed picture of the rise and fall of public housing is Bauman, John F. 1994. "Public Housing: The Dreadful Saga of a Durable Policy." *Journal of Planning Literature*, (8)4, while a thoughtful analysis of the forces affecting changes in low-income housing policy during recent decades is Erickson, David J. 2006. "Community Capitalism: How Housing Advocates, the Private Sector and Government Forged New Low-income Housing Policy, 1968–1996." *The Journal of Policy History*, (18) 2.

CHAPTER 3: DESIGNING AFFORDABLE HOUSING

Two valuable and largely complementary websites focus on the design of affordable housing. The Affordable Housing Design Advisor, available at http://www.designadvisor.org, hosted by the New Jersey School of Architecture, includes a catalog of model affordable housing developments (taken from Jones, Pettus, and Pyatok's *Good Neighbors: Affordable Family Housing*) but its greatest value lies in the many valuable documents and other tools that it offers to help interested individuals think through affordable housing design issues.

Design Matters, available at http://wall.aa.uic.edu:62730/ahc/catalog/home.html, is sponsored by the University of Illinois at Chicago. While it lacks the depth of background information offered by the former site, it has a more extensive catalog of projects, which can be searched by specific project features.

A different sort of catalog that brilliantly addresses the recurrent issue of development density is Campoli, Julie, and Alex S. MacLean. 2007. *Visualizing Density*. Cambridge, Mass.: Lincoln Institute of Land Policy. It provides visual images of a wide range of developments at densities from under one dwelling per acre to more than 200 per acre, as well as a valuable discussion of density-related issues. A second useful book on the topic is Wentling, James W., and Lloyd W. Bookout, eds. *Density by Design*. 1988. Washington, D.C.: Urban Land Institute. A new book, also from ULI is Haughey, Richard. *Getting Density Right*. 2008. Washington, D.C.: Urban Land Institute; it focuses on the process of planning for compact development and gaining community approval.

Two books offer an excellent overview of affordable housing design issues. Jones, Tom, William Pettus, and Michael Pyatok. 1997. *Good Neighbors: Affordable Family Housing*, New York: McGraw-Hill, is particularly strong on good examples, mostly from the West Coast. Davis, Sam. 1995. *The Architecture of Affordable Housing*, Berkeley: University of California Press, offers a thoughtful and insightful perspective based on Davis's years of experience as an architect in the Bay Area. *Affordable Housing: Designing an American Asset*. 2005. Washington D.C.: Urban Land Institute, contains a number of good case studies of projects, but otherwise offers less than the first two books mentioned.

There are many books that address specific design and site planning issues relevant to affordable housing. Although not specific to affordable housing, the writings of Christopher Alexander and his colleagues, in particular *A Pattern Language: Towns—Buildings—Construction*. 1977. New York: Oxford University Press, are a source of creative insight and inspiration for anyone who cares about the design of our built environment. Oscar Newman's seminal book on the relationship of design to security in affordable housing, *Defensible Space: Crime Prevention Through Urban Design*. 1972. New York: Macmillan, is difficult to obtain, but he addresses similar issues in *Creating Defensible Space* (1996), which can be downloaded from HUD User at http://www.huduser.org/publications/pdf/def.pdf. A second book by Newman, *Community of Interest*. 1975. New York: Anchor Books/Doubleday, addresses a broader range of issues.

CHAPTER 4: SELECTING SITES AND GAINING APPROVAL

Useful information on site selection can be obtained from the Affordable Housing Design Advisor website (see above). *Planning and Urban Design Standards*, edited by the American Planning Association and published by John Wiley & Co. (2006), provides detailed guidance for planners on site evaluation criteria, impact assessment, and land-use approval standards, and is an invaluable reference for anyone involved in land development.

In addition to the Babcock books cited under Chapter 7, a good layperson's introduction to zoning is Merriam, Dwight. 2005. *The Complete Guide to Zoning*. New York: McGraw-Hill. A variety of legal texts, casebooks, and treatises on land-use law, zoning, and related matters are available. A good one-volume casebook is Mandelker, Daniel. 2008. *Planning and Control of Land Development: Cases and Materials*. LexisNexis, while the classic multivolume treatise is Taylor, John M., and Norman Williams, Jr. 1975, updated annually. *American Land Planning Law*. Wilmette, Ill.: Callaghan & Co. Since land-use laws and procedures vary widely by state, the general literature cannot provide specific guidance to how to address land-use issues within a particular state. As a result, state-level educational institutions or professional organizations publish a variety of guidebooks, treatises, and the like, which should be consulted to help users through that state's distinctive labyrinth.

A good deal of research has been done on the impact of affordable housing on property values. Two publications that summarize that research are *Why Affordable Housing Does Not Lower Property Values*, prepared by HomeBase/The Center for Common Concerns for Habitat for Humanity, available at http://www.habitat.org/how/propertyvalues.aspx, and Galster, George C. 2002. *A Review of Existing Research on the Effects of Federally Assisted Housing Programs on Neighboring Residential Property Values*. Washington, D.C.: National Association of Realtors. The NAR offers further information and links to a variety of specific studies in its *Field Guide to the Effects of Low-Income Housing on Surrounding Property Values*, available at http://www.realtor.org/libweb.nsf/pages/fg504.

CHAPTER 5: MAKING THE NUMBERS WORK

The multiplicity of different financing programs requires a potential user to pull together information from many different sources. A good background analysis, although not entirely current, is Wallace, James E. 1995. "Financing Affordable Housing in the United States." *Housing Policy Debate*. (6)4. The National Alliance to End Homelessness provides a set of short, useful materials on financing affordable housing on their website at http://www.endhomelessness.org/content/article/detail/1721. Information on HUD programs including HOME, is available on their website, at http://www.hud.gov/offices/cpd/affordablehousing/programs/home, and on Housing Choice Vouchers at http://www.hud.gov/offices/pih/programs/hcv/about/fact_sheet.cfm.

Iglesias, Tim, and Rochelle E. Lento, eds. 2005. *The Legal Guide to Affordable Housing Development*. Chicago: ABA Publishing, has chapters outlining federal, state, and local affordable housing financing programs.

As befits its significance, there is a considerable body of literature on the Low Income Housing Tax Credit. Novogradac & Co., a certified public accounting and consulting firm, publishes an annually updated *Low Income Housing Tax Credit Handbook*, and offers a variety of links and other resources on its website, http://www.novoco.com. Another popular guide to the LIHTC program, also updated annually, is Guggenheim, Joseph. *Tax Credits for Low Income Housing*, 13th ed. Glen Echo, Md.: Simon Publications. Further information is available at http://www.housingtaxcredits.net/id36.html.

The National Association of Realtors offers a Field Guide to the LIHTC at http://www.realtor.org/libweb.nsf/pages/fg720. Affordable Housing Finance is a monthly publication that serves the diverse industry of developers, investors, lawyers, housing finance agencies, and others involved with the tax credit program. It is available at http://www.housingfinance.com. Although it concentrates on the tax credit program, it offers frequent articles and interviews on other housing finance and housing policy issues. A good background analysis of the program is McClure, Kirk. 2000. "The Low Income Housing Tax Credit as an Aid to Housing Finance: How Well has it Worked?" *Housing Policy Debate*. (11)1.

The Housing Trust Fund project of the Center for Community Change tracks state and local trust funds. Mary Brooks's *Housing Trust Fund*

Progress Report 2007 describes the current picture with respect to trust funds, including both an overview and numerous program descriptions. It can be ordered from the Center or downloaded from http://www.communitychange.org/our-projects/htf/other-media/HTF%2007%20final.pdf. The National Association of Realtors has a Field Guide to Housing Trust Funds, available at http://www.realtor.org/libweb.nsf/pages/fg322. Additional information about state housing programs comes from the Progressive States Network, http://www.progressivestates.org/content/654/promoting-affordable-housing-through-state-policy.

CHAPTER 6: DEVELOPING AFFORDABLE HOUSING, STEP-BY-STEP

Hecht, Bennett L. 2006. *Developing Affordable Housing: A Practical Guide for Non-Profit Organizations*. Hoboken, N.J.: John Wiley & Sons provides detailed information on all stages of the development process; a 1996 companion volume by Hecht and James Stockard, *Managing Affordable Housing: A Practical Guide to Creating Stable Communities,* also from John Wiley & Sons, provides details on managing affordable housing developments. Enterprise Community Partners, a national organization that supports the work on nonprofit community development corporations, has created a Program Operations Series in its Community Development Library with nine publications that focus on specific development types, such as single-family subdivisions, single-family infill, and multifamily new construction, available at http://www.enterprisecommunity.org/resources/publications_catalog/#housing.

A number of publications offer guidance to local governments on strategies to further affordable housing, including Lubell, Jeffrey. 2007. *Increasing the Availability of Affordable Homes: A Handbook of High-Impact State and Local Solutions*. Washington, D.C.: Center for Housing Policy, and White, S. Mark. 1992. *Affordable Housing: Proactive and Reactive Planning Strategies*. Planning Advisory Service Report no. 441. Chicago: American Planning Association.

Four detailed case studies of housing development projects using a variety of creative financing and development strategies are presented in *New Directions, Sustainable Solutions*. 2007. New York: Local Initiatives Support Corporation, It is available at http://www.lisc.org/content/publications/detail/6773.

CHAPTER 7. CONCENTRATION AND OPPORTUNITY: UNDOING THE EXCLUSION OF AFFORDABLE HOUSING

A classic book on suburban exclusion is Babcock, Richard. 1966. *The Zoning Game: Municipal Practices and Policies*. Madison: University of Wisconsin Press. Other valuable works are Danielson, Michael N. 1976. *The Politics of Exclusion*. New York: Columbia University Press, and a sequel by Babcock with Charles Siemon, 1985. *The Zoning Game Revisited*. Boston: Oelgeschlager, Gunn & Hain, All are highly readable. A useful social perspective on the same issues is Perin, Constance. 1977. *Everything in its Place: Social Order and Land Use in America*. Princeton, N.J.: Princeton University Press.

An early and unusually forward-looking essay on overcoming regional imbalances is Downs, Anthony. 1973. *Opening Up the Suburbs: An Urban Strategy for America*. New Haven, Conn.: Yale University Press, while a more recent perspective can be found in Dreier, Peter, John Mollenkopf, and Todd Swanstrom. 2001. *Place Matters: Metropolitics for the Twenty-first Century*. Lawrence: University Press of Kansas. Useful materials on regional equity issues are available from PolicyLink, a nonprofit national think tank that focuses on issues of social and economic equity: http://www.policylink.org.

A superb account of the *Mt. Laurel* story and its aftermath is Kirp, David ., John P. Dwyer, and Larry R. Rosenthal. 1995. *Our Town: Race, Housing and the Soul of Suburbia*. New Brunswick, N.J.: Rutgers University Press. Haar, Charles M. 1996. *Suburbs Under Siege: Race, Space and Audacious Judges*. Princeton, N. J.: Princeton University Press, covers similar ground, less vividly but with a broader policy perspective. An assessment of the effects on the Massachusetts "anti-snob-zoning" law is *The Record on 40B: The Effectiveness of the Massachusetts Affordable Housing Zoning Law*. 2003. Boston: Massachusetts Citizens' Housing and Planning Association, available at http://www.chapa.org/pdf/TheRecordon40B.pdf. No single publication adequately documents the scope of affordable housing strategies in California, but a compendium of resources can be found at the California Housing Law Project website, http://www.housingadvocates.org.

An assessment of regional affordable housing strategies can be found in Meck, Stuart, Rebecca Retzlaff, and James Schwab. 2003. *Regional Approaches to Affordable Housing*, Planning Advisory Service Report no. 513/514. Chicago: American Planning Association. Rusk, David. 1999. *Inside Game Outside Game: Winning Strategies for Saving Urban America*.

Washington, D.C.: Brookings Institution Press, offers a number of case studies of regional affordable housing strategies. The *Legal Guide to Affordable Housing Development* (see resources for Chapter 5) has good chapters on exclusionary zoning and affirmative state strategies.

CHAPTER 8. AFFORDABLE HOUSING AND NEIGHBORHOOD REVITALIZATION

The classic work on concentrated poverty is Wilson, William Julius. 1987. *The Truly Disadvantaged: The Inner City, the Underclass, and Public Policy*. Chicago: University of Chicago Press; another valuable work is Jargowsky, Paul A. *Poverty and Place: Ghettos, Barrios, and the American City*.1997. New York: Russell Sage Foundation. A recent analysis by Pettit, Kathryn L.S., and G. Thomas Kingsley. 2003. *Concentrated Poverty: A Change in Course*. Washington, D.C.: The Urban Institute, looks at recent trends in this area.

An assessment of the HOPE VI program to date is found in Popkin, Susan J., Bruce Katz, Mary K. Cunningham, Karen D. Brown, Jeremy Gustafson, and Margery Austin Turner. 2004. *A Decade of HOPE VI Research Findings and Policy Challenges*, published by the Urban Institute and available at http://www.urban.org/publications/411002.html.

There is a growing literature about neighborhood change, CDCs, and about the theme of communities of choice. Two good and highly readable books about urban neighborhood change are von Hoffman, Alexander. 2003. *House by Housing, Block by Block: The Rebirth of America's Urban Neighborhoods*, New York: Oxford University Press, and Kromer, John. 2000. *Neighborhood Recovery: Reinvestment Policy for the New Hometown*, New Brunswick, N.J.: Rutgers University Press, which weaves Kromer's experience as Philadelphia's community development director in the 1990s with broader observations on neighborhood change.

A highly readable but excessively one-sided and promotional picture of CDC-led neighborhood change is Grogan, Paul S., and Tony Proscio. 2000. *Comeback Cities*, Boulder Colo.: Westview Press. Valuable perspectives on community development generally, and CDCs in particular, can be found in the essays in Ferguson, Roland F., and William T. Dickens, eds. 1999. *Urban Problems and Community Development*. Washington, D.C.: The Brookings Institution Press. Two solid and thoughtful assessments of the network of CDCs are Vidal, Avis C. 1992. *Rebuilding Communities: A National Study of Urban Community Development Corporations*. New York:

New School for Social Research, and Walker, Christopher. 2002. *Community Development Corporations and their Support System*. Washington, D.C.: The Urban Institute. The former is no longer readily available, but the latter is available from http://www.urban.org/UploadedPDF/310638 _ChangingSupportSystems.pdf.

The author has written two short publications that focus on the role of housing strategies in neighborhood change. *Building a Better Urban Future: New Directions for Housing Policies in Weak Market Cities*, (2005) and *Managing Neighborhood Change: A Framework for Sustainable and Equitable Revitalization* (2008), are both available from the National Housing Institute at http://www.nhi.org/research. A good overview of the issue is Katz, Bruce. 2004. *Neighborhoods of Choice and Connection: The Evolution of American Neighborhood Policy and What it Means for the United Kingdom*. Washington, D.C.: The Brookings Institution. Another book, Varady, David P., and Jeffrey A. Raffel. 1995. *Selling Cities: Attracting Homebuyers Through Schools and Housing Programs*. Albany: State University of New York Press, addresses school-related issues in the context of marketing urban areas. A number of additional resources are available through the website of the Healthy Neighborhoods Group, a consortium of independent consultants working in this area, at http://www.fallcreek consultants.com/resources.php.

In addition to preserving affordable housing developments, an issue addressed in Chapter 10, issues of affordability and equity in appreciating neighborhoods are addressed in the author's *Managing Neighborhood Change*, and in the Equitable Development Toolkit developed by Policy Link, available at http://www.policylink.org/EDTK/default.html. An older book that contains much useful information is Hartman, Chester, Dennis Keating, and Richard LeGates. 1981. *Displacement: How To Fight It*. Washington, D.C.: National Housing Law Project.

CHAPTER 9: RISKS AND REWARDS OF AFFORDABLE HOME OWNERSHIP

A wide variety of valuable articles on different aspects of lower income home ownership is included in Belsky, Eric S., and Nicolas P. Retsinas, eds. 2002. *Low-Income Homeownership: Examining the Unexamined Goal*. Washington, D.C.: The Brookings Institution. Other articles and papers on home ownership are available from the Joint Center on Housing Studies at http://www.jchs.harvard.edu/publications/homeownership/index.html. The vast academic literature on the costs and benefits of home ownership is summarized in Rohe, William M., Shannon Van Zandt, and George McCarthy, "Social Benefits and Costs of Homeownership" in the Belsky and Retsinas volume, and in National Association of Realtors. 2006. *Social Benefits of Homeownership and Stable Housing*. Washington, D.C.: National Association of Realtors Research Division, available at http://www.realtor.org/Research.nsf/Pages/reportsbuysell?Open Document. A highly valuable paper takes a critical look at low-income homeownership: Shlay, Anne B. 2006. "Low-Income Homeownership: American Dream or Delusion." *Urban Studies*, (43)3.

NeighborWorks America has a long track record in developing creative strategies to foster low-income home ownership, and offers a wide variety of publications on the subject at http://www.nw.org/network/pubs/studies/default.asp#homeownership. Additional information can be obtained from the Local Initiatives Support Corporation Online Library at http://www.lisc.org/content/publications/?topic=53&year=&type=. The NeighborWorks site also contains many valuable resources about home ownership education and counseling and foreclosure prevention.

While the subprime industry and its catastrophic fallout have generated a plethora of articles and commentaries, a single book that does justice to the subject is not yet (as of September 2008) available. Adequate overviews can be found in Gramlich, Edward M. 2007. *Subprime Mortgages: America's Latest Boom and Bust*. Washington, D.C.: The Urban Institute Press, and Neighborhood Housing Services of Chicago. 2004 and *Preserving Homeownership: Community-Development Implications of the New Mortgage Market*, available at http://www.nhschicago.org/content/page.php?cat_id=3&content_id=33. The best account of the subprime industry, however, can be found in Bitner, Richard. 2008. *Confessions of a Subprime Lender*. Hoboken, N.J.: John Wiley & Sons. The publications of the Center for Responsible Lending, a Durham, North Carolina-based nonprofit organization that monitors the subprime industry, are a valuable resource to understand the dynamics of the industry and the impacts of the foreclosure crisis: http://www.responsiblelending.org.

CHAPTER 10: PRESERVING AFFORDABLE HOUSING

Excellent resources on preserving subsidized housing are Achtenberg, Emily P. 2002. *Stemming the Tide: A Handbook on Preserving Subsidized Multifamily Housing*. New York: Local Initiatives Support Corporation, and Atlas, John, and Ellen Shoshkes. 1997. *Saving Affordable Housing: What Community Groups Can Do and What Government Should Do*.

This report, which includes detailed case studies, appeared as a special issue of *Shelterforce*, and is available online at http://www.nhi.org/online/issues/sf90.html. More detailed information is available from the National Housing Trust, whose mission is to preserve and revitalize existing subsidized housing, at http://www.nhtinc.org, and at the MacArthur Foundation at http://www.macfound.org.

The issue of preserving affordable home ownership is discussed in detail in Davis, John E. 2006. *Shared Equity Homeownership: The Changing Landscape of Resale-Restricted, Owner-Occupied Housing*. Montclair, N.J.: National Housing Institute, available at http://www.nhi.org/pdf/SharedEquityHome.pdf. The Center for Housing Policy has issued a series of materials on preserving affordable home ownership, including *Preservation of Affordable Homeownership: A Continuum of Strategies* (2007), available at http://www.nhc.org/housing/sharedequity.

The use of Community Land Trusts as a vehicle for creating permanently affordable home ownership is described in detail in Institute for Community Economics. 1982. *The Community Land Trust Handbook*. Emmaus, Pa.: Rodale Press.

A recent publication from the Harvard Joint Center for Housing Studies offers a series of articles and essays illuminating different rental housing issues: Belsky, Eric S., and Nicholas P. Retsinas. 2007. *Revisiting Rental Housing: Policies, Programs and Priorities*. Washington, D.C.: The Brookings Institution Press. Additional papers on rental housing are available at http://www.jchs.harvard.edu/publications/rental/index.html, including the author's paper on the poorly understood one- to four-unit rental market: "Landlords at the Margins: Exploring the Dynamics of the One to Four Unit Rental Housing Industry," (2006).

CHAPTER 11: HOMELESSNESS AND AFFORDABLE HOUSING

Even more than most other housing-related topics, homelessness has spawned a vast literature of books, reports, and other publications. A historical overview is provided by Kusmer, Kenneth L. 2002. *Down and Out, On the Road: The Homeless in American History*, New York: Oxford University Press. Among the many books that provide an overview of the growth of homelessness in the 1970s and 1980s, noteworthy are Burt, Martha R. 1992. *Over the Edge: The Growth of Homelessness in the 1980s*, New York: Russell Sage Foundation; Jencks, Christopher. 1994. *The Homeless*. Cambridge, Mass.: Harvard University Press; and Rossi, Peter

H. 1989. *Down and Out in America: The Origins of Homelessness*. Chicago: University of Chicago Press.

A tighter focus is provided by O'Flaherty, Brendan. 1996. *Making Room: The Economics of Homelessness*. Cambridge, Mass.: Harvard University Press. Two recent books that bring recent research and analysis to bear are Burt, Martha R., Carol L. Pearson, and Ann Elizabeth Montgomery, eds. 2006. *Homelessness: Prevention, Strategies and Effectiveness*. Nova Science Publishers, and Levinson, David, and Marcy Ross, eds. 2007. *The Homelessness Handbook*. Great Barrington, Mass.: Berkshire Publishing Group.

The most detailed profile of the homeless appears in Burt, Martha R., et al. 1999. *Homelessness: Programs and the People They Serve*. Urban Institute for the Interagency Council on the Homeless, National Survey of Homeless Assistance Providers and Clients, conducted in 1996. Reprinted, Darby, Pa.: Diane Publishing Co. The HUD 2007 *Annual Homeless Assessment Report to Congress* provides an updated, although less detailed, picture. It is available at http://www.huduser.org/publications/povsoc/annual_assess.html. The two principal organizations providing current information on homelessness and the strategies being pursued to address the problem are the National Alliance to End Homelessness, http://www.endhomelessness.org, and the National Coalition for the Homeless, http://www.nationalhomeless.org. Both organizations offer a wide variety of publications, including useful succinct fact sheets and program descriptions as well as more extended reports.

CHAPTER 12: INCLUSIONARY HOUSING

The most comprehensive study of inclusionary housing, although out of date in many respects, remains the author's *Inclusionary Housing Programs: Policies and Practices*. 1984. New Brunswick, N.J.: Rutgers University Center for Urban Policy Research. Two more recent publications presenting a broad picture of the subject are Anderson, Mary. 2003. *Opening the Door to Inclusionary Housing*. Chicago: Business and Professional People for the Public Interest., available at http://www.bpichicago.org/documents/OpeningtheDoor.pdf, and Brunick, Nick. 2007. *Inclusionary Zoning: Lessons from the National Experience*; prepared for the New Jersey Council on Affordable Housing, it can be downloaded at http://www.state.nj.us/dca/coah/dec07proposal/task3a.pdf.

A number of other valuable publications on inclusionary housing can be found on the BPI website, http://www.bpichicago.org. The National

Association of Realtors offers a *Field Guide to Inclusionary Zoning*, available at http://www.realtor.org/libweb.nsf/pages/fg806.

Two recent research studies attempt to evaluate the effect of inclusionary zoning on housing markets, reaching different but in both cases preliminary conclusions: Schuetz, Jenny Rachel Meltzer, and Vicki Been, *The Effects of Inclusionary Zoning on Local Housing Markets: Lessons from the San Francisco, Washington DC and Suburban Boston Areas* published by the Center for Housing Policy (2008) and available at http://www.nhc.org/housing/iz, and *Housing Market Impacts of Inclusionary Zoning*, prepared by the University of Maryland National Center for Smart Growth Research and Education (2008), funded by the National Association of Home Builders and available at http://www.nahb.org/generic.aspx?genericContentID=90746.

The great majority of publications about inclusionary zoning focus on the experience in specific states. Many of them are valuable to readers outside those states, since they go beyond description to offer insights relevant to anyone interested in the subject. A thoughtful comparative analysis of trends in the two states with the most extensive history in this area is Calavita, Nico, Kenneth Grimes, and Alan Mallach. 1997. "Inclusionary Housing in California and New Jersey: A Comparative Analysis." *Housing Policy Debate*. (8)1. Two excellent compilations are available from the National Housing Conference: *Inclusionary Zoning: Lessons Learned in Massachusetts* (2002) and *Inclusionary Zoning: The California Experience* (2004), available at http://www.nhc.org/housing/pubs-descriptions. Detailed descriptions of the California experience can be found in *Inclusionary Housing in California: 30 Years of Innovation*. 2003. California Coalition for Rural Housing and Non-Profit Housing Association of Northern California, available at http://www.nonprofithousing.org/knowledgebank/publications/Inclusionary_Housing_CA_30years.pdf, and *Affordable by Choice: Trends in California Inclusionary Housing Programs*. 2007. Non-Profit Housing Association of Northern California. The latter report is not available for download, but can be ordered from NPH. An executive summary is available at http://www.nonprofithousing.org/AffordableByChoice/SampleIHReport.pdf.

An assessment of inclusionary programs in the Washington, D.C., area, including the much-publicized Montgomery County, Maryland, program is Destorel Brown, Karen. 2001. *Expanding Affordable Housing Through Inclusionary Zoning: Lessons from the Washington Metropolitan Area*. Washington, D.C.: Brookings Institution, Metropolitan

Policy Program, available at http://www.brookings.edu/reports/2001/10metropolitanpolicy_brown.aspx. Making the case for inclusionary zoning in a rapidly appreciating urban environment is Fox, Radhika K., and Kalima Rose. 2003. *Expanding Housing Opportunity in Washington, D.C.: The Case for Inclusionary Zoning*. Oakland, Calif.: PolicyLink. It is available at http://www.policylink.org/Research/DCIZ.

CHAPTER 13: POLICIES, POLITICS, AND THE FUTURE OF AFFORDABLE HOUSING

Two good analyses of changing demographic trends in the United States are Passel, Jeffrey S., and D'Vera Cohn. 2008. *United States Population Projections 2005–2050*. Washington, D.C.: Pew Research Center, and Shrestha, Laura B. 2006. *The Changing Demographic Profile of the United States*. Washington, D.C.: Congressional Research Service, available at http://www.fas.org/sgp/crs/misc/RL32701.pdf. The Brookings Institution has published three volumes of papers on the implications of the 2000 Census: Berube, Alan, Bruce Katz, and Robert E. Lang, eds. *Redefining Urban & Suburban America: Evidence from Census 2000*.

The "reurbanization" of America and the market shift toward urban living from the perspective of a real estate developer are described in Leinberger, Christopher. 2007. *The Option of Urbanism*. Washington, D.C.: Island Press, and in Breen, Ann, and Dick Rigby. 2004. *Intown Living: A Different American Dream*. Washington, D.C.: Island Press, which provides case studies of eight cities in the United States and Canada. The condition of America's first-ring suburbs is described in Hudnut, III, William H. 2003. *Halfway to Everywhere: A Portrait of America's First-Tier Suburbs*. Washington, D.C.: Urban Land Institute.

A good overview of the relationship between affordable housing and smart growth is *Affordable Housing and Smart Growth: Making the Connection*. 2001. Washington, D.C.: National Neighborhood Coalition, available from Smart Growth America at http://www.smartgrowthamerica.org/affordable_housing.pdf. An excellent collection of materials on smart growth and affordable housing has been compiled by the Citizens Housing and Planning Association, at http://www.chapa.org/smartgrowth.htm. While some of the material is specific to Massachusetts, it offers valuable lessons for users in other areas.

There is a growing body of information about green building, including resources from the United States Green Building Council, http://www.usgbc.org, and the Green Building Initiative of the National Association of Home Builders, http://www.thegbi.org. The National Association of Realtors offers a good collection of materials on green building at http://www.realtor.org/smart_growth.nsf/pages/greenbuilding?open document. A project of Enterprise Community Partners, http://www.greencommunitiesonline.org provides information directly aimed at the planners, designers, and developers of affordable housing. A valuable paper by Proscio, Tony. 2007. *Affordable Housing's Green Future*. Columbia, Md.: Enterprise Community Partners, can be downloaded from http://www.enterprisecommunity.org/resources/publications_catalog/#green. A thoughtful perspective on sustainable design and its relationship to the environment can be found in Williams, Daniel. 2007. *Sustainable Design: Ecology, Architecture and Planning*. Hoboken, N.J.: John Wiley & Sons, which also contains a variety of case studies.

Information about the proposed national housing trust fund is available from the National Low Income Housing Coalition, at http://www.nlihc.org/template/page.cfm?id=40. The Coalition tracks the Washington scene closely, and its website contains useful, up-to-date information about federal spending and policy shifts in housing. Both the *Report of the President's Commission on Housing*. 1982. Washington, D.C.: President's Commission on Housing, and *Meeting our Nation's Housing Challenges: Report of the Bipartisan Millennial Housing Commission*. 2002. Washington, D.C.: Millennial Housing Commission, are important documents in tracing the recent history of American housing policy, although the latter has had little effect on housing policy in the six years since its release. While the 1982 report is not available at present, its recommendations are analyzed in Weicher, John C. 1983. "Report of the President's Commission on Housing: Policy Proposals for Subsidized Housing." *Real Estate Economics*, (11)2. The Millennial Commission report is available at http://govinfo.library.unt.edu/mhc/MHCReport.pdf. The issue of the right to housing, as well as a variety of critical housing policy issues, is well addressed from a progressive political perspective in an important book: Bratt, Rachel G., Michael E. Stone, and Chester Hartman, eds. 2006. *A Right to Housing: Foundation for a New Social Agenda*. Philadelphia: Temple University Press.

Index

Abrams, Charles, 35, 351
Abt Associates, 182
adjustable rate mortgages (ARMs), 104, 230, 301
"affirmative" marketing, 149
affordability, 30–32, 102–6, 254–59, 350
affordable housing
    approval for, 89–99
    "attainable housing," ix
    the case for, 1–26, 349–51
    and communities of choice, 191–95
    and community development corporations, 186–91
    community opposition to, 84, 85, 95, 136
    cost assistance in, 106–18
    and the courts, 97–99, 162–65
    and demand-side approaches, 19–21, 24–25, 41–44
    and demographics, 16, 58–60, 80, 123, 192, 311, 312–14, 315, 363
    designing, 53–75
    developing, 133–54. *See also* development
    and existing housing, 15–17, 19–21, 43, 72–73, 158, 200, 220, 254, 303
    filling the gap in, 106–12
    financing, 101–31. *See also* financing
    future of, 319–42, 363–64
    history of, 29–50, 207–11
    and homelessness, 263–82
    and home ownership, 207–35, 358–59. *See also* home ownership
    as a housing problem, 17–25
    and inclusionary housing, 285–307
    as an income problem, 17–25
    in contrast to luxury housing, 64, 80, 82, 89, 97
    management of, 148–54
    mandates, 167–74
    and neighborhood revitalization, 195–203
    "normal people's housing," ix
    and open space, 65–67
    and poverty, 21–22, 179–85
    preserving, 239–59. *See also* preservation
    and the private market, 1–2, 10–17, 19, 25, 41–43, 47, 50, 64, 85–86, 109, 130, 136, 165, 178, 189, 194–97, 199, 202, 214, 218–20, 239, 241–43, 248, 254–59, 279, 285–86, 295, 394, 332–33, 335–37, 339–41
    and public policy, 29–50, 312–32, 363–64
    and renting. *See* rental housing
    as a right, 324
    and safe spaces, 69–72
    and state planning laws, 165–67
    and the subprime meltdown, 228–41
    and subsidy layering, 123–25
    and suburban exclusion, 158–65, 174–75, 356
    and traffic, 65–69
    and use restrictions, 242–46
Affordable Housing Design Advisor, 60, 65, 66, 83, 351–52, 353
Affordable Housing Program, 117, 144
Alinsky, Saul, 186

American Dream Down Payment Initiative, 207, 220, 222
American Housing Survey, 2, 350
"anti-snob zoning law." See Chapter 40B
area median income (AMI), 5, 19, 38, 120, 168, 182, 193, 195, 219, 223, 225, 254–55, 268, 296, 320, 334–35
Azalea Park, 193

Beach, The, 75
Bedford-Stuyvesant Restoration Corporation, 186
Bethel New Life, 188
Brooke Amendment (1969), 36
brownfield sites, 86
Builder's Choice Award, 151

California Housing Finance Agency (CalHFA), 111
Camden Regional Legal Services, 163
capital grants, 106–7, 112–18, 122, 146, 337
Carl Mackley Houses, 55
cars and traffic, 65–69
Case-Schiller index of house prices, 214
Center for Responsible Lending, 231
Chapter 40B, 89, 165, 168–69, 291, 356
Chapter 40R, 224–25
Chicago Rehab Network, 188
"city of neighborhoods," 186
Community Development Block Grant (CDBG), 113–14, 319, 337, 349
community development corporations (CDCs), 49, 186–91, 203, 286, 290, 305, 355, 357–58
Community Investment Corporation (CIC), 340–41
community land trust (CLT), 49, 212, 251–52, 320, 330–31, 360
Community Reinvestment Act (CRA), 142, 187, 210, 222, 226
Comprehensive Permit Law. See Chapter 40B
Consumer Price Index, 32
Council on Affordable Housing (COAH), 169, 250, 289, 296, 361

Danter Company, 121
deregulation, 11–12, 350
development
    approval process, 90–97, 353–54
    construction, 146–48
    costs, 107, 119, 124, 127–29, 141–42, 145–46
    designing affordable housing, 351–53
    development pro forma, 126–31
    "fast track" permitting, 224
    for-profit developers, 133–34
    involuntary displacement, 197
    and marketing, 48, 146–54, 192, 230, 337–38, 340–41, 358
    and new construction, 261
    predevelopment process, 140–46
    property management, 147–50, 340–41
    selecting sites for, 54, 65–69, 72, 73–75, 79–89, 96, 98, 113, 121, 127, 129, 135–43, 146–48, 151, 167, 202, 220, 224, 352–54
    step-by-step, 133–54, 355
    and type of housing, 60–65
disinvestment, 85, 188, 192
Downs, Tony, 193–94, 356
"dumbbell" buildings, 30

Emergency Low Income Housing Preservation Act of 1990, 242
Enterprise Community Partners, 141, 187, 355, 364
Enterprise Foundation, 49, 187
equity investments, 45, 106–7, 112, 118–22, 129, 145, 330
Euclid v. Ambler, 160–61
"exotic" mortgages, 230

Fair Housing Act, 97–98, 165, 169, 289, 306
Fair Market Rent, 42, 109, 334
Fall Creek Place, 193–94
Fannie Mae, 38, 209, 226–27, 319, 331, 348–49
"fast track" permitting, 224

Federal Housing Administration, 22, 158, 209, 234, 331
Federal National Mortgage Association. *See* Fannie Mae
Federal Reserve System, 234
"filtering down," 10–11, 15–17
financing
    adjustable rate mortgages (ARMs), 104, 230, 301
    capital cost assistance, 105, 106–8
    and capital grants, 106–7, 112–18, 122, 146, 337
    carrying cost assistance, 105, 108–9, 220
    demand-side programs, 19–21, 24–35, 41–44
    equity investments, 45, 106–7, 112, 118–22, 129, 145, 330
    "exotic" mortgages, 230
    housing trust funds, 44–45, 47, 48, 114–15, 131, 135, 251, 253, 279, 286–87, 291, 292–94, 299, 306–7, 319–21, 354–55, 364
    Low Income Housing Tax Credit (LIHTC), 44, 45, 47, 106, 118–22, 124, 129–30, 131, 137, 144, 181, 182, 183, 195, 198, 240, 244, 291, 319, 320, 330, 332, 335, 339, 341, 354
    Low Income Purchase Assistance, 223
    and low-interest mortgages, 37, 111–12, 226
    Mortgage Revenue Bonds (MRBs), 44, 111
    Multifamily Bonds, 111
    "no-doc" loans, 230, 234
    pari passu financing, 106
    PITI (principal, insurance, taxes, insurance) formula, 103, 105
    private mortgage insurance (PMI), 222
    private revenue sources, 117–18
    rehabilitation loans, 199
    second mortgages, 243, 339
    state and local government resources, 114–16, 354–55
    and the subprime meltdown, 228–41
    tax abatement, 103–4, 106, 109–11, 131, 225–26, 244, 297, 299, 300
    tax credit equity, 110, 112, 118–19, 129–30, 144–45, 150, 244
    tax increment financing (TIF), 115–16, 219, 300, 306
First Houses, 34
"floating zones," 87–88
foreclosure crisis, 231–35, 258–59, 311, 316, 319, 321–22, 331, 359
Freddie Mac, 226–27, 319–20, 331

Galster, George, 94, 353
Garden Homes, 44
grassroots organizations, 49, 186
"green" buildings, 147
Grigg's Farm, 151, 153

Habitat for Humanity, 93, 353
Harlem River Houses, 34
"hidden homelessness," 9, 264
high-rise towers, 55
Hismen Hin-nu Terrace, 75
homelessness, 9, 263–81, 360–61
Home Loan Banks, 112, 117, 144
Homeowners Emergency Mortgage Assistance Program (HEMAP), 228, 234
home ownership
    benefits of, 212–17
    costs of, 215
    home ownership education and counseling (HEC) programs, 226–28
    lower income home owners, 257–59
    public and nonprofit strategies to foster, 217–28
    and public policy, 328
    and regulatory barriers, 223–26
    and the subprime meltdown, 228–35
    subsidizing homeownership, 219–23
    today, 212
Homeownership Zone program, 47–48, 193, 219
Home Owners' Loan Corporation (HOLC), 208–210, 234

HOME program, 43–47, 113–14, 115, 117, 122, 131, 219, 222, 319–20, 337, 354
Hope VI program, 47–48, 157, 219
housing
    cost burden in, 4–7
    and the deconcentration of poverty, 21–22
    economic competitiveness in, 22–24
    economic segregation in, 21–22
    exclusion in, 157–74, 356–57
    existing, 15–16
    modern housing movement, 29–30
    needs, 349–50
    overcrowding, 3, 7–10
    for senior citizens, 84
    shortages, 24
    substandard, 2–7
    type of, 60–65
    "useful life" of, 53
    "workforce housing," ix, 23, 25, 59, 118, 211, 218–19, 226, 348
Housing & Mortgage Finance Agency, 111, 116, 141–42
Housing Act of 1949, 323
Housing and Community Development Network of New Jersey, 141, 187
Housing and Economic Recovery Act of 2008 (HR 3221), 234
Housing and Urban Development (HUD), 5, 18, 38, 44, 109, 122, 182–83, 193, 240–43, 325, 335, 348, 349, 350, 353, 354, 361
Housing Choice Vouchers. *See* Section 8
Housing Trust Fund Act of 2007, 320
housing trust funds, 44–45, 47, 48, 114–15, 131, 135, 251, 253, 279, 286–87, 291, 292–94, 299, 306–7, 319–21, 354–55, 364
Huntington Branch NAACP v. Town of Huntington, 97–98

inclusionary housing, 285–319, 361–63
income, 1–26, 58, 215
    area median (AMI), 5, 19, 38, 120, 168, 182, 193, 195, 219, 223, 225, 254–55, 268, 296, 320, 334–35
    and cost burden, 4–7
    and home ownership, 215–17
    low versus lower income, 4–5
Industrial Areas Foundation, 186
intermediaries, 48, 187, 305

Joint Committee on Taxation, 326

land banks, 89, 202, 286
land-use regulations, 12, 60, 62, 80, 82, 87–88, 90, 99, 137, 138, 140–44, 146, 161–64, 166–67, 174, 286, 292–95, 298–99, 317–18, 333, 353
Langham Court, 73
League of Women Voters, 162
Local Initiatives Support Corporation (LISC), 49, 141, 187, 359
Low Income Housing Preservation and Resident Home Ownership Act of 1990, 242
Low Income Housing Tax Credit (LIHTC), 44, 45, 47, 106, 118–22, 124, 129–30, 131, 137, 144, 181, 182, 183, 195, 198, 240, 244, 291, 319, 320, 330, 332, 335, 339, 341, 354
Low Income Purchase Assistance, 223
low-interest mortgage, 37, 111–12, 226

MacArthur Foundation, 118, 333, 339, 360
Maple Heights, 231–32
"Mark to Market" program, 243
"Mark-Up to Market" program, 243
McMansions, 90, 316–17, 326
Millennial Housing Commission, 48, 323, 364
Mortgage Revenue Bonds (MRBs), 44, 111
Mt. Laurel decisions, 12–13, 163–64, 169, 185, 288–89, 293, 356
Multifamily Assisted Housing Reform and Accountability Act, 243

National Affordable Housing Trust Fund Act of 2007, 321

National Alliance of Community Economic Development Associations, 188
National Association of Realtors, 214, 349, 353–54, 359, 364
National Center for Foreclosure Solutions, 228
National Commission on Urban Problems (Douglas Commission), 162
National Committee against Discrimination in Housing, 162
National Housing Act (1934), 209
National Housing Conference, 23, 348, 349, 362
National Low Income Housing Coalition, 320, 349, 364
Neighborhood Housing Services programs, 226, 359
Neighborhood Progress, Inc., 187
Neighborhood Reinvestment Corporation. *See* NeighborWorks America
Neighborhood Revitalization State Tax Credit, 122
neighborhood revitalization, 122, 179–203, 249, 336, 357–58
Neighborhoods Now, 187
NeighborWorks America, 227–28, 359
New Deal, 33–34, 38, 55, 208–9, 351
New Jersey Predevelopment Loan and Acquisition for Nonprofits (NJ-PLAN), 141
Newman, Oscar, 56, 70–71, 352–53
"no-doc" loans, 230, 234
"not in my backyard" (NIMBY), 158, 350

Oak Court Apartments, 151
online housing libraries, 347–49
open space, 11, 27, 55, 60, 65–68, 71, 84, 192
operating costs, 108, 112, 123–27, 130, 149, 255, 320, 335
Our Neighbors, Inc. (ONI), 135–50
"outdoor rooms," 66
overcrowding, 3, 7–10, 27, 30, 292, 332

"overlay zones," 87–88
Owner Service Program, 341

Palo Alto Housing Corporation (PAHC), 150–51
pari passu financing, 106
Patterson Park, 193
PILOT, 109–10
PITI (principal, insurance, taxes, insurance) formula, 103, 105
preservation, 239–59, 359–60
    and expiring use restrictions, 242–46
    using "index-based" resale prices, 251
    with resale controls, 241, 249–53
    resale prices, 241, 249–53, 304, 331
Presidential Commission on Housing (1982), 323
Princeton Community Housing, Inc. (PCH), 94–95, 151–53
private mortgage insurance (PMI), 222
Pruitt-Igoe project, x, 36, 55–57, 69
Public Housing Authorities (PHAs), 34, 109, 183
Public Works Administration, 34
Pyatok Associates, 75, 151, 352

Qualified Allocation Plan (QAP), 121, 336
Qualified Census Tracts, 119, 182

Rawn, William Boston, 73–74
real estate appreciation, 16, 194, 196, 199, 214–15, 241–51, 253, 256, 315, 319, 331, 340
refinancing, 208, 228, 230, 232, 234, 258
regulation, 10–12, 14–17, 89–90, 98, 158, 162, 198, 208, 233–34, 247, 292–95, 319, 350
rehabilitation loans, 199
rental housing, 5–7, 12–17, 38–40, 43, 70, 102–3, 110–11, 118–22, 148, 153–54, 182, 196, 217, 214, 241–42, 332–42, 360
    Fair Market Rent, 42, 109, 334
    and public policy, 332
    rent control, 194, 197–98, 292

Resolution Trust Corporation, 234
Riis, Jacob, 29
Robert Taylor Homes, 55

S.M.A.R.T. Housing Initiative, 224
Sadowski Act, 45, 49, 114–15
Scudder Homes, 55
Section 221(d)3 program, 37
Section 235, 38–42, 161, 219, 246
Section 236, 38–45, 161, 201, 240, 242, 260, 339
Section 8, 18, 20–22, 25, 42–44, 108–9, 181–82, 201, 240–44, 267, 276, 319, 339, 354
"shotgun houses," 73, 218, 334
Slavic Village, 233
Southern Burlington County v. Township of Mt. Laurel cases. See *Mt. Laurel* decisions
Standard Zoning Enabling Act, 160
Suburban Action Institute, 162–63
suburban communities, 14, 17–18, 21–22, 62, 65, 67, 83, 84–86, 89–90, 93–95, 137, 157, 177, 185, 209, 249, 356, 362, 263
   developing in, 72–75
   exclusion in, 158–65, 174–75, 356
   and inclusionary housing, 286–319

tax abatement, 103–4, 106, 109–11, 131, 225–26, 244, 297, 299, 300
tax credit equity, 110, 112, 118–19, 129–30, 144–45, 150, 244
tax increment financing (TIF), 115–16, 219, 300, 306
Tax Increment Set-Aside (TISA) fund, 116
Tax Reform Act of 1986, 45, 111, 118

Tenant Opportunity to Purchase Act (TOPA), 197–98
Tenement House Act of 1901, 30
tenements, 29–30
Tent City, 73
"towers in the park" design, 55, 71, 66

"use restrictions," 201–2, 240, 242–46, 256, 332, 339
"useful life," 53

vacant properties, 19, 56, 72, 85, 126–27, 191, 195, 201–2, 219–20, 233, 235, 305, 318, 334, 336, 337
vouchers, 18–19, 20–25, 41–43, 50, 108–9, 182–85, 243, 254, 267–68, 276, 279–80, 320–23, 326, 332, 334–35, 339, 354

Wagner Act, 34
White flight, 40, 188, 316
Wilson, William Julius, 179, 357
"workforce housing," ix, 23, 25, 59, 118, 211, 218–19, 226, 348
Wright, Gwendolyn, 30, 55, 351

Yale University, 225

zoning, 86–87, 92, 159–60
   exclusionary zoning practices, 12, 21–22, 83, 96–97, 157–74, 223, 286–87, 289, 317, 356–57
   "floating zones," 87–88
   inclusionary zoning ordinances, 48–49, 185, 201, 224, 289–90, 293–94, 298–300, 333, 348, 361–63
   rezoning, 82, 86, 92, 98, 136–44, 224–25, 298–300